To Jamie

From one Regimental Officer to another.

Nec Aspera Terrent.

Jeremy Wagstaff

28 May '06

With The
Prince of Wales's Own

Lieutenant-Colonel Boris Garside greets Lieutenant-Colonel Robert Laird (centre) commanding 1st East Yorkshires and Lieutenant-Colonel Dan Webber (right) commanding 1st West Yorkshires at Dover for amalgamation of the two regiments, 25 April 1958

With The Prince of Wales's Own

THE STORY OF
A YORKSHIRE REGIMENT
1958–1994

H. M. Tillotson

MICHAEL RUSSELL

By the same author

FINLAND AT PEACE AND WAR 1918-1993

© H. M. Tillotson 1995

First published in Great Britain 1995
by Michael Russell (Publishing) Ltd
Wilby Hall, Wilby, Norwich NR16 2JP

Typeset in Sabon by The Typesetting Bureau
Allen House, East Borough, Wimborne, Dorset
Printed and bound in Great Britain
by Biddles Ltd, Guildford and King's Lynn

All rights reserved

ISBN 0 85955 218 7

*To all who have served with
The Prince of Wales's Own*

Contents

Preface, *by Her Royal Highness The Duchess of Kent*, GCVO   xi

Author's Note and Acknowledgements   xiii

Prologue   1

1. In Aden   17
2. Beside the Sea   47
3. On the Rhine   65
4. In Berlin   81
5. In Northern Ireland 1969 and 1972–3   99
6. On Immediate Call   121
7. Back in the Troubled Province   138
8. In Yorkshire   155
9. On Detachment   175
10. In Competition   188
11. Wives and Children   203
12. In Bosnia   216

Epilogue   233

APPENDICES 239

1 Citation for the George Cross 236
2 Roll of Honour 238
3 Regimental Appointments 239
4 Battalion Locations 1958-1994 244
5 Honours and Awards 247
6 Sporting Achievements 254
7 Individual Sporting Champions 261
  Notes 266
  List of Abbreviations 274
  Bibliography 276
  Index 278

List of Maps

1	Aden	16
2	The Radfan and Dhala	21
3	Crater	23
4	Tawahi	44
5	Cyprus	58
6	Germany (1st British Corps area)	66
7	The Allied Sectors of Berlin	83
8	Northern Ireland	102-3
9	Londonderry	106
10	Belfast	112
11	AMF(L) Northern Contingencies Region	124
12	Yorkshire	157
13	The Liberation of Kuwait 1991	184
14	Bosnia-Herzegovina	219
15	Central Bosnia	222

YORK HOUSE
ST. JAMES'S PALACE
LONDON S.W.1

This history was commissioned by the Regimental Association of The Prince of Wales's Own Regiment of Yorkshire to record almost four decades of service to Crown and country. Also captured in this book is the quite exceptional catalogue of the Regiment's sporting achievements. The twin themes of professional competence and endeavour in competition are evident throughout the story.

On every occasion I visit our Regiment, I am constantly struck by the strong sense of regimental pride. In ourselves – on or off duty; in our achievements, and in our sense of history. Pride, too, in our belief in an end to suffering. We have felt privileged to have been able to play our part in recent times in many areas of the world where strife and anguish exists side by side with everyday life. We also respect our traditions of family solidarity and tolerance; much attention is given to the valuable support and encouragement given by the wives and children.

I have no hesitation in recommending this hitory to those men and women who soldiered with The Prince of Wales's Own, or had family members with the Regiment. The author tells a lively story, which combines close personal experience with critical analysis and wry humour.

Katharine

Colonel-in-Chief

Author's Note and Acknowledgements

The idea that a book might be written to record the thirty-six years of the regiment's history from 1958 arose out of consultations between Major-General Tony Crowfoot and Colonel David Hanson. I am grateful for their suggestion that I should write it and for their subsequent and significant advice, encouragement and help. I also recognize the confidence shown by the Executive Committee of the Regimental Association in asking me to prepare a manuscript for publication and I have appreciated the forbearance of the Committee in leaving me to undertake the research and writing with only the broadest of guidelines.

One of my main sources for research has been *The White Rose* – the regimental journal of The Prince of Wales's Own. I have drawn extensively on the journal, not only for photographs but for dates and for details of events. I am indebted to the former Regimental Secretaries, Major Harry Spencer, Major Bob Tomlinson and Brigadier Malcolm Cubiss, for their work as editors of *The White Rose* over more than three decades. This, together with the Historical Record of the 1st Battalion, made the writing of this book possible.

I am grateful to the surviving commanding officers of the regular and Territorial Army battalions for allowing me access to operational orders, maps and other papers and records relevant to their periods in command and for the care with which they have read and corrected the draft manuscript. I also acknowledge the additional help given by Lieutenant-Colonel Peter Taylor with the Prologue and thank him for his research into several areas where the facts proved elusive. I am indebted to Lieutenant-Colonel Peter Steel and to Major Neville Taylor for their advice on the first period in Aden and in Gibraltar and to Band Sergeant-Major David Cocker for his help on matters appertaining to the Regimental Band.

My special thanks are due to Lieutenant-Colonel Gerry Jarratt for advice on the history of the Leeds Rifles and for allowing me access to letters and papers that trace the vicissitudes of the Territorial Army over the past thirty years, to Lieutenant-Colonel Teddy Denison for information about the 3rd Battalion and to Major Tony Podmore for use of his lineage of the 'Volunteer Artillery and Infantry in the County of York'.

One of the more exhilarating aspects of research has been that into the regiment's sporting achievements, not least due to the full and lively manner in which events were reported at the time. In this field, I am indebted to Brigadier Peter Woolley, Major 'Lakri' Wood, Major Peter Blyth, Major David Moffat, Major Danny Matthews and Captain Byron Cawkwell for meticulously checking what I have written and recorded on the sporting triumphs brought about by their individual achievements, leadership and encouragement of others.

Many individuals have advised me on aspects of the story with which they were closely concerned. These contacts by letter or telephone have renewed friendships that had begun to fade; but the enthusiasm and vigour of every response has been inspirational. There are too many to name here but they will recognize their part in the story, as I hope will their comrades.

I owe most grateful thanks to Regimental Headquarters, and to Lieutenant-Colonel Tim Vines and Major Steve Kennedy in particular, for their painstaking research into many subjects, for seeking out the first names or nicknames of those who served with the regiment until very recently, and for their valuable comments on the manuscript as it was developed. Similarly, my thanks are due to Lieutenant-Colonel Charles Le Brun and Lieutenant-Colonel Christopher Wood, currently commanding the 1st and 3rd Battalions, and to their adjutants, Captains Tom Wagstaff and Howard Newson, for details of those now serving.

I am especially grateful to the wives and widows for their contribution to my research for chapter 11, 'Wives and Children', and for their subsequent comments on the draft. It was a delight to read their crystal-clear recollections of events long past, as was their insistence on deflecting attention away from themselves onto someone they believed more deserving of mention. But I think one must be wary of allowing a book such as this to become a catalogue of saints and saintly acts. In consequence, many of both have had to be left out.

There were sceptics who considered thirty-four years too brief a span for a history but the difficulty has not been any shortfall in material but a judgement as to what could reasonably be omitted. The history of a regiment is in part that of the nation it serves, so events have had to be placed in a political and sometimes an international context. Recognizing that most readers will be impatient to read of the part the regiment played in what occurred, I have relegated the more detailed background material to notes on each chapter, which appear towards the end of the book.

Presentation of the story in relation to places or situations in which the regiment served, rather than in a strict chronological sequence, is an experiment which carries a risk of confusion as to what happened next and where. To help the reader's orientation, the sequence of battalion locations with dates has been included at Appendix 4. I have also broken with custom by omitting abbreviations for decorations after the names of individuals in the text, as I consider they interrupt the flow of a narrative. But to avoid laborious repetition, I have used abbreviations for organizations, weapons and a few military terms, after explaining them when first mentioned. A complete list of abbreviations follows immediately after the Notes to Chapters.

The photographs have been placed in a chronological sequence, or very nearly so, as I believe that this helps to illustrate changes in modes of dress – and sometimes of manner – not only in the regiment but in the Army as a whole. I am grateful to Regimental Headquarters and to the 1st and 3rd Battalions for the help I have received in finding photographs for inclusion in the history and to members of the regiment who have lent personal photographs.

The spelling of foreign place names always gives difficulty, so, in an attempt to be consistent, I have used the spelling on the maps used in the particular campaign or country.

My own prejudices occasionally intrude; for example a lighthearted attitude towards military ceremonial, acquired while at Sandhurst and which sustained me throughout my service. The anecdotes are either from my memory or received at first hand from those who were principally concerned. This may have led to one or two imperfections in reported speech but the spirit of the moment will be clear.

Writing a part of the history of the regiment with which one has served is a great privilege. To me it has been as exacting as I imagine would be writing the biography of one of my dearest friends, when ties of affection might occasionally conflict with the need for objective analysis. Although many who have served are referred to by name, there are many times that number – equally deserving – who are not mentioned. I ask their forgiveness in recognition that this is essentially the story of a team.

Throughout, it has been my intention to inform, to record and sometimes to entertain, but never to give offence – well, not *serious* offence.

Chérencé le Roussel, Normandy, France.　　　　　　　　　　H.M.T.

Prologue

A regiment of the British Army is an enduring theme in the lives of those committed to it. The term 'The Regiment' means infinitely more than the sum of active units in the order of battle. It encompasses the families of those serving, men who have served and often their families too, together with the city and town associations through which the veterans keep in touch and to which they can turn in adversity. The term also describes a sense of comradeship, born from a mix of hardship and humour that the civilian mind can seldom comprehend. There is no room for mawkish sentiment in any of this. Personal relationships are often gritty, a grudge may be nursed long after a favour is forgotten but in danger or in stress The Regiment will stand as one.

Commentators and to an increasing extent British politicians, of whom only a handful have the least military experience, tend to confuse the regimental system and 'spirit' with pride in uniform and bearing on parade, which are but the outward manifestations of a much deeper ethos. This is loyalty to comrades and obligation to the group to which all belong, be it platoon or company or battalion, and its reputation. This is a key ingredient to success on operations, when the shout 'Stand fast, B Company' will stiffen the spine more than reference to some high-flown ideal or, it must be said, even to country. It is therefore necessary to mark out the identity of a regiment by title and a few trappings, so that other men may see and know its stamp.

Regiments of cavalry and infantry are relatively small parts of the army as a whole. An officer or soldier is a member of a regiment throughout his service, although he may serve with a unit of another regiment, particularly to replace a casualty in war or to fill a rank or specialist vacancy in peace. He may serve as an instructor at an army school or recruit training depot or on the staff. He will always wear the badges and uniform of his own regiment, except when on the strength of a field force unit of a regiment other than his own. Transfers are rare but are possible to allow brothers to serve together or when opportunities for promotion are markedly better for a deserving individual in one regiment than in another.

Many infantry regiments have had a county affiliation since before the Napoleonic Wars. Regional links were strengthened under Edward Cardwell's Army Regulation Act of 1871. This provided for each infantry regiment of the line to have two regular battalions, one serving overseas and the other at home, and also set up Regimental Districts and headquarters. The militia battalions from the affiliated county, the forerunners of the modern Territorial Army, were incorporated into the county regiment. Thus regular recruits were drawn from a region where two or more Volunteer battalions of the same name were present as key parts of the regimental infrastructure.

In his First World War autobiography *Goodbye to All That*, the poet Robert Graves records an assessment of the fighting qualities of British regiments made by a group of officers who had been wounded on the Western Front. All agreed that the most dependable in battle were those drawn from the industrial areas of Lancashire and Yorkshire.

This is the story of a Yorkshire regiment but it begins elsewhere in the aftermath of the disintegration of Cromwell's New Model Army. This well-organized force was virtually disbanded after the Lord Protector died in 1658. Only General George Monck's Regiment of Foot was retained in recognition of its march from Coldstream to London to secure the accession of Charles II, for which service it was retitled the Coldstream Regiment of Foot Guards. New regiments were formed, usually under command of Royalists who had supported the monarchy from abroad and named after them. This system of naming regiments after their commanding officer persisted until 1751, when they were numbered to mark the sequence in which they were raised.

The Duke of Monmouth's Rebellion of 1685 caused James II to raise several new regiments. Two of these were formed by royal ordinance of 22 June 1685, named Colonel Sir Edward Hales's Regiment of Foot and Sir William Clifton's Regiment of Foot and raised in Kent and Nottinghamshire respectively. Neither regiment saw service against the new King's bastard nephew, who was defeated at Sedgemoor and executed before they were ready for battle. They were kept in being at reduced strength and despatched on various peace-keeping duties around the kingdom. It is with these two regiments, raised on the same day to meet the same emergency, that this history begins.

The unbroken line of their separate existence can be traced through the tapestry of British military history until they became joined into one regiment almost three centuries later. Both continued to be known by the names of the commanding officers of the day until that custom ended in 1751, when they were numbered the 14th and 15th Regiments of Foot. The 14th, having been first raised in Kent, became the 14th (Bedfordshire) Foot in 1782, 14th (Buckinghamshire) (Prince of Wales's Own) Regiment of Foot in 1876 and The Prince of Wales's Own (West Yorkshire) Regiment in 1881. In contrast to these regional variations, the 15th Foot had a consistent affiliation with Yorkshire from 1782, when the title 15th (Yorkshire East Riding) Regiment of Foot was introduced. This was modified to The East Yorkshire Regiment in 1881 and the subtitle 'Duke of York's Own' granted in 1935.

Provenance of the subtitles is worth investigation, as they were to take on special significance in the amalgamation negotiations of 1957–8. Granting of the subtitle 'The Prince of Wales's Own' to the 14th Foot came about in a curious fashion. Edward, Prince of Wales was due to present new Colours to the 1st Battalion of the regiment at Lucknow in 1876. In common with others in India at the time, the battalion was divided into two wings or 'flanks', each comprising two or more companies. The parade was to be held at Lucknow, where battalion headquarters and the right flank were stationed, but HRH insisted that the left flank stationed at Benares (now Varanasi) should also be present. Receiving the order by telegram only half an hour before the train left for the 160-mile journey, the left flank arrived just one hour before the parade. Even so, the battalion so impressed HRH by its turnout and drill that he announced his intention to seek approval for the regiment to become 'The Prince of Wales's Own', which was granted. To date, he is the only Prince of Wales to have had any formal association with the regiment.

The second son of King George V, the Duke of York, was appointed Colonel-in-Chief of The East Yorkshires in 1922. The regiment was subsequently granted the subtitle 'The Duke of York's

Own' in recognition of its 250th anniversary in 1935, the year of King George V's Silver Jubilee.

Both regiments saw their fair share of action down the years. When presenting new Colours to the 1st Battalion in 1984, Field-Marshal Sir Edwin Bramall (later Lord Bramall of Bushfields) remarked 'Your Regiment has a proud and distinguished pedigree, which reads like the history of the British Army itself.' The 14th fought in the army of King William III against the French at Namur in 1695, at Corunna under Sir John Moore and at Waterloo. They were at Sevastapol in the Crimea. Both the 14th and 15th marched with General Sir Frank Roberts from Kabul to Kandahar in Afghanistan in 1879. Both fought in the South African War, the West Yorkshires taking part in the relief of Ladysmith.

The 15th served under Marlborough at Blenheim, Ramillies, Oudenarde and Malplaquet. During the Seven Years' War against the French in North America they were with Amherst at the capture of Louisburg in 1758. After scaling the Heights of Abraham, they were granted the honour position of left flank guard under Wolfe at Quebec, having caught the eye of that exacting young general during the assault on Louisburg the previous year. Quebec became the regiment's most prominent battle honour and is still celebrated today.

Two incidents during the eighteenth century had an impact that is still apparent in the last decade of the twentieth. The regimental badge now worn on the cap, the key symbol of British Army uniform for the last 200 years, was formerly worn in the centre of the crossbelt. On his cap or grenadier's mitre-like hat a soldier wore the badge of the reigning monarch. Thus from 1714 until the system changed, all regiments wore on their headgear the white horse of the reigning House of Hanover. When regimental cap badges were introduced in 1765, the 14th Foot were stationed at Windsor and Hampton Court. In recognition of the soldiers' conduct and bearing during this duty, King George III granted the regiment the privilege of adopting the King's badge as its own. The same Horse of Hanover with the accreditation 'Yorkshire' on the rough ground beneath is the regimental cap badge today.

At the outset of what were to become known as the Napoleonic Wars, Austria, Britain, Hanover and Holland formed an alliance against revolutionary France. The 14th Foot were a part of the

British expeditionary force under command of the Duke of York in Holland in 1793. During the approach march into France, the British column encountered a heavily fortified French camp at Famars blocking the route to Valenciennes, just south of what is now the Franco-Belgian frontier. The 14th and 53rd (Shropshire) Foot were ordered to clear the heights of Famars so as to open the route. The action was fierce with the French revolutionary troops tauntingly singing the current popular song 'Ça ira, ça ira, les aristos à la lanterne', referring to the pre-guillotine practice of stringing up aristocrats on street lamp posts. When checked by the French defenders, Lieutenant-Colonel Welbore Ellis Doyle rallied the 14th with the shout, 'Come on lads, let's break the scoundrels to their own damned tune. Drummers, strike up Ça Ira' – and so they did and the French broke.

By order of the Duke of York, 'Ça Ira' was adopted as the quick march of the 14th Foot, the only march known to be taken in battle. Today, 'Ça Ira' is the first part of the modern regimental march, the second being 'The Yorkshire Lass', adapted from a traditional tune that was the quick march of the 15th Foot. On parade, the march is played with a jaunty swing but after Beating Retreat in Berlin in 1984, following the presentation of new Colours, the regimental band stood fast, their instruments lowered. From behind a nearby barrack block came an eerie but strangely familiar sound. It was 'Ça Ira' but played as no one present had heard it played before. This was no jaunty swing but a menacing beat. Then onto the square marched a contingent of grim-faced men in the French revolutionary uniform of 1793. It seemed as if the French had come to seek revenge and recapture their tune, 200 years on! Everyone held his breath until a veteran in the audience gasped, 'Where did they get the bloody uniforms?' thinking the men were our own, dressed for the part. But they were real French soldiers of the 46ème Régiment d'Infanterie, our comrades in the Allied Garrison of then still-divided Berlin.

The First World War, or Great War as it was formerly known, saw a huge expansion in both regiments. Between them, the West and East Yorkshires had a total of fifty-two battalions in service during 1914-18. 1st West and 1st East Yorkshires served in the same brigade of the British Expeditionary Force of 1914, described by Kaiser Wilhelm II of Germany as 'that contemptible little army'. They fought with the 6th British Division on the River Aisne in September

1914 and both regiments won the battle honour 'Armentières 1914'. As with many others, neither regiment had room enough for the new battle honours on their Regimental Colours after the war. Instead, they were allowed to be worn on the King's Colour. The regiments won sixteen major honours in the Great War, including 'Neuve Chapelle', 'Ypres 1915, 17, 18', 'Loos', 'Somme 1916,18', 'Arras 1917, 18', 'Cambrai 1917, 18', 'Suvla and Gallipoli 1915'.

9th West Yorkshires and 6th East Yorkshires took part in the landing at Suvla Bay on 6 August 1915. This was the Allies' ill-fated attempt to revitalize the bogged-down Gallipoli campaign by a new landing to outflank the Turks still stubbornly holding the peninsula controlling the Dardanelles passage into the Black Sea. Subsequently, the same battalions fought with the 11th Division in the battle for Scimitar Hill, the final attempt to drive the Turks off the dominating ground. Major Cecil Estridge of the 6th East Yorkshires, wounded at Scimitar Hill, later commanded 9th West Yorkshires on the Somme.

The West Yorkshires had won two Victoria Crosses during the South African War of 1899 to 1902. Four more were won during the Great War and the East Yorkshires also won four. A huge price was paid by Britain and France, in terms of the casualties they sustained, for a victory which was to hold Germany in check for less than a generation. Few survived of the original regular and Volunteer battalions but, throughout the war, the training and discipline of the those pre-1914 soldiers proved invaluable. Many warrant officers and NCOs were commissioned, some in the field, and served with great distinction.

Afterwards the work of rebuilding the Army began at once, as Britain's burden of imperial policing was increased. Iraq and Palestine become League of Nations mandated territories under British control, requiring substantial garrisons. Egypt also needed British troops for protection of the strategically vital Suez Canal, and India for internal security and security of the North-West Frontier.

It was possibly during the inter-war years that the two very similar regiments began to develop different characteristics. The West Yorkshires adopted a down-to-earth approach, amused to see their title paraded daily by the West Yorkshire Bus Company and making no pretensions of being anything other than a good sporting county regiment. In contrast, the East Yorkshires became what was then known as a 'shiny regiment'. Much effort was spent on turnout and bearing. Soldiering was taken extremely seriously. One apocryphal story told how the professionalism of the 1st East Yorkshires was such that the Pathan tribesmen declined to attack them during a two month tour of duty on the North-West Frontier, thus preventing an award of the much-prized Frontier Medal, which could result only after action against the tribesmen had been joined.

This difference became accentuated during the Second World War when 1st Battalion The East Yorkshire Regiment was denied any opportunity for active service until the final months of the Burma campaign. Instead, it was kept as a first-line internal security battalion in Bombay and Poona. The remnants of these divergent attitudes were still apparent when the two regiments were amalgamated in 1958, with often amusing contrasts in approach to military life. Outside observers claimed that they could always tell from which former regiment anyone other than the most junior ranks had come.

The inter-war years also saw the Territorial battalions restored to the situation before 1914. Each had a stiffening of experienced veterans from the Great War and kept close contact with the regular battalions through regular permanent staff. The Cardwell 'home and away' system prevailed for the regular battalions, except in an emergency. The Palestine Revolt of 1936 resulted in the 2nd Battalions of both regiments being sent to Palestine while the 1st Battalions were in India.

As war with Germany became inevitable, the strength of the Territorial Army was doubled in April 1939 from thirteen to twenty-six infantry divisions, leading to the formation of new battalions. Earlier, existing TA infantry units were converted to other roles. 6th West Yorkshires had become a Royal Engineer Searchlight battalion, the 7th (Leeds Rifles) Battalion was re-roled as 45th (Leeds Rifles) Battalion Royal Tank Corps, while the 8th (Leeds Rifles) Battalion became 66th (Leeds Rifles) Heavy Anti-Aircraft Artillery Regiment RA. The Leeds Rifles battalions were to serve throughout the war in these roles, only handing in their tanks and Bofors guns in 1956 and 1961 respectively.

5th West Yorkshires were restyled the 1/5th and ordered to raise an additional TA battalion, the 2/5th. Similarly, 5th East Yorkshires were raised by the 4th Battalion. Although other battalions were raised for home and overseas garrison duties, it was the 5th West Yorkshires and the 4th and 5th East Yorkshires that were to bear the brunt of the hard fighting ahead, in which they distinguished themselves equally with the regular battalions.

2/5th West Yorkshires and the 9th (Overseas Defence) Battalion served with the British Expeditionary Force (BEF) in France before Dunkirk. Both regular battalions were already abroad: the 1st in India and the 2nd in Palestine. 2nd East Yorkshires went to France with Major-General Bernard Montgomery's 3rd Division in September 1939. The 4th and 5th Battalions followed in February 1940. All were heavily involved in resisting the German advance through Belgium, 2/5th West Yorkshires suffering a heavy mauling by enemy armour during the defence of the La Bassée Canal on 26 May 1940. Only thirty men of 2/5th West Yorkshires returned via Dunkirk. The other battalions got back with relatively few casualties; the most serious being sustained by 2nd East Yorkshires while waiting to be taken off the beach at La Panne.

Subsequently, Territorial battalions of the West Yorkshires served in Iceland and as the wartime garrison of the Falkland Islands. 4th and 5th East Yorkshires fought in the Western Desert, where the 4th were all but annihilated by Rommel's breakthrough of the Gazala Line in May 1942. This battalion was not reformed until after the war. 2nd West and 5th East Yorkshires were involved in the same battle and took part in the withdrawal to the Alamein Line. 2nd West Yorkshires found themselves unsupported by armour during the battle on Ruweisat Ridge and suffered serious casualties. They were then moved to Iraq with 5th Indian Division and were subsequently to distinguish themselves in the Burma campaign. 5th East Yorkshires remained with 8th Army and, after Alamein, formed part of the first wave of the attack on the Mareth Line. Later, this by then very experienced battalion fought with 50th (Tyne Tees) Division at Wadi Akarit and, still with 50th Division, took part in the invasion of Sicily, before being withdrawn to the United Kingdom to prepare for the invasion of Normandy.

Before the Western Desert battles, 2nd West Yorkshires had fought the Italians in the fiercely contested Battle of Keren, in Ethiopia. In contrast to their performance in the desert, the Italians fought well in this campaign but their forces under command of the Duke of Aosta were finally defeated, thus East Africa was secured for the remainder of the war. After leaving the Western Desert, 2nd West Yorkshires travelled via Iraq to India and the Arakan campaign of 1944 in Burma, where 1st West Yorkshires had already gained a formidable fighting reputation. It was with General Sir William Slim's 14th Army that the two regular West Yorkshire battalions won their most famous Second World War battle honour – at Imphal.

Commanded by Lieutenant-Colonel 'Munshi' Cree, 2nd West Yorkshires arrived in the Burmese Arakan in December 1943. After a stiff battle at Maungdaw as part of 5th Indian Division, they were tasked to hold the Ngakyedauk Pass in protection of the 'Admin Box', on which depended the whole of the XV Corps offensive. The battle lasted twenty-five days and, in a post-war speech, the Commander XV Corps – Sir Philip Christison – said of 2nd West Yorkshires, 'Never has any regiment counter-attacked so successfully and so often as in that battle. It is rare in history that one regiment can be said to have turned the scale of a whole campaign.'

From the Arakan, 2nd West Yorkshires were air-lifted direct to Dimapur and ordered to march north to Imphal. After a battle for the safe evacuation of administrative units north of the town, the 2nd Battalion met up with the 1st Battalion commanded by Lieutenant-Colonel Ashton Hunt, serving with 17th Indian Division. It was the first time that the two battalions had met for fifty years. A full account of the bitter and often confused, four-week-long defence of Imphal against the 15th and 33rd Japanese Divisions is given in chapter XI of the West Yorkshires' history of the Second World War. The siege was finally lifted by the arrival of 2nd British Division on 22 June 1944. This day has ever since been celebrated as 'Imphal Day', ranking with 'Quebec Day'.

Sixteen days before the relief of Imphal, 2nd and 5th Battalions of the East Yorkshires landed in the first wave of the invasion of Normandy. Alone of the sixty-nine infantry regiments of the Army, the East Yorkshires had two battalions in the first assault wave. Both commanding officers, Lieutenant-Colonel Frank Hutchinson of the 2nd Battalion and Lieutenant-Colonel Gilbert White of the 5th were wounded on D-Day, 6 June 1944. Sixty men of the 2nd Battalion and eighty-five of the 5th Battalion were killed on the beaches that first day. This was just the beginning of a series of battles that took the 2nd Battalion to Bremen by the end of the war in Europe.

Meanwhile, 1st East Yorkshires had finally shaken off the shackles of internal security duties in India and got themselves to Burma. There they joined 1st West Yorkshires in 17th Indian Division for the concluding phase of a bitter campaign to drive the Japanese out of the jungle and the forced march southwards to capture Rangoon before onset of the monsoon.

The five-year period following the end of the Second World War provided a holiday-like interlude for the regular battalions, although these were reduced to one for each regiment in the first post-war reductions of 1947. The 1st Battalions of both West and East Yorkshires formed part of the British garrison of Austria. The West Yorkshires' base was the resort of Pörtshach on the Wörthersee, which led to the adoption of the popular song, 'Du bist die Rose, die Rose von Wörthersee'. The East Yorkshires garrisoned Austria's second city of Graz and adopted the song 'Mariandl'. Both songs are still sung in the regiment today, although few people remember why.

Each battalion went twice every year for a two-month period to Vienna to carry out guard and ceremonial duties as part of the quadripartite Allied garrison. In the winters, all ranks learned to ski at the mountain training centre at Schmelz, in the hills overlooking Judenburg. Field firing was carried out in the same beautiful countryside each summer and there was mountain climbing for the more adventurous in the Tyrolean Grossglockner. Seats at the Viennese opera cost the equivalent of twenty pence, while the royal box of Emperor Franz-Josef at the Graz opera was free, when the commanding officer did not happen to be using it.

During this phase, the battalions comprised about thirty percent regular soldiers including virtually all the senior NCOs. Many had pre-war experience in India or Palestine, as well as a hard war under their belts. The remaining rank and file were men called up under wartime conscription measures. As these were released, their places were taken by National Servicemen.

National Service was introduced with a skilfully devised and successful public relations campaign. This emphasized that men were to serve for a predetermined period – initially this was for only eighteen months – and their role was to maintain the fighting capability of the armed forces in face of the growing threat from the Soviet Union and Communist subversion. The demeaning term 'conscript' was abolished, instructors at depots and with battalions were selected from the best young officers and NCOs available. The National Serviceman was made to feel, quite correctly, that he was a man of importance. The majority rose magnificently to the challenge, bringing zest and humour to a situation which was no particular choice of theirs. It is a great shame that a medal to mark National Service was not struck until thirty years after its abolition.

The Austrian holiday had to end. In 1950 1st West Yorkshires moved to Vienna to undertake guards and ceremonial duties. 1st East Yorkshires left at the end of that year for a gruelling training season as a lorried infantry battalion in Germany with 7th Armoured Division, followed by a fifteen-month tour with the Berlin Garrison. 1st West Yorkshires spent eighteen months in the Canal Zone of Eygpt, never a popular station, under command of 1st Guards Brigade, whom they surprised by winning every competition other than drill. The two battalions were not to remain apart for long. 1953 found both in Malaya.

The emergency in Malaya had begun five years earlier with a Communist insurrection against British rule in February 1948. Having been declared illegal, the troublesome Malayan Communist Party (MCP) went underground into the jungle with which more than three-quarters of the peninsula is covered. They dug up weapons supplied by the British to the 'Malayan Peoples Anti-Japanese Army' during the Second World War and set about murdering isolated British planters and officials. Sir Edward Gurney, the British High Commissioner, was ambushed and killed in October 1951. The situation continued to deteriorate until Gurney's successor, General Sir Gerald Templer, was appointed High Commissioner and Director of Operations, with absolute control over the civil and miliary authorities.

Templer was a clear-minded and utterly ruthless commander. He isolated the Communist-terrorists (CTs) from their supporting village cells by moving the Chinese rubber tappers squatting on the jungle edge into protected new villages. This forced the Communists onto a defensive stategy, in which acquisition of food became their prime need. From then onwards, it became a matter of hunting down the terrorists in the jungle, while 'winning the hearts and minds' of the civilian population and of the Chinese element of it in particular. Templer encouraged the indigenous Malays to aspire to independence within the Commonwealth, something to which no one else appeared to have given much serious consideration.

The tide had begun to turn by the time 1st West and 1st East Yorkshires joined the Commonwealth force. This amounted to two divisions: 1st Federal Division in the north and 17th Gurkha Division in the centre and south. Divisions comprised either Gurkha brigades, of two British battalions, two Gurkha battalions and an armoured car squadron for convoy escort on the main roads, or Malay brigades with a similar organization but with Malay Regiment battalions instead of Gurkha Rifles.

1st West Yorkshires were assigned to 48th Gurkha Brigade and based at Ipoh in the north-western state of Perak. The local population was predominantly Indian, with an interest in the emergency only to see it speedily concluded with defeat of the Communist insurgents. The latter used the swamps and jungle hills of Perak chiefly for retraining and regrouping units that had been weakened by serious casualties sustained elsewhere. 1st West Yorkshires therefore had a frustrating time hunting relatively few of the enemy over a vast and difficult area. In contrast, 1st East Yorkshires with 26th Gurkha Brigade and then 99th Gurkha Brigade in the predominantly Chinese southern state of Johore faced a population which supported the insurrection and the terrorists with equal enthusiasm.

There is no sound basis for comparison of the performance of the two battalions during their last campaign together. 1st West Yorkshires had a sparse and largely unaggressive enemy to hunt over a huge area. 1st East Yorkshires faced a strong and guileful opposition in the region where the terrorists enjoyed the steadfast support of the civilian population. National Servicemen played a critical part in operations with both battalions, as they provided virtually all the rank and file. Men from Bradford, Hull, Leeds and the industrial towns of the West and East Ridings seldom found themselves immediately at home in the silent primary jungle. A firefly seen by a night sentry was breathlessly reported as a man approaching the jungle base on a bicycle! Another who trod on a sleeping crocodile, while fording a muddy river, must still dine out on the outrage registered on the reptile's face as it reared out of the water.

Events proved that small groups of four or eight men, acting on good information, were the most effective. Operations on a large-scale against the jungle-based enemy seldom achieved surprise, so the quarry just melted away. 1st West Yorkshires accounted for relatively few terrorists but brought security to their area of Perak. In Johore, 1st East Yorkshires killed thirty-seven terrorists and captured five more, but at a cost of several men killed and others badly wounded.

Major Billy Robinson of the East Yorkshires was awarded the Military Cross for his part in a series of operations which led to the location of a huge but empty CT jungle base camp. This was eventually attacked by the battalion which relieved 1st East Yorkshires in Johore, 1st South Wales Borderers, causing significant CT casualties. Having already completed eighteen months overseas service in Egypt, 1st West Yorkshires left for Northern Ireland in mid-1954, while 1st East Yorkshires slogged on in the jungle until the end of the following year.

Regulars and National Servicemen from the West and East Yorkshires served with various other regiments in Korea. Lieutenant Malcolm Cubiss, a former National Serviceman recalled from the Reserve, was awarded an immediate Military Cross after the Battle of Sibyon-Ni in Korea in November 1950. Cubiss was wounded three times in the campaign. Two subalterns of the East Yorkshires also received the Military Cross: 2nd Lieutenant William Sheppard for gallantry at the Battle of the Imjin River in April 1951 and Lieutenant James Yeo for leadership, personal courage and example while commanding a platoon and driving off counter-attacks by the Chinese, in spite of being wounded in the head and chest, in October the same year. Extraordinary courage and determination in appalling circumstances were shown by Lieutenant Terry Waters of the West Yorkshire Regiment, while a prisoner of war of the Chinese in Korea. His resolution cost him his life but saved others. The citation for the George Cross awarded posthumously to Lieutenant Waters is reproduced in Appendix 1 of this book.

The Suez operation of 1956 was the catalyst for events that finally drew the two regiments together into one. Few would now argue that the Anglo-French invasion of Egypt, ostensibly to secure the Suez Canal, was anything other than a political fiasco. In spite of a long delay in concentrating the invasion force, the operation was well-conducted from a military point of view. 1st West Yorkshires were moved from Northern Ireland to land at Port Said with

19th Brigade of the 3rd Division. They were also the last unit to re-embark when withdrawal and handover to United Nations troops was ordered. The political set-back of Suez caused the fall of Anthony Eden and replacement as prime minister by Harold Macmillan, a man with ideas for change, one of which was the ending of National Service.

Radical changes in British defence policy stemming from the Review of 1957 were based not on deductions wrought from rational argument, but on predetermined solutions towards which policy and practice were obliged to march. The new Minister of Defence, Duncan Sandys, was a man in a hurry to make his name. He had concluded that a nuclear deterrent reduced the importance of conventional forces at sea and on land. The consequent reduction in the size of the Army was therefore based not on what might be needed but what might be recruited, given better pay and conditions following an end to National Service. The Army's manpower ceiling was initially set at 165,000 but later raised to 185,000 when the recruiting response was better than expected, permitting some regimental amalgamations to be postponed.

The rationale for the first round of infantry amalgamations was primarily based on joining up what were known as 'compass regiments', that is those with a point of the compass in their title. There was some logic in this, as it could be argued that the North and South Staffords could surely not object to becoming the Staffords nor the Queen's (West Surrey) and the East Surreys to becoming, inititially at least, the Queen's Surreys. This principle, if it deserves that status, could not be applied to an amalgamation of the Royal Scots Fusiliers and the Highland Light Infantry, with Scotland as the sole link between them. When the Colonels of these regiments pronounced an amalgamation impracticable they were promptly replaced by more amenable men.

On the face of it, an amalgamation of the West and East Yorkshires was a classic example of what should happen except, unlike the Staffords and Queen's Surreys, they did not share their whole county between them. A request for the title 'The Yorkshire Regiment' was refused on the ground, spurious as a later investigation was to prove, that the title was already lodged elsewhere. The Colonels of both Regiments were retired brigadiers and knew each other well. 'Munshi' Cree of Imphal fame was Colonel of the West Yorkshires and Robin Springhall Colonel of the East Yorkshires. Compared with today, these men had little historical precedent on which to draw when deciding what would be best for the combined regiment. Meanwhile, various serving and retired officers of both regiments began to fight for what they presumed was their own regimental corner as tenaciously as in a boxing final.

Gentlemanly and sporting to the last, the two Colonels agreed to toss a coin for first choice down a long list beginning with title and badge. Cree won the toss and chose the title 'The Prince of Wales's Own Yorkshire Regiment', with impeccable historical precedent to support him. Springhall then chose the Star of Brunswick as the badge. A representation by the Green Howards that the proposed title came too close to their subtitle 'Princess of Wales's Own Yorkshire Regiment' led to a change to what the amalgamation committee termed the 'French-sounding' Prince of Wales's Own Regiment of Yorkshire, which is how today's title came about.

Neither former regiment felt wholly satisfied with the outcome, although most of those directly involved in forming the new battalion put a brave face on the matter. Urgency was lent to their endeavour by the knowledge that they would leave for active service immediately after the amalgamation parade to be held in the Sports Arena in Dover on 31 July 1958.

Meanwhile, what of the three Territorial battalions? Duncan Sandys, rightly judging that cuts in the Territorial Army were likely to be at least as politically controversial as they had proved with regard to the regular forces, shrewdly left them for a later stage. Therefore, for the time being, the 5th West Yorkshires, 7th (Leeds Rifles) West Yorkshires and 4th East Yorkshires, together with TA battalions of other amalgamated regiments, were permitted to retain titles that the regular regiments had just been obliged to relinquish. This led to some sharp intakes of breath but, unknown to them at the time, the Territorial battalions faced a future full of uncertainty. As we shall see, they were to handle this with resolution. In one form or another and under a variety of names, they were to maintain the county links until they rejoined the regimental fold more than thirty years later.

Long before this would happen, at Dover in the summer of 1958 the final packing cases were being stuffed. At the last moment the stencils were changed – from Cyprus to Aden.

Map 1 *Aden*

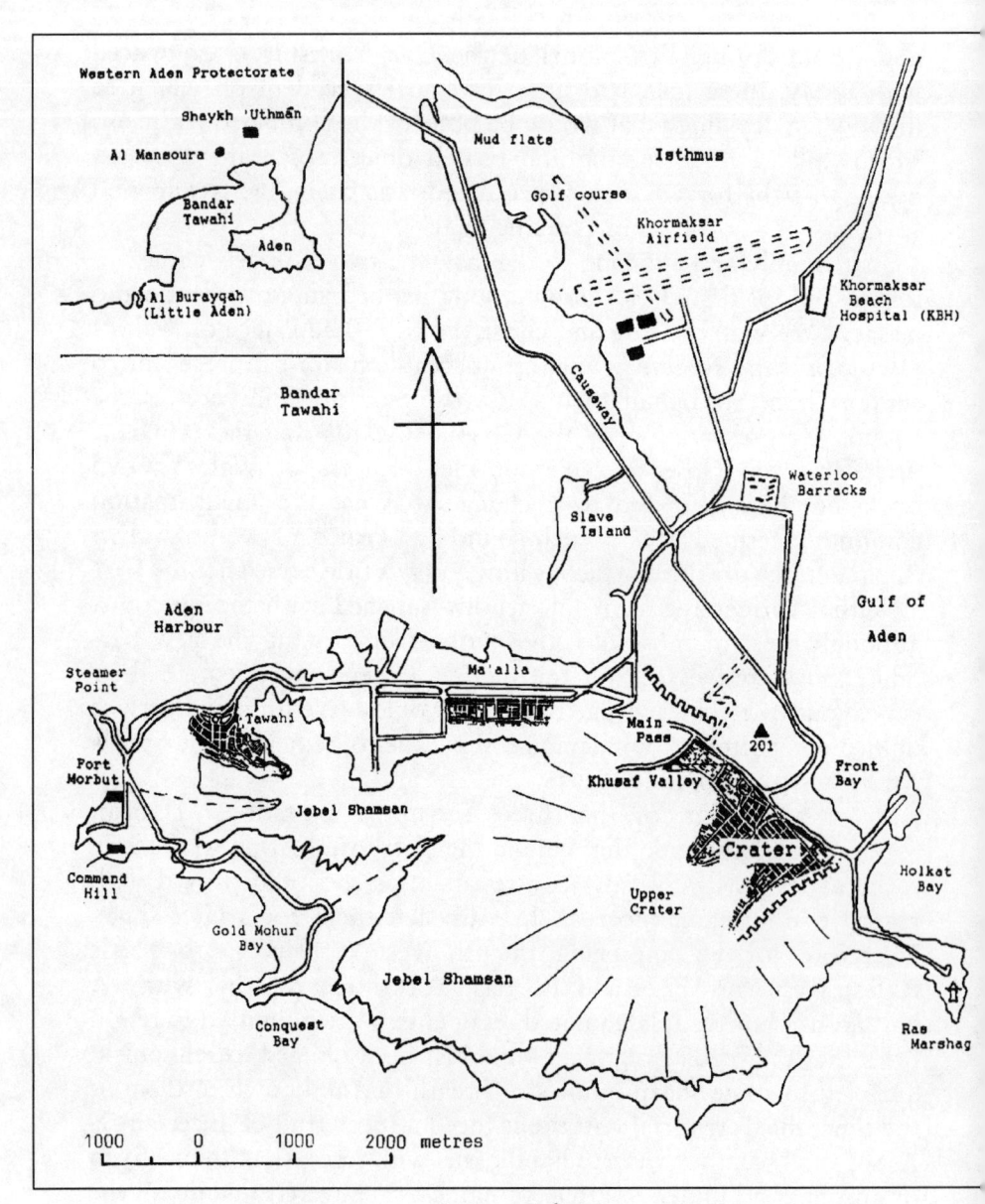

I

In Aden

'I have given my seal that Aden is yours.'
THE SULTAN OF LAHEJ, 1838

Such was the message the Sultan sent to Commander Stafford Haines of the Bombay Marine, having surrendered his claim to the place for an annual pension of 8,700 Maria Theresa dollars. Although the Sultan's son forcibly contested the cession, as the years went by many British soldiers would come to reckon that the Sultan had struck a good bargain.[1] Sent to survey the coast of south-west Arabia for a steamship coaling station between Suez and Bombay, after the garrison on Socotra Island has been decimated by fever in 1835, Haines chose Aden. Anxious lest France, Russia or even the bellicose Muhammad Ali of Egypt might seize the harbour while he continued negotiations, the Bombay authorities ordered Haines to occupy Aden and establish a fortress against all comers. He took the town with a loss of fifteen men on 19 January 1839.

The natural anchorage of Bandar Tawahi can hold a fleet and is well protected. Opposite the western Al Burayqah promontory – later renamed Little Aden – rise the walls of an extinct volcano from which Aden's 'foot' reaches into the bay. The volcano's eastern wall has collapsed into the sea, leaving a partly-enclosed crater where lies the old town of Aden. This is connected to the mainland by a mile-wide isthmus, sealed by massive fortifications, except for two narrow coast roads and a tunnel. Others bar the south-eastern approach from Ras Marshag point. Begun during the (Turkish) Yemeni Pashalik of 1538–1636, the fortifications were improved by Haines and his successors to withstand possible Ottoman attack. But the Turks never again got closer than the isthmus golf course, where a panicky British Resident reported them in July 1915.

Throughout her 128 years of involvement with Aden, Britain

the dilemma of needing the port while seeking to avoid any involvement with the incompatible hinterland. As Aden quickly developed as a free port, attracting merchants from the Middle East and India, the tribal areas to the north and east continued a way of life unchanged for centuries and with no coherent system of government, although overall title to the territory was variously claimed by the Ottoman Empire and the Imam of Yemen. Prudence suggested that so long as trade caravans passed through peacefully the hinterlands were best left to themselves. But British garrisons were reluctant to peer patiently over the fortifications in the hope of seeing that only the camels were coming. Intelligence was required about the extension of Ottoman control over Arabia and, from that, came the desire for treaties of friendship with tribes opposed to the Turks and perhaps able to delay their approach.

Treaties with the main tribes eventually led to British control over what became known as the Western and Eastern Aden Protectorates.[2] During the First World War, Turkish troops made deep incursions across the northern frontier of the Western Protectorate but, when they reached the Aden isthmus, a British force under General Sir George Younghusband drove them back beyond Shaykh 'Uthman. Between the wars, the tribes were kept in check by a balance of diplomacy and carefully measured punitive action when the tribesmen became too aggressive.

Commercial and British defence policy developments during the 1950s suddenly gave Aden increased importance. An oil refinery opened at Little Aden in 1951 and the labour demands of the increasingly busy port attracted thousands of foreign workers. Politically motivated trades unions sprang up to form the Aden Trades Union Confederation (ATUC), 40,000 of whose members had come south from the Yemen. Their presence upset the uneasy co-existence between Aden and the interior and, at much the same time, external pressures began to threaten the political stability of the region as a whole. Arab socialist Egypt and Syria joined with the then Kingdom of Yemen to form the 'United Arab States'. The external voice of this curious union, Radio Cairo, opened a tirade of abuse against the 'colonialist' regimes of Aden, Jordan and the Oman. Concurrently with all this, British defence policy switched from dependence on large overseas garrisons to a system of rapid reinforcement through a chain of bases, of which Aden was one, and the Middle East Command headquarters moved from Cyprus to Aden in 1958.

Political activity in the Protectorates at this time had some focus through the South Arabian League (SAL), with its headquarters in Lahej, some twenty miles north-west of Aden, but there was little cohesion. By contrast, the Aden-based United National Front (UNF) comprised fervent nationalists who found a foothold in the Protectorates by absorbing a radical breakaway faction of the League. Both groups demanded a union of Aden Colony and the Protectorates with Yemen, a call eagerly taken up by Radio Cairo with the introduction of the term 'Occupied South Yemen' to describe South Arabia. But it was Ali, Sultan of Lahej, descendant of he who had consigned Aden to Britain in 1838, who instigated events which led to the entry of the newly-formed 1st Battalion The Prince of Wales's Own into this fast-deteriorating situation.

When the Yemen joined the Egyptian-Syrian United Arab States in 1958, SAL demanded that South West Arabia should make up a foursome. Sultan Ali lent his support to this idea and was promptly dismissed from his post by the British Governor for breaking his treaty of friendship. Ali's followers fled to the Yemen, disturbances broke out in Aden Colony and a state of emergency was declared. The 1st Royal Lincolns, calling at Aden on their way home by sea from Malaya, were disembarked in haste to strengthen the garrison. 1st Battalion The Prince of Wales's Own, preparing for an emergency tour in Cyprus, were diverted to relieve them and sailed from Southampton in HMT *Devonshire* on 21 August.

The advance party, led by Lieutenant-Colonel Boris Garside, left by air on 22 August to arrive in Aden two weeks ahead of the main body. Garside was no stranger to the region, having served with the Aden Protectorate Levies (APL) in Beihan during the previous year. A compellingly calm and operationally experienced officer, he assessed that the main purpose of the reinforcement was to provide a deterrent against further outbreaks of violence and so, given a modicum of luck, he had a useful opportunity to pull his new battalion together against an operational background without too many distractions.

Aden's heat and humidity are at their worst in August and September. The body streams with sweat thoughout the twenty-four hours, night giving no respite. The *Devonshire* anchored off Tawahi early on 8 September to allow the battalion to disembark in lighters to the strains of military and other predictable music rendered by the Levies' band. A tented camp alongside Khormaksar airport became the battalion's temporary base, except for B Company (Major Peter Steel) which enjoyed a sea-breeze from Gold Mohur Bay in a still only partly built camp on the south-western shore of Aden's foot. On 9 October, C Company (Major Billy Robinson) became the first to deploy operationally into the Western Aden Protectorate (WAP) to set up a basecamp at Nawbat Dukaim, where the road from Aden leaves the Wadi Tiban to head northwards for Habilayn and Dhala.

Occupation of Nawbat Dukaim was a precursor to participation in an event to which every legitimate Aden veteran must lay claim – the Dhala convoy. Dhala is a small town, in fact a very small town, dramatically situated at 4,000 feet above sea level, sixty-five miles north of Aden and ten from the Yemeni frontier. Supply of the garrison on the high ground covering the northern approaches was chiefly by air but a ground convoy was needed every few weeks. This called for picketing of the heights overlooking the thirty-eight miles of road and track from Nawbat Dukaim. Techniques developed on the North-West Frontier of India were used and much sweat was sweated. Provided no one was blown up on a mine or shot while leaving a picket position, it was a useful military experience greatly enjoyed by all concerned including, so rumour had it, the hostile Haushabi and Radfan tribesmen. Arrangements rivalled those for staging the Grand March in Act II of *Aïda*.

The battalion, less D Company (Major Jack Skelton) left behind to ensure that no one stole the Khormaksar transit camp, concentrated at Nawbat Dukaim on 20 September. Colonel Garside, to whom such operations were no novelty, issued orders for the Nawbat Dukaim-Habilayn phase for which his battalion group was responsible. Under command were a squadron of The Life Guards (armoured cars), one section of 108 mm guns from 5 Field Regiment Royal Artillery and the forty-truck convoy, with a company of the Levies as close protection. The plan was for the battalion to picket the heights overlooking the route from Nawbat Dukaim to Habilayn, the halfway point to Dhala, hand over the convoy to 1st APL who were responsible for rest of the route, await the convoy's return and cover it safely back to Nawbat Dukaim. Rather to

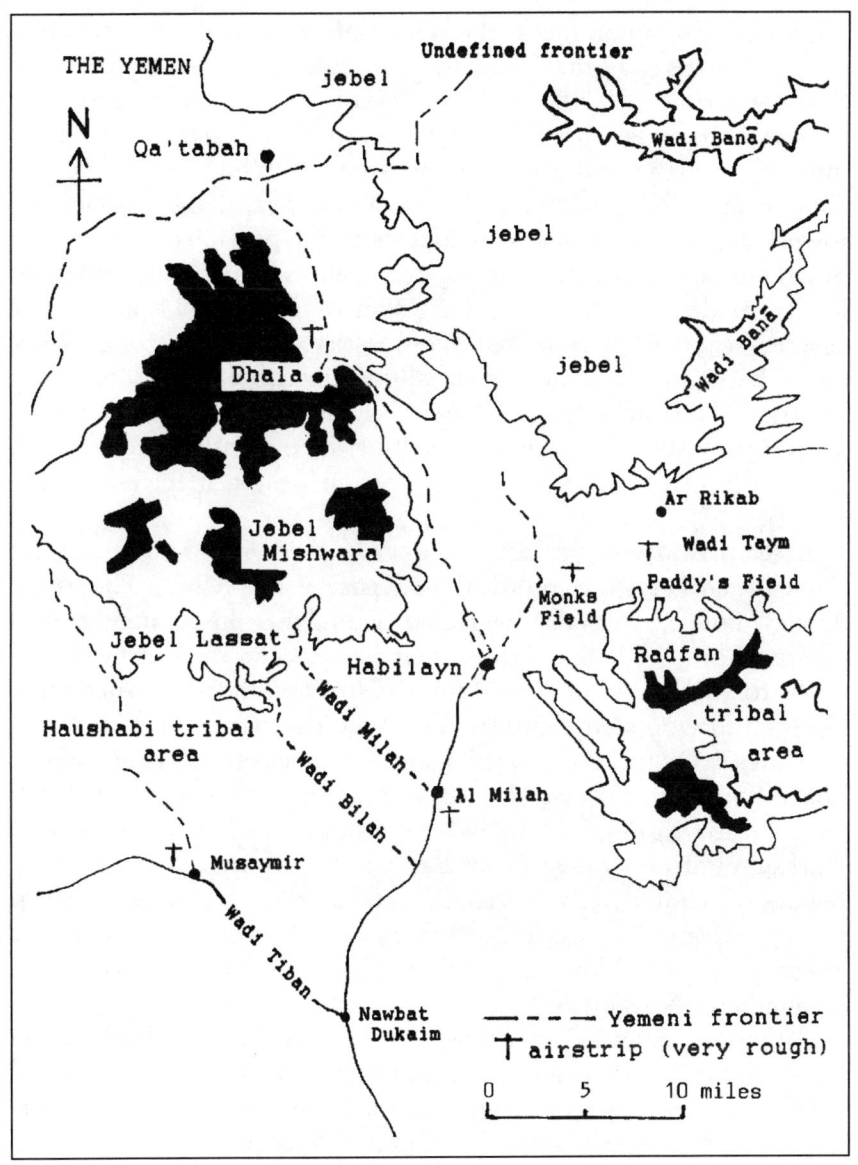

Map 2 *The Radfan and Dhala*

everyone's disappointment, the operation went without hitch or a shot fired. This was the first battalion-scale operation mounted by the new regiment. With this bit of up-country experience under the collective belt, the battalion next received a foretaste of urban internal security operations in the area for which it was to become responsible seven years later: Crater. This densely populated township had been laid out by Haines in the previous century with broad straight streets at right angles, much as Haussmann had done for the modernization and military control of Paris, but on a rather smaller scale. Although this layout assisted riot control, narrow alleys between the main streets allowed trouble-makers to avoid arrest and start up violence or fires elsewhere. When two journalists aligned with the ATUC were gaoled for three months on charges of sedition in October, violence broke out in Crater at the end of the month.

Crater prison was besieged by a stone-throwing mob incited by Yemeni workers and political activists of the UNF. The Aden Armed Police, specially recruited from the up-country tribes, deployed onto the streets from their barracks in the northern part of the township and in the course of dispersing the mob killed three rioters and wounded eighteen. Two rifle companies of The Prince of Wales's Own were moved from Khormaksar into the Armed Police Barracks and tasked with keeping open Queen Arwa Road, which leads through Main Pass to Ma'alla and Tawahi. Service married quarter areas in Front Bay and the isolated Khusaf Valley region of Crater were patrolled intensively but, after a sweep through Crater for curfew breakers on 1 November, order was restored and control handed back to the Armed Police at 0830 hours on Sunday, 2 November.

As the dust resettled in Crater, the battalion moved back to the Khormaksar transit camp while 240 Yemenis had the possibly less dispiriting experience of being repatriated to the Yemen, on the orders of the Governor, for their part in the violence.

At the beginning of November, B Company left Gold Mohur camp to relieve a company of the 1st York and Lancasters at Am Nu'am some seventy miles north-west of Aden, close to the WAP border with the Yemen and twenty-five miles from the coast at Dar am 'Umayrah, which was to prove handy for bathing. A few days later, D Company also moved up-country to relieve another York and

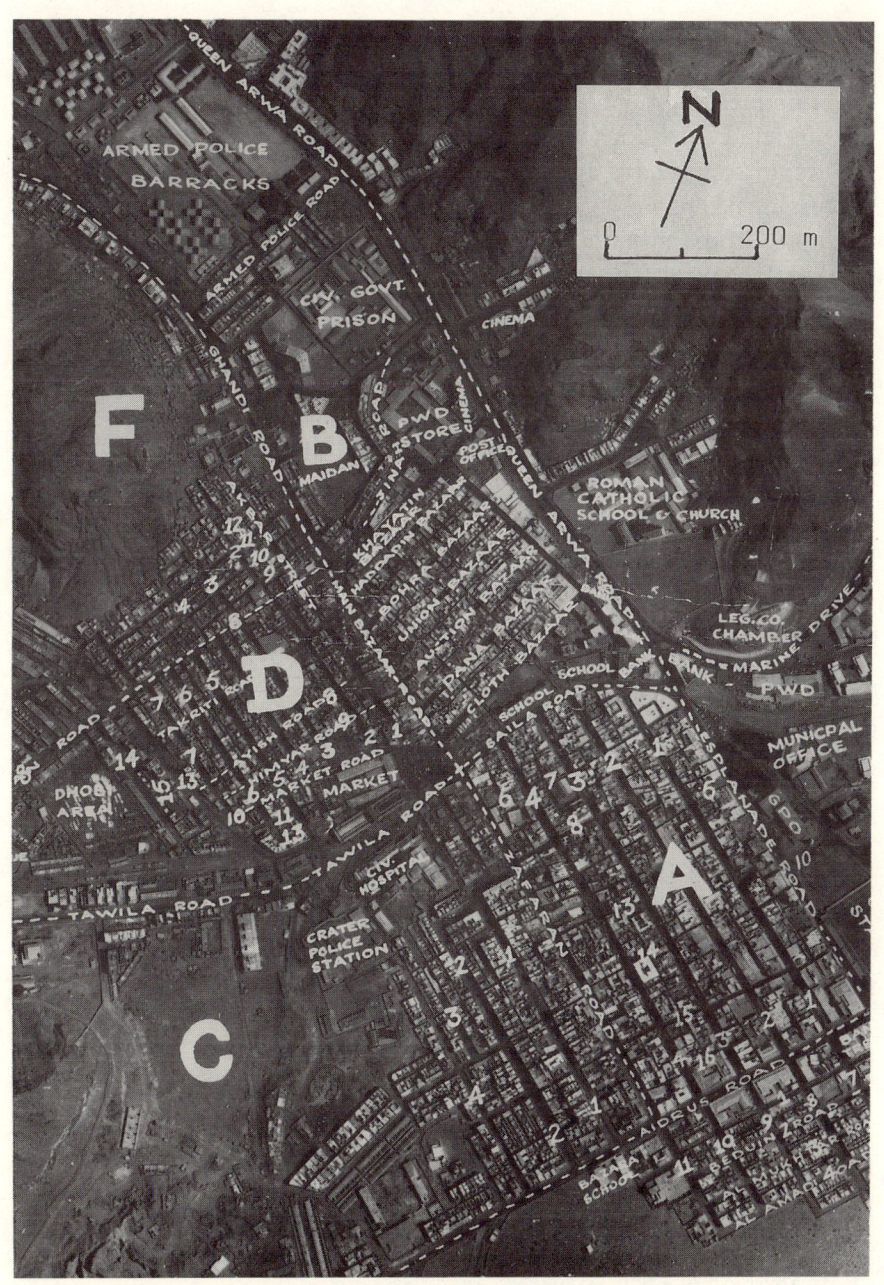

Map 3 *Crater* (Courtesy RAF Khormaksar)
The white capitals indicate the administrative districts.

Lancaster company at Mukeiras in the Western Protectorate, one hundred miles north-east of Aden. Standing on the edge of a 3,000-foot high escarpment with a stupendous view only a mile or so from an undefined border with the Yemen, Mukeiras has an ideal climate of warm sunny days and cold nights. The constant threat of border incursions kept everyone on his toes. A small airstrip allowed air-resupply and, in theory at least, the means of withdrawal on relief.

Shortly before Christmas, B Company was detailed to replace C Company at Nawbat Dukaim and stay there until the New Year. In mid-January C Company relieved D Company at Mukeiras but, as no airlift was available, the relief had to be conducted by march route through 150 miles of hostile territory up and down the escarpment and by truck along what was laughingly referred to as the Gulf of Aden 'coast road'. This performance was perhaps the most memorable event of the whole tour for those who took part. There was no reliable intelligence of the state of mind of the tribesmen of the Urqub Pass, which leads to the escarpment. Consequently, this had to be picketed by detachments from the battalion while ground-attack aircraft of the Royal Air Force patrolled overhead. Mercifully, the aerial firepower was not required.

The perils of a climb or descent of a 3,000-foot escarpment, by ledge-like tracks only wide enough to permit the passage of tiny nimble-footed mules in single file, may be left to the imagination. It was the so-called 'coast road' that caused the greatest excitement. In 1958 it was a road in name only, consisting of the strip of beach between the high and low tide marks firm enough to bear a vehicle's weight. Slight delay in starting the relief convoy led to a breathless race against the incoming tide, narrowly won by the battalion with loss of two vehicles to the Gulf of Aden.

Thankfully, battalion headquarters left Khormaksar's transit lines for a British Petroleum hutted camp in Little Aden in mid-November. The 1st Battalion's first tour of duty in South Arabia ended without further action up-country or in Aden Colony. B Company took over from C Company at Nawbat Dukaim and C Company replaced D Company at Mukeiras. Training, sport and the social round took on the tempo of a peacetime station until departure for Gibraltar on 6 April 1959.

One fatality was sustained during the tour. Sergeant Wilf Saville of the Signal Platoon, with which he had served continuously since he was a private soldier, was accidentally electrocuted on 6 October 1958 while directing the laying of line. He was buried with military honours in the Hejaf cemetery, the firing party being provided by his comrades.

Service in Aden for the 1958-9 state of emergency was marked by the award of the clasp 'Arabian Peninsula' on the General Service Medal. This medal had been first struck in 1918 in recognition of service in Iraq and was later awarded for Palestine, Malaya, Suez and a variety of similar campaigns deemed to fall short of war.

Some useful knowledge of Aden Colony and the Western Protectorate was carried forward by a handful of officers, warrant officers and senior NCOs for the two subsequent tours of duty during 1965-7. But the Army as a whole would see many changes during the intervening years. The all-regular battalion sent to the Colony in 1965 had not been hastily diverted from another destination but thoroughly trained for an altogether more dangerous situation.

1965-6

We must return to the political arena to set the scene for the second and third Aden tours. The concept of establishing some form of federation between Aden and the two Protectorates had been raised but set aside in the past due to the inherent incompatibility of the city and rural cultures. Nevertheless, some positive steps were put in train in 1953 with the granting of an elected majority in the Aden Municipal Council and the signing of treaties of friendship with two hitherto intractable rulers in the Western Aden Protectorate. In January 1954 the treaty rulers were invited to meet Governor Sir Tom Hickinbotham at Lahej, Sultan Ali being at that point still in Government favour, to discuss the possibility of federation. This was a flop. None of the rulers wished to see any erosion of his own authority. But later, in March 1959, the Western Protectorate rulers were persuaded to accept a federation of their states.[3]

A conference of the Federation rulers and members of Aden's Legislative Council, held in London in June 1961, heard proposals from Colonial Secretary Iain Macleod for constitutional reform in Aden designed to lead towards a merger of the Colony and the Federation. To Macleod's surprise, the rulers and councillors accepted his proposals without qualm but implementation on the ground was an altogether different affair. The ATUC, led by Abdullah al-Asnaj who had been thought not to merit a seat at the London conference, flatly rejected any British-sponsored solution for constitutional reform.

Duncan Sandys replaced Macleod as Colonial Secretary and convened a second London conference in July 1962. Time to find an agreed way forward was short, as the mandate of the elected Aden Legislative Council was due to expire in December 1962, after when there would be no elected body with whom to negotiate. By a risky piece of twin-track diplomacy, Sandys persuaded the two delegations to accept a merger of Aden and the Federation immediately after the next Aden Legislative Council elections. Complete Adenization of the Council was the prize offered to the councillors for their agreement to the merger, which they gave. As a safeguard for the fainter-hearted councillors, Aden was to be permitted to opt out of the enlarged Federation if it appeared unworkable after a six-year trial.

The merger was approved by a slender margin in the Legislative Council, in spite of violent demonstrations in Crater instigated by the ATUC's recently-formed political wing, the People's Socialist Party (PSP), with some raucous vocal encouragement from Radio Cairo. Al-Asnaj was arrested and detained for inciting unrest. After a year's pause to allow the new Federation to find its feet, a third London conference was called to discuss the surrender of British sovereignty over Aden Colony and its replacement by a treaty with the Federation to ensure the continued security of the Aden base. When the British High Commissioner to the Federation, Sir Kennedy Trevaskis, arrived at Khormaksar airport to fly to London for this meeting, a grenade was thrown. Trevaskis survived but one of his principal aides, George Henderson who had shielded him, was killed and around fifty people injured. This proved to be the death knell for the conference and a new state of emergency was declared throughout Aden and the Federated states.

With hindsight, it is apparent that this already desperate political situation was worsened by the mounting of a large-scale military riposte to a rebellion of the Radfan tribes in 1964–5. The rebellion had its roots in tribal interests but the scale of the British reaction allowed the hostile media in the Middle East to present it as a war of national liberation. A new Adeni political organization, the

National Liberation Front (NLF), seized the opportunity to establish common cause with the up-country tribes, infiltrate some of the APL battalions, now renamed the Federal Regular Army (FRA), and generally up-stage their rivals in the SAL and PSP. From the time of the Radfan campaign, the NLF maintained its lead in opposition to any negotiated settlement with Britain and became the eventual inheritors of power.[4]

On 30 August 1965 the advance party of the 1st Battalion The Prince of Wales's Own arrived in Aden to begin taking over from 1st Battalion The Royal Anglian Regiment at the start of a one year's unaccompanied tour of duty. The advance party was led by Lieutenant-Colonel Roy Birkett and comprised nine officers, RSM Ben Campey and fifty warrant officers, NCOs and men. Four days after their arrival, the Speaker of the Aden Legislative Council, Sir Arthur Charles, was murdered outside his house in Crater. Lieutenant Peter Woolley, commander of the battalion's reconnaissance platoon and accompanying a Royal Anglian patrol in Crater at the time, was the first officer on the scene.

When the President of the Federation Supreme Council, Abdull al-Qawi Meccawi,[5] refused to condemn the assassination, the High Commissioner dismissed both him and his government and, with London's approval, reimposed direct British rule over Aden state. From 3 September a curfew was imposed in Crater, Ma'alla and the Tawahi port area from 1800 to 0500 hours. Enforcement of the curfew in Crater became the battalion's first responsibility after arrival of the main body by five separate flights over the period 18–24 September. The temperature was around 86 degrees and rifle companies had two hours in which to organize themselves before deploying onto the streets.

On 22 September C Company (Captain Tony Nevile) was placed under command of the 1st Royal Sussex for a cordon and search of the Shaykh 'Uthman area. On the same day Battalion tactical headquarters (Tac HQ) with B and D Companies (Majors Keith Robinson and David Hanson) were ordered to cordon and search the Lahej village of Al Waht, where a known terrorist was believed to be hiding. Hanson's command vehicle became bogged down in the desert and his company completed the operation without him which, one might argue, demonstrated how well he had trained it. The terrorist had already left for the Yemen.

A general strike called by the ATUC in protest at the suspension of the constitution was followed by widespread rioting in Crater in early October. In anticipation, Battalion Tac HQ, D Company and the reconnaissance platoon moved into Armed Police Barracks before first light on 2 October. Disturbances began soon after 0900 hours and by midday all Armed Police riot squads had been committed, the civil police had been stoned and cars overturned and burned. Police attempts to impose a curfew failed and at 1530 hours the battalion was instructed to enforce the curfew and restore order. B Company was called into Crater from reserve and D Company of the 1st Parachute Regiment, plus two platoons of the FRA, were placed under command. The curfew was imposed by 1700 hours, except for sporadic burning of cars and property, 248 rioters or curfew breakers were arrested. Of those arrested, ninety-seven were deported to the Yemen on the following day.

Dawn on 3 October revealed the streets of Crater strewn with boulders, although barricades and burned-out vehicles had been demolished or towed away by military recovery vehicles during the night. The vehicle hulks were pushed into a huge refuse pit between Crater and Ras Marshag, including a few closer to being cars than hulks which had to be discreetly winched out, dusted down and restored to their owners.

The curfew was lifted at noon on 3 October with the intention of reimposing it at 1500 hours. Crowds quickly reformed, fires were started and a synagogue was burned. The battalion was further reinforced by a company of 2nd Coldstream Guards and another of the Federal National Guard (FNG), a loosely-knit, tribal-based force. The Armed Police clashed with a violent mob and one rioter was shot. The FNG company and a section of the reconnaissance platoon were fired on, the former sustaining one man wounded. The curfew was reimposed shortly after 1500 hours with 351 people arrested and detained. Of these, 148 were subsequently deported to the Yemen.

During the disturbances on 2 October, the inmates of Crater prison had occupied a cell block roof and flung bottles and stones at security force units moving along Queen Arwa Road. As most of the inmates were awaiting transfer to the Al Mansoura detention centre near Shaykh 'Uthman, it was decided to move them without delay. This was done in the early hours of 3 October when the streets were deserted, so as to avoid the inevitable rioting, and when troops were readily available for escort duties. The detainees at first refused to move and some gentle manhandling became necessary but all were safely delivered to Al Mansoura before first light. An inquiry by Roderic Bowen QC, made at the direction of the British Foreign Secretary in 1966, examined this action along with others following allegations of misconduct by the security forces when arresting, detaining and interrogating terrorist suspects in Aden. No charges were brought against troops involved in the transfer of detainees to Al Mansoura.

The riots of 2/3 October 1965 were the most violent and destructive of property of the battalion's second tour in Aden. Others took place or were anticipated but the lessons learned during early October made it possible, on virtually all future occasions, to confine the mob to areas of Crater where the rioters' own property would be most vulnerable to damage while overall control remained firmly with the security forces. An airborne command post, using a Scout helicopter of 3 Wing Army Air Corps, was used to excellent effect on 2/3 October. This practice became a standard feature of all subsequent riot control operations, usually using a Sioux helicopter from the battalion's own air platoon formed in February 1966 under command of Captain Spencer Holtom.[6]

The battalion was again fortunate in having a very professional commanding officer. Roy Birkett had been trained in internal security operations in the Indian Army, had three years' experience of the Malayan Emergency and had taken over command immediately after being the Staff College, Camberley instructor responsible for internal security and counter-insurgency operations. His identification with all ranks was marked. His presence at a knife-rest barricade, cigarette-holder clamped between his teeth as his soldiers confronted a howling mob, was an unfailing source of confidence that an ugly situation was being calmly and professionally controlled.

Terrorist activity changed to a more sinister theme as the NLF strengthened its hold in the Colony during October and November. Demonstrations and riots gave way to selective assassination and random murder. The entire on-the-ground complement of the Aden Police Special Branch were tracked down and shot, their bodies left in the street. Close-range automatic pistol attacks began against local officials and expatriate businessmen, usually as they left their workplace for home. Grenades were thrown at off-duty servicemen and their families, often injuring passing local civilians rather than the intended victim. Small but potentially lethal time bombs were left in civilian garages and stores. In spite of the publicity given to such incidents, many expatriates believed themselves immune, relying on either their jobs or local friends for protection. The careless and over-confident were killed.

The insidious threat of pistol or grenade attack was difficult to counter. Either weapon was easily discarded when a security force patrol appeared, as hiding places amongst the bolt-holes and rubbish in Crater and Ma'alla were unlimited. The narrow lanes connecting the streets of Crater gave the grenade-thrower a handy escape route and, as he could drop the pin as soon as he had thrown his grenade, no evidence stood against him. Closure of these passages by breeze-block walls was only partially effective, as the walls were easily broken through in preparation for a grenade attack. While rooftop observation posts, foot and mobile patrols 'maintained a presence' in Crater, such tactics were essentially defensive in nature and left the initiative with the terrorist.

Cordon and search operations, occasionally based on intelligence but more usually on just a hunch, were Aden Brigade's favoured means of demonstrating security force intitiative. Such tactics were worthwhile only if the chosen area could be successfully isolated before the persons or weapons being sought were spirited away. This seldom happened, at least to an extent to justify a large-scale deployment of troops. Rummaging through pitiful dwellings after their owners had been turned into the street, often in the early hours, was not an uplifting experience either. Humour sometimes came to the rescue. During one pre-dawn cordon and search in Crater, a soldier of C Company accidentally fired his Sterling SMG. The round entered the ground floor of a block of flats and ricocheted upwards into a refrigerator on the third floor. The owner of the 'fridge was a large, very handsome but very, very angry Somali woman. 'This one', said the company commander to Sergeant Chas Elliott commanding the platoon, 'is entirely yours to do with as you will.' 'We're sorry about this, luv,' Elliott began, as his commander callously turned away.

In addition to security duties in Crater, the battalion was responsible for close protection of installations elesewhere. These included Ma'alla police station, the Fort Morbut interrogation centre and

Command Hill, where the residence of the C-in-C Middle East Command and those of the Army and Air Force commanders were sited overlooking Steamer Point. These duties absorbed an entire company every twenty-four hours and were a constant scource of friction between the battalion and the brigade and superior staff. Not only had the men to be turned out in starched shirts and shorts, hosetops and puttees of a byegone age, totally unsuited to protection duties, but watching for the right car to salute was infinitely more important than giving warning of attack.

Years later Roy Birkett reflected, 'Command Hill guard gave me the real problems. Compared to that, dealing with riots and terrorism was easy.' This situation persisted until Admiral Sir Michael Le Fanu took over as C-in-C. On his first day he walked down to the Command Hill guard house wearing a T-shirt, shorts and sandals. 'I'm Ginger Le Fanu,' he announced to Sergeant George Prosser, who instantly recognized him from a press photograph, 'tell me about The Prince of Wales's Own.' Our guardian angel had delivered the new C-in-C into the hands of a man able to give the story exactly as it was, with humour thrown in. From shortly afterwards, Command Hill and similar guards became operational rather than ceremonial duties.

Development of a coherent pattern of operations against the NLF was inhibited in the early months of the tour by the daily rotation of the Crater company at 1700 hours, under a system adopted from the previous unit. In common with others, the battalion had a BAOR-orientated organization of four rifle companies (one to be fully implemented only on mobilization), each of which had its own support platoon of two 81 mm mortars and two 120 mm Wombat anti-tank guns. While this large company structure suited company-level operational demands well, lack of a fourth rifle company or a support company limited flexibility at battalion level.

A Company, commanded from November by Captain Tony Nevile and in cadre strength, occupied Mukeiras and became responsible for the acclimatization and training of reinforcement drafts. C Company, commanded by the author from November, was temporarily detached to the Radfan for operations under command of 1st Welsh Guards from mid-November to early December. Thus B and D Companies were left to alternate daily between Crater and guard duties and no significant change of system could be made before C Company returned to Aden.

After consulting his company commanders, Colonel Birkett adopted a system which allowed each rifle company in turn to run operations in Crater for a period of six days and nights. This was unless a strike or threat of riot called for reinforcement and control by Battalion Tac HQ. At the same time, he directed that operations should be orientated towards the acquisition of intelligence of NLF methods and intentions and towards taking the initiative against the NLF, so far as this was compatible with an internal security role. These policies were to bring some far-reaching results later in the tour.

Mukeiras, although used for reinforcement, acclimatization and training, had its local dissident element. A visit by the Band and Drums was thought to be a useful hearts and minds-winning enterprise but after they had Beat Retreat on the maidan, performing innovative marching manoeuvres to avoid the camel droppings, a grenade was thrown into one of the trucks taking the musicians to their next engagement. As it was dusk, the object was only identified when Bandsman Ian Plaice picked it up. 'I don't think we want that,' he remarked and lobbed it over the tailboard. It failed to explode. The band frequently moonlighted as a rifle platoon during security operations in Crater and provided the small garrison on Perim Island.

Two political developments in early 1966 took analysts by surprise. The NLF briefly made common cause with the PSP and SAL to form FLOSY, the 'Front for the Liberation of Occupied South Yemen'. Grass-root levels of the NLF never accepted this merger and the organization split up in November 1966, with the rump left by the NLF's departure retaining the FLOSY title. In February 1966 Lord Beswick, a junior minister in the Colonial Office, brought news that the British Cabinet had decided to abandon Aden and the Protectorates by 1968, no defence agreement would be signed with the successor regime, whatever that might be, and a much reduced British Middle East base was to be set up in Bahrain. Thus the supporters of a federation and the up-country tribal rulers were left, if not actually dead in the water, flat on the desert floor.

When Lord Beswick's message leaked out, terrorist activity intensified as the various political groupings sought to establish superiority. Individuals previously involved in confrontation with the British administration were targeted as 'moderates'. An ATUC senior official was shot dead outside his home in Ma'alla at the end of February. On 16 April a charge exploded under the Sultan of Lahej's car, fracturing his leg and injuring his bodyguards. The period November 1965–May 1966 drew to a close revealing a relentlessly worsening security situation in Aden Colony. Cooperation with the civil police was by then little more than a formality, so seriously were they penetrated or threatened by the NLF. When making a call at a police station, a company commander was wise to keep his back to the wall and a rifle section deployed round the doorway. On 10 January, two bursts of automatic fire marked Major Keith Robinson's departure from Crater police station, but possibly this was simply a *feu de joie*!

Grenade attacks, particularly during the hours of darkness, switched from soft targets to security patrols. During these seven months, the battalion sustained fifteen casualties from grenades but none was serious. There were several narrow escapes. The commanding officer had a grenade thrown into his Land Rover on the evening of 8 June but it failed to explode. Earlier the same day, a grenade was thrown at a vehicle patrol of D Company driving through Crater's Cloth Bazaar. It struck Lance-Corporal Pete Ralph on the neck, bounced into the road and exploded, wounding fifteen civilian bystanders, one of whom later died. Undeterred by his narrow escape, Corporal Ralph and two other members of his patrol pursued three suspects, capturing one and wounding another.

Virtually all grenades used by the NLF during this period were the British-made No. 36, huge quantities of which had been handed over to local forces on withdrawal from various Middle Eastern countries since the Second World War. Unless the working parts are cleaned of the thick preservative grease and tested, the grenades seldom explode when thrown. Failure by terrorists to clean and test the grenades undoubtedly saved many soldiers from injury or death. The need to hold down the firing-pin release lever after the pin is removed, before the grenade is thrown, led to hours being spent searching for the levers at sites of grenades incidents in the hope of finding one bearing incriminating fingerprints. The more cynically-minded regarded this as a scheme devised by the NLF faction in the Aden police to waste the Army's time.

For some weeks the battalion had been looking forward to a change of role, with a switch to up-country operations in the area Al Milah-Habilayn-Dhala. Before this welcome change came about, two events – one grimly amusing and the other operationally significant – occurred in Crater. At 1220 hours on 14 June B and C Company commanders had just exchanged responsibility for Crater when an explosion was heard in the Khusaf Valley. Investigation revealed human remains spread around the walls and ceiling of a room in a house from which smoke continued to pour. After attaching a clockwork timing device to 20 lb of TNT, one of the less technically-minded NLF members had tried to turn the clock to the correct time and, in so doing, had passed the points to which the electric terminals were soldered – and blown himself to bits. Besides this very nasty mess, the house contained Soviet-made explosives, automatic weapons, grenades and grenade launchers.[7]

In the late evening of 20 June a tactic designed to take the initiative against the NLF brought results. An obvious road block with concealed cut-offs on the coast road out of Crater, under command of Lieutenant Duncan Green, trapped a civilian car attempting to avoid the block. When halted by Privates Bob Burgin and Henry Irvin who formed the cut-off group, the car was found to contain three men, 18 lb of TNT, a fuse and time pencil. While valuable in itself, the full significance of this event was not to become apparent for several weeks. Meanwhile, the 1st Battalion moved up-country.

Operations in the Western Aden Protectorate in mid-1966 had the spice of uncertainty about them. The Haushabi and Radfan tribes had not been informed that the Radfan campaign had been brought to an official close by a Whitehall committee, which had ended the period of eligibility for the General Service Medal clasp 'Radfan'. Therefore the tribesmen fought on, oblivious of the fact that their foes would not receive the coveted clasp. Further north, various groups of dissidents against authority of any kind operated out of the Wadi Bana and the Wadi Taym, attacking the airfield at Habilayn and mining the airstrip at Monks Field,[8] just over five miles to the NNE. (See Map 2 on page 21.) The influence of FLOSY was growing in these regions but not as strongly as in the Yemeni frontier region, from where well-armed guerrillas ventured to attack Dhala. These security force bases, together with those at Al Milah and Mukeiras, were frequently subjected to mortar and *blindecide* rocket attacks under cover of darkness.

There were also uncertainties amongst the so-called security forces. Federal Regular Army relationships with the Federal National

Guard (FNG), with whom the FRA was due to amalgamate, were steadily worsening. The Federal Guard was structured and run on a tribal basis. Battalion 'O Groups' were gatherings of the entire unit, in which the voice of the most persuasive speaker held sway. Appointments and promotions turned on family and tribal loyalties, rather than on military merit. Units of both forces were penetrated by terrorist organizations, FLOSY concentrating chiefly on the Federal Guard to counter the influence of the NLF in the FRA. In such circumstances, it was impossible to be certain whether one was in the company of friend or foe or one or both enemy factions at any one time.

Having left Crater, Command Hill and Ma'alla police station in the care of 42 Commando Royal Marines, the battalion deployed up-country at the end of June. Battalion Headquarters set up alongside the Habilayn airstrip with B Company manning surrounding picket positions. C Company went to Dhala under command of 2 FRA, while D Company remained free for offensive operations against the Haushabi dissidents harassing Sappers working on the Al Milah-Habilayn road. An FRA company at Monks Field was placed under command of the battalion, E Battery 1st Royal Horse Artillery (1st RHA) was in direct support and RAF Hunter ground-attack jets and Wessex transport helicopters on call.

The reconnaissance platoon, having patrolled Crater for nine months with a mixture of stoicism and verve, was despatched on what was expected to be a holiday by comparison. Lieutenant Peter Woolley took his dismounted platoon to Wadi Ayn, seventy miles north-east of Aden, to provide infantry protection for detachments of the 4th/7th Royal Dragoon Guards and the 1st RHA. The locals of Wadi Ayn were reputedly friendly, as were the Yemeni Royalists beyond the unmarked frontier. A request by a local headman for help in repairing an ancient Soviet anti-aircraft gun was consequently received with amusement. Next day two unidentified MiG jet aircraft strafed his village, indicating that the headman had good intelligence sources if little else.

Action was joined near Habilayn within twenty-four hours of the battalion's arrival. On the night of 29 June a dissident force attacked a Federal Guard position some 600 yards south of Battalion HQ. An OP on the spot, manned by Corporal Geoff Auker and three men of B Company for the purpose of directing supporting fire from the battalion main position, was struck by rocket-launched missiles and intense small-arms fire. Finding it impossible to get a bearing on the direction of attack from the OP, Corporal Auker ran across open ground to a Federal Guard sangar, from where he radioed instructions to bring down 81 mm mortar fire from Habilayn and directed machine-gun fire from a neighbouring picket. He finally won the fire-fight by engaging the dissidents with GPMG fire from his own OP. For his leadership, calmness and courage, Corporal Auker was subsequently awarded the Military Medal.

With a support platoon of the 2nd Parachute Regiment under command and a handful of the local 'Special Guard' (armed civilians believed to be friendly) in support, D Company made light work of defending Al Milah and protecting the Sappers working on the road to Habilayn. This made it possible to launch several company-scale offensive sorties into the surrounding hills. The first brought contact with dissidents up the Wadi Bilah, which joins the Aden road four miles SSW of Al Milah. There were no casualties, although a scream from one dissident position suggested someone might have been winged.

A more ambitious operation codenamed Cover Point was directed against a group of dissidents thought to be in the village of Ar Rikab in the Wadi Taym. The Special Guards, supposedly responsible for security of the village, were in some doubt as to whose side they were on, so they had to be disarmed. Battalion Tac HQ deployed with under command D Company, elements of Patrol Company the 2nd Parachute Regiment, a platoon of the Federal Guard, two armoured car troops of the 4th/7th Royal Dragoon Guards as escort and a couple of Hunter ground-attack aircraft on call, as well as helicopter lift for troops, ammunition, mortars and stores. An FOO from E Battery 1st RHA deployed with Battalion Tac HQ.

Phase 1 began on 10 July with the despatch of 'Lukeforce', comprising 13 Platoon (2nd Lieutenant Robert Woolsey), one section of mortars and another of assault pioneers in Wessex helicopters, to secure Paddy's Field as the airhead. Meanwhile, the main body of D Company laboured up the wadi in Stalwart troop carriers escorted by the 4th/7th armoured cars. Phases 2 and 3 involved D Company being lifted by helicopters to high ground overlooking Ar Rikab, to cover the entry of the Political Officer, Mr Godfrey Mennell, and his Federal Guard escort into the village. There was an exchange of fire as Mennell's party approached the outskirts. Several dissidents were killed, others captured and the surly-looking Special Guards disarmed.

Withdrawal to Paddy's Field was followed by a dissident night attack on D Company's position using mortars and *blindecide* rocket-launchers. 13 Platoon received several missiles around their sangars but return of fire was inhibited by difficulty in identifying points from which the attack came. Finally, Lance-Corporal Fitz 'The Baron' Fitzgerald located the enemy's position and directed the platoon's fire onto it. Action was abruptly broken off and the dissidents withdrew. 14 Platoon (2nd Lieutenant Tony Phelan) received a few 'overs', but had been unable to join in as 13 Platoon lay betweem them and the enemy. No casualties were sustained and the whole force returned to base on 14 July.

D Company also took part in Operations Full Time in the Radfan hills and Springboard in the little-known territory between Jebel Lassat and Jebel Miswarah, some twelve miles west of Habilayn. (See Map 2 on page 21.) Neither resulted in direct contact with the enemy, although a Saladin escort vehicle ran over a mine when returning down the Wadi Milah at the end of Springboard.

B Company patrolled intensively throughout July, concentrating on the area east of Habilayn and ambushing the airfield approaches at night. On the night of 27 July an ambush under command of Lieutenant Peter Orwin was sprung by a group of dissidents, estimated to be fifteen to twenty strong, which entered the fire zone of the section protecting the rear of the ambush position. The enemy immediately retaliated with rocket-launchers. The first *blindecide* killed Lance-Corporal Bryan Foley and stunned Sergeant Ron Davison, the ambush second-in-command. A fierce fire-fight ensued, which Orwin won by a combination of GPMG and grenade attack, until he was able to bring down fire from B Company's 81 mm mortars. Privates John Berryman, 'Spam' Spammer and 'Spider' Webb were wounded in the exchanges of fire, John Berryman seriously. It was later reported that the dissidents suffered two killed and six wounded. Lieutenant Orwin was awarded the Military Cross for his leadership and personal example during this action.

On the night of 28/9 July it was the turn of C Company to engage the enemy. Dhala had been unusually quiet until then, except for the serious wounding of Privates Ken Proctor and George Cornell by a

No. 6 anti-personnel 'pencil' mine. At the end of a day when the two had been with a section covering a well outlying the company position to the north, Proctor had taken out his cigarettes to offer one to the younger soldier and, in doing so, put his hand on a sandbag concealing the mine. Proctor's hand was blown off into Cornell's face, together with stones and debris. Both soldiers were remarkably stoical. Proctor came into the company position holding up his bloody stump, while Cornell remained composed in spite of the certain loss of one eye and serious damage to the other.

At 0220 hours on 29 July a group of dissidents of unknown strength attacked the Emir of Dhala's palace and the local Political Officer's house with *blindecide* rockets and mortar fire. The Political Officer was Peter Hinchcliffe,[9] who had served at Suez as a National Service subaltern with 1st West Yorkshires. His house was built to withstand attack, with walls two feet thick, but he very reasonably called for fire support. This was not easy to provide, as both his house and the Emir's palace lay to the south of C Company's position, with the Dhala souk between them. Mortar defensive fire tasks near the PO's house were fired and 11 Platoon (2nd Lieutenant Michael Garside) was despatched to ambush what was judged to be the dissidents' most likely withdrawal route to the hills.

A possibly unique feature of this action was its direction by the commander of C Company (the author) sitting on a bucket. He had been an active casualty to gastro-enteritis throughout the previous twenty-four hours, a condition which the dissident attack did nothing to calm. The mortar defensive fire (DF) tasks drew small-arms fire and two mortar bombs from the attackers, but no casualties or damage were sustained. The action ended at 0315 hours when, according to intelligence later received, the dissidents withdrew southwards – away from Garside's ambush waiting near the foothills – taking two of their wounded with them, one of whom died the next day.

The Radfan-Dhala period ended on 6 August 1966 with a return to operations in Crater. In addition to Corporal Foley killed, three men had been seriously wounded and four slightly injured. These included Private Mick Campbell of B Company, who was thrown out of a Stalwart when it ran over a mine near Habilayn on 29 June. Reporting on the usefulness of operations in the Radfan, Colonel Birkett pointed to the lack or total unreliability of intelligence of enemy intentions or movements, the difficulties of hunting him down in his tribal territory and of distinguishing friend from foe. Movement or reconnaissance by helicopter declared our own intentions and, except from really high ground, fields of fire were short. All that said, the battalion unquestionably controlled its area by day and was stimulated by the change from the enervating and dispiriting atmosphere of Aden, where the political high ground was already lost.

The rate of terrorist-inspired incidents in the Colony had risen from the previous high point of twenty-seven per day in March to forty in July. Against this, forty-seven terrorists had been arrested as a result of the quick reactions of Bob Burgin and Henry Irvin at the Crater road block on 20 June. (See page 34.) The arrested thugs had sung like canaries. This was the sort of intelligence breakthrough that Birkett had urged his company commanders to seek. The same source revealed the rift between FLOSY and the NLF but this news came too late for the battalion to exploit, beyond the whimsical replacement of NLF graffiti by FLOSY slogans on walls in Crater. Meanwhile the Colonial Office mused as to which of the terrorist groups was best suited to take over power.

Lance-Corporal Bob Blythe and Private Mick Thackeray of the reconnaissance platoon were slightly wounded by a grenade in Crater on 11 August and Private John Render of A Company was injured in the same incident. Two grenades were thrown, indicating increased NLF confidence and aggression. In separate grenade incidents on 14 and 15 August, Company Sergeant-Major Mick Dillon and Privates Dave Hamilton and Bernie Willingham, all of D Company, were slightly wounded. On 26 August Lieutenant Rory Forsyth and Privates Tommy Addlington and 'Smiler' Edwards of B Company were all cut by grenade splinters while on one of their last foot patrols in Crater.

In a farewell talk before the battalion had left Colchester, Brigadier 'Munshi' Cree, Colonel of the Regiment, had warned the men that the final weeks of the operational tour would be the most dangerous, when they may be feeling over-confident and thinking of home. Colonel Birkett reminded the battalion of these wise words and pointed to the increasing terrorist activity. It became daily more essential to insist on strict security drills, with lookout sentries and patrol groups to provide cover for each other to move in Crater's streets. A grenade thrown into a patrol of 14 Platoon, which had paused in a confined area, killed Private Fred Langrick and wounded eight of his comrades, Lance-Corporal John Anthony and Privates Tony Laverick and Barry Renardson seriously. Langrick was a fine sportsman and a promising soldier. He was buried at Little Aden military cemetery on 6 September, when the firing party was provided by his comrades of D Company.

As the RAF VC10s flew the battalion home in early September, it seems most unlikely that the thought crossed anyone's mind that they would return to Aden within the year. Those looking back over 1965-6 probably reflected that the battalion had put up its most professional performance to date. In an operational tour it is the rifle companies and specialist platoons who receive the most acclaim. But no operational success would have been possible without the administrative support that Headquarter Company never failed to provide, often in exasperating and exhausting circumstances but without complaint. The phrase, 'If only the bloody rifle companies would...', cropped up only once. Birkett cut the speaker short, reminding him that his job was to serve the rifle companies, not to whinge.

Almost everyone gave of his best but a few let down their comrades and the battalion. Two men of C Company narrowly escaped death whilst whoring in an out of bounds area of Ma'alla in December 1965. Miraculously, in view of the close range at which they were shot, both survived to serve as useful reminders of where such recklessness could lead. In sharp contrast, casualties of two killed, six seriously and thirty-six slightly wounded indicated a high state of training on arrival in Aden and of security discipline throughout twelve months of intensive active duty.

Due to a weird Whitehall-devised arrangement, the battalion was on active service while up-country in the Radfan area but not while on security duties in Aden Colony. In consequence, operational awards were not permissible for bravery or leadership in Crater but Colonel Roy Birkett and Major David Hanson were appointed OBE and MBE respectively in the New Year Honours List for 1967. The undercover work of the battalion's Special Branch section was recognized by an award of the Queen's Commendation for brave conduct to Lieutenant Shane Lucas, who commanded it throughout the twelve months' tour. Faced with a terrorist suspect aiming a pistol from the bed from which he had been aroused, Lucas launched himself at the man, overpowered and captured him single-handed.

Nine warrant officers and NCOs were awarded the Commander-in-Chief's Commendation, including Lance-Corporal Pete Ralph who had led the pursuit of three terrorists in Crater on 8 June. A full list of recipients of C-in-C's Commendations for the second Aden tour appears in Appendix 5. Had active service conditions been declared for Aden Colony, as they were towards the end of the battalion's third tour, many recipients of the C-in-C's Commendation would have been mentioned in despatches, if not recommended for a decoration. Everyone who had served continuously for thirty days in South Arabia after 1 August 1964 became entitled to the new clasp 'South Arabia' on the new General Service Medal (1962).

1967

Crater was handed over to the 1st Royal Northumberland Fusiliers, who were due to serve a nine-month tour in Aden before relief in June 1967 by 1st Argyll and Sutherland Highlanders. The rupture betwen FLOSY and the NLF became common knowledge in November 1966, after when the two factions fought each other with increasing intensity. A United Nations mission arrived in Aden on 2 April the following year, coinciding with the Colony's heaviest rainfall in living memory. Scenes of high farce ensued. The UN mission demanded to interview the terrorists held in Al Mansoura detention centre, but the detainees refused to receive the delegates. After having been denied permission to question the legality of the Federal Administration over the official radio network, the UN mission left in fury. Its Afghan leader declared at the airport, 'You British are bloody sight contributing to the bloodshed in the world more than anyone else', thereby demonstrating the moderation and objectivity of his position.

The visit of this UN mission had been an unwise suggestion of the Foreign Office. Even so, it was the High Commissioner who was sacked and replaced by Sir Humphrey Trevelyan, a tough ex-ambassador with a background of difficult posts. Tasked with the orderly withdrawal of British troops and handover of power to a broad-based and stable government, he realistically concentrated his efforts on the first of these objectives. Then the crushing defeat of Egypt in the Six Days War in June encouraged the British Government to offer Aden a military aid package, with independence to follow in

January 1968. This news became public on 19 June but next day Crater was seized by the NLF as a result of a series of miscalculations and misunderstandings, amidst scenes of appalling violence.

In May the FRA and FNG had reluctantly amalgamated to form the South Arabian Armed Forces (SAAF). This arrangement had failed to take account of tribal aspirations which led to an appeal to the Ministry of Defence by a delegation of four ex-FNG colonels. When the colonels were suspended by the British commander of SAAF, some of their supporters began a disturbance at a camp adjacent to a rifle range from which a group of British soldiers happened to be returning. Mistakenly believing that the latter were coming to quell the disturbance, the perpetrators opened fire, killing or wounding most of the range party, but were themselves shortly afterwards overcome by a British rifle company sent for that purpose. A breathless telephone call to fellow tribesmen in the Crater Armed Police, to the effect that 'The British are killing us', brought that hitherto loyal and steady force fatally into the conflict. A group of officers and NCOs of the 5th Fusiliers and the 1st Argylls, driving up Queen Arwa Road during their operational handover, were fired on and killed to the last man. With the Armed Police committed, the NLF seized control of Crater.

Recently returned to Colchester from cleaning up Cornish beaches after the *Torrey Canyon* oil-slick disaster,[10] 1st Battalion The Prince of Wales's Own was undertaking one month's duty as the Army's 'Spearhead battalion' at seventy-two hours' notice to deploy to meet an emergency. Two changes of significance had recently occurred. The battalion had reorganized onto an air-portable establishment of three rifle companies, a support company, command and headquarter companies and command had passed from Lieutenant-Colonel Roy Birkett to Lieutenant-Colonel Bill Todd. The latter had been battalion second-in-command during the 1965-6 Aden tour and, incidently, was the last commanding officer of the 1st Battalion with Second World War combat experience.

The Ministry of Defence ordered the Spearhead battalion to move to Aden on 28 June and Tac HQ and the leading rifle company left six hours later. It was confidently expected that arrival of the remaining companies by 30 June would be followed by the battalion being orderd to recover Crater, with which it had some familiarity. Instead, this duty fell to 1st Argylls, who completed a professional and bloodless occupation by night after the NLF leadership had been smuggled out in an ambulance with the connivance of British officials. While Crater was still under NLF control, 1st Prince of Wales's Own were made responsible for security of the newly vulnerable area of the Isthmus, lying between Crater and Khormaksar airfield, and the Al Mansoura detention centre close to what had become Aden's defensive perimeter. By that stage FLOSY and the NLF shared control of the up-country territories in a loose form of alliance with some of the tribes and SAAF battalions. The situation in Aden Colony was close to siege, but with air and sea routes still open. All the service families had left.

Once Crater had been retaken on 3 July, the battalion was freed from the Isthmus security task and redeployed to the Tawahi-Steamer Point area, which included Command Hill plus the Government and Command headquarters. Tawahi is laid out with a symmetry not unlike that of Crater, but is even more narrowly confined between the Jebel Shamsan and the sea. (See Map 4 on page 44.) As in 1965–6, the most dangerous adversaries were the pistol assassin and grenade thrower. Rioting would not have been difficult to control in the restricted street areas of Tawahi but, by mid-1967, the struggle for power between FLOSY and the NLF dominated the scene, with nightly fire-fights between them.

The battalion set up a protected main base in six blocks of flats in Ma'alla, while Battalion Tac HQ took over the managing director's house of an Aden trading company on Clocktower Hill, providing a commanding view over much of the operational area. Two tactics from the 1965-6 tour were revived, one successfully on the single occasion it was used but the other less so. The mobility of the reconnaissance platoon had been a source of information and quick reaction in Crater out of all proportion to its strength. The much more closely confined area of Tawahi significantly limited the platoon's scope and, especially in the narrow streets and hutted shanty town, made slow-moving mobile patrols vulnerable to grenade attack.

The reconnaissance platoon incurred eight casualties during the tour. Corporal Vick Goodall received multiple wounds from a grenade on 6 August. Private Phil Davison lost both legs when he was wounded for the second time and Corporal Jim Tattersfield suffered multiple injuries. Lance-Corporal Leslie Roberts died of burns as the result of a collision between one of the platoon's patrol

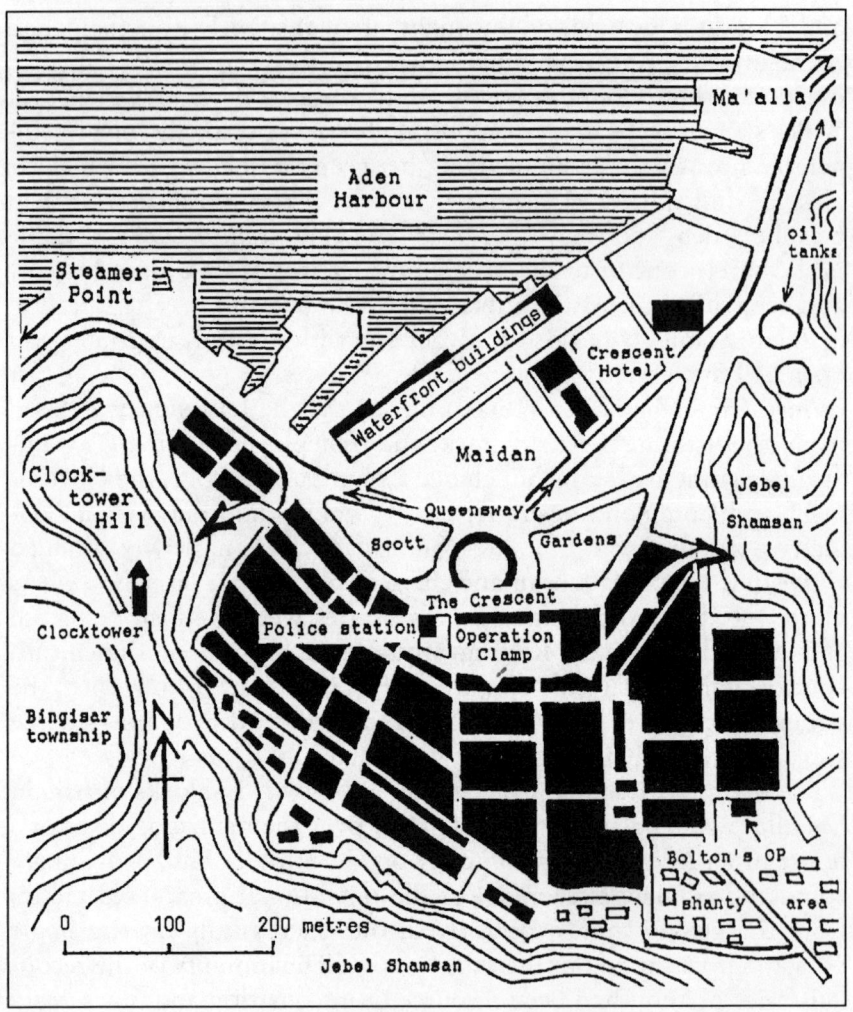

Map 4 *Tawahi*

vehicles and another security force vehicle. Sergeant Colin Jackson and Privates Mick Barker and Stew Milnes were injured in the same incident. Sergeant Jackson was badly burned whilst trying to extricate Roberts from the fiercely burning vehicle amidst exploding ammunition. He was subsequently awarded the British Empire Medal for gallantry for this action. Thus, although the reconnaissance platoon apprehended several terrorist suspects, the price was high.

A new form of impact grenade, reportedly of Russian origin, made its appearance. Corporal Wally Walford of the assault pioneer platoon was wounded in the head by one of these missiles while wiring in Tawahi on Sunday, 16 July. A fragment lodged against his brain but, after surgery and care, he was able to make the squeamish wilt by an account of an operation involving peeling back part of his skull. The old adversary, the pistol assassin, also took his toll. Lance-Corporal Trevor Holmes of Support Company was shot dead in a bookshop alongside the Bingisar post office on 21 August. None of the local witnesses to his murder made any attempt to identify his killer amongst the suspects rounded up.

An 81 mm mortar attack on Middle East Command Headquarters on 26 August gave rise to some amusement amongst those who had long been in the thick of it. Counter-measures were clearly required and quickly. Jebel Shamsan 'Rimrock' patrolling became a new operational commitment, helped by helicopter lift to the high ground and Sioux helicopters searching for likely baseplate positions. No further mortar attack was made on Command Headquarters but an intelligence report suggested that the NLF mortar team had been banished up-country for missing a truly sitting target!

Interfactional fighting between the NLF and FLOSY became a nightly occurrence in which the battalion took no side. The end of the tour was marked by a concerted terrorist attack on Tawahi and Steamer Point on 14 October, which both the NLF and FLOSY declared to be the 'anniversary of the revolution'. At 0905 hours Battalion Tac HQ on Clocktower Hill and four OPs came under intensive automatic fire. Privates Lance Hepworth and David Yates of A Company, manning an OP on a block of flats at the rear of Tawahi, were wounded in the head. The OP was commanded by Corporal Ken Bolton, who calmly reported them unconscious and unlikely to survive.

This was the occasion for reuse of Operation Clamp, which had been devised to confine rioters in Crater but planned to limit terrorist fire positions in Tawahi and keep open the route to the harbour. A Company (Major Dick Glazebrook) was already in position on the rooftops of the Tawahi Crescent, Support Company (Major Donald Hall) was ordered to picket a route to Corporal Bolton's OP and evacuate it, while C Company (Captain Edwin Beckett) was despatched up the Jebel Shamsan to dominate the situation from there. Arrival of B Company (Major Peter Wade) from reserve to join A Company on the rooftops brought all four companies into the fire-fight, which was won without difficulty.

Privates Terry Carter and Henry Irvin of Support Company were slightly wounded by a grenade thrown in the final moments of the picketing operation to recover Corporal Bolton's section and his two wounded. Private 'Huggy' Hugill was wounded by another grenade as Support Company completed this task. Fire on terrorist positions, including that from a troop of The Queen's Own Hussars under command, was intensive throughout. Later, intelligence reports put the enemy dead and wounded in the seventies but this was probably a misinterpretation by Radio Cairo of the casualties the NLF alleged they had inflicted on the battalion.

The battalion's third and last Aden tour ended on 20 October when Tawahi and Steamer Point were handed over to 45 Commando Royal Marines, who had been flown from Singapore in anticipation of the doubtful privilege of walking backwards into the sea, firing as they went. In the event, this proved an unnecessary precaution, as FLOSY and the NLF were still too busy fighting each other when the Marines left.

The 1st Battalion sustained twenty-nine casualties during the four months in Aden, including two killed and five seriously injured. There were 821 terrorist incidents in Aden Brigade area in August 1967, compared with fifty-two for the previous August. This increased tempo was recognized by a declaration of active service on 15 August and authority for operational awards. Corporal Ron Bradley and Private Phil Davison, both of the reconnaissance platoon, each received the Military Medal for gallantry. Colonel Bill Todd and eight officers and soldiers were mentioned in despatches. A full list of awards for the final tour of duty in Aden appears in Appendix 5.

Aden 1958 to 1967 was not a situation susceptible to a military solution. Britain's influence in South Arabia was lost through political neglect and ineptitude.

2
Beside the Sea

'Where the brass band plays tiddly om pom pom.'

The 1st Battalion's tours of duty in Gibraltar and Cyprus had more points in common than barracks overlooking the Mediterranean. Sun and sea induced a holiday atmosphere, which almost everyone appreciated and set out to enjoy. But in each station the battalion was the only one present, on a permanent basis, with a self-important headquarters watching closely over every move. An old-style colonial atmosphere, in Gibraltar in particular, encouraged a preoccupation with military non-essentials developed in the past to keep soldiers busy in outposts where training opportunities were restricted. For much of the year the sun discouraged vigorous activity; strong drink was cheap and readily available. But none of these matters gave rise to serious concern.

Lieutenant-Colonel Boris Garside brought the battalion to Gibraltar from Aden by sea in the spring of 1959. Spirits were high at the prospect of a more predictable programme, improved sporting facilities and, for the married men, being reunited with their families. There was no significant restriction on travel to Spain at that time, so even the less adventurous were planning expeditions to Grenada, Seville and Madrid. Training in Tripolitania and travel to Morocco were on the cards, so there was no concern about being cooped up on the Rock. All these expectations were to be fulfilled and more. Gibraltar proved ideal for bringing the still relatively new battalion into closer cohesion, after the frequently changing detachments in South Arabia. Near-complete isolation from the rest of the Army, for what turned out to be longer than the anticipated two years, was perhaps less of an advantage.

The role of the infantry battalion in Gibraltar was protection of the Colony from outside threat and to support the civil power in the event of internal unrest. Neither possibility was considered very likely in 1959, but the widening scope of extremist Middle East terrorist activity had to be kept in mind. Much later the Provisional IRA became a danger. Gibraltar was still important as a base for the Royal Navy and was to become increasingly so, when it was decided to switch the main Mediterranean naval base there from Malta. Major units of the fleet staged through the port frequently, providing welcome and strong competition for the battalion sports teams. On the Rock, the Fortress Engineer Regiment Royal Engineers and RAF Gibraltar had keen and high-standard teams for almost every sport except rugby football. The Colony had no rugby pitch but one was discovered across the frontier in Spain in the season before the battalion left in 1961.

Ceremonial absorbed much of the battalion's time but not an equivalent proportion of its energies. The routine guards were on the Governor's residence, the Convent, and at the only land frontier crossing into Spain, known as the Four Corners Guard from the days when it was the guardhouse for sentries stationed at the four corners of the Fortress. These duties were performed in a high profile manner that invited the curiosity and criticism of senior officials, tourists and others equally pressed as to how to spend their day. The forbearance of the British soldier in such circumstances is remarkable, thanks to his awareness of the irony of his situation. Telephoning a guard commander to inquire how an inspection by a senior visiting officer had passed off, Regimental Sergeant-Major Neville Taylor concluded, 'Where's he gone now then?' 'For a bloody 'aircut, I 'ope, sir,' came the prompt response.

At routine intervals the battalion provided a platoon in blue or white ceremonial costume, depending on the season, to perform the ancient 'Ceremony of the Keys', together with the Band and Corps of Drums. This ritual dates from the end of the four-year 'Great Siege' of Gibraltar in 1783, when the then Governor – Sir George Elliott – decided to make the fortress impregnable against *coup-de-main* attack, the means by which the British had captured the Rock in the first place in 1704. Elliott decreed that the three main gates should be locked at sunset after all 'aliens and non-residents' had been safely shut out. So keen was Sir George to ensure that no alien should disturb his sleep that he kept the keys on his own belt. A 'Keys Sergeant' was appointed to lock the gates and deliver the keys to the Governor at sunset.

Inauguration parade of the 1st Battalion at Dover on 31 July 1958. ABOVE The Colonel-in-Chief, Her Royal Highness The Princess Royal, with the Colonel of the Regiment, Brigadier R. J. Springhall (left) and the Deputy Colonel, Brigadier G. H. Cree. BELOW The Colours of the 1st Battalions of the two former regiments are marched past.

ABOVE, LEFT Aden 1958. Major Peter Steel, Lieutenant Roy Quinn, CSM Ben Campey and Lieutenant Tony Jackson with a group of Special Guards in the Western Aden Protectorate. RIGHT Vickers machine-gunners at Mukeiras.

BELOW British Forces Aden Protectorate Boxing Champions 1958-9. Back row: NK, Private T. Burke, NK, Corporal K. Bowman, Lieutenant Tony Nevile, Privates N. Burns, A. Wray, N. Andrews, G. Doran and A. Kirk. Front row: NK, Private G. Callan, Corporals D. S. Kenny, L. Waters and K. A. Bolton, Privates N. Wilkin, 'Rocky' Neal and Corporal P. J. Russell.

ABOVE, LEFT Regimental Sergeant-Major N. D. Taylor. Right HRH The Princess Royal speaking to Colour-Sergeant 'Spike' Saywell, when inspecting the 1st Battalion Guard of Honour outside the Convent on her arrival in Gibraltar.

BELOW The old Colours of the West and East Yorkshire Regiments march off parade for the last time, 7 June 1960.

ABOVE, LEFT Inauguration parade of the 3rd Battalion at Beverley on 15 July 1961. Number 3 Guard commanded by Major Charles Rennie. RIGHT. HQ Company, 1st Battalion marching through Homs (Tripolitania) November 1960. Left to right: Captain David Dodd (Adjutant), Corporal Basil Dilcock and Drum-Major Lionel Hornby.

BELOW 3rd Battalion recruits exercising on Salisbury Plain, summer 1961.

ABOVE Winners Gibraltar Command Athletics Championships 1961. Back row: Lance-Corporal Beaumont, Private Colley, Lance-Corporals Chappelow and Brindle, Private Atkinson and Corporal Clark. Centre row: Privates Davis and Mason, Lance-Corporal Lumb, Private Davis, Lance-Corporal Blyth, Corporal Elsey and Private Prince. Front row: Private North, Major M. A. Stevenson, Major R. M. Johnson, Lieutenant-Colonel W. S. G. Armour, Captain D. H. Holmes, CSMI Browning, Captain W. C. A. Battey.

BELOW Winners BAOR Cross-Country Championship 1963-4. Left to right: Lance-Corporal Mick Conroy, Corporal Tony Waterhouse, Private Bill Waddington, Lance-Corporal Billy Walters, Private 'Blackie' Broadhurst and Herman Brecht, the team's ex-Olympic coach.

ABOVE Farewell to Wuppertal parade, June 1963. C Company commanded by Lieutenant T. C. E. Vines, with Lieutenant J. H. Desmond. (The officers are carrying swords, not umbrellas.)

BELOW Lieutenant Ivan Scott Lewis ready to lead the Berlin-Helmstedt convoy through the Soviet zone, November 1963.

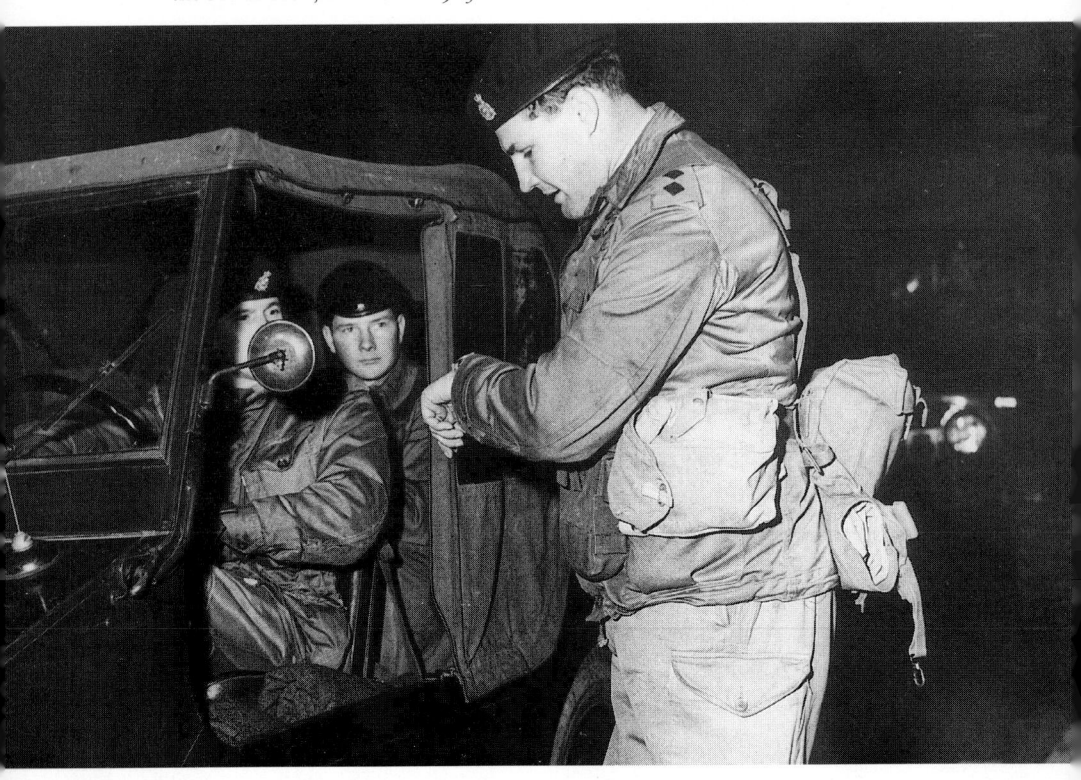

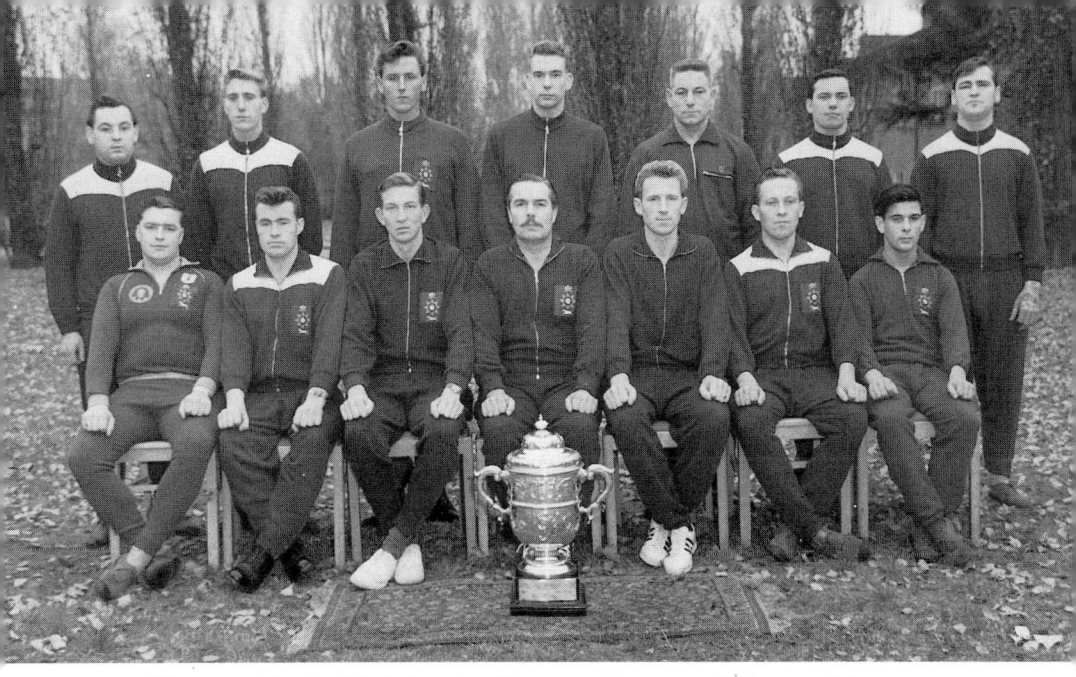

ABOVE Winners of the BAOR Swimming Championships 1964. Back row: Privates M. Cunningham, A Henderson, B. King, S. J. V. Cossins, Corporal B. Hunter and Privates H. Isles and S. Moy. Front row: Lance-Corporal M. F. Uscroft. Private J. Berry, Lieutenant J. S. Eaton, Lieutenant H. Rushworth, Corporal J. H. Bennett and Privates M. Page and B. Fox.

BELOW The 1st Battalion Cub and Brownie Packs. Back row, left to right Joan Sherratt, Bridget Crowfoot, Battalion Padre, 'Jimmie' Brooks and Peggy Hardaker.

ABOVE, LEFT Sergeant Mick Garrigan receiving the welterweight prize, which secured the Berlin inter-unit boxing trophy for the 1st Battalion, from Brigadier Alan Taylor.
RIGHT Lieutenant-Colonel Peter Taylor with Prime Minister Harold Wilson, Berlin 7 March 1965.

BELOW The PM with Regimental Sergeant-Major Tommy Wall (left), Colour-Sergeant George Hardaker (with mug), who had heard the story before, and Company Sergeant-Major Sid Shepherd.

Like not a few events that have their origin in sound military precautions, this one had received some embroidery over the years. By the mid-twentieth century, the keys were held by the Governor, handed over to the Escort to the Keys (a platoon of the Garrison battalion or the local volunteer Gibraltar Regiment) and used to effect a ceremonial locking of the Waterport Gate on one occasion every six weeks. After the escort had been challenged, 'Who goes there?' and the guard had received the predictable and stirring reply 'Queen Elizabeth's Keys', the keys were marched up Main Street and handed back to the Governor waiting on the steps of the Convent. Each move was accompanied by a fanfare or piece of military music. The whole event was evidently much appreciated by the citizens of Gibraltar, the increasing number of tourists and everyone else who rejoices in occasions of this kind.

Guards of honour for visiting dignitaries also came thick and fast. For the officers and men of the guard, these functions presented few hazards, other than the weather. It is difficult to look keen and 'guarding' with rain streaming off the end of your nose. Generals or politicians in crumpled grey suits are small beer to the experienced guard of honour soldier. He much prefers to turn out for a foreign dignitary in exotic rig, who might startle him and those around by asking in an Oxbridge voice, 'How do you fancy our chances in the World Cup?' 'Well, since you ask . . .' the soldier begins, as the guard commander holds his breath.

Appreciation of a ceremonial performance is a minor art form that possibly merits development. In a letter to Colonel Boris Garside after the battalion had provided a guard for the opening of the Gibraltar Legislative Council on 16 October 1959, the Governor wrote, 'I was particularly impressed by the guard of honour, who were extremely well turned out and carried out the drill movements very well indeed. They were a first-class guard of honour and I was very impressed by them.' It seems that the ADC had not reached far into his *Golden Treasury* when composing that draft. Another side of the coin was reflected in the words of a visiting admiral who took Garside by the shoulder and said, 'My God, you must be a proud man to command a regiment like this.'

Well before 1960 was under way it was formally announced that the Colonel-in-Chief, Her Royal Highness The Princess Royal, would present new Colours to the 1st Battalion in Gibraltar on

7 June that year. Since amalgamation the battalion had carried the Colours of the former 1st West and 1st East Yorkshires. Colours of infantry regiments of the line are expected to endure the ravages of wind and rain for twenty-five years, after when their silk fades and the embroidery by the ladies of the Royal College of Needlework begins to come away. As it happened, both sets of 'old' Colours were quite new. The West Yorkshires had received theirs on a warm sunny day at Spittal, Austria in July 1951 and the East Yorkshires on a paralysingly cold one at Osnabruck, in Germany, in November 1956. Even so, new Colours were required for the now single regiment and the date soon became central in everyone's calendar.

An earlier date to which the battalion was keenly looking forward was 22 February, when the former Colonel of the West Yorkshires – Field-Marshal Sir William Slim, KG – and Lady Slim were due to call on the Rock. They were on their way home by sea on the SS *Arcadia* from Australia, where Sir William had been a most popular Governor-General for almost seven years. Foul cold and wet weather, such as the Mediterranean always has up her sleeve, began in mid-February and persisted until the end of March. This delayed the *Arcadia* by twenty-four hours and caused her to anchor at the far side of Algeciras Bay. Undeterred, the Field-Marshal crossed the bay by launch in a rough sea to spend just over an hour with the officers, warrant officers and sergeants, when he returned the silver Horse of Hanover centrepiece which the regiment had lent to him to use on his dining table in Canberra. The serving veterans of Imphal and other battles with 14th Army glowed with pride in their association with the great soldier.

While Gibraltar was still referred to occasionally as 'The Fortress', it no longer had any artillerymen to fire salutes. Thus when the Commander of the American 4th Cruiser Squadron arrived in USS *Boston*, on one of the few fine days in February, it fell to Support Company to fire a twenty-one-gun salute from the King's Bastion saluting station with 25-pounder guns held on the Rock for that purpose. The 'gunners' acquitted themselves well in this unusual infantry duty and were subsequently called upon to fire many more gun salutes, including those to mark Her Majesty The Queen's Birthday. Hearing of all this, the then Regimental Secretary – Major Harry Spencer – looked into the histories and discovered that 1st East Yorkshires had carried out an exactly similar commitment when providing the British Legation Guard at Peking from 1925 to 1928.

Harry Spencer brought an immense knowledge of regimental history to his post of Regimental Secretary and was the author of the first handbook on the founder regiments and the present one up until 1966. He served as Regimental Secretary from the formation of Regimental Headquarters in 1959, and as curator of the museum and editor of the regimental journal, until his retirement at the end of 1976. His dedication to the history of the regiment and to all its interests was remarkable – even for a mind as inquiring and responsive as his.

There were precious few sites suitable for tactical training on the Rock, in particular for preparing and testing younger officers for their practical promotion examinations. This difficulty was overcome by a series of plain-clothes picnics in the countryside across the border in Spain. Short walks into the hills allowed appreciations of the ground to be made and theoretical questions to be posed and answered. A sprinkling of wives and one or two girlfriends added authenticity to the picnic scene, while ensuring – indirectly – that questions were answered against the pressure of time.

Even the more cynically-minded found little to complain of in Gibraltar and the increasing number of sportsmen of all kinds were delighted with the facilities and opportunities for team and individual activities. The battalion had established the foundations of sound athletics, boxing, rugby, soccer and swimming teams while in Aden. In Gibraltar, all of these other than the rugby team were trained and tested against the tough opposition of the Fortress Engineer Regiment, RAF Gibraltar and visiting units of the Royal Navy.

In the first season on the Rock, a representative boxing team from the battalion met opponents from the aircraft-carrier HMS *Victorious*, with a crew strength of 2,000, and were narrowly beaten seven bouts to five. The Gibraltar Garrison novices boxing competition was won decisively against RAF Gibraltar and the battalion provided six boxers for a Combined Services (Gibraltar) team against Cambridge University. The University won eight bouts to two but both Corporal Ken Bolton and Lance-Corporal Danny Davis won their bouts with knockouts in the first and second rounds respectively. The competitions against HMS *Victorious* and

Cambridge gave battalion boxers valuable experience and both occasions were greatly enjoyed by those supporting the teams. More details of the sporting achievements of the 1st Battalion in these early years can be found in chapter 10 and Appendices 6 and 7.

The week 6 to 12 June 1960 was a momentous one. Her Royal Highness The Colonel-in-Chief arrived in Gibraltar at 1815 hours on Monday 6 June in an aircraft of the Queen's Flight. She was received at the Convent by a guard of honour under command of Captain W. C. A (Bill) Battey and on which the Regimental Colour of 1st West Yorkshires was carried by Lieutenant Allan Bower. The weather was uppermost in every mind, as an unseasonably strong westerly wind had blown the Egyptian tanker *Cleopatra* aground on her way through the straits on the Sunday and continued to blow hard next day.

Tuesday dawned bright and clear but with the westerly persisting. The spectators, many of them from England visiting Gibraltar for the occasion, were in their places by a quarter past nine, the ladies elegant in 'hats suitable for parade'.

Timings were precise. At 1016 hours exactly the four guards of the battalion, wearing white No. 3 Dress with matching belts and rifle slings, marched on parade to a new march composed to mark the birth of Prince Andrew, 'Royal Event'. The Governor, General Sir Charles Keightley, arrived at 1028 hours to be followed two minutes later by Her Royal Highness, each being received with a Royal Salute. The weather stood to hold, the dignitaries were in place and everyone settled themselves as comfortably as possible to enjoy the spectacle.

The presentation parade was held on Europa Point, with the peak of the Rock as a backdrop on the landward side and the Pillars of Hercules visible through the summer haze across the straits to the south. It was a fine setting. After the Colonel-in-Chief had inspected the parade, the Band and Drums carried out the slow and quick-march trooping across the front of the guards before the four old Colours were marched off for the last time. Invariably an emotionally charged event, this one was made particularly so by the westerly wind unfurling the Colours so that they streamed out horizontally with every detail visible, in front of the Ensigns, as they were slow-marched away to 'Auld Lang Syne'.

The piling of drums and the service of dedication, conducted by the Deputy Assistant Chaplain-General Gibraltar, followed. At the outset, Colonel Boris Garside requested, 'Reverend Sir, on behalf of the Regiment we ask you to bid God's blessing on these Colours.' The Reverend Edward Morris replied, on behalf of himself and padres of the various denominations, 'We are ready so to do.' Then he continued:

> Forasmuch as men in all ages have made themselves signs and emblems of their allegiance to their rulers, and of their duty to uphold those laws and institutions which God's providence has called them to obey: we, following this ancient and honoured custom, stand before God this day to ask His blessing on these Colours and to pray that they may be an abiding symbol of our duty towards our Sovereign and our Country, and as sign of our resolve to guard, preserve and sustain the great traditions of bravery and self-sacrifice of which we are the proud inheritors.

After the words of consecration had been spoken, a prayer and the blessing, the new Colours were handed in turn to Her Royal Highness by Major W. S. G. (Billy) Armour and Major Peter Steel. Her Royal Highness then presented them to the ensigns. The Colour Party had been chosen with due sense of the occasion. The ensign of the Queen's Colour was Lieutenant David Dodd who had been with 1st West Yorkshires at Suez in 1956. The ensign of the Regimental Colour was 2nd Lieutenant John Beckett, the first regular officer to be commissioned into the combined regiment. Company Sergeant-Major Tom O'Brien had served with both the founder regiments, Colour-Sergeant 'Spike' Saywell had served in Burma with the West Yorkshires and Sergeant Sid Jasper was an East Yorkshire veteran.

Her Royal Highness then addressed the parade:

> Since I last saw the Regiment on its amalgamation parade at Dover nearly two years ago, I have watched with pride and satisfaction your activities in Aden and Gibraltar. I have heard nothing but praise for the way you have settled down together and carried out your military tasks which you have been called on to perform. Here in Gibraltar, where many of you must feel somewhat restricted in your activities after your experiences in Aden, you are on view as ambassadors of your country to people of many nations who pass through on their travels. You

therefore have the very special privilege of demonstrating to them the traditional standards of the British soldier. From all I have seen of you today, I know that you are worthy of this trust.

In his reply, Colonel Garside said, 'Since the inaugural parade, we have striven in both Aden and Gibraltar to uphold the proud traditions of the two great Yorkshire Regiments which passed into our keeping and whose regular battalion Colours today were marched off parade for the last time. Our new Colours will be guarded and served in the highest traditions which are the heritage of The Prince of Wales's Own Regiment of Yorkshire.'

That afternoon, an alfresco tea-party was held on Europa Point, during which many members of the battalion and their families were presented to the Colonel-in-Chief. Later, Her Royal Highness and the Governor dined with the officers before joining Regimental Sergeant-Major Neville and Mrs Nolwyn Taylor as guests at the Warrant Officers and Sergeants' ball held at Imperial Court on Queensway. At midnight the Colonelcy of the Regiment passed from Brigadier Robin Springhall to Brigadier 'Munshi' Cree and command of the 1st Battalion from Lieutenant-Colonel Boris Garside to Lieutenant-Colonel Billy Armour. It had been a long but momentous day.

Next morning the *Gibraltar Chronicle* carried the headline 'Smartest Ceremonial Seen in Gibraltar for Years', below which was a report that the battalion had 'carried out a long and complicated parade in a manner regarded by old soldiers among the 2,500 spectators as the smartest seen in Gibraltar for a generation'. But the week was far from over. Although Wednesday was a holiday, Thursday saw rehearsals for another ceremonial on Friday 10 June: Her Majesty The Queen's Birthday parade, on which the battalion carried its new Colours.

The Presentation of Colours over, for the next twenty-five or so years anyway, the battalion was able to turn its attention to summer sports. The annual athletics meeting was held on the Europa sports ground on 23 June and was won by C Company. Lieutenant Allan Bower established a new discus record of 114 feet 10 inches and an own personal best. The Gibraltar Command athletics competition was won with a lead of thirty-six points over RAF Gibraltar, with the Fortress Engineers running them to a close finish for second place. Training for the swimming gala met with more enthusiasm than it might have been if held in Catterick. D Company won both the swimming and water polo competition and the battalion team the Command Challenge Cup. Three battalion teams entered the Rowing Regatta with short odds. A Company reached the final in the gigs but just failed to match the RAF for speed. D Company came third in the whalers which, to the immense relief of all present, the Navy won.

The final major event of the Gibraltar period was a four-week training visit to Libya, then quietly ruled by the good King Idris, during October–November 1960. The change proved to be more useful in anticipation than in reality but some valuable lessons were learned. The horrors of the expedition were neatly suppressed in one company report, 'A Company's efficiency, adaptability, team work and humour have all come to the fore and made life great fun.' Oh yes! The flies were expected but not the desert winds that blew down the tents or the rain that fell on the tentless.

The advance party with the ammunition, heavy equipment and vehicles crossed a tranquil Mediterranean in LST *Empire Guillemot* and bright sunshine. They enjoyed the voyage but, after docking at Tripoli, there was something of a rush to prepare to receive the main body due to arrive a few hours later by air. A single BOAC Britannia had been hired to transport the main body to Libya, which was achieved in six flights spread over several days. All began well enough but a demand for the reception base to be moved from the Italian-built barracks at Tarhuna to a bare and windswept hillside tested a sense of humour or two.

A workmanlike training sequence had been developed. A and D Companies established close-quarter battle and grenade ranges and what was quaintly referred to as the 'musketry camp' at Homs. They and the other companies passed through these in turn to fire their SLR, SMG and GPMG annual range courses and to throw their yearly quota of two No. 36 grenades. Those not engaged on the ranges tried tactical training in the desert, with varying degrees of success in finding their way back to their blown-down tents. Support Company fired their heavy weapons in remoter parts of the desert before driving to Homs to fire small arms. Everyone was united in their praise of the cooks, who produced good food almost free of flies.

The visit also had an intellectual stimulus. Everyone, other than those cooks who could not be spared, visited the Roman ruins of Leptis Magna and had their photographs taken relaxing on the broad steps of the 2,000-year-old amphitheatre. Tarhuna barracks also contained some specialist murals, which the new padre was thoughtfully advised to leave undiscovered. Headquarter Company was here, there and everywhere providing communications and administrative support, as well as firing their range courses. At the end of the training period, Headquarter Company HQ, with the Corps of Drums and accompanied by the adjutant, Captain David Dodd, marched from their inland camp through Homs to the sea, a distance of sixteen miles, for a final bathe before flying or voyaging back to Gibraltar. No one in the battalion returned in any doubt that the change had been good for him, but everyone was glad to be back.

Coincident with the early part of the Libya training period, a party led by Lieutenant Edwin Beckett drove through the Pyrenees and the south of France to Rome – to see the Olympic Games. Camping by the roadside and eating rations cooked by Sergeant Geoff Kennerdale, the party covered the 2,000 miles to Rome in seven days, saw most of the athletic finals and returned to Gibraltar via Capri, Naples and Sorrento within a month. The whole expedition was accomplished for £45 per head.

This is but one example of the manner in which groups from the battalion took advantage of the opportunities available from the Rock. There was mountain climbing in Spain within half a day's drive from the crossing point at La Linea and also in the northern Atlas range in Morocco. Sergeant Geoffrey Broadman, an Army individual ski champion, taught soldiers how to climb in summer and to ski in winter, from huts on the Sierra d'Lun and the Moyen Atlas. The ski training stood the battalion well after moving to Germany in September 1961.

The end of the Gibraltar period saw a loss to the 1st Battalion, for a few years at least, of a significant personality. Regimental Sergeant-Major Neville Taylor had held that post since the amalgamation parade at Dover. 'Spud', as he was universally known – although never within his hearing – appeared at first sight the archetypal RSM: tall, gravel-voiced and pugnaciously handsome. When young, someone had told him that he looked like Clark Gable and no one subsequently had the courage to tell him that the ears were the chief similarity. He had enlisted in the West Yorkshires two days before outbreak of the Second World War, then served with 1st East Yorkshires in India, Burma and later in the Malayan campaign. He was a highly efficient and much respected RSM but his twinkling blue eyes were the giveaway. Laughter was always just around the corner when Spud was present. Luckily, he was to rejoin the battalion as a Captain Quartermaster in time for the second Aden tour, which began in 1965.

Cyprus 1968-72

The 1st Battalion first returned to the Mediterranean seven years after leaving Gibraltar. This was for an excercise in Cyprus in the summer of 1968, when part of the United Kingdom Strategic Reserve. This proved to be a fortuitous visit to the island as, although not known at the time, the battalion was to begin a two-year period of service there in early 1970. The commanding officer, Lieutenant-Colonel Bill Todd, sent a post-exercise report to Headquarters Strategic Reserve which was to prove of particular value to his successor. It was a well-crafted document, to which no one could take exception, but reading between the lines made clear that arrangements in Cyprus fell well short of excellent and the mid-summer climate was much more enervating than almost everyone anticipated.

Cyprus had been an independent member of the Commonwealth since 1959, following the vicious EOKA campaign conducted by Greek-Cypriot terrorists led by Colonel George Grivas with the aim of uniting Cyprus with Greece (*Enosis*). The constitution imposed upon the Cypriots by the combined pressure of Britain, Greece, Turkey and the United States[1] was flawed, in that Turkish-Cypriot interests were protected only by a blocking veto in cabinet, in which the Greek-Cypriots had a seven to three majority – as they also had in parliament. Bearing in mind the animosity between the two communities on the island, it was a recipe for confrontation. Nudged on by Grivas and his unfettered ex-terrorists, President Archbishop Makarios laid a new draft constitution before Parliament in 1963. This was flatly rejected by the Turkish-Cypriots who walked out of both cabinet and parliament. Whereupon fighting between the two communities broke out in the captial, Nicosia, and other main towns immediately before Christmas that year.

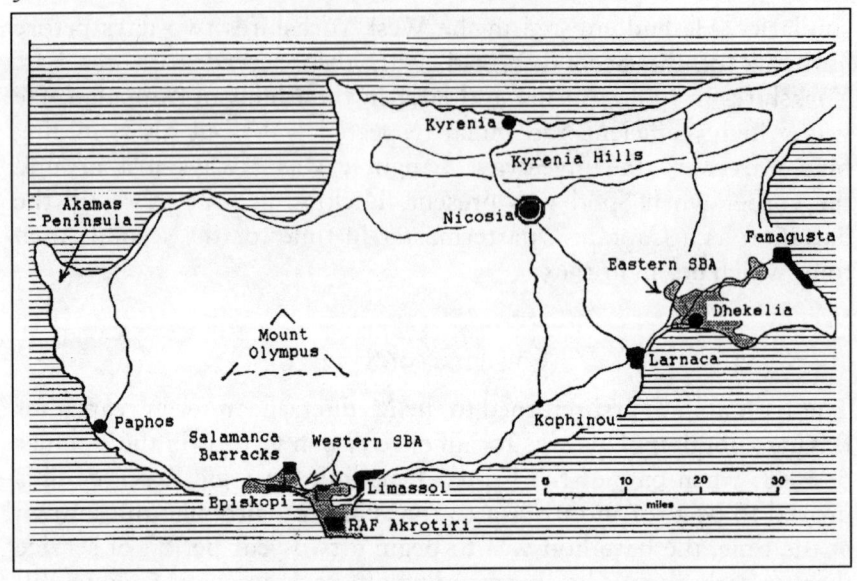

Map 5 *Cyprus*

Attempts by Britain, Greece and Turkey to restore peace and harmony having failed,[2] an appeal by Britain and the rump of the Cypriot Government to the UN Security Council led to the setting up of a UN force, UNFICYP, in March 1964. It was tasked 'to use its best efforts to prevent the recurrence of fighting and contribute to the restoration of law and order'. This force was still in Cyprus when the 1st Battalion The Prince of Wales's Own exercised there in 1968. It is still there, at the time of writing, thirty-one years after being first established.

Under the 1959 Treaty of Establishment[3] Britain retained two Sovereign Base Areas (SBAs) on Cyprus. As their name suggests, these remained British Sovereign territory, although Cypriots were allowed to continue living in them and travel on their public roads. The western SBA was required for the RAF base of Akrotiri, then of strategic importance to the Central Treaty Organization,[4] and the site of what had been chosen to be the joint headquarters of the British Army and Royal Air Force in the Middle East at Episkopi. Sixty miles away the untidily shaped eastern SBA contained the Army administrative base of Dhekelia and, at the end of the tendril reaching out towards Famagusta, a strategic communications complex run by 9th Regiment Royal Signals.

When the advance party of the 1st Battalion arrived in Cyprus in January 1970, there had just been an explosion against the wall of a small electricity substation in the Western SBA. Only the detonator had gone off and the damage was repaired a few minutes after being examined by an explosives expert and whitewashed over by someone from RAF Episkopi, as that part of the SBA was then known. Against all the dictates of the Army Staff College and other seats of military learning, this event led to instructions being given to the resident battalion to mount guards on isolated British facilities all over the SBAs. Whoever had planted the explosive thereby learned that he had caused concern out of all proportion to his efforts to excite terror and the resident battalion was handed a commitment that, unaided, it would be unable to sustain for long.

This was the situation that the battalion inherited when it flew into Cyprus in February. With characteristic disrespect for the judgement of his superiors in office, the commanding officer (the author) suggested that, rather than wasting men and time guarding things, it might be more useful to find out who had planted the explosive, then send him an invitation to the Administrator's annual garden party or put right whatever other omission had given rise to his grievance. Not surprisingly, he was instructed to do as he was told.

As is not infrequently the case, this matter was apparently solved more by accident than design. Determined to to a job well if at all, the battalion mounted mobile patrols in the SBAs during the dark hours. One of these stopped the car of a Greek-Cypriot dignitary, reputed to be in touch with all shades of Cypriot political opinion, who was on his way home to Limassol after having had dinner with the General Officer Commanding, no less. The patrol included two of the three Haggan brothers[5] with which the battalion was stiffened at the time. They had both served in Aden and knew a thing or two about searching suspects for concealed arms and explosives. The dignitary was sent on his way after having been given a comprehensive going over with his arms stretched over the roof of his limousine.

Power of speech having been restored by the time he reached home, the man telephoned the GOC in a state of some concern. Although it was by then the middle of the night, the General thoughtfully telephoned the commanding officer to make sure that he was acquainted with all details of what had taken place. Relations between

Command and battalion headquarters were cool for a few days after this incident. Then intelligence was received that for the foreseeable future the SBAs had nothing to fear from explosive devices. It may have been a coincidence but the dignitary was reputedly in touch with all shades of political opinion. Instructions for the guarding of installations were withdrawn.

The battalion was based at Episkopi but required to detach one company to the Eastern SBA for its security and protection. During discussions in Cyprus in the autumn of 1969 the commanding officer of the outgoing battalion had suggested that the resident battalion's support company would be ideal for the detachment, as it was stronger than a rifle company, and comprised the more mature men suitable to be on detachment. The anti-tank and mortar ranges, too, were both on the fringes of the Eastern SBA. This proposal was knocked smartly on the head by the Command headquarters on the grounds that no one had previously suggested it but had nevertheless managed very well. Hence, A Company commanded by Major Tony Crowfoot went to Dhekelia and gave a very good account of themselves there. Halfway through the tour, due to a Ministry of Defence inquiry about retaining use of ranges, the battalion was asked to produce an appreciation of the advantages that might accrue from the resident battalion having its support company at Dhekelia. The paper was written and A and Support Companies changed places.

Cyprus was of course a delightful place to visit, especially during the English winter. Consequently a stream of senior officers, politicians and the like made the short drive from Command headquarters to Salamanca Barracks to be briefed or otherwise entertained. One senior visitor remarked to the CO, 'I am sorry to see that you already have two officers awaiting trial by court-martial.' Inquiries revealed that a large chart in the GOC's office headed 'Courts-Martial' included an entry 'awaiting trial: 2 officers 1 PWO'. These were two subalterns left behind by the previous regiment and put on the battalion strength, because their offences were civil ones that had to be tried in Cyprus. They had dented the roof of a taxi by dancing on it because the driver had demanded an exorbitant fare to drive them back to barracks late at night.

Few of these curiosities intruded into the day-to-day lives of the soldiers, who settled down to enjoy the sun, sea and magnificent sporting facilities. The site for the future headquarters Middle East Command had been chosen for the suitable nature of the nearby 'Happy Valley' as a polo ground. Within it also lay six soccer pitches, plus others for cricket, rugby and hockey. The athletics stadium was a joy to use. Sadly, the only available Olympic-sized swimming pool was ninety miles away at Nicosia, as the RAF were a bit touchy about sweaty soldiers using their pool at Akrotiri.

Such falls in sporting achievements as had inevitably been sustained during five years in Colchester, which included three emergency operational deployments as well as exercises abroad, were quickly turned around. Sport came to dominate almost everyone's thinking and military activity, as far as possible, was scheduled around the key events. Individuals who were to take part and influence regimental sport for years ahead came to the forefront during this period. Notable among these were Company Sergeant-Major Peter Blyth, Sergeants Dave Moffat and Byron Cawkwell, of the reconnaissance and signals platoons respectively, and Orderly-Room Sergeant Johnny Emms.

Also very influential was Corporal Benny Bates of the RAPC Pay Team, who ate, drank and slept football without ever failing to balance his ledger. He was a totally unsuppressed dynamo of enthusiasm and swept aside any triviality of service protocol that appeared likely to get between him and the match.

An entry in the 1st Battalion's *Digest of Service* for June 1970 reads, 'There is insufficient space to record in detail the tremendous volume of sport in which the battalion is now participating. For the record, it is actively and successfully represented in athletics, cricket, hockey, polo, sailing, skiing, soccer, sub-aqua, swimming, water polo and free-fall parachuting.' Polo was something new and the battalion had six or seven regular players. Under the captaincy of Major David Hanson, a team consisting of himself, Captain Tony Hincks and Lance-Corporals Len Hutton and 'Gran' Marsh defeated C Squadron Royal Scots Greys by seven goals to two in the semi-final of the Inniskilling Cup.[6] The final against A Squadron 17th/21st Lancers opened dramatically with Hanson scoring a goal in the first twenty seconds, but the Lancers scored the next six to win. Neither match was played on handicap.

Outside competition of a good standard was sometimes a problem, although RAF Akrotiri could usually be relied upon to provide a strong side for almost any sport. Fortunately, the battalion was well above establishment strength due to having received a contingent of over a hundred officers, NCOs and men from 1st York and Lancaster Regiment, on its disbandment shortly before the move to Cyprus.

The island presents the observer with a curious contrast of ancient history, with Roman ruins and tiny Byzantine churches nestling alongside wide, almost dried-up watercourses. Some Cypriots attribute the low rainfall to the Crusaders cutting down trees to build ships, but the more likely explanation is the clearing of the central plain, to plant crops, during the Lusignan period, which began after Richard I had left Cyprus on his way to the Third Crusade in June 1191. For a people who set so much store on their Greek ancestry, most Greek-Cypriots have surprisingly scant regard for preserving their heritage. While there are still quiet valleys with vineyards reaching to the horizon, almost all the accessible coastline is hemmed in by hotels and tavernas to draw the tourist trade.

Operational issues seldom upset the even tempo of life after the Western SBA explosive device affair. Someone, not from the battalion, tried to shoot down the helicopter taking President Makarios from Nicosia to look in on the Limassol wine festival but the British pilot managed to land the machine, even though he had a couple of bullets in his belly, and the matter seemed to blow over without further excitement.

Concern did arise, however, when a breakaway faction of the PLO sent a message to say that an aircraft packed with high explosive was to be crash-landed on Akrotiri runway with the aim of causing it serious damage. The same faction had hijacked three passenger 'planes, diverted them to a disused airstrip in Jordan and, after disembarking the passengers, blown up the aircraft. Activity at Akrotiri, in preparation for possibly recovering the stranded passengers was interpreted as hostile, hence the suicide-bomber threat.

Those in higher authority, in the Royal Air Force in particular, declared this to be an ideal chance for the resident battalion to show that it could do something other than win sporting competitions. 'But surely,' argued the commanding officer, who had once attended a course run by the Royal Australian Air Force, 'as soon as you pick up the aircraft on radar from Mount Olympus you can scramble a couple of Lightnings to shoot it down over the sea – and avoid a lot of mess?' Maybe this was part of the plan, but B Company and the reconnaissance platoon found themselves patrolling Akrotiri's fourteen kilometre perimeter for a few nights, peering anxiously into the night sky, until the passengers were rescued some other way and the fuss died down.

A battalion-scale exercise, the first since arrival on the island, was planned for November 1970. A relief battalion was flown in from Malta to cover any internal security requirements and all appeared set fair for a tactical approach march from near Paphos to the Akamas training area in the rugged extreme west of the island. Suddenly the British High Commissioner and the GOC were summoned to see the acting President. This was the genial Glavkos Clerides,[7] who was performing the duties of Head of State while President Makarios was on post-assassination attempt vacation. Accompanied by the commanding officer with map, His Excellency and the General called at the Presidential Palace in Nicosia to be told that the approach march would take the battalion through a region in which the Greek-Cypriot National Guard had heavy weapons, by inference in excess of treaty entitlement, concealed in the undergrowth. The exercise was switched to the opposite end of the island at twenty-four hours' notice and went tolerably well.

By early 1971 all the routine events of the Cyprus calendar had been negotiated through, round or over at least once and everyone was eagerly seeking a change. This materialized in the form of an exercise in Kenya during June and July. Thorough preparation was clearly necessary, but training for the African rain forest in Cyprus is not easy. Orange groves were tried but the trees were too small. It was fortunate that a company from the battalion had exercised in Kenya on a previous occasion, in January 1969 from Colchester, and in much the same area. The Quartermaster was therefore aware of the wrinkles. It was also an advantage to have the advice on living in the rain forest from Lieutenants Tony Blanch and Michael Watson, who had spent their boyhood in East Africa.

It had been hoped that the whole battalion would go to Kenya together but, due to pressure on the UK Strategic Reserve caused by the Northern Ireland emergency, no battalion could be provided to take on the Cyprus security commitments. Two Ordnance Corps sub-units, temporarily converted to the infantry role, were provided instead and the battalion went to Kenya two companies at a time.

The expedition was a great success and no one was eaten, or even frightened, by a lion.

Four base camps had been chosen within fifty-mile radius of Nanyuki, to the west of Mount Kenya. They varied in location from open savannah, scrubland and dense rain forest. Access to one of the forest sites became impossible after heavy rain, so only three were used. Even then, the last company to leave the Kathendini forest had to cut and log a new vehicle track to extricate themselves, which proved excellent training. Tactical field firing with minimum restrictions, patrolling in the rain forest and keeping healthy in a warm wet climate, as well as resisting temptations of the flesh, were all valuable experience. The few remaining expatriates living locally made everyone feel welcome and no one returned to Cyprus believing he had been cheated of his summer holiday.

During the second half of the Kenya training period, a signal was received announcing that the battalion would begin an eighteen-month tour of duty in Northern Ireland in April the following year. The emergency tour of 1969 was still fresh in many minds but there were no groans. 'Well,' someone remarked, 'we've had it pretty good for two years. It's time to get stuck in again.' Shortly after return to Cyprus, Lieutenant-Colonel David Hanson took over command of the battalion and began to train it for the situation it would face in Belfast. At that stage of the Ulster emergency, there was no specialist touring team to advise or help. Training concentrated on all aspects of internal security operations and officers, NCOs and men were sent on intelligence, dog-handling, booby-trap and other relevant courses. The advance party left for Belfast on 21 March 1972 and the main body quickly followed on.

Gibraltar and Cyprus gave the 1st Battalion some halcyon days. Their environments, in many ways similar but in other ways different, provided opportunities for constructive achievement. Both periods fell between turbulent times and were used to consolidate effort on the path that the regiment had chosen: that of professional soldiering and sporting excellence.

3
On the Rhine

'General, all they need are shoes.'
GENERAL AL GRUENTHER, US Army

The first British Army of the Rhine was primarily concerned with the river. The Armistice terms at the end of the Great War in 1918 required Germany to evacuate all troops from the Rhineland – her lands west of the Rhine – and for the Allies to hold key bridgeheads on both banks of the river. The purpose was to calm France's fear of a resurgent Germany and to provide a safeguard against surprise attack. Together with a larger French contingent, British troops held the bridgeheads for ten years. Under the Treaty of Versailles, occupation should have been for fifteen years but The Hague Conference of 1929, called to moderate German war reparations, decided on withdrawal five years ahead of schedule. Combined with other measures, this was intended to encourage the German economy and so strengthen the Weimar Republic's resistance to Communism. But it was the Nazis who overthrew the Weimar Republic in 1933. The German Army reoccupied the demilitarized Rhineland in 1936.

When victory came at the end of the Second World War, the Western Allies fulfilled the terms agreed at Yalta[1] and occupied Germany up to a line from Hamburg to the Czech frontier. This put around 190 miles between the Rhine and the new inner-German border (IGB) in the British sector of occupation in Westphalia in the north but only seventy miles at the nearest point, through the Fulda Gap leading to Frankfurt, in the US Army sector. The Rhine assumed a new significance when NATO was formed to present a united defence against any Soviet attempt to overrun Western Europe. When General Dwight Eisenhower, the first SACEUR, arrived at his temporary headquarters in the Astoria Hotel in Paris, in March 1951, he inquired of General Al Gruenther, his chief of

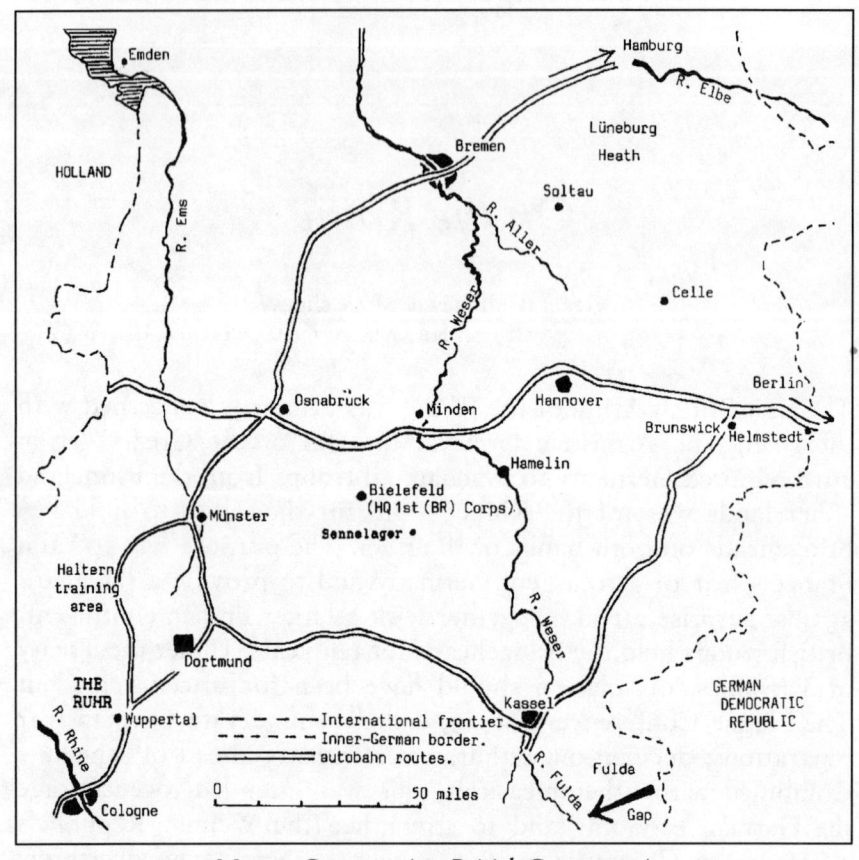

Map 6 *Germany (1st British Corps area)*

staff, 'What do the Russians need to march to the Rhine?' 'General,' came the reply, 'all they need are shoes.'

The initial NATO strategy was based on a withdrawal to the Rhine, where the Allies would make a united stand supported by a threat to use nuclear weapons against the Soviet Army. By the time 1st Battalion The Prince of Wales's Own joined BAOR for the first time – in 1961 – there had been significant changes. The West German Federal Republic had become a key partner in the NATO alliance and, not surprisingly, objected to the abandonment of seventy-five percent of its territory as the first defensive move. The strategy of 'defence of the river line' was consequently shifted eastwards to the Weser, which for much of its length is rather less deep and wide than the Pied Piper allegedly found it at Hamelin.

Nowhere does it present a military obstacle comparable to the lower Rhine.

A brief review of the strategy of the day is worthwhile, as the battalion was from time to time required to rehearse the part it would play in the event of war. The doctrine, by then unequivocally termed 'nuclear defence of the river line', was based on forcing advancing Soviet tank divisions to pause and concentrate on a river line, then annihilate them using nuclear weapons. The part to be played by infantry in the sector of 1st British Corps was to crouch in holes in the near bank of the river and report when sufficient Russians were assembled on the far bank to warrant a nuclear strike. Few expressed confidence in this plan, although practice in the construction of observation posts with four feet of overhead cover was accorded a high priority.

The battalion had arrived in Germany from Gibraltar via the United Kingdom, where everyone took his due share of leave. As a result, individuals joined the advance party at the new station – Wuppertal – as their leave period ended, rather than as their particular talents might to be required. This process, imposed on the battalion as a measure of financial economy,[2] hindered preparations for the new role. So far as is known it was not used again.

Two BAOR battalions serving with armoured brigades were then undertaking trials with the new tracked FV 432 (originally termed the armoured fighting vehicle 432 – the 'armoured' had to be dropped when it became apparent that the armour gave protection only against shell splinters and small-arms fire from an oblique angle). In common with all remaining infantry in 1st British Corps, the battalion was tactically mobile in what was unaffectionately known as the 'Humber armoured Pig'. Later, this snout-nosed wheeled vehicle was to earn honourable retirement via the Northern Ireland campaign, in which it afforded welcome protection against bottles and stones, provided someone shut the hatches and rear doors.

The consequences of the Duncan Sandys-driven Defence Review of 1956-7[3] were beginning to show in the financial constraints imposed upon the Army's modernization programme. Except for the relatively new 7.62 mm GPMG and self-loading rifle, the infantry still had the weapons and equipment of the period immediately following the Second World War. The main anti-tank weapon, the 120 mm Wombat, was recognized as having only a single-shot capability against the

Soviet T-55's 100 mm main armament, which had twice the range of the Wombat. The 3-inch mortar had not then been replaced by the much longer-range and more powerful 81 mm variety and the greatly prized Vickers machine-guns, with a range in excess of 4,000 metres, had been withdrawn and replaced with GPMGs with half that range when fixed onto tripods. New radios were in service but were seldom reliable except at short range.

Nor, it must be said, were the new regular recruits the cream of the nation's youth. Many were to develop well, physically and in motivation, thanks to good diet, exercise and training, but few were impressive on first viewing. This period, which saw the last National Servicemen leave by 31 March 1962, was probably the British Army's ebb-tide, post-1945.

The 1st Battalion had at this time a man who still stands out – more than thirty years later – as a most unusual commanding officer. Billy Armour looked ten years older than his forty-two years. He had been wounded in action against the Italians, Germans and Japanese during the Second World War and despised all of them. He spoke slowly and rather seldom, rarely walked other than on a golf course or grouse moor and, curiously because he had a reputation for always being late, had a shrewd sense of timing as well as of the relative importance of things. Without actually saying so, Armour let it be known that 'nuclear defence of the river line' was for the birds. He set the battalion to work shooting, marching and on realistic tactical training to company level. In this he was assisted by a strong team of middle-ranking officers and some experienced warrant officers and sergeants.

There was another problem – Wuppertal. This conurbation of seven towns linked by the River Wupper, and the overhead railway that runs above it, covers the western slope of a ridge in the industrial Ruhr attracting the highest rainfall in the Federal Republic. The battalion's barracks were on top of this ridge and, unlike the majority of ex-Wehrmacht establishments, was almost devoid of trees. This may have been due in part to the firestorm that resulted from an RAF raid, on 20 June 1943, in which 3,000 local people died. Even the seven *bürgermeisters*, when pressed, conceded that Wuppertal had never enjoyed much popularity as a garrison in the German Army. A REME warrant officer, appointed to command the LAD, described the main married quarters patch as a 'disaster area, which should be razed to the ground and built elsewhere'. As the first winter set in under a leaden sky, it was appreciated that the battalion had a potential Achilles' heel in the morale of the families, in particular those fresh from Gibraltar, in this grim, wet and unwelcoming place.

If the regiment owes anything to Wuppertal, it is thanks for providing the conditions which led to the flourishing of what shortly afterwards became known as the White Rose Club. Having set the military priorities, Colonel Armour asked his wife and the wives of other officers, warrant officers and senior NCOs to draw together the threads by which arrangements for the welfare and entertainment of families had been made in Gibraltar. The wives of company commanders took to visiting the wives of their husbands' junior NCOs and soldiers to establish a ready helpline in case of difficulty. From this grew the idea of a club to arrange gatherings and social outings – all with a view to fostering a strong community spirit and to avoid any sense of individual isolation, especially in the case of very young wives and those who would otherwise be kept at home by small children when their husbands were away.

Absence of any local entertainment for the single men, other than the AKC cinema and the odd *gasthaus*, performed a useful function in bringing the young officers and soldiers together while off duty. Games that could be played in the evenings, for example roller-skating hockey in the gymnasium, darts and most of the English pub pursuits, soon had inter-platoon rivalry running at a high pitch. The battalion sports teams got into their stride without perceptible pause. 4th Guards Brigade provided the geographically nearest opponents as all the units of 12th Infantry Brigade, of which the battalion was part, were at Osnabrück, some eighty miles away. 1st Welsh Guards were defeated four goals to three at soccer and 1st Irish Guards three-one. The 12th Brigade cross-counry competition, in which five major units took part, was won with a decisive margin of 134 points. Lance-Corporal John Redfern came second and all the other members of the team in the first twelve.

In the middle of a December night Sergeant Kenneth Johansson, commanding the quarter guard, was confronted by an armed German civilian demanding ammunition. This was available in the guardroom but was not for giving away and, as Johansson pointed out to the gunman, it was unlikely to fit the automatic pistol being held a few inches from his nose. This was long before the taking of hostages by armed lunatics became prevalent in Western society but

Johansson knew exactly what to do. For an hour he faced the gunman with calm resolution and eventually persuaded him to surrender his weapon and himself. He was subsequently awarded the Queen's Commendation for brave conduct in recognition of his action that night.

Individual training during the first winter was dominated by preparation for a competition between all the rifle companies in 12th Brigade involving a forced march, shooting, night orienteering, radio communication, battlefield first-aid, decontamination from nuclear fallout and a variety of other military skills. Excitement was generated less by the competition, appropriately named 'Last Straw', than by the selection of a team of one officer and twenty men from each company by the brigade commander himself. The aim was to prevent any team being 'packed' and to ensure that everyone was equally well trained, which was what happened – more or less. C Company's team, which happened to contain several battalion cross-country runners, opened up an early lead by winning the night-orienteering but came second overall at the end. The B Company team commanded by 2nd Lieutenant Peter Rogerson won the forced march with a panache that drew the grudging applause of teams that had already failed to match the time limit.

The Brigade Shooting Competition was approached with rather more enthusiasm. Demonstrating his infallible sense of timing, Colonel Armour arrived only for the prize-giving. Noticing that other commanding officers who had been present throughout the day were looking a bit tense, he asked, 'Who's won?' 'You have!' growled one.

The summer was taken up with battalion and then brigade-level training at Soltau and elsewhere. The weather to the east was a welcome change from Wuppertal and everyone enjoyed the clear skies and sunshine. The only excitement occurred during a two-sided exercise controlled by commander 12th Brigade. One of the company commanders sent the armoured squadron he had under command forward by a route that, so it transpired, it had not been intended he should choose. The 16th/5th Lancers' squadron outflanked the 'enemy' and enveloped exercise control headquarters in a dust storm. Senses of humour and proportion were briefly suspended with the brigade commander demanding instant dismissal of the company commander responsible. Calm was restored when Colonel

Armour stepped in with an assurance that a repeat performance was unlikely.

The second winter was markedly better than the first, with many crisp clear days. Exercise Last Straw had departed with the previous brigade commander, providing an opportunity to revive an alternative, well-tried institution. The Geddes Cup marching and shooting competition had been the annual test of individual and platoon training in the former East Yorkshires since 1928.[4] The new commanding officer, Lieutenant-Colonel Peter Taylor, extended the range of tests to include those covered by the brigade competition but with all soldiers of the rifle and support platoons taking part. The coveted cup was won that first year by a combined assault pioneer and reconnaissance platoon commanded by Sergeant 'Chick' Doran Thorpe. Except when active service has intervened, the competition has been conducted annually ever since.

Escape from Wuppertal to Denmark was granted to D Company in 1962 and to B Company in the following spring. The purpose was to provide part of an invading force to test the preparedness of Denmark's reserves. Under command of 1st Lancashire Fusiliers on each occasion, the companies motored to the Danish frontier in their armoured 'pigs' and then to the five-mile-long bridge leading to Odense on the island of Funen. (See Map 11 on page 124.) Having heard of D Company's ecstatic welcome there the previous year, B Company were disconcerted on reaching Odense on 4 May 1963 to see a candle burning in every ground floor window facing the street. 'Looks like being a quiet night,' said someone, 'there's a religious festival on.' It proved to be the anniversary of the 'coming of the light' when the British Army entered Denmark on 4 May 1945. No one had any sleep before the 'pigs' had to be driven onto the ferry at 0400 hours next day, for shipment to Zealand.

After each exercise the companies were most generously hosted by the Danish Army in Copenhagen for a week. Danish hospitality has to be experienced to be believed. A visit to the combined Carlsberg and Tuborg breweries looked potentially dangerous, not least as everyone was promised as much beer as he could drink. Possibly the slowly rocking tank of fermenting lager had the required salutary effect; no one drank too much.

The first of the three tours of duty with the Army of the Rhine undertaken by the 1st Battalion within the span of this story ended after only twenty-two months. It had been known since the autumn of 1962 that there would be a move to Berlin in the following June. Farewell was paid to Wuppertal with a march past for the *Oberbürgermeister* in the pouring rain and a speech in German by the commanding officer from the steps of the Rathaus. Peter Taylor was not seriously put out to be informed by the *Oberbürgermeister* that he spoke German with a marked English accent. Everyone was looking forward to Berlin.

Celle 1974-78

The 1st Battalion's second tour of duty with the Army of the Rhine, which began in June 1974, made a striking contrast with the first. By then all battalions of 1st British Corps were mobile under the protection of the FV 432 and the weapons inventory included the Swingfire command-controlled anti-tank guided missile, capable of destroying any known tank at realistic battlefield ranges. As a mechanized infantry battalion with 7th Armoured Brigade of the 1st Division, tasked to cover the area of front likely to receive a main Soviet thrust in war, there could be no question of anything other than the best in equipment, training and motivation.

This was not a role which could be taken up by individuals trickling in from leave and learning on the job, as in Wuppertal. The battalion left Belfast at the end of 1973 and then spent five months in Dover, from where links with Yorkshire were reforged. Contingents from the battalion exercised their Freedom rights to march through Bradford, Leeds and Morley to coincide with changes in their municipal status. From Dover, instructors and specialists went away for courses on all the new weapons and equipment. The instructors returned to teach the main body of men, while eighty drivers went to the Army School of Transport at Bordon to convert to the FV 432. Behind all this lay the knowledge that the battalion would spend four years in the mechanized infantry role – and in Celle.

This attractive German town had avoided being bombed, shelled or fought over throughout the Second World War. In 1945 there was a touching belief amongst some of the local inhabitants that this had been due to the town's tenuous connection with the British Royal Family.[5] Situated only thirty miles from the IGB, there was a distinct sense of being close to any potential action and the local population had proved themselves to be friendly and hospitable to the succession of British units that had lived amongst them. It was not a crowded garrison. The battalion shared it only with a locating regiment, Royal Artillery. The surrounding countryside was varied and the training areas more than adequate.

During the Celle period the battalion could look forward to three major breaks in routine. It was known that at least two Operation Banner tours of four months each would have to be undertaken in Northern Ireland and that an opportunity would arise for full battle-group training at Suffield in Canada. The commanding officer, Lieutenant-Colonel Tony Crowfoot, was very professionally minded, thorough in all to which he turned his hand and familiar with the demands of the Army of the Rhine in the 1970s. At this stage there was no relaxation in the threatening stance of the Soviet Union or the Warsaw Pact. The stone-faced Brezhnev was still in power in the Kremlin and the smile of Mikhail Gorbachev as yet unknown in the West.

The manner in which the battalion tackled its early commitments quickly gained the favourable attention of the commanders of 7th Armoured Brigade, 1st Division and 1st British Corps. The sporting opportunities presented by four years of relative stability, excellent facilities and tough opponents were inspirational. The rugby XV got off to a good start, under the captaincy of Major Ivan Scott Lewis, playing eight matches in quick succession in the 1st Division knock-out competition. The first tactical test came in the form of Exercise Red Rat 74 in the late summer. The battalion deployed with 7th Armoured Brigade at Soltau. Among several distinguished visitors was the Chief of the General Staff, Sir Peter Hunt, who was later to distinguish himself further by declining his due promotion to Field-Marshal on the grounds that the Army had been reduced below a safe level by Government cuts during his stewardship.

An unusual feature of Trenchard Barracks in Celle was the experimental single-soldier accommodation block in the form of apartments for three or four men. Each had individual sleeping areas, a kitchen, shower, sitting room and front door complete with bell. Not surprisingly, the apartments were very popular, although the men of C Company – who occupied them – were obliged to keep them in an unnaturally tidy state, as visitors to the battalion invariably wished to see them.

Aware that time would be short for individual training during the first winter, Colonel Crowfoot regrouped the battalion into 'wings' for trained soldiers, advanced infantrymen, support weapons, driving and maintenance and sports. In this way the expertise of battalion instructors was used to best effect, no one was retaught anything in which he was already competent and sport was not neglected. The spring of 1975 was dense with mechanized training exercises in the field, quickly followed by preparation for the first Operation Banner tour of duty in Northern Ireland. Experience gained in the first five years of the emergency had been applied in the development of a comprehensive training sequence at Sennelager, where a mock urban area had been built for use by BAOR battalions. The first Operation Banner tour in Londonderry is described in chapter 7.

The centrepiece of 1976 was all-arms training in the mechanized infantry role at Suffield in Alberta. This 700 square miles area of Canada's treeless prairie was leased for realistic training in armoured and mechanized infantry battle-groups with live firing, including artillery and tank main armament, in a tactical setting. Total absence of any local agriculture or population allowed the relaxation of range safety measures, so that they applied only to the military participants. As with prairie anywhere, fire remained an unavoidable hazard and much time and energy was expended in putting out fires started by live firing. The battalion went to Suffield in two groups. The first group comprised battalion headquarters, A Company, the reconnaissance platoon and support weapons elements, plus an armoured squadron each from the 13th/18th Royal Hussars and 3rd Royal Tank Regiment and Toombs Troop, Royal Artillery.

Unbelievably, the battle-group was based on a camp site named after Crowfoot, Chief of the Blackfoot tribe in the 1870s, who had brought peace to the Canadian West by signing a treaty with the Crown in 1877. His descendant, Chief Leo Pretty Youngman, travelled from his air-conditioned tepee at Gleichen in Alberta and, on arrival, changed into full costume, headdress and all, to meet Chief Not-Quite-So-Pretty Tony Crowfoot and smoke a pipe of peace on the open prairie. Once aboard the commander's FV 432, Chief Pretty put on his sunglasses and lit a long Marlboro'. Pipes of peace take some getting used to!

The other companies of the battalion followed in a second group to train as part of an armoured regiment battle-group. After each phase, around eighty men from The Prince of Wales's Own set out for adventure training in the Rocky Mountains of western Alberta. Based on the Daniel Thompson Resort, they climbed mountains and canoed in swift-flowing icy rivers. A height of 7,000 feet was achieved on two mountains, under the instruction of Captain David Howell and 2nd Lieutenant James Allen. The reputed presence of brown bears encouraged even the less agile to struggle to reach high ground. One party of the second group scaled Mount Elliot's 9,452 feet. Another group tried ice and snow climbing on the Athabasca Glacier, during which expedition Privates Paul Astbury and Paul Haynes spent thirty-six hours living in a snow hole, just to see whether they liked it. No one got frostbitten or seriously hurt.

Victory in the 1st Division skill-at-arms meeting at Horsten ranges over the period 4 to 6 May 1976 slipped from the grasp of the battalion by the narrowest of margins. End to the first day's shooting, in which the GPMG pairs was the main event, saw the battalion in the lead by a single point over 1st Division Headquarters and Signal Regiment. Pistol matches on the morning of the second day gave the Signallers a brief one point lead but the rifle match in the afternoon restored the position to exactly that at the end of the first day. The SMG match on the third and last day initially confirmed victory but an objection against Corporal Alan Wright's use of the sling to steady his weapon led to a re-shoot. Without a sling, Corporal Wright just failed to achieve his first score, so the battalion slipped into second place overall.

No such fate awaited the battalion soccer team, which won the BAOR Infantry Challenge Cup. The final was against 1st Queen's Own Highlanders at Sennelager and resulted in a three-one victory. Two goals were scored by Sergeant Byron Cawkwell and the other by Sergeant Dave Moffat. This was a satisfactory end to a season that had not started well, with defeat in the Army Cup by 1st Black Watch in the first round.

Command of the 1st Battalion passed to Lieutenant-Colonel Edwin Beckett in July 1976. As second-in-command earlier in the Celle period, he was familiar with the cries and had no difficulty in launching the battalion into a series of attack-orientated exercises, including a night river-crossing. After two training seasons in which defence had predominated, this was a stimulating change and, in many ways, Beckett was the ideal man to make it. The 1st Division was commanded at this time by Major-General David Alexander Sinclair, who had a sure grasp of armoured warfare and who would doubtless have reached the Army Board but for a devastating heart attack, which led to his early retirement. Speaking to the author about Colonel Beckett's extrovert style, he said, 'We were all waiting for Edwin to trip himself up – but he didn't. He just left everyone else standing.' The remaining two-and-a-half years in Celle capitalized on the sound investment, in the way of organization and training, put in during the first two years.

The shooting team returned from Bisley with improved team and individual scores. Lieutenant Nicholas Allbeury was 15th in Stage 1 of the rifle match and 59th in the Army 100. Sergeants 'Amos' Burke and Mally Hawes were 7th in the GPMG match and the GPMG team 7th overall. Lance-Corporal John 'Legs' Diamond and Private Roy Dickson both proved their worth in the rifle match and were placed in the Army's first 250 shots. These were good results in this invariably difficult competition, which even the most experienced marksmen find intimidating.

Lance-Corporal Peter O'Shaughnessy acted decisively when in command of the fire picket by putting out a potentially very dangerous fire. On hearing the alarm on the evening of 29 July he led the picket to the cookhouse and, on seeing the extent of the blaze, sent a soldier to turn off the gas main while he personally smothered the fire, in spite of intense heat from a burning cooker, using an asbestos blanket. He received the Commander-in-Chief's Commendation for his prompt action which saved the members of the picket from possible injury and the cookhouse from further damage.

New Year 1977 found everyone's thoughts turning to the next Operation Banner tour of duty in Northern Ireland, due to begin in mid-March and last until mid-July. Originally planned to be in the so-called bandit territory of Armagh, there was some disappointment when the venue was switched to Londonderry where the battalion had served during the immediately previous tour. There had been a major change in emphasis, however, in that the bogus PIRA ceasefire of 1975 had ended and full-scale hostilities resumed. An account of the second tour of duty in Londonderry is included in chapter 7.

The battalion ski team, and novices who aspired to join it, had enjoyed the winters of 1974, 75 and 76 as much as anyone. A ski hut in Bavaria had been used as a training base during the first winter, when creditable results for newcomers had been achieved in the 1st Division competition. Exercise Snow Queen organized by Captain Christopher Eddison, also in Bavaria, from November 75 to March 76 was designed to find new talent and develop a credible racing team to take part in the 1st Division and Army Ski Championships. The team was formed, trained and took part but brought home no trophy. Two teams were formed for the following winter, the Alpine team of experienced skiers and the Nordic team of novices, to compete in the Army Nordic Championships in Austria. The only first place was won by Private Guy Mellors in Group B of the parallel slalom but much valuable experience was gained. In the winter of 1977–8, over 120 soldiers spent two weeks at the battalion's ski hut at Kranzegg in Bavaria, whose *bürgermeister* presented a stainless steel vase as the inter-company trophy.

The highlight of the battalion's final year in Celle was the regimental reunion, organized by the 1st Battalion over the weekend 23–25 June. The Regimental Colour was trooped and the salute was taken by Lieutenant-General Sir Richard Worsley, Commander 1st British Corps, who had taken such a close and friendly interest in battalion affairs. Among the regimental guests was Major-General Sir Francis de Guingand, Field-Marshal Lord Montgomery's chief of staff from Alamein to Luneburg Heath. General Freddie unveiled a portrait of himself by Carlos Sancha at a special ceremony, complete with fanfare. Other distinguished guests included the Lord Mayors and Mayors of five of the regiment's six Freedom cities and towns – Beverley, Bradford, Harrogate, Hull and Leeds – with their wives and a huge contingent from the Regimental Association. It was a fitting climax for an outstandingly successful four-year tour of duty, in which everyone could take pride.

It was a great shame that the 1st Battalion had to leave Germany in 1978, at a point when it had reached such a level of operational competence in the mechanized infantry role. Ironically, the Army was shortly to extend the tours of duty for infantry battalions in the Army of the Rhine from four to five years or longer, so as to take full advantage of the costs of training and retraining. This change came too late to delay the move of the battalion to England in August 1978.

Osnabrück 1990 – 94

It was to be twelve years before the 1st Battalion would next be stationed in Germany, although returns for exercises in the air-mobile role with 24th Air-Mobile Brigade occurred in the interim. When the time came, the battalion again joined the 1st Division but with 12th Armoured Brigade in Osnabrück and at a time when the politico-military landscape was changing dramatically. The winter of 1989–90 had seen the fall of the Berlin Wall and Germany would soon be a united country. There was talk of Russia and other ex-members of the defunct Warsaw Pact joining NATO. As things turned out, these changes did not lead to any lack of excitement.

Lieutenant-Colonel John King, who had come to the regiment from the Green Howards to command the 1st Battalion at Catterick, brought it to Osnabrück. Initially the battalion was to be equipped with versions of the FV 432 similar to those left behind in Celle in 1978 but not for long. Conversion to the Warrior mechanized combat vehicle – which had been under development for more years than most experts wished to remember – was a priority for 1992. Every fifty years or so the British Army designs or adopts a piece of fighting equipment that is the envy of other armies. The Churchill tank is a good example, reworked models of which were used by the Israelis to defeat modern Soviet tanks used by the Syrians in the Yom Kippur War of 1973. The Warrior could prove equally durable.

The third and final tour of duty of the 1st Battalion in Germany, within the span of this story, began in August 1990 and ended almost exactly four years later. It had been anticipated that the tour would last for six years, in line with the new policy on the length of time that infantry battalions would serve in Germany. The earlier than expected return to England arose from the euphemistically termed *Options for Change* in the structure of the Army. This review led to substantial reductions, including a contraction of the army in Germany from a corps to a single armoured division. It was the redeployment consequent on this change that brought the battalion home, to Warminster, in July 1994. The principal recollections of those who served in Osnabrück during the years 1990–94 are likely to be of operations in the Gulf War, in Belfast and in Bosnia, rather than of the German city where units of the British Army had been stationed since 1945.

Accounts of these operations appear in chapters 7, 9 and 12. Saddam Hussain's Iraqi army and air force invaded Kuwait while the battalion main body was making final preparations to leave Catterick for Osnabrück. The advance party was already there. As soon as the so-called Coalition Forces began to assemble in Saudi Arabia, it became clear than any substantial British ground force contribution could be drawn only from the Army of the Rhine. In all, the commanding officer and 148 members of the 1st Battalion left Osnabruck to serve in the Gulf War but there was activity enough for those left behind.

The 7th Armoured Brigade was the first to leave for the Gulf, soon to be followed by the 4th. Coincidentally, these same formations were together in Britain's first victory in the Second World War – General Sir Richard O'Connor's defeat of Marshal Graziani's Italian army in Cyrenaica in the winter of 1940–41. Their departure from Germany left empty 'Granby garrisons'[6] which needed guards. Deployment to the Gulf also revealed gaps in battle-readiness in the follow-up elements, which had to be supplemented by weapons, armoured vehicles and equipment from units left behind. Thus the battalion found itself guarding barracks, spraying vehicles desert yellow and training administrative units in anti-chemical and gas attack techniques. These were not idle times.

A winter with many husbands absent in the Gulf and with others guarding other peoples' wives and children in remote parts of Germany was not a cheerful prospect. The Snow Queen and Her Royal Highness the Duchess of Kent both came to the rescue. It had all along been the intention to take a ski hut in Bavaria and Tiefenbach was chosen for the winter of 1990–91. Not only were the skiing enthusiasts, experts and novices, welcomed there but also those wives and children of men in the Gulf who were willing to risk their lives and limbs on the planks under instruction from Sergeant Brian 'Knocker' Knowles.

The Colonel-in-Chief visited the battalion in Osnabrück on 12 February 1991, expressly to meet the wives and children of men serving in the Gulf. Her Royal Highness was met at the airport by the new commanding officer, Lieutenant-Colonel Alastair Duncan, and Regimental Sergeant-Major Michael Haynes, who had been detained by the Iraqis while serving with the British Liaison Team in Kuwait. As always during her visits, Her Royal Highness found time to listen to everyone and give encouragement to those anxious about their husbands. Her visit provided exactly the uplift that was needed before action was joined in Kuwait just five days later.

No sooner were the men back from Kuwait than preparations and training had to be put in hand for the Operation Banner tour of duty in Belfast, now extended from the earlier four to six months. It seemed impossible to come to grips with what had to be done in Germany. A break came on 8 June, when the battalion exercised the garrison's Freedom of Osnabrück. The Band, Drums and a guard for the Regimental Colour, comprising the junior leaders' cadre, marched through the city and past the Rathaus, where the *bürgermeister* took the salute. Time was also found to win the BAOR and Army cross-country championships before training for Northern Ireland began in earnest.

On return from Belfast in May 1992, the battalion started the training programme for conversion from the FV 432 to the new Warrior mechanized fighting vehicle and its associated weapon and communication systems. This was a demanding challenge and everyone appreciated the distinction of being in the group of infantry battalions selected for this conversion. Training began only just in time and something of a supercharge had to be applied to the later stages. During live-firing exercises in the autumn, the battalion was put on stand-by to join the United Nations Protection Force (UNPROFOR) in Bosnia in May 1993. Specialist training for this new role began in January.

The six months in Bosnia are described in chapter 12. On return, the battalion was tasked to assist in the training of 2nd Battalion The Royal Anglian Regiment, which had also been stood-by to join UNPROFOR. Then the contraction decided upon under *Options for Change* required a return to England to start a new task as the demonstration battalion at Warminster.

When the 1st Battalion left Catterick for Osnabrück in August 1990, no one expected it would return to England in four years' time with three campaign medals and forty-five decorations, mentions in despatches or certificates of commendation. Of the three tours of duty on the Rhine over thirty years, this was certainly the most varied. More significantly, return to England marked the end of the Cold War. Except under the Brandenburg Gate, there was no widespread jubilation. This had been a long, quiet war that the West had won.

4
In Berlin

'Ich bin ein Berliner.'
PRESIDENT JOHN F. KENNEDY

Prussia's former capital has a holiday atmosphere in spring, summer and autumn. The waters of the Havelsee, glimpsed through trees in the south-west of the city, are bright with small sailing craft and the wide avenues of the city centre are thronged with well-dressed visitors. In winter the scene is bleak. Leafless trees reveal pretentious architecture of the Third Reich, a sense of space is replaced by one of emptiness and the east wind brings biting cold. Always a city of contrasts, it was never more so than when the western and eastern sectors were divided by the Brandenburg Gate and the infamous Berlin Wall until the wall came down in November 1989. When 1st Battalion The Prince of Wales's Own joined the British garrison in June 1963, nerves were still on edge in the aftermath of the 'Berlin Note' crisis two years earlier and were being kept there by the wall by then dividing the city.

In June 1961 Soviet Premier Nikita Khrushchev had unilaterally announced a prospective peace treaty with the (East) German Democratic Republic in the form of a note addressed to leaders of the wartime allies. One direct consequence of such a treaty would be Berlin becoming a 'free city', thus ending its Allied quadripartite status and closing a chink in the Iron Curtain. Khrushchev was successfully faced down by President John Kennedy of the United States but the Russian took his revenge on Berlin. During the night of Sunday 13 August 1961, while Western leaders were on holiday or away electioneering, a wall of concrete and breezeblock was thrown up along the dividing line between east and west Berlin. All windows overlooking the wall from the eastern side were blocked up, but not before thousands of East Germans had escaped through them or other still open exits to the West: 2,400 people fled in a single day.

Cold War tensions had begun in earnest in Berlin with the Soviet road and rail blockade of the city which led to the Berlin Air Lift of 1948–9. They found a focus there again in the early 1960s, following the Khrushchev Note and the building of the Wall. How best to react to the ongoing crisis became a source of dissension between the Western Allies. A poll conducted in the United States during 1961 had suggested that seventy-one percent of the adult population was ready, if necessary, to see their country go to war over Berlin. Charles de Gaulle and Konrad Adenauer had made bellicose statements on behalf of France and West Germany, without actually committing themselves as to what form action might take. Britain's Prime Minister, Harold Macmillan, was more circumspect, commenting, 'With both sides bluffing, disaster may come by mistake.'

As the battalion main body flew into Berlin between 24 June and 1 July 1963, President John Kennedy received a rapturous welcome when he declared to a huge crowd gathered to greet him, 'All free men, wherever they may live, are citizens of Berlin and, therefore, as a free man I take pride in the words – Ich bin ein Berliner.'[1] Allied military staffs remained nervous, being unable to forget that Soviet and American tanks had confronted each other, only a hundred yards apart, on the perimeter of the western sector of the city in October 1961. Berlin jitters were well demonstrated by the furious reaction of the British Military Headquarters when two young officers of the battalion were arrested for venturing onto the Soviet war memorial, inconveniently placed just inside West Berlin, so as to get a better look at the Wall. This incident occurred while the battalion was still taking over from the 1st Durham Light Infantry. The subalterns' misdemeanour, while thoughtless, arose more out of curiosity than recklessness. In other times or circumstances, their action and arrest might well have been greeted with amusement and cries of 'Good form', but in this instance it was not. Perhaps someone should produce a military maxim of 'Beware commanders and staffs who have lost their sense of humour'.

Of all the garrison units, the battalion occupying Montgomery Barracks in Kladow, in the extreme south-west of the British sector, had best reason to be aware of the Soviet presence. As may be seen from Map 7 opposite, the barracks lay alongside the outer perimeter fence separating Berlin from the territory of the so-called Democratic

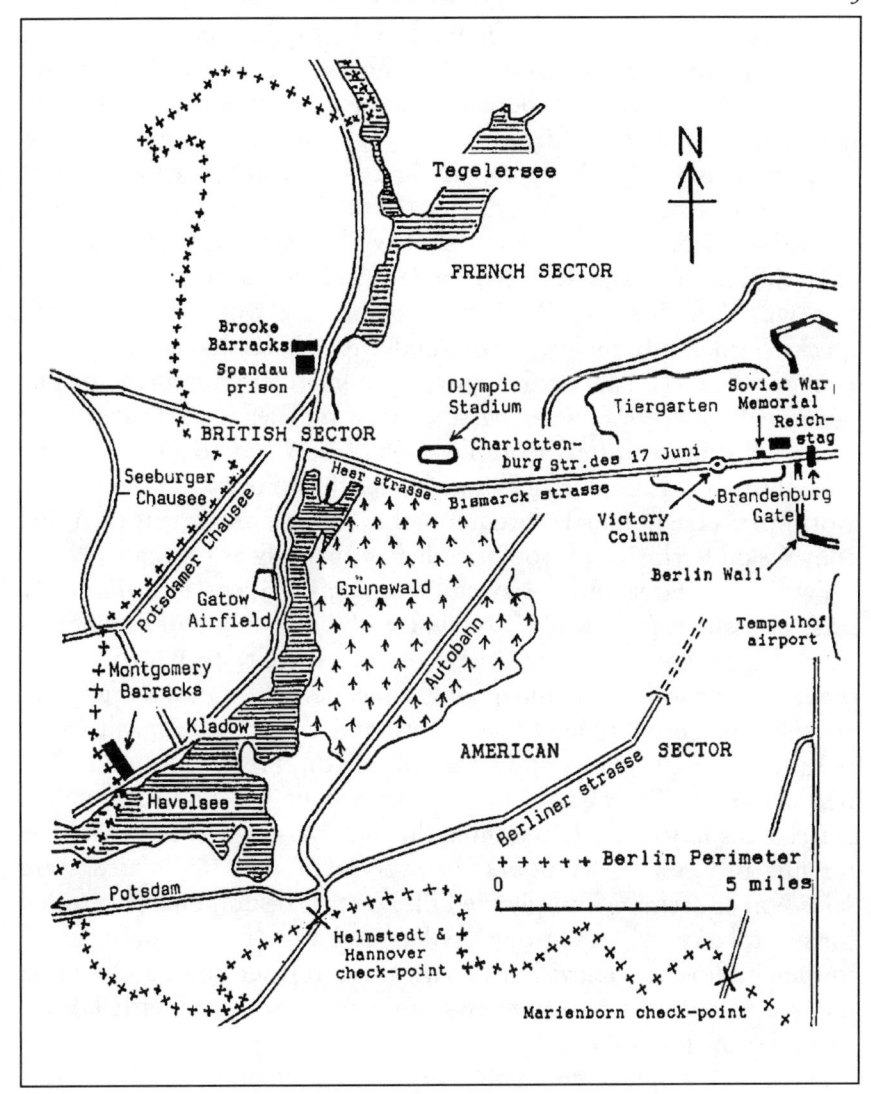

Map 7 *The Allied Sectors of Berlin*

Republic. Green-coated police of the Volks-Polizei (VOPO) were often to be seen peering wistfully through the wire into the barracks, not infrequently and disconcertingly at a point immediately above the targets of the thirty-metre range!

Soviet harassment of the Allied garrison took a variety of forms. In November 1963, road convoys on the autobahn through the

Helmstedt checkpoint between West and East Germany, and at the exit point from Berlin onto the autobahn, were halted and the troops invited to dismount to be counted. Although seemingly trivial in itself, this demand hinted broadly at interference with Allied right of access to Berlin. After a US Army convoy had been held up at the Marienborn checkpoint exit from Berlin for thirty-six hours, when the troops refused to dismount to be counted, it was decided that a test convoy from the battalion should make the Berlin-Helmstedt run. This operation was mounted on 5 November before the world press, always quick to smell a Berlin crisis, and under the leadership of Lieutenant Ivan Scott Lewis. Maybe the convoy commander's forename on the documents acted as a *laissez-passer*, as the vehicles were delayed only forty-five minutes after Scott Lewis had declined to dismount his men. Driving through thick fog, he reached Helmstedt and more world press flashbulbs before midnight. Soviet harassment of Allied convoys on Berlin access routes ended as abruptly as it began.

Two weeks later, on 22 November 1963, President John Kennedy was assassinated in Dallas. Nowhere did the news of Kennedy's death have a more stunning effect than in the city to which he had made his personal and unequivocal pledge. The news came in at 1945 hours Berlin time. Immediately and spontaneously all cafés, restaurants, night clubs and other places of entertainment in West Berlin closed. Their staffs joined the rest of the population in a massive display of grief, marching through the main streets in a huge torchlit procession. Rumours that the KGB was implicated were seized on as seeming entirely credible. A state of numbness prevailed for several days with everyone, civilian and military, remaining glued to their radios and television sets awaiting further news and fearing the worst. Then, as no more news came, the city slowly settled down to its routine level of tension.

Three events of a ceremonial or quasi-ceremonial nature dominated the programmes of all three battalions of the British Berlin Brigade and, such was the news media attention given to each one, only the very best would do. The first such duty encountered after the battalion's arrival was the taking over of the Spandau Prison Guard from 2nd Battalion, 6th United States Infantry on New Year's Day 1964. By then Rudolf Hess, Albert Speer – the former Nazi minister of war – and Baldur von Shirach – the one-time Gauleiter of Vienna and Hitler Youth leader – were the only prisoners remaining in the fortress-prison of those convicted of war crimes at Nuremberg. It fell to B Company to mount the first Spandau guard from 1 to 16 January. After inspecting the guard during this tour of duty, the General Officer Commanding the British Sector, Major-General David Peel Yates, remarked that the men 'were probably the finest guard he had seen since his appointment'.

Allied Forces Day, held on St George's Day in 1964, was the next test of ceremonial nerves. This event was a 'flag march' by the Allied garrison to remind the population, other than the nightclub proprietors who needed no reminding, that Allied troops still garrisoned the city. American, British and French contingents marched westwards from the massive Victory Column,[2] which stands within sight of the Brandenburg Gate, between the linden trees of the Tiergarten flanking Strasse des 17 Juni into Bismarck Strasse. The route is thirty yards wide, so the three-rank columns appeared a little thin until they passed between the Inter-Allied Guards of Honour and the densely packed spectators near the saluting base. Twenty years later, when the battalion next formed a part of the Berlin Garrison, the contingents marched six files abreast followed by tanks of the Allied armoured squadrons and a motorized column.

The ceremonial highlight of 1964, at least so far as the British element of the garrison was concerned, was Her Majesty The Queen's Birthday Parade on 13 June, with the temperature at 102 degrees in the shade. The form of parade closely resembled the annual Proclamation Parades in British India and had a not dissimilar motive. Virtually the entire brigade was on parade for trooping of the Regimental Colour of 1st Battalion The King's Regiment, a *feu de joie* by the infantrymen and a twenty-one gun salute by the tanks in honour of the Queen's birthday. The occasion was certain to be impressive so long as no calamity occurred and the weather held.

Perhaps quaintly in view of the epoch, the reviewing officer – General Sir William Stirling, C-in-C British Army of the Rhine – the brigade commander and the commanding officer, second-in-command and adjutant of 1st King's were mounted. This was the prime hazard as, although well-schooled police mounts, the possibility of a horse bolting during the *feu de joie* inevitably lent an air of additional excitement to the ceremonial. An officer of the Foot

Guards, reputed to bet on anything, had started a book on the event in the early 1950s. Odds were available on each horse for the form that any embarrassment might take: bolting, unseating its rider, defecating while passing the saluting base, and so on. By 1964 there was a rich patina of precedent but the parade was executed impeccably, no rider was unseated and the Commander-in-Chief remarked favourably on the bearing and drill of The Prince of Wales's Own. Because it arrived in Berlin in late June 1963 and remained only until April 1965, the battalion was involved in this pageant only in 1964. Two guards, each of 100 men, and a Colour Party were provided. The Queen's Colour was carried by Lieutenant Ivan Scott Lewis and the Regimental Colour by Lieutenant Peter Woolley; escorts to the Colours were Company Sergeant-Major Sid Jasper, Colour-Sergeant Michael Orum and Sergeant Bill Atkin. Having had the C-in-C's comments passed on to them, they and the officers and men of the guards were proud of having completed an exacting job well.

In Lieutenant-Colonel Peter Taylor the battalion had a commanding officer suited to the Berlin scene, although it is unlikely that he always saw it that way. Tall, striking-looking and well read, he walked the stage with perfect ease, pausing only to make some oblique comment that the listener usually only half-understood. The formal nature of garrison life and the almost hysterical reaction of the staff to anything with a whiff of 'badness' about it amused him, as being ridiculous and far removed from Army life as it really is. He was well supported by RSM Tommy Wall, who had rejoined the battalion in Wuppertal. Tommy had fought with the 2nd West Yorkshires at the Battle of Keren, in the Western Desert and at Imphal. He regarded the Army rather like a pantomime, that is something to be tackled very professionally but thoroughly enjoyed. He was a popular and highly effective Regimental Sergeant-Major.

Contrary to expectations, the training opportunities in and around Berlin were good. There was the Grünewald on the east bank of the Havelsee, plenty of open ground north of Kladow, river-crossing sites and two mock villages for training in street fighting. Nor was the battalion confined to the area of the garrison. At least twice each year all or a large part of the battalion left for field firing at the Sennelager all-arms training centre or for the Soltau tactical training area, both of which were familiar to those who had served in Wuppertal. Each year the battalion participated with armoured and other supporting arms in a test exercise at Soltau, set by the commander of Berlin Brigade. It was while the battalion was at Sennelager in 1964 that intelligence was received by the staff of Berlin Brigade that the nearby Soviet 10th Guards Tank Division was heading along the supposedly closed Seeburger Chausee straight for Montgomery Barracks. A telephone call from the brigade major alerted Major John Hart commanding the rear party, comprising the Regimental Band and a handful of administrators. With these Hart manned the perimeter fence and prepared to die bravely. Luckily, he was not called upon to make the supreme sacrifice, as the Russians lost either their nerve or interest and turned aside at the last moment. Operational readiness was rightly taken very seriously. One fully-manned platoon had to be maintained, armed and dressed, ready for immediate deployment throughout the twenty-four hours. This imposed no small strain, as courses and leave left gaps that had to be filled from elsewhere. On receipt of the codeword 'Rocking Horse' – usually in the early hours of the morning – the entire battalion, including men at home in their married quarters, were required to move out fully armed and equipped to man one of several predetermined action stations. These demands kept everyone rather on edge, as a Yorkshireman might say; or maybe he would put it a little differently!

The sporting facilities in Berlin were outstandingly good. The previous twenty-two months spent with The 12th Brigade in Wuppertal had provided little opportunity to carry forward the sporting skills built up in Gibraltar or make good the hiatus caused by the switch from National Service to an all-regular Army. Regular recruits in the early 1960s were seldom of the physical standard of the best National Servicemen and they needed building up. Effort was concentrated on rugby football, swimming and cross-country, in which the commanding officer took a personal part by leading the battalion run each week, at the start of the run if not at the finishing line.

By winning the Berlin Brigade cross-country championship in December 1963 the battalion qualified for and then won the British Army of the Rhine team competition in January 1964, beating 1st Royal Canadian Regiment by thirty-one points. Lance-Corporal Paddy O'Brien challenged the BAOR individual champion for first place up to the final twenty yards. This began the battalion's ascent to a dominant position in Army cross-country, winning the Middle East Command competition in 1966, being runners-up in the Army championship of 1983 and winners in 1984, 1985, 1986 and 1987. The captain of the successful team of 1963–4 was Sergeant Russ Pask, who began a tradition carried forward by Paddy O'Brien as an outstanding runner and later by Majors Peter Blyth and Dave Moffat as runners, captains and coaches of outstanding achievement. While efforts to establish a strong rugby football side were frustrated by the limited following the game enjoyed in the battalion, the swimming team came from behind also to win the BAOR Championships in 1964. Heavy Berlin commitments precluded a battalion swimming competition but some inspired training of individual swimmers by the team captain and coach, Lieutenant 'Cobber' Rushworth, won a place in the 1st Division competition by being runners-up in the Berlin championships. Runners-up to 1st King's again in the next round, the team qualified to go forward to the BAOR championships. After an intense day, the battalion beat 1st King's by half a point to become the BAOR champions. Whatever may be said about the sometimes irritating aspects of service in Berlin, the bedrock of the battalion's future sporting prowess was laid there in 1963–5.

Promptly on New Year's Day 1965 the battalion took over the Spandau Prison guard for the last time. The guard commander was Lieutenant Rory Forsyth who had joined the battalion during the tour and was to command it during the next period in Berlin, beginning in 1983. The winter of 1964–5 was marked by two occasions for mourning. A memorial service for Sir Winston Churchill was held in the Berlin Kuppelsaal on 28 January, when the draped Colours of the three battalions of the Berlin Brigade were placed on the draped drums. President Lubke of the German Federal Republic and a host of British and foreign dignitaries attended. The battalion provided the lining party at the main entrance to the Kuppersaal.

While Sir Winston's death at the age of ninety was not unexpected, the death of the regiment's Colonel-in-Chief, Her Royal Highness Princess Mary The Princess Royal, on 29 March 1965, came as a deeply saddening shock. Her Royal Highness had always kept in close touch with the regiment. She had visited Regimental Headquarters in York as recently as 27 February 1964 and presented new Colours to the 3rd Battalion on 27 June. Once again the Colours were draped, the officers and warrant officers wore mourning armbands and a message of sympathy was sent to Princess Mary's immediate family.

Even though the end of the battalion's tour was approaching, there was no relaxation in the stream of visitors. There was always someone to be briefed, given a demonstration or wined and dined. Prime Minister Harold Wilson called on 7 March but declined to drink in the officers' mess. He choose the NAAFI instead, little dreaming what a hotbed of reactionary opinion he would encounter there. He was photographed looking bemused by the response to one of his sallies: 'I don't know about that,' said Private Rosie Rosenquest of B Company, who enjoyed stirring the pot, 'I always vote Tory myself.'

The close proximity of the Russians just beyond the barrack perimeter wire had long been the basis for hoax telephone calls or similar tricks played on newly-joined junior officers undertaking their first stint as duty officer. The telephone calls usually purported to be from the commander of 10th Guards Tank Division expressing an urgent desire to defect to the West. The inevitable happened. In the early hours 2nd Lieutenant Duncan Green was awakened by a figure dressed in unfamiliar uniform standing by his bed – with snow on his boots! 'Oh bugger off and let me get some sleep,' grunted Green with an insouciance for which he was later to become well known. No doubt accustomed to doing as he was told by an officer, the would-be defector left and surrendered to a nearby post manned by the Berlin civilian police, thereby provoking another sense of humour failure on the part of brigade headquarters. The defector, who was East German, compounded the problem by reporting that the British officer had kicked him downstairs, but that would not have been in Green's nature.

Departure of the flight taking the first company to England on 5 April coincided with a meeting of the West German Parliament in the ruined Reichstag building within a few yards of the Berlin Wall. This incited scenes of well-orchestrated protest by East Germans beyond the wall, the autobahn access routes were closed for several hours in the succeeding days and Russian fighter-jet aircraft made passes over the city at heights below 500 feet, causing supersonic bangs. One MiG was seen to streak across the runway of RAF Gatow directly in the path of a transport aircraft bringing in families of the relieving battalion. Thus the battalion left Berlin in a state of tension equally acute as when it had arrived almost two years earlier.

One soldier lost his life during the tour. Private Alan Fieldhouse was drowned on 21 July 1964 and buried in the British Commonwealth Cemetery, Berlin with military honours, the firing party being provided by his comrades of C Company.

1983-5

Eighteen years later the 1st Battalion returned to a city strikingly similar to the one it had left. Although Yuri Andropov had succeeded Leonid Brezhnev in 1982 and was clearly grooming the youthful Mikhail Gorbachev as a future leader,[3] there were no indications of the dramatic changes in East-West relations that were to occur in 1989-90. The Cold War continued to be systematically waged. When the battalion returned to Berlin on 23 June 1983 under command of Lieutenant-Colonel Peter Woolley, the Berlin Wall was still in place. In spite of Andropov's nascent reforms in Moscow, the German Democratic Republic remained one of the most hard-line Communist states of the Warsaw Pact. The only glimmer of change was a conscious attempt by the authorities of East Berlin to improve the tourist facilities, to the extent of publicizing the names and location of restaurants serving 'international cuisine'.

Oblivious of such temptations, the battalion immediately set about establishing its reputation in the garrison. Militarily, Berlin was still a goldfish bowl in which the least mistake or misadventure was severely judged and sanctioned. Those who had served during the previous tour noted a quickening in tempo, especially in the competition to excel. This time, situated in Brooke Barracks in centrally-placed Charlottenburg, there was no escaping the closest scrutiny. But the Russians were still nearby. During the summer nights their sentries could be heard calling to each other from the watch-towers of Spandau Prison. There only the pathetic Rudolf Hess remained, von Shirach and Speer having completed their sentences and been released.

Two days after arrival the battalion narrowly missed winning the Berlin Brigade swimming championships, but swept the board in the athletics competition in August, setting seven new records. The cricket team won the BAOR Infantry competition on 2 September, beating 2nd Royal Green Jackets by eighty-three runs. Private John Willerton obligingly took six Green Jacket wickets for seven runs. Sport and a wide range of other forms of competition were to become a predominant feature of the second tour in Berlin, thereby capitalizing on foundations begun twenty years earlier.

Otherwise the scene had a Kafkaesque familiarity to those who had served in the city during 1963–65. Battalion deployments in the dead of night were just as frequent and as exacting. Contingency emergency deployment positions had to be reconnoitred and fighting in built up area (FIBUA) skills relearned and practised. Border patrols were tense operations and the reconnaissance platoon vehicle crews were as alert and ready to react as were their predecessors of 1964. The Spandau Prison Guard, Allied Forces Day Parade and the Queen's Birthday Parade loomed ahead largely unchanged. The battalion's international affiliations, which involved joint operational planning, training and shared sporting events, were familiar. Although the 2nd Battalion 6th US Infantry Regiment had been replaced by the 4th Battalion of the same regiment, the French affiliated unit remained the 46ème Régiment de l'Infanterie as in 1963–5. The sporting aspects of the Queen's Birthday Parade had not been diminished. Indeed there was an even wider selection of potential embarrassments on which to bet. In 1977 the brigadier commanding the parade had given the wrong word of command which half the parade had attempted to obey while the remainder had correctly stood fast, with a resulting shambles. The French Commanding General was reported to have walked to his car still weeping with silent laughter and murmuring to his American counterpart, 'Oh, these Engleesh, they know 'ow to make the best of the ceremonies.'

On 5 September 1983, the by then Lieutenant-Colonel Rory Forsyth returned to take command of the battalion he had joined there almost exactly twenty years earlier. He knew the scene from what he termed 'a worm's eye view', and set himself to use that experience to his battalion's advantage. The son of Lieutenant-Colonel John Forsyth of the regiment, a noted military sceptic and raconteur, Forsyth junior brought a robust sense of humour to a station where that quality was often in distinctly short supply. He inherited a strong and highly motivated battalion, which had used the previous five years in the United Kingdom-based ACE Mobile Force to burnish its military skills and sporting prowess.

The Brigade inter-platoon competition, remembered from the 1963–5 tour as Exercise Shooting Star, was as much a test of humour as of military competence. Rivalry between the three battalions of the brigade was intense and one misjudgement could put a platoon out of the running. A tortuous night march, an obstacle course through ruined buildings and sewers and the shooting tests with all platoon weapons were designed to separate the tough and the skilled from those with only enthusiasm. Before the competition began, the battalion had established a position as the unquestioned leaders in Berlin Brigade sport. The commanding officer of the battalion next door was unwise enough to remark over the local radio, 'Forget the sporting heroes, now the blankshires will show you what proper soldiering is about.' 1st Battalion The Prince of Wales's Own won the competition with three platoons in the first four. Training outside Berlin, usually in the 1st British Corps sector of West Germany, remained one of the key features of the calendar. Shortly after taking over command, Forsyth was surprised to discover that he, or at least one of his minions, was responsible for arranging the area where the brigade commander's test exercise was to be held. May 1984 was the month chosen but every remotely suitable training area was found to be already booked by someone else. With more immediate matters on his mind, Forsyth sent his operations and signals officers, Captains Graham Binns and Martin Dransfield, to find a piece of ground and not to return until they had done so. They found the Hochsauerland, the rugged and wooded countryside lying in the shadow of the Mohne Dam. In spite of misgivings in Berlin Brigade headquarters, Exercise Spring Gallop was a remarkable success. Mountain air, some glorious weather and the scenery of the Sauerland put everyone in the right frame of mind to resist armoured and helicopter attack, in which they were to be tested. Striving hard to get into true operational mode, battalion headquarters established itself in Schloss Laer, home of the Graf von Westphalen with whom Captain Ken Miles had negotiated the arrangements.

The Berlin tour of 1983–5 was set to include an event of major regimental importance: the presentation of new Colours. The first set of Colours had been presented by Her Royal Highness Princess Mary, The Princess Royal in Gibraltar in 1960 and twenty-five years is the estimated life span of the silk and gold wire with which they had been embroidered by the Royal College of Needlework. The form of parade for Presentation of Colours is precise and the formal and international atmosphere of the Berlin setting was in many ways ideal. The GOC of the British Sector was of the Foot Guards and sympathetic to the time the battalion had to set aside in preparation. He was also skilled in detecting an imperfect military stance in the rear rank of Number 3 Guard and thoughtfully attended rehearsals equipped with binoculars, so as to provide the commanding officer with expert advice on this and related matters.

Long before rehearsals began, there were important policy issues to be considered. It is usual for a regiment to receive new Colours from its Colonel-in-Chief but the regiment had been without one since the death of HRH Princess Mary in 1965. This was a matter of long-standing concern to the Regimental Council, composed of previous commanding officers under the chairmanship of the Colonel of the Regiment. Two schools of thought emerged in the Council. One advocated a request for HRH The Prince of Wales to present the Colours, expressing an implicit hope that this might spark the idea that he should perhaps become the Colonel-in-Chief of the regiment bearing his title. The other school opposed both aspects of this suggestion, arguing that the Prince of Wales was already Colonel-in-Chief of several regiments, including the Gordon Highlanders and the Parachute Regiment to which he was known to be greatly attached. Moreover, his presence in Berlin could lead to an inordinate fuss that might obscure its main purpose.

The Council eventually agreed that it would be polite to submit a request for the Prince of Wales, as to ask for anyone else might be thought discourteous. The Prince was only very recently married at this time, he and his bride were in the spotlight of world attention and both enjoyed widespread popularity. Unknown to the Council, a cosy cavalry cabal was working on a similar theme and two members of the cabal were in the chain along which the regiment's request was to pass. The exchange of formally couched letters that followed reads more amusingly in the light of this later knowledge than it did at the time. The outcome was nevertheless most satisfactory.

After a seemly delay, the Colonel of the Regiment received a letter explaining that 'The Prince of Wales feels unable to accept this commitment to a Regiment of which he is not Colonel-in-Chief'. This silenced one school of thought in the Regimental Council, on both points of its argument, and opened up the options. Delicate inquiries ensued and in due course Field-Marshal Sir Edwin Bramall, Chief of the Defence Staff, accepted an invitation to present the new Colours. Although the Field-Marshal had no close connection with the regiment, he did know a few members of it extremely well. Several had served on his staff, one had been his brigade major and another his chief of staff. He was also widely admired, throughout the Army, for his friendly and relaxed manner with all ranks and total scorn for pomposity or military brouhaha of any kind. The date for the Colours presentation was set for 12 July 1984. That spring and early summer already promised to be demanding enough, with operational readiness, training in and outside Berlin and ceremonial and sporting rivalry jostling for attention. Fortunately, Allied Forces Day and the Queen's Birthday parades preceded the presentation of Colours so, as Regimental Sergeant-Major Michael Sullivan pointed out with his customary awesome humour, 'The lads can't complain that they have been short of drill practice.' But as large a contingent of the Regimental Association as could be persuaded to make the journey to Berlin was to be invited to attend the parade, as well as 2,000 other guests, there were plenty of arrangements to be made.

Final rehearsals for the presentation of Colours took up the early days of July. Last-minute changes to the march on, march off and other details were helpfully suggested by GOC Berlin, the Colonel of the Regiment and anyone else who happened to be passing. The reconnaissance for the benefit of the Field-Marshal was carried out virtually incognito with Sir Edwin, the Colonel of the Regiment and Colonel Forsyth walking the ground wearing shirt sleeve order.

After discussing the form of parade, Sir Edwin suggested that they should stroll over to have a closer look at the Olympic Stadium behind the Maifeld, on which the presentation was to be made. They soon encountered a barrier of wire some eight feet high with a young American tourist on the other side trying to get out. Assuming the three lightly uniformed figures were park attendants or groundsmen, he protested vigorously about his impeded progress until the Field-Marshal asked whether he had seen the track on which Jesse Owens had won the 100 metres in 1936. 'You know about Jesse Owens?' gasped the young man. 'Gee, this is something else!' But it proved impossible for either party to breach the German wire on this occasion.

The anniversary of the Battle of the Boyne[4] was perfect for a parade, with bright sunshine but a stiff breeze to lift the flags of the nations on the rim of the Olympic Stadium and make the Colours fly. White roses for special regimental occasions topped the pikes of the old Colours, on parade for the last time. A crowd of 2,500 spectators watched the battalion march on, two guards abreast, to 'On the Square', straightening many an old soldier's back, followed by 'On the Quarter-deck'. The old Colours took up position on the left flank of the parade and the new Colours, still cased, at the centre rear, under command of the Battalion Quartermaster, Captain Peter Blyth, who had been on parade at the presentation of the old Colours at Europa Point, Gibraltar, on 7 June 1960. At 1100 hours exactly, Field-Marshal Sir Edwin Bramall was received by a General Salute. The great day had begun.

The commanding officer marched forward to invite the Field-Marshal to inspect the parade, which he duly did, pausing every few paces to ask a soldier about his medals, his family or where he came from. After return to the saluting dais, Sir Edwin watched the Regimental Band and Drums 'troop' across the front of the parade under the direction of Bandmaster Kenneth Shell, who was to lose his life so tragically just a few weeks later.[5] Then the old Colours were trooped. A drummer sounded for Regimental Sergeant-Major Michael Sullivan to join the Escort, under command of Captain Simon Caley, which took up station facing the old Colours to the march 'British Grenadiers'. The RSM took each of the Colours in turn, the Queen's Colour from Sergeant David Hill and the Regimental Colour from Sergeant David Biggs, who had carried them onto the parade, and handed them to the two ensigns, Lieutenant Henry Middleton and 2nd Lieutenant Richard Sawtell. The ensigns bore the old Colours through the ranks of the battalion for the last time, then finally off parade to the Regimental slow march 'XVth von England', followed by 'Auld Lang Syne'.

The battalion formed hollow square in which Drum-Major Tony Froggatt quickly supervised the piling of drums to form an altar. Captain Blyth marched forward Sergeants Tony Wilkinson and John Diamond, bearing the new and still-cased Colours. Captain Blyth uncased each Colour and fixed each pike with white roses before laying the Colours across the drums ready for consecration. The Colours were consecrated by the Chaplain-General, the Venerable

Archdeacon Frank Johnston, a friend of the regiment from Cyprus days, attended by the Principal Roman Catholic Chaplain to the Army, Monsignor John Moran, the Senior Chaplain Berlin, the Reverend Paul Abram, a former chaplain to the battalion, and the Reverend David Wilkes, the current chaplain to the battalion. Following the consecration, Major Charles Hepworth handed the Queen's Colour to the Field-Marshal for him to present it to the ensign, Lieutenant Graham Jackson. Major Tony Blanch then handed the Regimental Colour to Sir Edwin for him to present to the ensign, Lieutenant Christopher Dockerty.

The new Colours presented, the Field-Marshal then addressed the parade:

> Commanding officer, officers and men of The Prince of Wales's Own Regiment of Yorkshire, distinguished guests, I consider it a very great and singular privilege to present this regiment with new Colours, on behalf of Her Majesty The Queen.
>
> Your regiment has a proud and distinguished pedigree, which reads like the history of the British Army itself; indeed, next year you will be celebrating your 300th anniversary in the service of the Crown.
>
> The regiment also, as you would expect from the county which provides you with your roots, has a very strong spirit, which is amply demonstrated today by the presence of many former members who have made the journey to Berlin to see you perform so excellently on this impressive parade, and on such a memorable day. Many of them fought in battles such as Imphal, in Burma, and in the Normandy landings which are commemorated on these Colours. And, of course, the spirit also extends to the friends of the regiment; and it is indeed good to see representatives from your affiliated units from the towns and boroughs of Yorkshire; I know that they will be proud of you.
>
> You are also honoured by the presence of friends from amongst the people of West Berlin, and from our French and American Allies. To all of them I would just like to say: Es freut uns sehr, dass Freunde des Regiment aus Berlin; sind mit uns heute; nous sommes très contents, que vous pouvez être ici aujourd'hui avec nous; and we are so glad to have you with us today.

Certainly all those who are watching have an understandably deep affection for this regiment, which can hold up its head in any company. Fortified by its past splendid history, it is making the most distinguished contribution to a British Army which today is in particularly good shape. It looks and feels good in public and private, is decently paid, well equipped and up to strength, and has proved its professionalism, stamina and gallantry in a wide variety of diverse tasks, as is so well illustrated by the fact that, in the twenty-four years which have elapsed since your old Colours were presented to you, this battalion has itself served with skill and dedication all over the world, in Gibraltar, in Aden, with the British Army of the Rhine, in Cyprus, in Northern Ireland no less than four times and where it was the first to be brought in, in the current emergency, in Norway in the highly-trained ski-borne role of the Allied Mobile Force, and now it is proud to be in this outpost of freedom, Berlin.

Thank you for all that you have done and congratulations for the way that you have done it, of which this parade is a typical example, carried out splendidly. I wish you good fortune for the future, confident that you are prepared for the commitment our profession demands and that you will always maintain the high standard for which your regiment is well known. And I hope that you will continue to get great satisfaction from your service as well.

In presenting these new Colours, on behalf of Her Majesty, I charge you all to honour and respect them as symbols of your duty to the Crown and to our country.

On completion of the Field-Marshal's address, Colonel Forsyth replied, 'Sir, it is my privilege, on behalf of the battalion, to thank you for presenting the Colours on behalf of Her Majesty The Queen. These Colours will take the battalion into the twenty-first century. We would ask you, Sir, to convey to Her Majesty that we will protect them, care for them and carry them with pride wherever we may serve.'

The Field-Marshal returned to the saluting dais, the battalion reformed into guards and marched past in quick time, Sir Edwin taking the salute. Finally, the battalion advanced in review order, giving a General Salute and thanked the Field-Marshal with three rousing cheers. Bearing the new Colours, the battalion marched off to 'Ilkla Moor', to the surprise of no one present, followed by 'Berliner Luft' and then 'Rose von Wörthersee' to the delight of many veterans who had served in the old regiments in Austria after the Second World War. As the battalion disappeared into the distance, Sir Edwin reviewed the members of the Regimental Association accompanied by Colonel Boris Garside, Chairman of the Association.

The final months in Berlin were underscored by the necessity to train for the battalion's next destination – Northern Ireland again, for a second resident tour. There was no reduction in other duties or responsibilities and counter-insurgency training had to be given a low profile in Berlin. Much of it was done within the perimeter of RAF Gatow and at Sennelager.

Proof that the battalion played its part in Berlin to the end came in the farewell message from Brigadier Patrick Stone, commanding Berlin Brigade. He wrote:

> The time has come to say farewell to one of the most popular battalions to have served in Berlin for many years. Since its arrival two years ago it has constantly striven for and achieved excellence on training in and outside Berlin, on the sports field as their impressive display of awards and trophies demonstrates, and as good honest tough ambassadors for their country in this unique city.

There is an even happier tailpiece to this chapter. A few days later the Colonel of the Regiment received a letter from the Adjutant-General which read:

> I am delighted to inform you that Her Royal Highness The Duchess of Kent has accepted from Her Majesty The Queen the invitation to become the Colonel-in-Chief of The Prince of Wales's Own Regiment of Yorkshire. Her Royal Highness hopes to attend the Regiment's Tercentenary in York and therefore The Queen has approved an early announcement, which is planned for Tuesday 7 May [1985].'

5
In Northern Ireland 1969 and 1972–3

'Proceed at once to Lamlash.'
WINSTON CHURCHILL

In March 1914 the General Officer Commanding British troops in Ireland declined to send additional units to Ulster to guard four arms and ammunition depots, suspected to be in danger of seizure by Ulster 'volunteers' opposed to Irish Home Rule, on grounds that such a move could precipitate a crisis. As First Lord of the Admiralty and before consulting his Cabinet colleagues, Churchill sent the above message to the 3rd Battle Squadron of the British Home Fleet. He chose Lamlash anchorage, in the Firth of Clyde, for the squadron to wait ready to transport the requisite units from the mainland.[1]

1st Battalion The Prince of Wales's Own was the first unit of the British Army to be deployed on the streets of Northern Ireland in the troubles that began in 1969. It was in Londonderry on Thursday 14 August. Forty-eight hours after the Apprentice Boys' March through the city had provoked the Catholic population from the Bogside to riot, the Royal Ulster Constabulary (RUC) were exhausted and the Army was brought to thirty minutes' notice to relieve them on the streets.

The battalion moved at 1700 hours with Major David Hanson's C Company immediately behind the reconnaissance platoon in the lead. Thanks to two recent Aden tours and a thorough briefing as to what was required, they quickly established control over the Strand and Waterloo Place. Exits from the Bogside were closed with 'knife-rest' barriers and barbed wire. C Company set up its headquarters in the public lavatories in the middle of Waterloo Place, which proved in every way convenient. After this brisk entry, which took rioters and onlookers equally by surprise, control was maintained of the old city area without a shot being fired or any of the populace stepping out of line until 19 August, when the battalion was relieved by the 1st Queen's who had sailed up the River Foyle into the city centre.

These events, dramatic for their time, came towards the end of four months' emergency duty in the Province which began with a no less dramatic move from England. In 1914 Churchill had qualified his message with the words 'at ordinary speed' but the commanding officer of the 1st Battalion was given no such leeway fifty-five years later. '1 PWO to deploy to Northern Ireland ASP' was the message handed to Lieutenant-Colonel Bill Todd at the Stanford Training Area in Norfolk on 25 April 1969. The battalion packed at once, returned to Colchester and was deployed in Northern Ireland by the following afternoon. This was the first emergency reinforcement of the Northern Ireland garrison in the troubles which began in 1969. Writing about it afterwards, the adjutant at the time – Captain Tim Vines – concluded that the move was accomplished so quickly because 'we did not have time to make mistakes and the Movements staffs did not have time to make difficulties at the departure and arrival airfields'. On 27 April Colonel Todd received a second message reading: 'Personal for CO 1 PWO from CGS. Congratulations on speed and efficiency with which your battalion has reacted. My best wishes to you all for your new assignment. George Baker.'

The April reinforcement had not been prompted by any threat from the IRA. At that time the virtually moribund movement was locked in internal debate on matters of Marxist principle. The Provisional IRA (PIRA or the 'Provos') did not then exist. The threat was thought to come from the so-called 'loyalists' of Ulster. When a breakaway faction of the Catholic-based Northern Ireland Civil Rights Association (NICRA) had attempted a protest march from Belfast to Londonderry in early January, the marchers had been set upon by a Protestant gang en route, at Burntollet, and mercilessly beaten. This incident led the Stormont Government of Terence O'Neill to begin giving serious thought to the need for social reform and a *de facto* truce in interfactional violence came into effect.

When news of the intended reforms started to circulate, the RUC picked up rumours that a sabotage campaign was planned as a signal to Stormont by Protestant extremists that any significant concessions to Catholic protest groups would not be acceptable. An electricity substation at Castlereagh was destroyed by an explosion on 30 March. As with later acts of sabotage, this was almost certainly the work of hirelings, although precise responsibility for their payment has remained in doubt. The campaign was resumed on 20 April with attacks on the County Down reservoir in Silent Valley (see Map 8 overleaf) which cut the water supply to two-thirds of Belfast. Further explosions damaged water pipes leading from Lough Neagh in County Down on 23 and 24 April.

At this point the GOC Northern Ireland, Lieutenant-General Sir Ian Harris, asked London for reinforcement of his single-brigade garrison of two infantry battalions and an armoured car regiment, for protection of key installations in the Province. On the day after the 1st Prince of Wales's Own had arrived in Northern Ireland, widespread Protestant opposition to O'Neill's proposed reforms led to his resignation as Prime Minister and replacement by James Chichester-Clark. Violence and the threat of violence had won their first victory over political moderation.

Having got himself to Belfast by the early evening of the day the order to move was issued, Colonel Todd was taken aback by the atmosphere of normalcy that greeted him. He had shifted his battalion to Aden at short notice when the NLF had taken over Crater, in 1967, but the contrast was marked. Everyone here was friendly and welcoming and not a shot or explosion disturbed the mild spring evening. Close police-military cooperation, the cornerstone of counter-insurgency operations, was conspicuously absent and Todd was advised not to visit a police station while in uniform. Rules for opening fire verged on the bizarre. In Aden a soldier was required not to open fire unless he believed that his life or that of someone under his immediate protection was threatened. In Northern Ireland in 1969 a criterion of 'equivalent force' was introduced.[2]

In comparison with later tours of duty in Ulster and the violence which other battalions would shortly face, the summer of 1969 was something of a dress rehearsal. There was, nevertheless, a sense of tension created by uncertainty as to what to expect, on the one hand, and the sensitivity of the local authorities and Downing Street[3] on the other. As usual at the outset of a security emergency, and in spite of centuries of experience, the army was dispersed in small groups guarding what were believed to be vulnerable points all over the countryside. Thereby showing where they were – and where they were not. No uncertainty was left to deter the would-be saboteur.

From April until late June the battalion was based at a Territorial

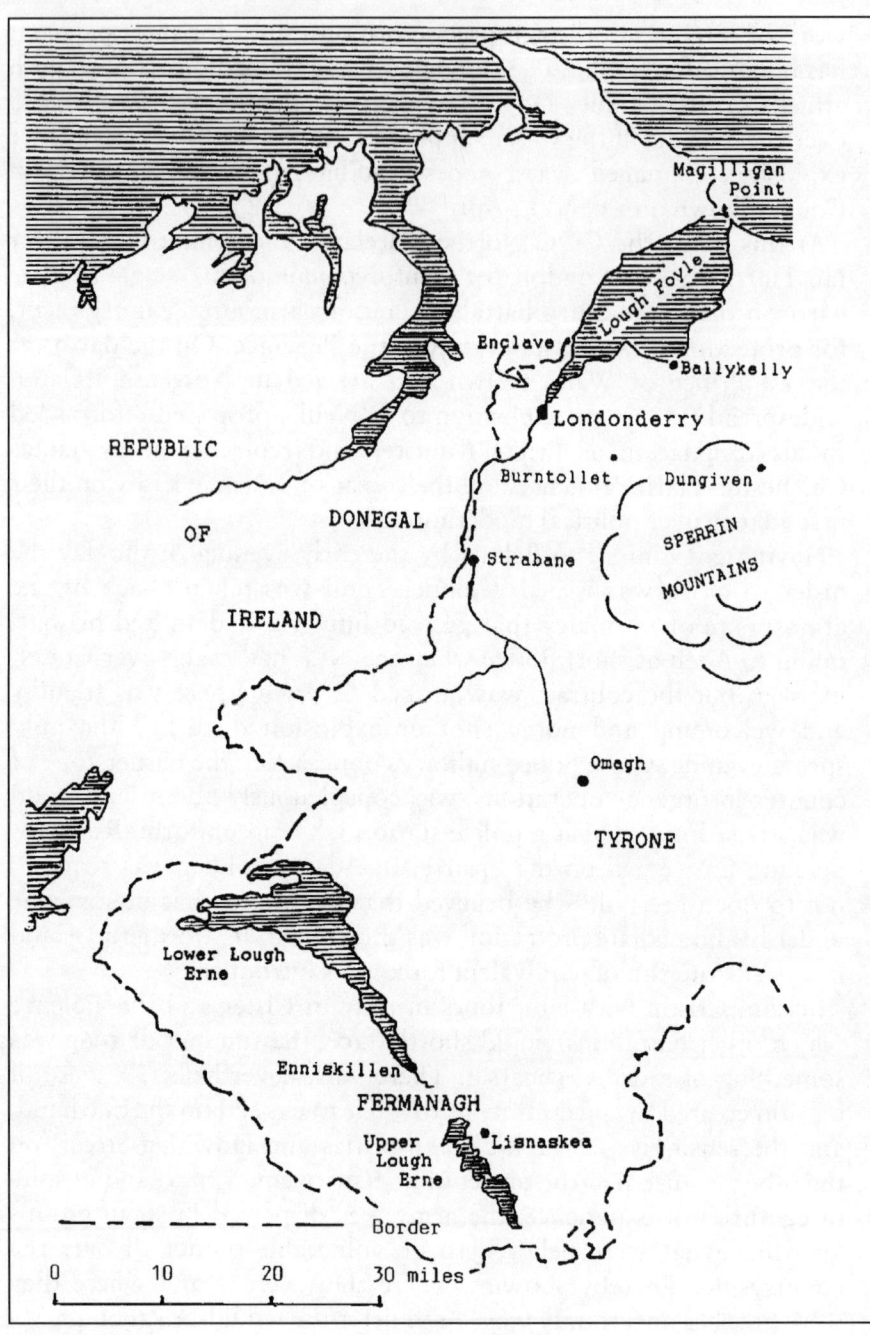

Map 8 *Northern Ireland*

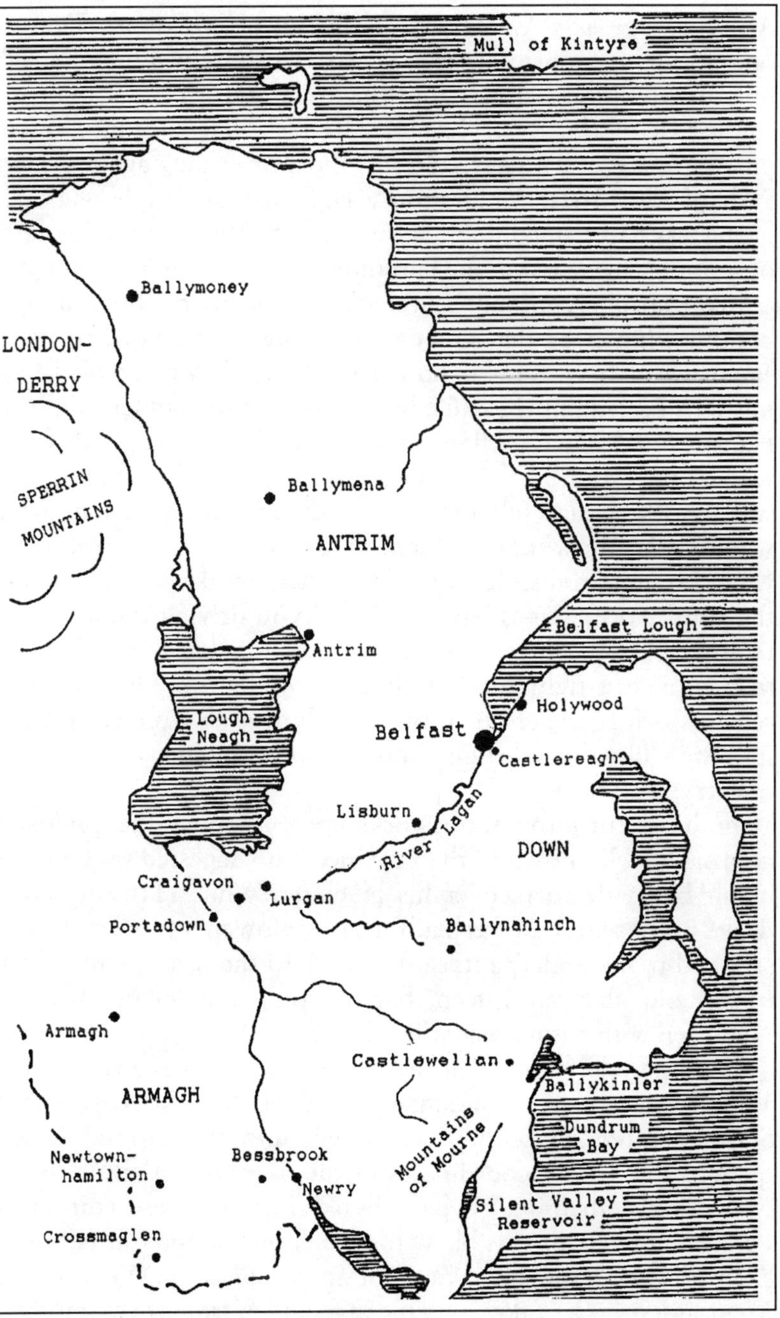
Mull of Kintyre
Ballymoney
LONDON-
DERRY
SPERRIN
MOUNTAINS
Ballymena
ANTRIM
Belfast Lough
Antrim
Lough
Neagh
Holywood
Belfast
Castlereagh
Lisburn
River Lagan
DOWN
Craigavon
Lurgan
Portadown
Ballynahinch
Armagh
Castlewellan
ARMAGH
Ballykinler
Dundrum
Bay
Newtown-
hamilton
Bessbrook
Newry
Mountains
of Mourne
Silent Valley
Reservoir
Crossmaglen

Army camp (105 WETC) at Ballykinler in County Down with operational responsibility for the eastern shore of Lough Neagh, the hills overlooking Belfast from the west and central County Down south-east of the River Lagan. The task was to guard reservoirs, pipelines, electric power stations and powerlines against sabotage. Perhaps due to the battalion's vigilance or maybe because the protesters had gained publicity without further personal risk, no act of sabotage occurred in the battalion's area during May and June.

An atmosphere of unnatural calm was briefly broken by what became known as the 'great motor-mower drama'. Private 'Jesse' James was left with his Land Rover alongside a reservoir just to the north of Ballynahinch, while his company commander, Major David Hanson, and Major Allan Bower commanding Support Company walked the ground before exchanging responsibility for guarding the water-hole. James fell into conversation with the man from the waterworks mowing the acres of grass round the reservoir and, when he prepared to leave for his lunch-break, offered to continue the good work. James had no difficulty in driving the mower in the required straight lines, but the art of manoeuvre eluded him. Failing to complete a tight turn, he flung himself from the controls only seconds before the entire apparatus plunged down a steep bank and into the still waters, leaving only a trail of bubbles to mark its point of entry.

On his return the waterworks man adopted the philosophical approach well known in the Province but suggested that some effort might be made to recover his machine. While Hanson and James drove off in search of fresh adventures, Bower, a powerful swimmer, stripped to his underpants and dived into the water, which he found to be cold, dark and deep, but he could not locate the machine. Night fell with the mower still submerged.

Cautious telephone inquiries were put out that evening by Tim Vines, the adjutant, including one to a friend at the Royal Naval Air Station at Lossiemouth. Keen to get into the action, 'Lossie' requested the precise coordinates of the reservoir to allow two Royal Marines frogmen to be parachuted into the reservoir at dawn. Perceiving that this was likely to attract unnecessary attention, Vines sadly declined the offer but put in a call to HMS *Sea Eagle* in Londonderry. Next day, two naval frogmen from there got a grapnel round something in the water and, with the aid of a Scammel recovery vehicle, hauled up the grid protecting the reservoir's outflow. A second attempt located the mower, which was then quickly recovered, apparently no worse for wear but in need of a quick blow-dry.

More serious issues were at hand. Dissatisfied with the package of social reforms tabled by Chichester-Clark, the Civil Rights Association announced that there would be a protest march from Strabane to Londonderry on 28 June. The date was carefully chosen to upstage the march of the Orange Orders on 12 July, an annual triumphant celebration to mark the anniversary of the never-to-be-forgotten Protestant victory over the Irish and French Catholics at the Battle of the River Boyne in 1690.[4] In anticipation of renewed outbreaks of violence, the battalion was redeployed. One company was left guarding the Lough Neagh water supply complex, one at Ballykinler with a platoon at five minutes' notice to move, one was held in reserve and the fourth made ready for redeployment to Londonderry, if required for the 28 June or 12 July marches.

A system of rotation through these duties found C Company at Magilligan Point camp, twenty-five miles north-east of Londonderry city centre, for the 12 July celebrations. No serious trouble occurred in Belfast but rioting broke out in Derry and twenty miles away in Dungiven. By 2300 hours the violence in Derry had reached such a pitch that C Company was brought to five minutes' notice to move. The RUC managed to cope on this occasion but A and Support Companies were also moved from Ballykinler to Magilligan Point early next day. On 14 July A Company relieved a detachment of 2nd Queen's, which had been at readiness in the Royal Navy's shore station HMS *Sea Eagle*, close to the city centre. A tense situation prevailed for ten days, at the end of which A Company returned to Magilligan Point. Earlier, on 15 July, the battalion's planned return to Colchester was postponed for one month.

The government of Northern Ireland faced a no-win decision as to whether the Protestant Apprentice Boys' march should be permitted in Londonderry on 12 August. The occasion was as emotive and potentially provocative as the anniversary of the Battle of the Boyne. Thirteen Protestant apprentices had slammed shut the main gates of Derry in the face of a Catholic army in May 1689 and the city withstood the subsequent siege for 105 days, thereby coining the slogan 'No surrender'. If the march were to be banned, Protestant

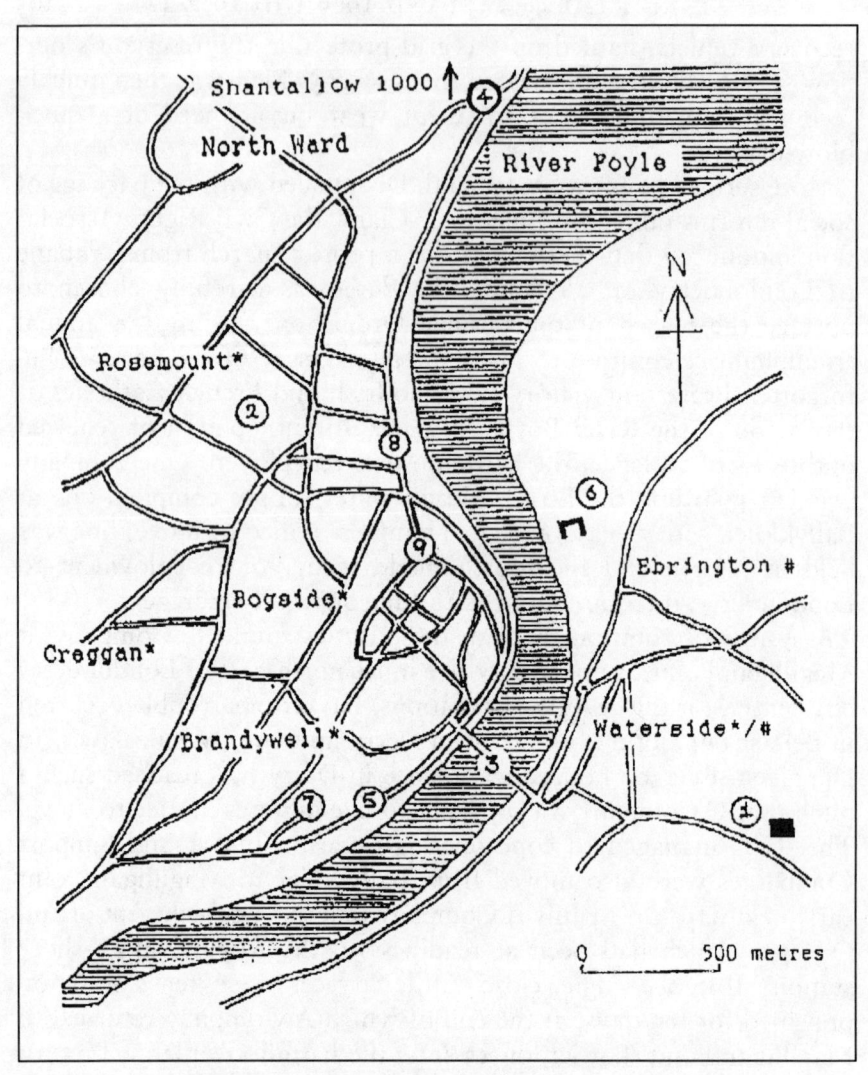

Map 9 *Londonderry*

*	Catholic district	5	Foyle Road
#	Protestant district	6	HMS *Sea Eagle*
1	Altnagelvin Hospital		(Ebrington Bks)
2	Brooke Park	7	Sloans Terrace
3	Craigavon Bridge	8	Strand Road
4	Fort George	9	Waterloo Place

reaction could bring the Government down, while if permitted it would be certain to provoke the Bogside Catholics to riot. On 11 August Stormont authorized the march to go ahead. In anticipation of trouble, Colonel Todd and his company commanders made a plain-clothes reconnaissance of the city centre where the march was forming up on 12 August. Unaware of the protocol of the occasion, he made to cross the road by stepping through the waiting ranks only to be crudely struck to the ground by two of the stewards organizing the march. Severely bruised and with a black eye developing, he got up and completed his reconnaissance.

As expected, the march was attacked as it marched around the Bogside. While it can be argued that if the march had not been permitted there would have been no one to attack, there is no doubt that the Bogside population was prepared for a full-scale assault on the marchers and on the RUC. Once the march gave them an excuse, violence was unleashed without restraint. When giving evidence to the Scarman Tribunal[5] after order was restored, Lieutenant Kevin Robbin – the battalion intelligence officer – reported seeing petrol bombs being flung from the roof of a seven-storey block of flats and stolen GPO vans being pushed down a steep slope towards a line of riot police. In a move to commit the Bogsiders to an irrevocable course, their leaders announced the innovation of 'Free Derry'.

Reinforced by the B Special Constabulary, the RUC initially contained the situation. At the instigation of Colonel Todd, CS tear-smoke and respirators were supplied to the police, with a view to avoiding any premature use of firearms. Although tear-smoke was not used on this occasion, the republican press subsequently sought to make capital out of its availability and the fact that the Army had supplied it to the RUC.

At 1500 hours on 14 August Prime Minister Chichester-Clark called 10 Downing Street and after only ninety minutes' delay the British Cabinet's authorization for troops to be used was received. In anticipation of this development, Colonel Todd had prepared a simple plan to interpose troops between the contestants and to seal off the Bogside from Londonderry city centre, while leaving access to and from the Creggan Estate on the western side. Half an hour after authority had been received from Westminster, the battalion entered the City Centre and the RUC withdrew.

Events of that evening and the next five days have already been described. The men of the battalion were welcomed as protectors by the people of Bogside. Nonetheless, dawn on 15 August revealed whole rows of Catholic houses in the Bogside burned out before the Army had intervened, some in direct consequence of action by the rioters. In Belfast continued rioting during the night of 14/15 August had left ten civilians dead. More than a hundred more were wounded by gunfire, together with four policemen. The troubles were getting into their stride but the battalion flew back to Colchester between 18 and 20 August.

The first Northern Ireland tour was significant in three particular respects: the IRA was initially dormant and became only covertly involved once violence had broken out in Belfast and Londonderry,[6] British newspaper and television journalists generally displayed a positive attitude in the interviews they demanded of commanders on the ground and the British Army was deployed on the streets of the British Isles, in an internal security role, for the first time since the Irish troubles of 1922. Four officers of the battalion gave evidence before Mr Justice Scarman as part of Lord Hunt's Commission of Inquiry into policing in Northern Ireland. The Commission's report led to the disbandment of the B Special Constabulary and formation of the Ulster Defence Regiment (UDR) in early 1970.

In spite of sabotage and riot, the Army was not regarded as being on active service in Northern Ireland at this time. As a result, no entitlement to a campaign medal or clasp on the General Service Medal was authorized. The single exception to this rule was Private Pat Coffey who, together with Corporal Steve Kennedy and Private Tony Middlesworth, was travelling in a 4-ton truck belonging to the battalion when it struck and almost completely demolished a pub in Ballymoney. The others escaped with minor injuries but Coffey sustained several fractures to both legs and had most of his scalp torn off. In consequence, he remained in hospital in the Province long enough to qualify for the General Service Medal with clasp 'Northern Ireland', when this was eventually authorized.

In the New Year honours of 1970 Colonel Todd was appointed an OBE, Captain Graham Longdon, who had served as Operations Officer throughout the tour, an MBE and Colour-Sergeant Eric Ross, who had done sterling work in supplying the many isolated detachments, received the BEM.

Province Reserve 1972–73

In the intervening two years and nine months before the 1st Battalion returned to Northern Ireland, the security situation in the Province changed dramatically for the worse. The honeymoon period when the Army was seen as the protector of the Catholic population was short-lived. Soldiers patrolling the Republican sectors of Belfast and Derry soon became targets for indiscriminate abuse and stoning by unemployed youths. Stormont did nothing to help, allowing every decision on whether or not to permit each proposed or traditional march to hang fire and develop into a major crisis of confidence, then making a compromise certain to inflame both factions. The Army found itself in the familiar pig-in-the-middle role of trying to keep one highly-charged mob from the throats of another – and taking casualties from both.

The winter of 1969/70 and the following spring were marked by an increasing scale and intensity of intercommunal rioting, which the security forces could only barely contain, then the IRA joined in.[7] After a lengthy internal wrangle, a breakaway faction had declared themselves the 'Provisional Army Council' (PIRA) in January 1970, while the Marxist rump of the movement became known as the 'Official IRA' (OIRA).

Pitched battles in Belfast between Catholic and Protestant mobs in late June and early July gave both IRA factions their chance. A handful of men of PIRA's 'Belfast Brigade' held off a Protestant mob attacking a Catholic church in the Short Strand, thus establishing PIRA's claim to be the defenders of the oppressed community and, shortly afterwards, fuelling a successful recruiting campaign amongst the Catholic urban working class. The 'Officials' made only one serious venture, attacking the Army when several small groups were isolated and off balance in the Catholic Falls area of Belfast on 3 July. An intensive and productive arms search throughout the area followed, after which the 'Officials' avoided direct confrontation with the security forces.

By the end of 1970 PIRA strength exceeded 1,000 volunteers and a campaign of terror was being prepared to make Northern Ireland appear ungovernable under British rule. Riot, the car bomb and the sniper rifle induced an atmosphere of fear and uncertainty, for which there was no effective counter. Hunting down and killing known terrorists, a method used with effect in more distant places, was ruled unacceptable in the United Kingdom. Suspects had to be arrested and evidence brought at a proper trial. But civilians giving evidence risked death. Internment without trial, proven effective in Ireland before, was reluctantly reintroduced by the government of Mr Edward Heath in 1971. On 9 August that year 342 suspects of the 450 on the wanted list were arrested, but the move met with widespread international condemnation and new volunteers quickly filled the gaps left by those interned.

On Sunday 30 January 1972 a march of some 3,000 Catholics in Londonderry was infiltrated by PIRA activists intent upon a confrontation with the security forces detailed to control the march. When the 1st Parachute Regiment was ordered to arrest the activists, thirteen civilians, including some of the PIRA activists, were shot dead in the ensuing action. Thus 'Bloody Sunday' entered the annals of Irish folklore. The Parachute battalion was not part of 8th Brigade responsible for Londonderry, but the Province Reserve based in Palace Barracks, Belfast and nearing the end of a 'resident' tour of eighteen months. 1st Battalion The Prince of Wales's Own took over that role on 20 May 1972. In the meantime, on 24 March 1972, the Northern Ireland Government at Stormont had been suspended and direct rule from London imposed. William Whitelaw became the first Secretary of State.

By the spring of 1972 the Northern Ireland garrison had been increased to a strength of three infantry brigades. 3rd Brigade was responsible for the border counties of Armagh, Fermanagh and Tyrone, 8th Brigade was based on Londonderry with operational responsibility for the city and the countryside up to the northern edge of the Sperrins and 39th Brigade in Belfast responsible for the city and its environs. 8th and 39th Brigades each had one eighteen-month tour resident battalion and a third such battalion, based in Palace Barracks outside Belfast, was the Province reserve. The brigades were brought up to strength by units on four, later four and a half, months' tours from Great Britain and Rhine Army. These were the 'roulement' (rotation) units, a term taken from the First World War when battalions were rotated through periods of duty in the trenches. At the height of the troop commitment, gaps between roulement tours of duty fell to as low as nine months for units in Britain.

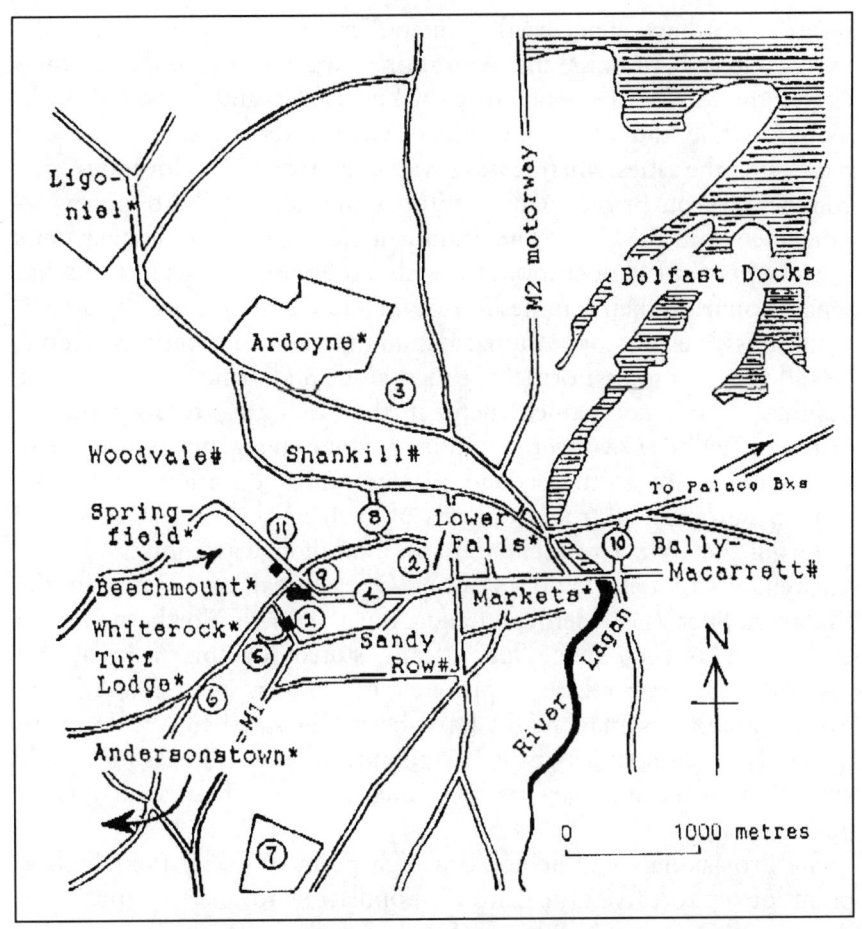

Map 10 *Belfast*

* Catholic district
# Protestant district
1 Broadway Tower
2 Divis Flats
3 Girdwood Park
4 Grosvenor Road
5 Iveagh Crescent
6 Milltown cemetery
7 Musgrave Park
8 North Howard Street
9 Royal Victoria Hospital
10 Short Strand
11 Springfield Road Police Station

One might have expected that the policy would have been to make the resident battalions the operational framework, utilizing their longer time in the Province to gain knowledge and to perfect techniques, while the roulement units covered the quieter areas and reinforced the cities when rioting was at its worst. It is an interesting commentary on British Army attitudes that almost the opposite arrangement was adopted. The argument ran that the roulement units must be kept at full operational stretch, otherwise they would feel that separation from their families in Britain and Germany was unjustified, while less intensive operational demands on the resident battalions would permit a more normal regimental life and some time with their families, who accompanied them. In the years 1969 to 1993 the 1st Prince of Wales's Own were to undertake one emergency tour in 1969, two resident tours, the second of two years' duration, and three roulement tours – all from the Army of the Rhine.

During the 1972-3 resident tour the battalion was commanded by Lieutenant-Colonel David Hanson. Operational experience in the Malayan, Suez and Aden campaigns together with Northern Ireland experience in 1969 made him ideally suited for this task, as did his forthright but relaxed approach to military matters. A more overtly ambitious man might have been frustrated by the frequent demands for companies of the battalion to reinforce others in trouble even though he and they received due credit for consistently good performance.

The Provisionals had achieved a high point, possibly their highest point, of support from the Catholic population around the time when the battalion arrived. 'Bloody Sunday' had given the terrorists a propaganda victory and they controlled sectors of Belfast and Londonderry, which had become so-called 'No-Go' areas for the RUC and which the Army could not penetrate without a politically unacceptable degree of bloodshed.

Impatient of security force interest in removing barricades and barriers from the streets, the Protestant para-military Ulster Defence Association (UDA) declared an intention to remove the barriers at the line of Catholic/Protestant interface on the Springfield Road in Belfast on 4 July, starting at 1900 hours. A Company, commanded by Major John Filor, was in position by 1700 hours to ensure that the barriers stayed in place, at least pro tem, and to keep the situation cool while talks were held. Perhaps predictably, talks broke down just before

ABOVE Aden 1965: Sergeant Ron Davison views Crater from the old fortifications.

BELOW, LEFT H. M. The Queen inspects the Guard of Honour of the Leeds Rifles, accompanied by Major Gerald Jarratt, outside the Civic Hall, Leeds, 22 October 1965.
BELOW, RIGHT Aden. Lieutenant-Colonel Roy Birkett, commanding officer 1st Battalion 1965-7.

Aden 1965-6. ABOVE Lads of the Recce Platoon, left to right John Gwilliams, Les Roberts (killed 1967), Ron Bradley, Chris Saunders, Brian Hopkinson, Steve Quarmby and Ray Wade at Armed Police Barracks, Crater.

BELOW Bandsmen from Hull, left to right Mike McKinder, Pete Quibell, John Fletcher, Mally Hindle, Harry Remblance, Pete Scholes, Pete Dunne, Johnny Towle, Dick Ledgeway, Mally Bird and Brian Fletcher.

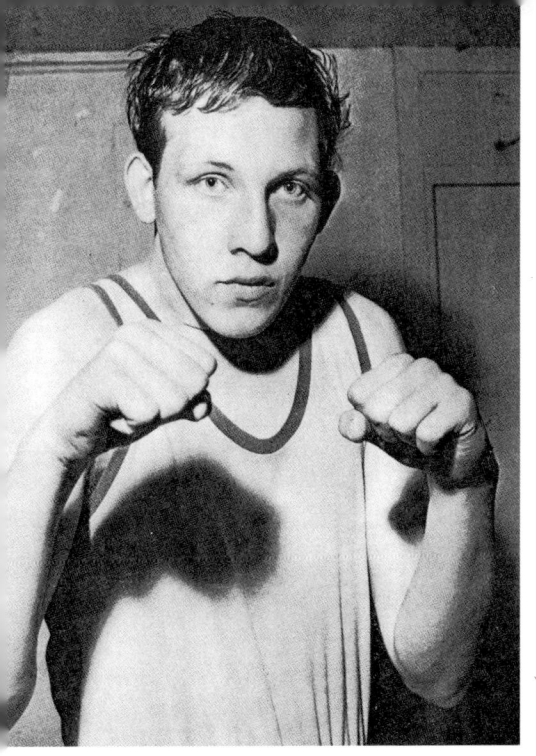

ABOVE, LEFT Private Roger Tighe, 3rd Battalion, British Empire and Commonwealth Games Gold Medal and Territorial Army light heavyweight champion 1966. RIGHT Aden 1966. Sergeant Frank Jackson and Lance-Corporal Bob Latto check workers entering Waterloo Barracks. BELOW Corporal Geoff Auker, MM and Lieutenant Peter Orwin, MC.

ABOVE Aden 1967. Lieutenant-Colonel Bill Todd taking the British High Commissioner, Sir Humphrey Trevelyan, round the 1st Battalion sector of Tawahi, accompanied by Captain Edwin Beckett, commander C Company.

BELOW Colchester 1968. 1st Battalion rugby team, winners of the District Cup. Left to right: 'Moose' Buckley, Roger Grannum, Pete Gibbons, John Filor, Arnie Arnold, Jim Wood, Bob Woolsey (with cup), Ivan Scott Lewis, Semi Korotoga, Howard Robinson, Johnny Tallon, Peter Wood, Danny Matthews and kneeling Ted Wilkins and Vic Scott.

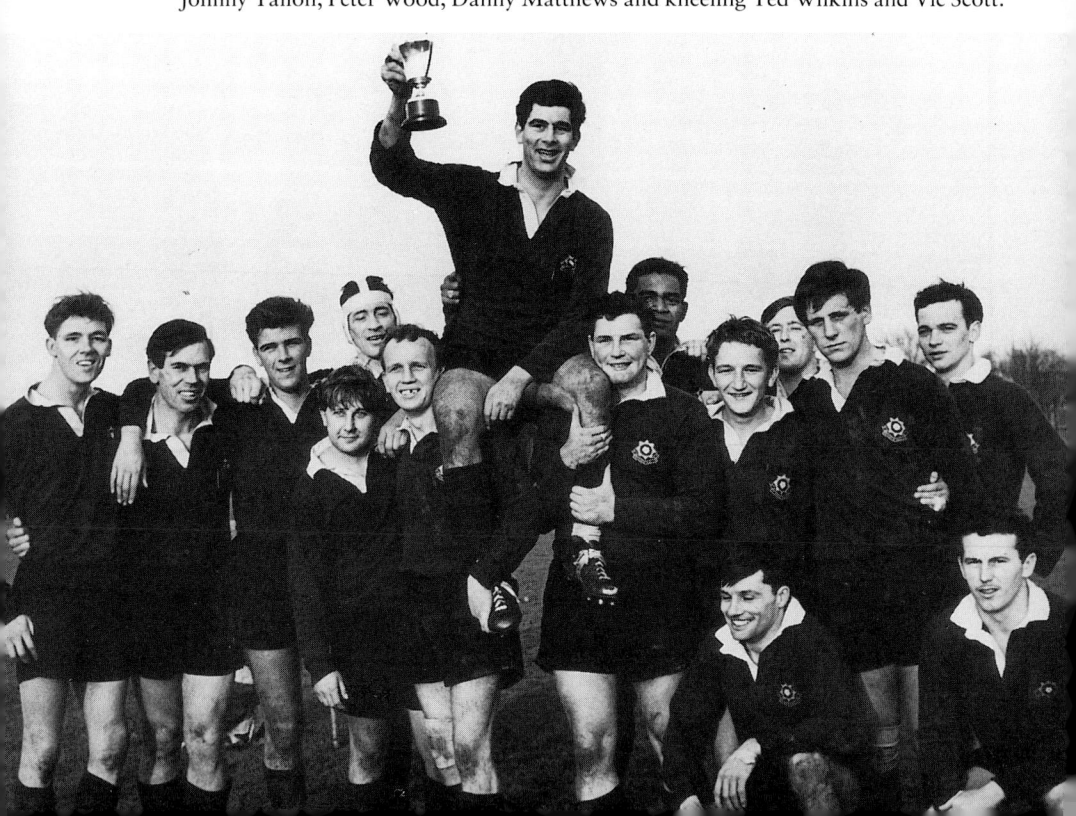

Londonderry 14 August 1969. ABOVE, LEFT and BELOW Soldiers of C Company 1st Battalion confronting republican rioters at the entrance to the Bogside. ABOVE, RIGHT. Tempers cool as the RUC is replaced by the military. Sergeant 'Rocky' Neal and two soldiers of C Company with a happy housewife.

Cyprus. ABOVE, LEFT Mrs Penelope Armour (left) with Mrs Sandra Linskey June 1971. RIGHT Private Ralph Johnson and Lance-Corporal Mally Hawes during the Geddes Cup forced march, March 1972.

BELOW, LEFT Lance-Corporal Mick Folan followed by CSM Peter Blyth in the inter-services cross-country championships February 1972, RIGHT. Addis Ababa. Drum-Major Nigel Elliott receives a gold medal from the Emperor Haile Selassie, February 1972.

Northern Ireland 1972-3. ABOVE. 1st Battalion cricket team, Army finalists 1972, back row Clint Hyman, John Evans, Mick Garnett, Ted Drake, Dennis Butel, Dave Bennett, Bob Wilde. Front row Captain Duncan Green, Bob Shaw, Major Steve Burnip, Mack Clarke and Kelvin Boynton.

BELOW 1st Battalion command team, left to right: RSM Laurie Linskey, Lieutenant-Colonel David Hanson, Brigadier Billy Armour (Colonel of the Regiment) and Captain Peter Orwin (Adjutant) in the Springfield Road, Belfast, 2 September 1972.

Northern Ireland 1973. ABOVE Palace Barracks Brownie Pack. Behind (left) Mrs Brenda McGarrell and Mrs Brenda Garrigan.

BELOW, LEFT Major John Filor on his way to the border area – March 1973. RIGHT Segment patrol, Privates Pete Oxley (left) and Jesse James (see page 104).

1900 hours and some 1,500 masked UDA volunteers confronted A Company at the appointed place of parade. Milk bottles were collected from doorsteps and paving stones wrenched up for breaking into missiles. Support Company, with Major Edwin Beckett in command, arrived to give a bit of depth to A Company's position. The stalemate was broken by A Company allowing the UDA leadership to use its public address equipment to regain control over its increasingly restless members and to withdraw them. As Company Sergeant-Major Peter Blyth of A Company remarked, 'It was a simple matter of standing firm', but he was well-known for seeing the nub of the problem.

The battalion had some familiarity with almost every part of Belfast by mid-July, giving those concerned a knowledge of the city and its inhabitants that no roulement unit could hope to achieve. This was an invaluable investment for the months ahead but the overall security situation in the Province could not improve while the No-Go areas remained. Operation Motorman was devised for this purpose and the strength of the garrison raised to twenty infantry battalions, plus additional engineer and transport units, for the occasion. At 0400 hours 31 July, after a broadcast warning to the population to stay indoors and giving the terrorists an opportunity to sneak away, the barricades were bulldozed and removed, the streets taken back under security force control and order ostensibly restored.

Motorman was a complete success in its limited aim to end the No-Go areas and, of equal importance, represented the start of a resolute climb back from the low point reached in the fortunes of the security forces. 1st Prince of Wales's Own operated as a complete unit and, together with 2nd Royal Regiment of Fusiliers, was responsible for the reoccupation of Andersonstown. Much of the battalion's work in this operation was accomplished before H Hour. During the previous week, several operations were mounted to allow Sappers to take down barriers and other obstacles. For one of these, in what was afterwards described as a magnificent public relations exercise, Colonel Hanson provided a Saracen APC exclusively for the press, so that they could see what was happening and report accurately. His action won great appreciation, as the press were inclined to believe they were kept in the dark.

The battalion was tasked to take over the eastern part of

Andersonstown and left Palace Barracks at 0326 hours on the morning of 31 July. The start line was crossed at 0350 and all four companies had achieved their objectives by 0415. Entry was unopposed but the battalion immediately began an intensive patrol programme to maintain absolute control of the the area. Each company was allocated selected houses to search and a file of PIRA documents, which subsequently revealed valuable intelligence, was discovered by A Company. Two schools were taken over as bases and fortified with some 12,000 sandbags that had been filled during the previous twenty-four hours.

Stoning of the base at the School of the Holy Child began during the morning and a brick smashed the windscreen of a Land Rover entering the gate. Just before 1600 hours a PIRA funeral party arrived at the Milltown cemetery. It was allowed to go ahead but, with soldiers standing amongst the headstones, no shots were fired over the coffin. Evening brought desultory shooting from the area of the Falls Road and at 2205 hours C Company had to fire baton rounds to disperse a crowd stoning another unit in Roger Casement Park. A few minor explosions occurred during the late evening but all was quiet when 1st Royal Green Jackets arrived at 0400 hours on 1 August to take over the area as their permanent patch.

An end to No-Go areas marked the beginning of a phase of offensive operations against the Provisionals with the aim of making the movement of arms and explosives in the city more difficult and dangerous for the terrorist. The tactics were immediately familiar to those who had served in Aden 1965-7. Under the appropriately-named Operation Random, pedestrians and parked cars were searched in the street and road blocks thrown up without warning to check vehicles on the move. It was intensely tiring work but, for the main part, everyone reacted with good humour. Some finds resulted. Private 'Jay-Jay' Waterhouse noticed a man pull a handkerchief from his pocket bringing a .303 round with it. He was seized, searched and found to be carrying a loaded pistol. Red-handed arrests were rare but welcome, as conviction was virtually certain.

The PIRA sniper posed the most deadly threat to security force patrols and deployment on the street, while gunmen firing indiscriminately were only slightly less dangerous. Privates Roger Bruce, Stephen Eastwood and Ernie Hare, all of C Company, were wounded by random fire while confronting a stone-throwing mob in Andersonstown in August. Fortunately, they were hit only in the legs, but Eastwood's injuries led to his spending a long time in hospital, where he was visited by Prime Minister Edward Heath.[8] Intervention to prevent Protestant mobs destroying Catholic property was also dangerous work. Lieutenant Neil Porter needed twenty stitches after being hit in the face by a Protestant-thrown bottle in Ballymacarret, where a Catholic enclave was on the point of being razed.

Close cooperation with the RUC was ensured by formation of a small team under the command of Major Brian Stead comprising Colour-Sergeant Ted Robinson, Sergeant John Prosser – younger brother of Sergeant George Prosser – and ten junior NCOs and men. Wearing civilian clothes and located at the RUC County Antrim headquarters, they were responsible for coordination of all military and police anti-terrorist tasks in the 1,000 square miles of RUC 'R' Division, from which the team took its name. Several arms and ammunition finds were a direct result of swift interchange of information, as was the interception of a would-be car bomber complete with bomb.

The autumn of 1972 saw the introduction of Operation Segment to deny terrorist access to Belfast city centre and Operation Lollipop for the escorting of schoolchildren safely home. The bomb threat to the business and shopping districts was on the point of bringing commercial life of the city to a standstill. The whole area was surrounded by a high security fence and the interior divided into segments with a few, easily controlled gates permitting pedestrians to move from one to another. Just as minefields must be covered by fire to be effective, so the perimeter and the segment gates had to be manned by patrols and checkpoints to stop and search civilians.

The problem of searching female pedestrians was overcome by introduction of 'Greenfinch' women soldiers of the Ulster Defence Regiment (UDR) for this express purpose. This called for an amendment of the Act of Parliament which had brought the UDR into being. When the amendment came before the House of Lords for approval, an English lady life peer took the opportunity to criticize the 'male chauvinistic nature' of the original Act. It is nevertheless surprising, as the problem of searching women had been encountered in both Palestine and Malaya and overcome by using women police constables, that the need for female soldiers in the UDR was not foreseen when the Act was drafted in 1970 and recruitment of women specifically precluded. The amendment allowed every handbag, shopping bag, pocket and person to be thoroughly examined.

Operation Lollipop cannot be better described than as in the regimental journal for February 1973, where a telling point on the thankless task of trying to keep the peace is also made.

> Once upon a time there were four schools, two for boys and two for girls – one of each for Catholics and Protestants. Every day just after 3 o'clock the teachers rang the bells and the children put away their books, put on their coats and picked up armfuls of bottles and stones and went home. The Protestant children walked on the right-hand pavement and the Catholic children on the left-hand pavement. As they walked home they shouted rude names and threw things at each other. They were happy playful children.
>
> One day the parents of these happy children said, 'This cannot go on, our children are being insulted.' So next day when the school bells rang, the parents were gathered outside to take their children safely home. After a few days of this, the parents became bored. To keep up their spirits, they began to shout rude names and throw stones at each other and many people were hurt. Next day the soldiers came to keep the peace and everyone behaved and went home peacefully. After a few days, the children got bored with behaving themselves and were unhappy. Now when the school bells ring, the children put away their books, put on their coats and pick up armfuls of stones and bottles. As they walk home they call the soldiers rude names and throw things at them and they are all now happy, contented children.

There was, however, a deadly aspect to this duty. While acting as 'lollipop men', the soldiers were slow-moving targets for the PIRA gunmen, who fired whenever they saw a safe opportunity.

Those of the 1st Battalion to whom the bogs of Ireland were still just a myth were given a taste of the real thing during the early months of 1973. Each of the rifle companies in turn was detached under command of 3rd Infantry Brigade in the countryside. Company headquarters and two platoons were based at Lisnaskea in

County Fermanagh and the third platoon at Lurgan in County Down. In Fermanagh the task was border security under the direction of the Province armoured reconnaissance regiment, 16th/5th The Queen's Royal Lancers. In the border areas the PIRA threat came from across the border with the Republic, from where forays could be made to attack isolated farms, mine roads and ambush security force patrols and soft-skinned resupply vehicles. After each such foray the terrorists could take refuge in the south.

Border security operations were overt, to give confidence in security force protection to the small isolated communities, and covert to discover PIRA border crossing points and rendezvous. Vigils of several days' duration in abandoned buildings overlooking the border, although testing of individual alertness, were a welcome contrast to Belfast city centre patrols and riot control. The platoons at Lurgan came under command of the 1st Staffordshires with the more mundane task of countryside and village searches for explosive devices left on roadsides, railways and, on one macabre occasion, in a graveyard. Waterborne patrols from 6 Platoon of B Company crossed and recrossed the lakes on the estate of Crom Castle, close to the border and unquestionably the most up-market of any patrol base used during border security operations.

Grim news reached Palace Barracks in May 1973. Staff-Sergeant Arthur Place, who had served with the regiment before becoming a pilot in the Army Air Corps, was killed by a PIRA bomb in a car park in Omagh on 18 May, together with three of his comrades. Place was an outstanding young man, who had distinguished himself in Aden when he and Sergeant Colin Jackson had attempted to rescue Lance-Corporal Leslie Roberts from a burning Land Rover (see page 44), for which he received a commendation from the Commander-in-Chief Middle East. The funeral at Staff-Sergeant Place's home town of Pocklington on 25 May 1973 was attended by many of his friends in the regiment and Regimental Association, as well as people of the small market town who turned out in respect.

A scheme inherited by the battalion in 1972-3 led to the award of the Wilkinson Sword for Peace for 1973 to five senior NCOs. Appreciating that security force relations with the community could be improved, Colonel Hanson appointed Colour-Sergeants Phil Hinds and Jim Wood and Sergeants Ron Bradley, Brian Dent and Henry Holmes to start up community relations projects in and around Belfast. They concentrated their efforts on forming youth clubs in ravaged areas of high unemployment and reported directly to the commanding officer.

There was significant risk involved. The NCOs travelled in plain clothes but in their easily identified private cars, chiefly at night. Sergeant Dent was set upon in the dark, shot five times in the legs and left for dead. He read about his 'killing' in a copy of a Dublin newspaper sent to him in hospital. He subsequently received the BEM. In spite of intimidation from hard liners in the popoulation, the clubs were formed with the NCOs handling up to fifteen projects each at the same time. Youths were kept off the street and out of drinking dens. Mixed religion groups met in some clubs and a summer camp for 940 children, Catholic and Protestant, was run by Colour-Sergeant Wood. One club formed by Sergeant Dent was named the Dent Centre in recognition of his service to the community of Thorburn. The Wilkinson Sword is awarded annually to a unit of each of the three armed services for outstanding efforts to foster good relations with its local community. The 1st Battalion received the award for 1973, based solely on the achievements of the five senior NCOs. The sword is now displayed in the Warrant Officers' and Sergeants' Mess.

Reductions in the Northern Ireland force level in mid-1973 and consequent changes in areas of operational responsibility required the battalion to cover some temporary gaps. Each company in turn deployed to the Blackmountain School in the Protestant Woodvale district of West Belfast. One platoon was detached to the Catholic Ligoniel estate to the north-west and came under command of the 3rd Parachute Regiment. Shootings, stonings, checks on stolen and suspicious cars, funerals and one rocket attack on a sangar overlooking the Springfield Road enlivened these detachments. The difference beween these and other operations lay not in the activities of the terrorists or the populace but in the fact that, in rotation, companies had a patch of their own for a while. It could scarcely be said that this led to a rise in affection for either Woodvale or Ligoniel, but the sense of having continuous responsibility for them was certainly worthwhile.

The July-August 'marching season' permitted no thought of a steady rundown to the close of the tour in November. Even when the season was over, emergency deployments continued but the nature of the emergencies showed signs of change. Anti-bombing patrols in and around Belfast city centre became increasingly frequent, as the Provisionals stepped up their campaign to counter the success of Operation Segment. Quick reaction by a C Company patrol near the Catholic Grosvenor Road led to the capture of a youth and a girl attempting to drive a car containing a 50lb bomb to an undisclosed destination. It was not possible to prevent the explosion but the area was immediately cleared so no one was hurt.

In November the weather turned bitterly cold. An entry in the B Company log sets the scene well, 'Under command 42 Heavy Regiment RA, Task anti-bomb patrols. No incidents. Cold and miserable.' Fourteen years before the outrage at Enniskillen, in November 1987, the same company log records, 'Sunday 11 November: Stood down. Remembrance Day.' Sunday could seldom be observed as either a Holy Day or a holiday, so it was fortunate that the Reverend Paul Abram was the battalion chaplain at this time. He had served as a National Service officer with the East Yorkshires and so knew Yorkshire soldiers well. He spent rather more of his time on the streets of Belfast than in church.

The first resident tour ended in November 1973. While it had been a fragmented experience in many respects, the battalion had drawn ever closer together in an operational environment where families were present, sport could be played and the essential domestic life of a regiment continued. It presented challenges in ever-changing priority of importance and where virtually every effort was on behalf of someone else.

A saddle club was run for the benefit of all ranks and their families and an indoor heated swimming pool built and similarly enjoyed. The wives' White Rose Club assumed an even greater importance than usual and flourished under the kind and caring leadership of Mrs Anne Hanson. The Club became the information centre when the men were away, keeping wives up to date on where their husbands were, what they were doing and when they might be expected home. A kindergarten was open on all weekday mornings. The Palace Barracks Brownie Pack, gathered and cajoled by Brown Owls Brenda Garrigan and Brenda McGarrell, reached a new record strength and Jo Longdon enrolled twelve young ladies who had outgrown their Brownie uniforms into the 5th Holywood Guide Company. The battalion cricket team entered the Army competition for the first time and reached the final.

Every man of the battalion who had served twenty-eight days in the Province during the tour received the clasp 'Northern Ireland' and the General Service Medal if he did not already hold it. Colonel David Hanson was appointed an OBE for his period of command in Northern Ireland. The Quartermaster, Captain John Long, who had achieved near-miracles of improvisation to ensure that no one went without what was essential for operations and was as comfortable as possible in even the grimmest of circumstances, was rewarded with the MBE. Colour-Sergeant Jim Wood and Sergeant Brian Dent, two of the community project leaders, were awarded the BEM. Majors Chris Day, John Filor, Roy Goble and Michael Sharpe, Company Sergeant-Major Mick Barham, Colour-Sergeant Phil Hinds and Sergeant Ron Bradley were all mentioned in despatches in recognition of their distinguished service. During the same period Colour-Sergeant Allan Simpson of the regiment was also mentioned in despatches while serving with the 1st Duke of Wellington's in Northern Ireland. Lance-Corporal Richard Sleight, who had been detached to Headquarters Northern Ireland, received the GOC's Commendation in person from General Sir Frank King.

Although not a few members of the battalion were wounded or injured by terrorist action or in riots during the eighteen months' tour, no fatal casualty was sustained. While this may be attributed in part to good fortune, credit is also due to the manner in which Colonel David Hanson had trained his battalion for its task and, as the months wore on, ensured that leaders at all levels resolutely maintained the measures essential for the security of their men, as well as for the success of operations. Only a few days before the battalion was due to leave Belfast, a visitor noted that security measures were as strict as when he had last visited, more than a year before.

The commanding officer was himself injured, although not in consequence of terrorist action. Seeking a refreshing change, he borrowed a horse and took a day off to go hunting with the North Down. After an hour or so, the horse refused to jump a thick hedge which Hanson cleared with ease, breaking a collar bone on impact. Arriving at the casualty section of the military hospital at Warringfield, in pain and with his arm in a temporary sling, he was greeted with sympathy and warm sweet tea – until the origin of his injury was revealed. He was then directed through a side entrance to a hut serving as the X-ray department and invited to join the end of the queue.

6
On Immediate Call

'There are in warfare no constant conditions.'
SUN TZU, *THE ART OF WAR*, 400 BC

The extreme flanks of NATO, in the north and south-east, were sources of unease from the first days of the alliance. Not only were they geographically remote and ill-suited for the stationing of large forces in peacetime, they included areas in which local disputes could be fermented and orchestrated from Moscow by proxy. Greek Thrace, narrowly separating Bulgaria from access to the Mediterranean, and eastern Turkey where the Kurdish population straddles the border with Syria are obvious examples. In the far north, Norway's frontier runs for more than 400 miles with that of Finland, denied a port on the Barents Sea since the Second World War, and for a further 120 miles with that of the Murmansk Military District.[1]

International tension in any of these regions would face NATO staffs with two difficulties. First, how to demonstrate resolution and solidarity against an essentially localized threat and, second, how to back up the national forces opposing it. A contingency plan for each perceived eventuality could be drawn up, but from where would come the men, aircraft and warships when the emergency arose? The assignment of naval and air forces at short notice presented no serious difficulty, so long as adequate contingency plans and facilities, air bases in particular, were prepared. Modern war at sea and in the air demands much the same expertise wherever it is conducted and warships and aircraft could be quickly diverted to the crisis zone from NATO command elsewhere.

In contrast, ground forces need highly specialized equipment and training if they are to be effective in the Arctic or in mountainous country. After more than a decade of research as to how best to match this requirement, the Allied Command Europe (ACE) Mobile

Force (Land) was established in 1961. Most of the assigned forces were to remain based in their own country and under national command. The catch was that they could not be used for non-AMF(L) operations without the prior consent of the Supreme Allied Commander Europe (SACEUR). For this reason the UK Ministry of Defence decided to assign a battalion-group to the AMF(L) role and keep it Arctic-trained, equipped and on stand-by for a four-year period. The 1st Prince of Wales's Own took over this responsibility after moving from Celle to Bulford, on the edge of Salisbury Plain, in August 1978.

In professional and sporting terms, the four years in Celle had been highly successful but any expectations of anti-climax in the next station were extinguished by the pressing demands of the AMF(L) role. Everyone had to learn to ski, live for weeks or even months in Arctic conditions and master techniques of air-mobility tactically by helicopter and strategically in NATO transport aircraft. Time was short. The first Hardfall exercises in snow were scheduled for February-March 1979 in Norway, during which the rifle companies had to achieve skiing proficiency – properly armed and equipped – in time for a formation-level exercise with the Norwegian forces in the second half of the period. A two-month exercise in Greece was forecast for the following autumn.

Command of the battalion had changed on the move from Celle, Lieutenant-Colonel John Filor succeeding Lieutenant-Colonel Edwin Beckett. They had contrasting styles of command that in many ways suited their different circumstances. Filor, always robustly down to earth, had no difficulty in getting training for the Arctic in hand but permitted himself some exasperation with the local District Headquarters, a mere stone's throw away, which plagued him with distracting demands for soldiers to do this and that. Drastic cuts in the Territorial Army had deprived all the United Kingdom regional headquarters of their cherished Division/District status, leaving them with more parochially motivated staffs. The chain of command down to the battalion was scarcely clear-cut. Operational and training policy came from AMF(L) Headquarters in Germany, the local brigade commander at Tidworth had a hand in overseeing the training, while the close-by Headquarters South-West District dealt with administration and complained about staff cars not being saluted.

AMF(L) Headquarters was situated at Mannheim-Seckenheim in West Germany. The force was commanded by Major-General Alexander Weyand, US Army, and comprised units from Belgium, Britain, Canada, Germany, Italy, Luxembourg and the United States. Brigadier Malcom Cubiss served as chief of staff of AMF(L) headqarters, in the rank of colonel, during 1975–7. Later he was chief of the Crisis Management Staff at SHAPE, responsible for AMF(L) contingency plans and training. In this post he was succeeded by Colonel (later Brigadier) Michael Sharpe of the regiment in 1980. They certainly had a clear understanding of what membership of the AMF(L) entailed, while other British officers regarded the skiing in Norway as 'a bit of a swan'.

It is true that soldiers learning to ski on grass on a sunny afternoon could leave a casual observer thinking that this was all rather remote from war. Seeing the same men after they had been living for weeks in Norway's deep snow conveyed a distinctly different impression. As did the strike-interceptor aircraft screeching overhead, those with the von Richthofen black cross markings giving a particularly curious sensation down one's spine. Air-support was closely coordinated with ground force aspects of excercises. Number 609 Forward Air Control (FAC) unit, commanded by an experienced RAF ground-attack pilot, was there to make certain that allied air forces knew exactly where AMF(L) units were on the ground and to direct the support they needed in the exercise battle. These were not aircraft making abstract supersonic passes through the heavens.

The battalion's first Arctic winter went well. No one made a complete fool of himself on skis and, more importantly, no one got frostbitten. The period ended with a sea deployment of 650 miles from Bergen to Narvik in northern Norway to join the Norwegian Brigade North for a formation exercise in the neck of the Lofoten Islands archipelago. There was some disappointment amongst the more extreme enthusiasts for the new operational environment that this region, although almost 150 miles north of the Arctic Circle, provided only four feet of snow in which to dig and live that winter. One essential infantry activity that cannot be satisfactorily simulated is the siting of weapons in snow. There can be few more persuasive reminders of the advantages of enfilade fire than four feet of snow to one's immediate front. Colonel Filor had an engaging way of dealing with those who perched their weapons on what appeared to

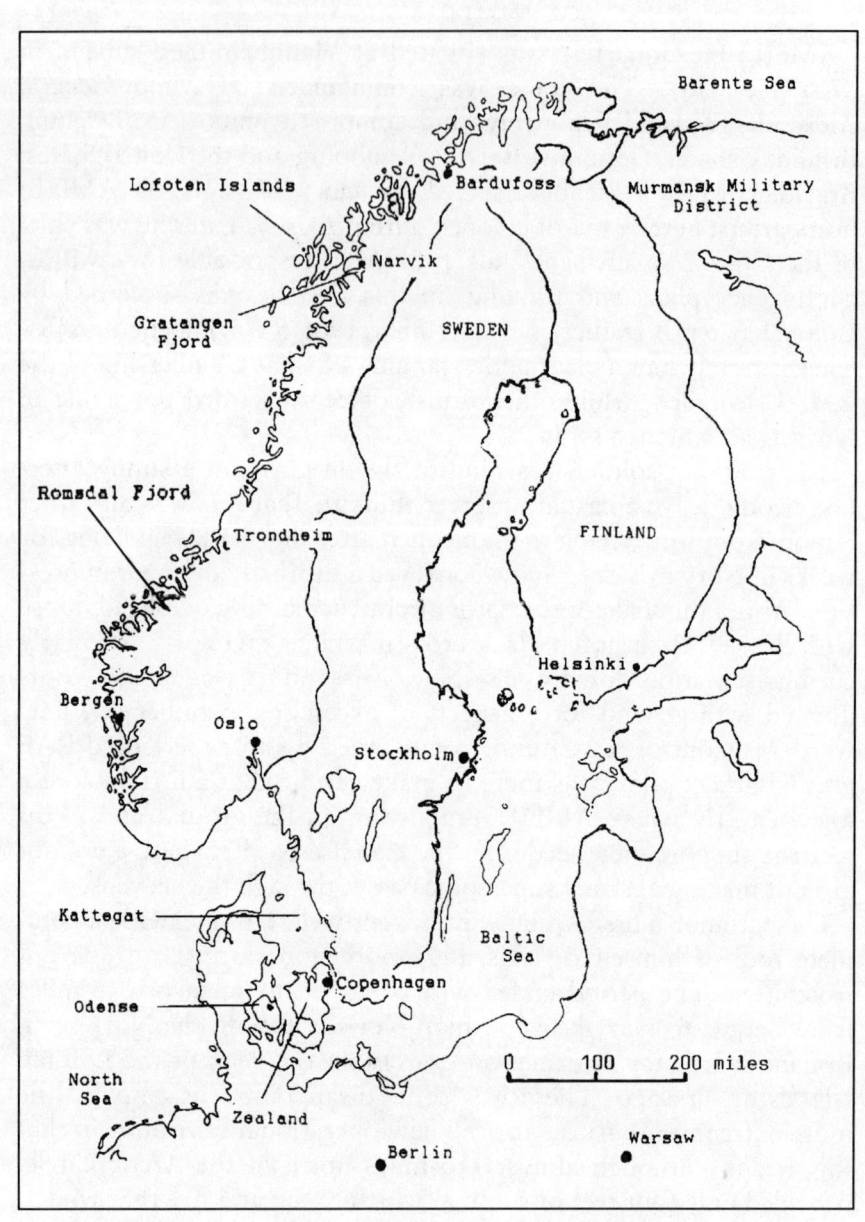

Map 11 *AMF(L) Northern Contingencies Region*

be horizontal snowmen. 'This stuff isn't bulletproof you know,' he would remark – as he gently kicked it through.

The battalion returned to Bulford to begin user-trials on the 'uniform of the 80s'. This was not a cold-resistant or snow camouflage suit but a ceremonial or walking-out dress. Provenance of the design has proved difficult to research and it is not inconceivable that all records have been destroyed. The basic design was not unlike that of Number 2 or Service Dress, but in an olive green similar to the costume in which the Canadian armed forces found themselves when combined into what became derogatorily known as the 'Green Machine' in 1968.[2] Chocolate éclair-type epaulettes were available for ceremonial occasions and what the soldiers rudely dubbed 'flasher-macs' for – well – walking-out, one must suppose!

No matter who thought of this ridiculous and unnecessary experiment, someone else showed a glimmer of genius in tasking the 1st Battalion to wear the uniform for trial. The job was taken seriously. When each of a seemingly endless stream of visitors arrived to check for quality and thickness, he was not allowed simply to observe a few soldiers standing about looking green. He was obliged to witness a fashion parade in which the flasher-macs were the culminating *pièce de résistance*, worn by three soldiers well aware of the fashion appeal of a contrasting lining.

The battalion wore the trial uniform when in barracks for a year, while a handful of volunteers – carefully selected by the Regimental Sergeant-Major in light of their recent conduct – were sent out to test the reactions of the citizens of Amesbury and Salisbury to what the Army of the 80s might wear. Two such volunteers never returned from their mission. Finally, the Adjutant-General himself – General Sir Robert Ford – asked for the battalion to parade for a final decision. John Filor often wears an expression suggesting that he knows a joke that he may or may not share with you. He was wearing it as he led the great man out to inspect his all-green battalion.

'Well, what do you think of the new uniform?' demanded the AG of number one in the front rank. 'Rubbish, sir, just rubbish,' came the candid response. The next man questioned simply rolled his eyes heavenwards. 'Is there any point in going on?' asked Sir Robert. 'I think the men have been looking forward to seeing you,' lied Filor politely. The inspection was completed in good humour without further questions about the trial uniform – and there the matter ended.

Although unconnected with the tri-service environment of the ACE Mobile Force, affiliation with the Royal Navy frigate HMS *Cleopatra* began in 1978 when the 1st Battalion arrived at Bulford. Seven officers and fifty members of the ship's company made the introductory visit to Picton Barracks on 22 November that year. After a briefing on the AMF(L) place in the NATO scheme of things, the visitors were invited to don their sports kit for a series of 'friendlies'. *Cleopatra*'s crew won the rugby and soccer matches, brought the battalion team to a hard-fought draw on the hockey field and only narrowly lost the squash competition. Everyone agreed that this was an outfit worthy of the battalion's comradeship; indeed *Cleopatra* might have a few useful tips to pass on. Six soldiers from C Company spent three weeks at sea in the frigate during the summer of 1979 and thoroughly enjoyed the experience. Contacts and exchange visits followed with increasing regularity. HMS *Cleopatra* and the regiment share the Freedom of Harrogate, which is how the affiliation was first brought about.

After the Arctic cold in February-March, the promised autumn exercise in Greece was anticipated with enthusiasm and a large reconnaissance party went to Greece to look at the ground. The battalion was therefore disenchanted to hear during the summer that the exercise had been cancelled 'for political reasons'. This was to prove a not-unusual occurrence when forays to the Mediterranean sun were in prospect. Fortunately, deployment to the Danish island of Zealand in June for a CPX with the other AMF(L) allied units was the next scheduled trip abroad. Legendary stories of visits to Denmark in the early 1960s, passed down over the years, built up a healthy head of steam for this expedition. When the time came, no one was disappointed.

The strategic significance of Zealand is that it closes the only exit from the Baltic Sea, the Kattegat, other than for four narrow channels. In war, NATO control of these would be crucial for keeping the Soviet Baltic Fleet where it belongs.

The exercise, codenamed 'Agate Exchange', involved over 200 men from the battalion and 50 vehicles, mainly for purposes of command, communications and reconnaissance. For the first time the affiliated units – 'O' Battery, 2nd Field Regiment RA, The Queen's Royal Irish Hussars close reconnaissance troop and a field troop from 22 Engineer Regiment – joined in to complete the AMF(L) battalion group. The exercise was held in southern Zealand after a voyage in a tank landing ship (LST) from Harwich to the Danish western seaboard port of Esbjerg. Defensive tactical digging was one of the exercise themes and a series of air sorties flown at the request of 609 FAC demonstrated how well the positions had been sited and concealed. The digging worked up exactly the thirsts appropriate for the battalion to renew acquaintance with the Tuborg brewery in Copenhagen.

The stability of the AMF(L) role, in that absences from the United Kingdom could be forecast reasonably well, provided a sound basis for planning the battalion's sporting programme, although the winter seasons suffered severely from the annual Hardfall exercises in February and March. In spite of this handicap the battalion soccer team moved from ending the 1978–9 season as runners-up in the Salisbury Plain League to the final in the Army Challenge Cup in the winter of 1980–1. The final was played against the School of Electrical and Mechanical Engineers, which for decades had attracted star performers to its staff.[3] Goals by Company Sergeant-Major Byron Cawkwell and Private John Johnson left the battalion team still down 3–2 after extra time. The game was reported by Army soccer experts as the most exciting final for a decade.

Athletics training continued to prosper through best use of the excellent local facilities and less disruption by overseas exercises. The South-West District inter-unit Athletics Competition was won decisively in 1981 and the United Kingdom Zone B Championship in 1982. The athletics team captain at this time was Captain Peter Blyth, who continued to achieve outstanding personal performances, for example as the Army 5,000 metres individual veteran champion in 1981. Athletics received an additional boost in the form of Sergeant Kris Akabusi as the battalion physical training instructor. He made an immense contribution to battalion sport during years 1981–5 and everyone basked in reflected glory when he won the 400 metres hurdles bronze medal in the 1992 Olympic Games.

Expertise in the snow had reached a high standard after two winters in the Arctic. During the concentration phase of the third Exercise Hardfall, in February 1981, the battalion was tasked with preparing a series of demonstration fire positions around the NATO airfield at Bardufoss. Never a man for half-measures, Filor ordered the felling of a sizeable tract of Norwegian pine for the overhead cover. The enthusiasm of the AMF(L) hierarchy for the final results appeared boundless and a request was made for the construction of a complete platoon position at a central point, to which VIP visitors could tip-toe from their helicopters without getting too much snow in their shoes. Again shouts of 'Timber' startled the northern tree pipits about their lawful, early-spring occasion, but not quite as much as the bill for the trees startled Filor when it turned up in Bulford that summer. Shrewdly, he re-addressed it to one of the allied battalions, without comment. It may well still be circulating today.

A vehicle sometimes difficult to keep circulating was the tracked Volvo Snowcat and its articulated trailer. The battalion was equipped with ninety-six of these expensive and sophisticated machines. Although specifically designed for Arctic conditions, each required cherishing with a degree of care and attention usually reserved for a prima ballerina. Intended for use as command vehicles or as weapon and ammunition carriers, they became the victims of overload when the ski-going was especially difficult. On firm snow a Snowcat could tow two sections of skiers without difficulty, while carrying a full internal load. On hard-packed snow, energy could be saved by fitting skids to the trailer tracks, but this technique carried a penalty of reduced control over the trailer.

During an exercise in 1982 the main command-post vehicle was dragged from a narrow bridge by its trailer while taking evasive action in an ambush. The Volvo plunged twenty feet onto its nose, ruptured a fuel tank and burned out completely within three minutes. Miraculously, the trailer did not block the towing vehicle's exit, allowing the entire crew to escape unhurt. The charred shell of the adjutant's Browning pistol, eventually recovered from the wreck, was a salutary reminder of how fortunate the vehicle crew were to have escaped with their lives and without injury.

Initial enthusiasm at being on emergency call, as the AMF(L) invariably was, began to pall when the call never came, while the annual pilgrimages to the Arctic continued remorselessly. Lieutenant-Colonel Peter Woolley succeeded Lieutenant-Colonel John Filor in command of the 1st Battalion in April 1981. When the Falkland Islands' crisis broke out with the Argentinian invasion one year later and the task force was being assembled, Woolley telephoned the chief of staff at Headquarters UK Land Forces. 'This must be the job for us,' he argued. 'We have all the training and equipment for the South Atlantic.' Woolley was not alone in this view, but the battalion was committed to SACEUR and – in the early stages of deployment – most people in Whitehall thought that 3rrd Commando Brigade RM was enough to frighten the 'Argies' into surrender. Adherence to the NATO obligation did not prevent the MoD ordering the battalion to hand over cold-weather clothing and equipment for use by Army units that did eventually join the Falklands task force.[4]

News of an extension of the battalion's period in the AMF(L) role until June 1983, adding a fifth winter season to the expected four, was received with mixed feelings. The lustre had long gone from the snows of Norway for all but the most recent reinforcements, keen to try their luck at winter sports. News that the next station would be Berlin was welcomed everywhere.

The winter exercise period of 1982 proved an exceptionally tough test of nerve and endurance. In addition to the Volvo accident already described, two troop-carrying helicopters met 'white-out' conditions which prevented the pilots from orientating themselves with the ground. The first aircraft, an RAF Puma, was able to achieve an abrupt hard landing, while the second, an Army Air Corps Gazelle taking technicians to check the Puma, flew into a hillside. The crew and three passengers escaped with their lives but were injured. The helicopter lifting the medical officer, Captain John Sheardown, and his team to the scene crashed on landing, throwing the doctor and his assistant, Corporal Tom 'Tupper' Hegney, through the windscreen. Amazingly, they sustained only cuts and bruises. The three crashes occurred with one hour, during which twenty-two men in all escaped with only minor injuries.

The Volvo accident and the helicopter crashes served as useful reminders that the Arctic cannot be ignored with impunity. This is not to suggest that the battalion was becoming blasé about snow conditions. After three years of winter training, British regular soldiers outclassed Norwegian conscripts on their home ground. The 1982 winter season closed with a major defence exercise in the region of Gratangen Fjord, where the German navy had skilfully put ashore the troops who took Narvik, in the early hours of 9 April 1940, thus forestalling the Allied intention of doing much the same thing.

The 'invaders' on Exercise Alloy Express were a US Marine

brigade and 42 Commando Royal Marines supported by a US assault helicopter carrier. 1st Prince of Wales's Own were placed forward with Canadian and Italian battalions in depth. The first US Marine probing move was ambushed by C Company, commanded by Major David Lyburn, with a consequent delay in the progress scheduled in the exercise 'pink'. Three helicopter assaults at battalion strength launched by the marines were 'destroyed' when they obligingly landed in areas chosen by the AMF(L) brigade as the killing ground. A long-range patrol led by Corporal Alf 'Stumpy' McKenzie reached the US Tac HQ and took the unguarded American brigade commander prisoner. There was a major sense of humour failure, of course, but these had become commonplace – and much enjoyed.

Colonel Peter Woolley had made a detailed study of the 1940 Norwegian campaign around Narvik and the *motti-tactics*[5] used by the Finns to inflict huge casualties on the invading Soviet Army in the 1939/40 Winter War. The lessons of both campaigns were explained to his officers and senior NCOs, thereby giving a fresh impetus to battalion training, for all ranks, as preparations were made for the fifth and final Arctic winter.

Woolley fostered the battalion's seemingly insatiable appetite for sporting competition. Although not his personal forte, preferring squash and tennis, he decided that athletics should have priority because they involved so many men in the battalion and constantly drew in fresh talent. Appropriately, he was to become Chairman of Army Athletics some years later. It was during this period that the battalion established a formidable reputation in the Army cross-country championships, improving from third team position in 1982 to second place in 1983. The Army team marathon championship was won in 1982 and the Army cross-country relay championship in 1983. From there the battalion went on to win the Army cross-country championships for four successive years: 1984, 1985, 1986 and 1987, establishing an Army record.

Individual performers also did well. In 1983 Private Graham Birdsall was the Army junior steeplechase champion, Sergeant Kris Akabusi the Army 400 metres champion and Colour-Sergeant Tom Copperwaite the Army surf canoe champion. The athletics team won the Army Zone B championship in 1982. No sport for which there were facilities was neglected during the final two seasons at Bulford, when the foundations for many of the battalion's subsequent sporting achievements were laid.

After the major two-sided exercise which ended each winter training period, everyone gathered for the NATO Challenge Cup march and shoot competition. This was conducted in that cheerful atmosphere of cut-throat rivalry customary between close allies. British battalions with the AMF(L) had established a tradition of winning this contest over the years, so there was a reputation to be maintained. The 1st Battalion won in 1979 and took first, second and third places in 1980. The Cup was retained in 1981 but success in 1982 seemed uncertain when it became known that the German Field Hospital team – of all people – were to compete armed with a new Heckler-Koch rifle. The competition was run in Denmark over a twelve-kilometre obstacle course before the shooting began, but performance over the ground provided the decisive edge. After almost closing the gap between the team which had set off earlier in the staggered start, 2nd Lieutenant Graham Jackson's Number 1 platoon of A Company claimed the Cup to give the battalion a win for the fourth successive year. The first three places were taken that year and also in 1983 – thus completing a five-year term in the AMF(L) with a straight run of victories.

Names and addresses were exchanged as the battalion prepared to leave Norway for the last time. A host of friends had been made there and amongst the allied units of the AMF(L). Many private return visits followed. Olav Garen, the owner of the hotel at Fossli, invariably chosen by battalion headquarters for its spectacular view, remains in Christmas card touch.

Air-Mobile Operations 1987–90

The British Army is studiously cautious about adopting methods or tactics proved in combat by someone else. Reasons for this probably lie between a reluctance to discard systems that have served well in the past and the near-certainty that the Ministry of Defence will kick for touch whenever extra cash is required. Tactical air-mobility was used to advantage during the Second World War; the move by air of 2nd West Yorkshires from the Arakan to Imphal providing a salutary example. Tactical use of helicopters in support of the land battle, although costly in men and machines and not invariably successful, became the principal battlefield regime of the United States in

Vietnam. These techniques received study in Britain and the author can recall arranging, when second-in-command of the 1st Battalion, an exercise without troops but *with helicopters*, in a Vietnam-type setting, in East Anglia in 1967.

News that the 1st Battalion was to move to Catterick from Ballykinler in the spring of 1987 was met not by the question 'What for?' but by 'For how long?' The two years in Northern Ireland had been operationally varied and Ballykinler popular with the wives and children, as well as with the men when off-duty. The beach is within easy reach and sailing and fishing there for everyone. Catterick can be a delight in summer but one needs an extra greatcoat in winter. The garrison town has an atmosphere of suspended military history about it, rather as if ghosts of the pre-1914 cavalry division are still exercising the horses before breakfast. To men who had served in demanding stations for years, Catterick seemed likely to be a place between places, where one waited to be called to something more exciting.

That appreciation proved not entirely mistaken. The task of 24th Infantry Brigade based at Catterick was emergency reinforcement of 1st British Corps in Germany. As in the AMF(L) some years earlier, the battalion was again on immediate call. At first it was equipped with Saxon wheeled armoured personnel carriers, which did not have much of an air of immediacy about them. Bought as a stopgap when it became known that the Army's new infantry AFV – the Warrior – would be delayed into service, the Saxon was simply a means of protected road transport mounting a self-defence 7.62mm anti-aircraft machine-gun in a roof cupola. As it gave protection only against small-arms fire and shell splinters, it was litle more than an updated and mechanically more reliable Humber armoured 'Pig'.

One advantage of the Saxon, which did not become apparent until the battalion deployed with them to Germany on Exercise Keystone, is that each can carry ten supermarket trolley-loads of bottled beer. Not that the exercise scenario allowed much time for utilization of this handy facility. 24th Brigade was tested in all phases of war over an exacting three-week period, including crossing the Weser both ways, on the second occasion in the form of an assault river crossing. Immediately on return from the Continent, two rifle companies were detached to protect a US Air Force cruise missile unit from the attentions of the CND and 'Cruisewatch' while exercising on

Salisbury Plain. Three female protesters were intercepted attempting to wriggle under the dannert wire and courteously returned through the gate to their own side.

Thankfully, the Saxons were handed over to another battalion in the late autumn of 1987, when it was announced that 24th Brigade was to become air-mobile. It was also to be commanded by Brigadier Peter Woolley of the regiment. The new role remained one of rapid reinforcement of 1st British Corps, but by air and helicopter-borne into battle rather than sedately trundled to war in the Saxons. The athletics team ran the winners to a needle finish in the Army Championship, a team was entered for Bisley for the first time for seven years and the commanding officer, Lieutenant-Colonel Duncan Green, led the cricket team in the Army and Infantry competitions.

Training began in the autumn with the new SA (Small-Arms) 80 weapons. The 5.56 mm 'individual weapon' replaced the 7.62 mm SLR with which the battalion had been armed for thirty years and also the 8 mm SMG. The light support weapon (LSW) superseded the 7.62 mm GPMG, except in the sustained-fire or anti-aircraft role. SA80 had been delayed coming into service due to an accuracy fault at a certain range. With this difficulty overcome, the weapons were warmly welcomed. Infantry versions of both weapons were fitted with Trilax X4 magnification sights, which trials had shown give a 30 percent improvement in accuracy over the SLR. The much smaller calibre ammunition allowed for many more rounds to be carried on the man and greatly reduced the overall infantry ammunition load.

In spite of the schedule of exercises being less predictable than during the AMF(L) period in Bulford, the upward spiral of sporting success continued. The 1987–8 season brought victory in the Army Team Marathon, the North-East District Grade III Novices and the Northern Zone Novices' Team Boxing Championships. A great effort was also made to achieve success on the rugby field. Confidence increased after an early season triumph over the redoubtable 38 Engineer Regiment from Ripon. The zone final was very narrowly lost to 1st Royal Welch Fusiliers after a nail-biting match on the familiar pitch at Ballykinler, which the Royal Welch had inherited when they relieved the 1st Battalion in Northern Ireland.

38 Engineer Regiment's team were co-finalists with the 1st Battalion in the North-East District novices' boxing competition in January 1988. This was a needle match in its own right but also because,

prior to their defeat on the rugby field, 38 Regiment had knocked the battalion out of the District soccer competition. Hence the boxing teams gathered at Catterick in an atmosphere of 'one each and one to go'. The account in the regimental journal written by Captain Danny Matthews, who trained the battalion team, tells the story.

At 1930 hours the first bout started with Private John McSherry evenly matched. The bout was very fast with both boxers equally determined but McSherry had the edge, gaining a unanimous verdict. Both boxers received the referee's congratulations and the spectators' appreciation. Each bout that followed saw the same determination from the battalion boxers. The final result of eight bouts to one, for the battalion, may appear one-sided but the opposition had come to win and hard blows were given and taken on both sides. It was the superior fitness that enabled our boxers to absorb blows and immediately retaliate, which won the night.

Acts of gallantry by two NCOs of the battalion received recognition during this period. On 9 July 1987 Corporal Peter Davidson of the REME light aid detachment (LAD) was cycling to barracks when he saw flames and smoke billowing from a married quarter. Hearing screams from the upper storey, he crawled onto the roof of the garden shed, rescued two small children from a bedroom window and then their mother, the wife of a corporal in 3rd Royal Regiment of Fusiliers who was away, and called the fire brigade. Corporal Charlie Pearce was driving to barracks from his home in Northallerton when he came across a serious traffic accident with several vehicles on fire. At serious risk to himself, he dragged the occupants of the burning cars to safety. Subsequently, Corporal Davidson received the North Yorkshire Fire Brigade Chief Officer's certificate for outstanding performance, while Corporal Pearce received The Queen's Commendation for brave conduct.

The entire battalion moved to Fort Lewis in Washington state, USA for training and a series of exercises in March and April 1988. The Fort Lewis training area extends over some 200,000 acres of scrubland and forest, where firing restrictions are few and opportunities for getting lost are boundless. The companies rotated through camps with different challenges to offer, in much the same manner as in former times in Libya and Kenya. The Geddes Cup competition provided the climax to three weeks of preparation under rugged conditions. Conducted in half-platoons, the test began with a twenty-mile approach march against time over a route demanding exacting map-reading skill. Only the group led by Sergeant 'Ginger' Burton reached the end within the bogey time. Individual tests in the military skills followed and what was widely agreed as the most rugged Geddes Cup for years concluded with a platoon attack with live artillery and mortar fire support, followed by another forced march of six miles and a snap-shooting competition. The Cup was won by Number 6 Platoon commanded by Lieutenant Tony Wilson.

Command of the 1st Battalion changed on 21 September 1988, when Lieutenant-Colonel Duncan Green handed over to Lieutenant-Colonel John King. Green had commanded the battalion for the latter part of the two-year tour in Ballykinler, for which he was mentioned in despatches. His detached manner concealed a knowledge and understanding of the battalion to the last man. This brought him respect and affection, as did his unswervingly relaxed approach to military matters, while keeping a firm grip of essentials. The battalion wished him well in his next appointment at Sandhurst. John King was the first commanding officer of the 1st Battalion to come from another regiment. He had an exceptional reputation with the Green Howards and had been an instructor at the Staff College, Camberley immediately before his appointment to command.

Demands for demonstrations of the battalion's air-mobile capability came thick and fast. Under the direction of Commander 24th Air-Mobile Brigade (Brigadier Peter Woolley) one was given on Salisbury Plain for the benefit of the members of the NATO Military Committee and the international press. It was highly praised afterwards for its professionalism and precision. On a visit to Catterick the Chief of the General Staff – General Sir Nigel Bagnall – remarked, 'I like this battalion and always have. They are not afraid to say what they think.' Then he turned to Dave Moffat for a bit of an update.

The final two years in Catterick, before the battalion moved to Germany in August 1990, were spent primarily in developing air-mobility skills through exercises of increasing complexity in the United Kingdom and Germany. The reality of being called to climb aboard the huge Chinook helicopters and thunder away to battle, even if only an exercise battle, kept the adrenalin pumping. There were vignette events, often unexpected, which impinged upon battalion life more significantly than their duration might suggest.

Unquestionably, the saddest event was the search for bodies of the victims of the Lockerbie air disaster, personal effects and forensic evidence. Parties from C Company, under command of Major Nick Evans and based on the village of Moffat some thirty miles from the search area, worked from first until last light for seven days in January 1989, searching forest and moorland on a sixty-man front at a rate of advance of 400 metres per hour. The teams found personal effects to fill sixty-five sacks, an aircraft panel embedded with shrapnel fragments and part of the luggage container in which the bomb had been stowed. It was grim work, but the people of Moffat made everyone feel welcome to Scotland.

Although Spearhead duty came round in the usual way, in each instance preceded by refresher training for Northern Ireland, only one platoon actually reached the Province. For six months between September 1988 and February 1989 a composite platoon of volunteers from the battalion under command of Lieutenant Boris Cowen served with 1st Royal Irish Rangers in the wilds of Enniskillen and the wetlands of Fermanagh. This helped 1st Royal Irish to put a full battalion into the field during a period in which they were undermanned and gave the volunteers from the 1st Battalion up-to-date Northern Ireland experience.

A happy vignette was a visit to the Royal Montreal Regiment – one of the allied regiments – on the occasion of its seventy-fifth anniversary and presentation of new Colours in May 1989. The Colonel of the Regiment was represented by Major-General Edwin Beckett, then Head of British Defence Staff in Washington, and by Lieutenant-Colonel John and Mrs Sue King, Major Richard Watson and Regimental Sergeant-Major Brian and Mrs Jenny Atkinson from the 1st Battalion. Two silver mustard pots were presented to the Royal Montreal Regiment to mark the occasion.

Private Richard Singleton of B Company distinguished himself by rescuing an old lady from drowning in Hull, for which act of bravery and initiative he received the GOC's Commendation, and the 1st Battalion acquired a young lady of its very own. The serene 2nd Lieutenant Claire Pridgeon of the Womens' Royal Army Corps joined for a two-year span of duty as assistant adjutant, which put an altogether new gloss on visits to battalion headquarters for those who had striven for years to give the place the widest possible berth.

The 1st Battalion achieved remarkable success in the boxing ring while at Catterick. Credit for this was chiefly due to the unrelenting efforts of Captain Danny Matthews in seeking out new talent, training the team and master-minding the contests. After being beaten six bouts to three by the 1st Parachute Regiment in the 1988 season, after some terrific bouts and one stopped fight, the battalion became the Army Grade II novices boxing champions in 1989 and Corporal Errol Tyrell the Army featherweight champion. He and Privates David Wilson and Jamie Yule, at light middleweight and lightweight respectively, were selected to represent the Army that year.

The cricket and soccer teams added to the laurels won by the boxers and distance-running champions, without reaching their Army-level championship victories. In the final of the Infantry Cricket Cup, victory was snatched by fellow Yorkshiremen of the 1st Duke of Wellington's by the barely credible margin of 0.2 of an over. This was the average scoring rate difference after both teams had the same score when the last wicket fell. The sports team photographs of the Catterick period show something of the disciplined authority of the Edwardian period but not everyone has a moustache! Determination and, above all, team solidarity is exuded by the straight-faced, identically-dressed young men.

The visit of Her Royal Highness The Duchess of Kent, the Colonel-in-Chief, to Catterick on 30 March 1990 provided the climax to this period. It was her second visit to the 1st Battalion since her appointment as Colonel-in-Chief and there was a great sense of occasion. C Company, commanded by Major Simon Caley, gave a dramatic demonstration of a helicopter-borne assault supported by a (simulated) artillery barrage. The Colonel-in-Chief's enjoyment of this spectacle, also watched by many of the wives and children of the battalion, is apparent from the photograph of her with General Tony Crowfoot and Colonel John King between pages 208 and 209. Afterwards, Her Royal Highness talked with the men of the battalion and their wives and children.

7
Back in the Troubled Province

'The Irish remain, in the Irish phrase, sorry for your troubles.'
MARY ELLEN SYNON

The Provisional IRA declared a unilateral ceasefire for eleven days just before Christmas 1974. This move followed a meeting in the Republic between the Provisionals and Protestant church leaders and the British Government set free some 300 suspects detained without trial at around the same time. Although ostensibly intended to cover only the period of Christmas and the New Year, the ceasefire was resumed – again unilaterally – by the Provisionals on 10 February 1975. Despite many violations, attributed to splinter groups or feuding between the Official and Provisional IRA, this ceasefire was supposedly still in place six months later when the 1st Prince of Wales's Own took over from the 2nd Light Infantry in Londonderry on 7 July.

After the resident tour in Belfast of 1972–3, the battalion had moved to Celle in Germany and joined the 7th Armoured Brigade of 1st Armoured Division. With no indications of thaw at that stage, the Cold War headed British defence priorities and the battalion's job in the mechanized infantry role was top of the league in the Army of the Rhine. Nonetheless, like other units in Germany, the battalion had to take its turn under Operation Banner – roulement tours of four months' duty in Ulster. Two such tours were mounted from Celle, both to Londonderry. The first – from July to November 1975 – came towards the end of the initial phase of the Northern Ireland campaign, while the second – from March to July 1977 – began at the time of a significant change in security force tactics.

In a situation of rising tension as sectarian tit for tat killings increased in the Province, the battalion – commanded by Lieutenant-Colonel Tony Crowfoot – took over responsibility for the westerly of the two operational sectors of Londonderry west of the River

Foyle. This sector included the Creggan, the Rosemount and Shantallow estates, together with countryside between the city and the border with the Republic, known as the 'Enclave'. Each company was allotted to a specific area for the whole tour: A Company (Major Ivan Scott Lewis) to the Creggan estate, B Company (Major John Desmond) to Rosemount and North Ward, C Company (Major Tony Hincks) to Fort George and the Shantallow estate, and Support Company (Major Tim Vines) to the Enclave, with the reconnaissance platoon under command for the additional task of border security.

In view of the PIRA ceasefire supposedly still in place, the Army was instructed to adopt a low profile and the incident rate was initially exceptionally low. Only twelve worth recording occurred in the battalion area between 10 July and 30 August and seven of these were bomb hoaxes. A Company patrols in the Creggan were regularly stoned and, as a variation, a gang in the Rosemount stoned a gang stoning B Company. On the third anniversary of Operation Motorman, 31 July, a crowd of around a hundred stoned the battalion base in the Creggan, which housed battalion headquarters and A and B Companies. The stoning began at exactly 0400 hours – H Hour for Motorman – and continued for only a few minutes. This was reported as the 'Siege of Creggan' by BBC news four hours later, no doubt in response to a PIRA press statement. Other light relief was provided when Private Cornelius Cross, while checking a car at a Support Company vehicle checkpoint, remarked to one of the girls inside, 'I like your skinny-rib jersey.' 'Would you like it,' came the prompt reply?' And it was quickly revealed that the 'no-bra' look was catching on well in Londonderry.

Following a spate of PIRA bomb attacks during the first half of September, the Secretary of State for Northern Ireland, Mr Merlyn Rees, spoke of the events as 'a mockery and travesty of any ceasefire, to which the security forces would respond vigorously'. An upsurge in terrorist activity began over the weekend 20–22 September and there were ten shooting incidents in the battalion's area between 22 and 27 September. A sniper fired a single shot from a silenced Armalite carbine at a patrol from 2 Platoon of A Company in the Creggan on 26 September, hitting Private David Wray in the chest. He was taken at once to Altnagelvin hospital but, in spite of emergency surgery, he died on 10 October. Private Wray's funeral at the Church of Our Lady of Good Counsel, Seacroft, Leeds on

15 October was attended by his platoon commander, 2nd Lieutenant Richard Watson, and five NCOs and men from his platoon and many members of the Regimental Association.

Any pretence of a ceasefire continuation was shattered by the massive explosion of a 200 lb PIRA lorry bomb outside the RUC's Castlereagh police station in Belfast on 15 October. The rate of bomb incidents and hoaxes in Londonderry had been mounting during the previous two weeks. A part-time soldier of the Ulster Defence Regiment was seriously injured when a bomb exploded beneath his car on 10 October. As a result of tip-offs, the battalion made three arrests and gathered useful intelligence in the form of PIRA documents found during searches of a house on 7 October and three houses in the Creggan on 15 October.

Four days later the sound of a shot led a patrol of C Company to an upper room of a house in the Carn Hill estate, two miles north of the city centre, where they found a young girl shot in the head but still alive. Weapons including a sub machine-gun and ammunition, most of it 5.56 mm calibre, were also found in the house. The wounded girl was taken to Altnagelvin hospital and the finds handed over to the RUC. Subsequent investigation by the RUC suggested that the house was either a training centre for the Provisionals or an arms distribution point. The girl had been accidentally wounded by one of her own group; all fled when the shot was fired, leaving her alone.

Colonel Crowfoot summarized activities during the final two weeks of the tour as surprisingly quiet. An arrest and arms find was made by A Company as a result of a snap road block in the Creggan, B Company unearthed an ancient siege cannon in Brooke Park and C Company recaptured an escapee from the Maze prison in the Shantallow. There was a suspected retaliation for the 7 October arrest of terrorist suspect John Coyle. On 4 November, a van containing a 280 lb proxy bomb was driven up to one of Support Company's vehicle checkpoints in the Enclave. The driver of the hijacked van shouted a warning, causing the terrorist in the front seat to jump out and flee. The checkpoint team forced open the back to discover a second terrorist locked inside, hastily defusing the bomb!

There were only 111 incidents during the four months of what everyone agreed was an unusually quiet Northern Ireland tour of duty. Searches and follow up operations had led to twenty-six arrests where screening had resulted in those arrested being handed over to the RUC, the score of arms and ammunition finds was impressive and the battalion's patch had at no time been other than under complete control. Lieutenant Charles Le Brun, Corporal David Austin, Lance-Corporal Brian McAnulty and Private Jock Kelly were all subsequently mentioned in despatches for their part in operations.

The future outlook for the Province remained grim, however. Four days before the battalion left on 11 November, the Northern Ireland Convention was dissolved after only six months of existence, as its members could not agree on the form of a devolved government. Army intelligence had reliable evidence that released detainees were taking up their old positions in the PIRA organization, which was regrouping for a new offensive. The only good news was the continuing feud between the Official and Provisional factions of the IRA, whose members were busy slaughtering each other. Four were killed and four more seriously injured on the day the battalion left.

Londonderry 1977

Commanded by Lieutenant-Colonel Edwin Beckett, the battalion returned to Londonderry on 16 March 1977. The situation in the Province had changed radically in the intervening sixteen months. After receiving back selected ex-detainees, the Provisionals had reorganized for a long campaign designed to bring sustained political and public pressure on the British Government. A structure of three- to five-man cells was introduced to make penetration by intelligence agents more difficult. Also appreciating that a long haul lay ahead, the security forces introduced a policy of gradually restoring police primacy. This required the Army to remain in support of the RUC but, wherever and whenever feasible, not to take the lead. At the start of this phase of the campaign, there were many 'hard' Republican areas, such as the Bogside and the Creggan, where the police were unable to enter except under close military escort. This situation would take a long time to change.

As in 1975, the battalion's operational area lay to the west of the River Foyle but, with the advent of police primacy, it was increased to include the Brandywell estate and the Bogside. A Company (Major Duncan Green) returned to the Creggan while B Company

(Major Peter Woolley) became responsible for the city centre and the area west of Strand Road. C Company (Major Kevin Robbin) had the Bogside and Support Company (Major Howard Holroyd) controlled both Brandywell and the approaches to Craigavon Bridge. Battalion Tac HQ was co-located with the RUC in Strand Road police station. As the area was was twice the size of that of 1975, it was necessary to reinforce one company's patch with troops from another when a concentration of force was required for a specific operation or follow up.

Police primacy notwithstanding, the battalion dominated the city west of the Foyle from the outset, while every effort was made to stimulate RUC self-confidence in areas were they had been reluctant to enter without escort. Unrestrained by ceasefire considerations, which had limited his predecessor's scope in 1975, Colonel Beckett determined on a policy of offensive action against the Provisionals in his area of operations. But to counterbalance the likely effect of this on the Catholic population, he had forcefully impressed on all ranks under his command the importance of maintaining a firm but friendly and, above all, considerate approach to the people of Londonderry – no matter how provoking they might be.

This attitude, revolutionary in its dual approach, began to pay off when A Company found some bomb-making equipment in the Creggan on 1 April. Five suspects were arrested, but a representative of the local community stated later how impressed onlookers had been by the smooth and efficient handling of the incident. There can be little doubt that the Provisionals found themselves wrong-footed by Beckett's strategy. Shots fired at patrols and search groups were the principal indication of their presence in the early stages, although these were fired from ranges long enough to make clear that a firefight was not being sought. This stand-off attitude may well have been a direct result of the battalion's technique of immediately backing up any patrol involved in an incident with support from the parent platoon or company.

On Saturday 16 April a mortar attack was mounted against Support Company's base at Craigavon Bridge Camp. Five home-made mortar barrels were set up in a street 150 yards to the west. One bomb exploded on hitting a tree, two fell into a nearby street, injuring three children, while a fourth exploded in its tube, causing the fifth tube to shift and fire its bomb into the Foyle. The children were whisked away to Altnagelvin hospital while the medical officer, Captain Phil Bolton, gave immediate aid to a woman who had suffered a heart attack. There were no military casualties and only superficial damage to the camp.

Arms and ammunition finds, mixed with hoax calls and the occasional bomb explosion, were routine occurrences in all company areas up to early May. Then the Pakistani contractor, who served the battalion bases where the NAAFI could not operate, played an indirect part in a future operational success. To stimulate inter-company competition, the commanding officer had offered the battalion's share of the contractor's profit in prizes for analysis leading to improved operational effectiveness. Provoked by lack of operational activity in Support Comany's sector to analyse, Major Howard Holroyd decided that his patch must be hiding the Provisionals' pivotal activity.

Observation led to attention being focused on Sloans Terrace just off the Foyle Road in the Brandywell Estate and specialist OPs came in from 8 Infantry Brigade to assist. An operation on the night of 5 May led to the arrest of the entire explosives cell of the Londonderry PIRA brigade at 12 Sloans Terrace. After the suspect house had been identified, Corporal John 'Legs' Diamond led the way in from the front while Company Sergeant-Major Peter McMennum opened the back door with a butt stroke. The PIRA 'Explosives Officer' tried to make a bolt for it but Holroyd floored him with a rugger tackle. In their haste to dispose of the evidence, the bomb-makers threw their materials into the fire! Eleven people inside the house were arrested and, when this led to a vociferous protest from the locals, a priest and a women heckler were taken inside to witness the bomb-making materials being gingerly removed from the fire. This quietened the protesting voices to a deathly hush. Of those arrested, five were subsequently convicted and sentenced to a total of forty-six years' imprisonment.

Trouble of some kind was anticipated when the United Ulster Action Council called a Province-wide strike from midnight on 2 May. This was in support of their demands for restoration of the Stormont Government and an all-out security force offensive against the Provisionals. There was little response in Londonderry, although several hundred Protestants led by Ian Paisley marched over the Craigavon Bridge from the Waterside on 4 May and then marched back again when invited by an RUC officer to do so. Saturday 28 May saw Londonderry's Civic Week start with a traditional carnival parade through the city centre. The spectacle was watched by closely packed spectators in holiday mood, with many chatting amicably to soldiers guarding the route. Ireland is nothing if not unpredictable.

Major Graham Longdon, the battalion second-in-command, had responsibility for community relations and found that one way of keeping a finger on the pulse was to leave the door to his office unlocked and unguarded until late each evening. Callers varied in reliability and sobriety and it was not unusual for a dram to be introduced if conversation flagged. Advice and intelligence was gratefully accepted and one practical tip undoubtedly avoided injury or loss of life. Longdon was also to find himself having a friendly chat with Bishop Cahal Daly after a helicopter patrol, maintaining aerial surveillance for tell-tale signs of change in the back areas, tracked a suspect into Derry Cathedral on 10 June. The priest invited to check the inside protested that no one could be found but, when the Bishop became involved, it was conceded that perhaps after all a mistake might have been made. But by then the suspect had disappeared.

Dogs played a lively part in security force activity. Local curs frequently demonstrated an aggressive attitude towards anyone in combat kit, which could be countered either by a well-placed boot or retaliatory tactics from a mongrel stray who had attached himself to Support Company. 'Mutley' became a welcome addition to foot patrols, earning an honorary single stripe for his aggressive response to canine harassment early in the tour and being advanced to honorary sergeant at the end. Each company had search dogs trained to sniff out concealed explosives and to attempt to follow any scent when a find was made. Results were patchy and, on one occasion, A Company's dog failed to indicate a batch of explosive that had already been discovered and which the company commander – Major Duncan Green – admitted that even he could smell.[1]

A reduction in the incident level in Londonderry during the final six weeks of the battalion's tour was not reflected in the Province as a whole. It was acknowledged that the relative quiet in Londonderry was largely attributable to the dual approach policy of aggressive action against the Provisionals linked to a firm but friendly attitude towards the population. In his farewell signal the Commander Land Forces Northern Ireland at the time, Major-General Dick Trant,

ABOVE Winners of the Wilkinson Sword 1973. Four of the five Belfast community relations NCOs, left to right, Sergeant Henry Holmes, Colour-Sergeant Phil Hinds, Sergeant Brian Dent, BEM and Colour-Sergeant Jim Wood, BEM being congratulated by Lieutenant-Colonel Tony Crowfoot. (The fifth NCO of the team was Sergeant Ron Bradley, MM).

BELOW, LEFT Celle 1974. Learning about 'Swingfire', left to right Private Charlie Pearce (see page 134), Lance-Corporal Paddy Conway, Corporal Keith 'Smiler' Stocks, Lance-Corporal Dave Jackson, Corporal Ralph Morton and, giving the instruction, Corporal Mally Hawes. RIGHT 1st Battalion ladies netball team, back row: Pat White, Jean Allen and Heidi Leigh; front row: Janet Kennedy, Sue Leslie, Lynn Barlow and Carol Morrison.

Londonderry 1975. ABOVE, LEFT Corporals Phil Stainthorpe and Pete Heaton on a quarry search. RIGHT Lance-Corporal 'Eggy' Stier with a B Company patrol in the Rosemount.

BELOW Vehicle patrol in the 'Enclave'. Private Jimmy Rodgers and Corporal George Hopper.

ABOVE Celle 1st Battalion shooting team 1976. Back row: Private Ken Wilson, Lance-Corporal John 'Legs' Diamond, Lieutenant Nick Allbeury, Corporal Ian 'Fritz' Worrall, Sergeant Pete Ambler. Front row: Sergeant 'Amos' Burke, Private Paul Harrison, Lance-Corporal Alan Wright, Private Paul Wood and Corporal Mally Hawes.

BELOW Crowfoot pow-wow in Alberta 1976. Left, with sun-glasses, Chief of the Blackfeet; right, indicating the way to the pass, Chief Tony 'Paleface' Crowfoot.

ABOVE Winners 1st Armoured Division novices' boxing competition, back row: Lance-Corporal Tommy Sprangle, Sergeant Robbno Robinson, Colour-Sergeant Dave Moffat, Lieutenant-Colonel Edwin Beckett, Captain John Davies, Lance-Corporal Dave Frank; front row: Private Chippy Chippendale, Private 'Boo-Boo' Alderslade, Private Terry Hudson, Private Paul Astbury, Lance-Corporal Trevor Oldfield, Privates Jimmy Hyam and Adj Adjei.

BELOW Trooping the Regimental Colour in Celle, 1978. The inspection by Lieutenant-General Sir Richard Worsley – (Lieutenant-Colonel Edwin Beckett behind), left Sergeant Roger Bruce, left guide: Colour-Sergeant Gerry Taylor.

ABOVE, LEFT AMF(L) Ski patrol in Norway 1980, front to rear: Privates Paul Dean, Karl Moorehouse, Garry Steel and Martin Woodhouse. RIGHT Rhodesia, Christmas 1979, Comrade Chris explains the location of his guerrilla friends to 2nd Lieutenant David Hill and Company Sergeant-Major Pip Hall.

BELOW The Regimental Band under Bandmaster Richard Martin Beating Retreat, Vigo, Spain, 8 May 1980.

ABOVE The 1st Battalion cross-country team 1980-1. Back row: Corporal Tony Wilson, Lieutenant Roy Hunter, Lance-Corporal Chris Smithson, Privates Andy Phillips, Norman Middlemass and Jimmy Clune, Corporal Bernie Dowson, Private Wes Westbury. front row: Lance-Corporal Wassie Wasden, Private Kevin Horton, Captain Peter Blyth, Lieutenant-Colonel Peter Woolley, CSM Dave Moffat, Sergeant Paul Margison, Private Andy Bishop, Corporal Paul Clark.

BELOW D Company command element Norway March 1981. From left Captain Karl Howard, Colour-Sergeant Tony Froggatt, Major Rory Forsyth, Sergeant Dave Frank, Lieutenant Vaughan Kent-Payne, Sergeant Martin Doyle, Lieutenant Christian Schofield

ABOVE Winners of the Geddes Cup 1981-4: Platoon, B Company, whose commander – Warrant Officer 2 Pete Ambler – is seen receiving the cup from Lieutenant-Colonel Peter Woolley.

BELOW 1st Battalion Football Team Bulford 1982-4. Back row: Corporal Alan Jones, Lance-Corporal Colin McNichol, Privates Lance Middleton, Carl Parker, 'Scouse' Halliday, Mick Murray and Dave Skelton; front row: Privates Andy Johnson, Keith Jarvis, Lance-Corporal Kevin Blagdon, RSM Terry Darley, CSM Byron Cawkwell, Corporal Paul Haynes and Drummer Paul Dean.

ABOVE 1st Battalion novices' boxing team 1982-3. Back row: Privates Phil Quantock, Monkey Monkman, Colin Sharp, Andy Crammond, Andy Calvert and 'Olly' Hollingsworth, Sergeant Robbo Robinson and Lance-Corporal Woody Woodhouse. Front row: Private Errol Tyrell, Sergeant Dave Frank, CSM Dave Moffat, Lieutenant-Colonel Peter Woolley, Colour-Sergeant Brian Atkinson, Privates Gavin Pickering and 'Ginge' Mulvey.

BELOW Molars in the snow, Norway March 1983, Left to right Colour-Sergeants Andy Adair, Kevin Hutchinson and Mick Winspear, Captain Terry Darley, Colour-Sergeants Robbo Robinson and Malcolm Polhill, Captain Ken Miles.

described the reduction in violence as a remarkable achievement and forecast that the battalion's approach would set a pattern for the future. Londonderry is well suited to the tactics that Edwin Beckett adopted on his arrival and for which he had trained his battalion. The city is divided by the Foyle with Loyalist and Republican confrontation lines few and well-defined on the west bank. Except in the run up to the annual Derry Boys' march, a siege mentality amongst the Catholic population is not such a feature as it is in Belfast, perhaps because Londonderry is so close to the border.

The Headquarters Northern Ireland decision to send the 1st Battalion to Belfast on 8 July, to reinforce various sectors for the marches on 'The Twelfth', reflected a current appreciation of the likely scale of potential trouble there and in Londonderry. It was considered safe to leave the sector west of the Foyle in the hands of a newly arrived and relatively inexperienced unit. In the event, the Belfast marches passed peacefully and the battalion returned to Celle in mid-July. No decorations were awarded to members of the battalion for this tour of duty but Lieutenant-Colonel Edwin Beckett and Colour-Sergeant Dave Moffat, commander of one of the special patrol groups, were mentioned in despatches. All ranks received the clasp 'Northern Ireland' for the General Service Medal.

Ballykinler and South Armagh 1985–7

The 'Arms Plot'[2] system delayed the return of the 1st Battalion to the Province for almost eight years after the 1977 roulement tour. On leaving Germany in August 1978, the battalion was based at Bulford as part of the NATO AMF(L), which precluded deployment to Northern Ireland or on any non-NATO emergency duty. Service with the AMF(L) was extended from the usual four years to five and followed by two years in Berlin, from where battalions could be only briefly moved for training elsewhere in Germany. Even so, a few officers and soldiers of the regiment served with other units and on the staff in Ireland during this time, as is apparent from the list of awards in Appendix 5. Prominent amongst these was Brigadier Tony Crowfoot who commanded 39th Infantry Brigade in Belfast from September 1980 to March 1982, for which he was appointed CBE.

The 1st Battalion began a two-year resident tour in Ballykinler in April 1985 as a unit of 39th Brigade. Lieutenant-Colonel Rory

Forsyth, who had served in Aden 1965–6 and in Northern Ireland during two previous tours, commanded the battalion for the first year. A Ministry of Defence decision to extend resident tours fron eighteen months to two years provided an element of much-welcomed stability. Moreover, Belisha-style, Abercorn Barracks was well-found and in a spectacular setting. The Mountains of Mourne are clearly visible to the south-west, a large sandy beach lies within easy walking distance and Inner Dundrum Bay, rich in salmon and sea trout, is close by.

Much had changed in the Province since 1977. The policy of police primacy had reached a certain level but, short of some form of political settlement, there appeared little chance of further advance. The battalion's arrival in the Province coincided with a shift of emphasis towards rural operations, with South Armagh as the key area. This region south of the line Newtownhamilton–Newry (see Map 8 on pages 102–3) had been solidly Republican for decades. It was fundamentally lawless by tradition and maintained active links across the border with the Republic. Except where the Army had bases or men on the ground, the Provisional IRA had dominated the area since 1974. Their activities were criminal as well as terrorist. They were experienced terrorists, who selected and prepared their operations with meticulous care and they had their successes. So close to the border, they were hard to catch.

Although attitudes were to change later, in mid-1985 rural operations were the first priority in the minds of Commander Land Forces, Major-General Tony Jeapes, and Brigadier Michael Rose commanding 39th Brigade. The battalion was required to form a forty-eight-man-strong close observation platoon (COP) and, by a rigorous slimming down of Headquarter Company, strengthen Support Company so that it could provide 39th Brigade with a patrol company for South Armagh. In addition, each rifle company in turn spent five weeks at a stretch there – monitoring and recording every movement of known and suspected terrorists. The Headquarters Northern Ireland appreciation was that Belfast was so closely controlled by security forces as to leave virtually no potential for any offensive against the Provisionals. But the whole battalion, other than the company in South Armagh, remained on call to reinforce roulement units under pressure in the city and during the marching seasons.

Based on the nineteenth-century mill at Bessbrook alongside the Armagh roulement battalion, it was the task of the South Armagh company to patrol the countryside of small hillside farms in the Bessbrook area and maintain a twenty-four-hour watch on the movements of known PIRA terrorists and supporters in the small towns. For the latter purpose, dug-in positions fortified against mortar attack were occupied and equipped with the latest observation and recording devices. This work called for dedicated attention but was infinitely preferable and more rewarding than dodging round the street corners of Belfast or Londonderry. Every coming and going of a suspect was noted and collated for use as evidence when required. At times, it was not without entertainment value. The South Armagh company also kept a small helicopter-borne rapid reaction force at immediate notice to move to meet an emergency situation.

The intelligence platoon operated under direction from Headquarters 39th Brigade, working out of Armagh city and collating information drawn from throughout the county. Four-man teams from the COP endured the most punishing observation routines, invariably in close proximity to the opposition, for periods of up to ten days at a time. After the end of the tour, COP operations were recognized by award of the BEM to Sergeant Donald McBurney and mentions in despatches for Corporals Kevin Burton and Kim Fowler. Captain Henry Middleton, who commanded the COP, was made an MBE for his services; he also remained in Northern Ireland for several months after the battalion had left to continue working with special units and the RUC.

Pressure was stepped up in South Armagh in 1985 by two battalion-scale operations. The first, codenamed 'Dundee', lasted for eight days across mid-June. The central purpose was to allow the Sappers to rebuild and repair the security force base at Crossmaglen. This carried with it a need to secure the ten-mile route from Newtownhamilton, along which the Sappers' equipment and materials had to be brought. This latter task allowed scope for some aggressive activity on the fringes.

The operation saw a force of 900 men under control of the commanding officer of the 1st Battalion, including companies of 1st King's Own Border, 1st Royal Regiment of Fusiliers, the Ulster Defence Regiment and two Sapper squadrons. The RUC appeared in South Armagh in strength for the first time in many years. Deployment and extraction of this considerable force was done almost entirely by helicopter. Later, the Staff College, Camberley was to use Operation Dundee as a model for rural counter-insurgency operations.

Later, in October, Operation Turner was launched with the aim of establishing strict control over border crossing points and carrying out a census of men and vehicles using them. The plan encompassed the whole of the Newry RUC sub-division and lasted for seven days. The battalion was reinforced by three additional companies and had Support (Patrol) Company and the COP released from under command 39th Brigade. Counter-insurgency operations on battalion-scale tend to be self-defeating through loss of surprise during the mounting phase. To avoid this, the battalion was divided into teams, termed 'multiples' of twelve men each and ferried into key nodal points by helicopter at dawn. While the helicopters themselves were readily apparent, the places where they put down and the subsequent deployment of the troops were not. Each multiple set up a vehicle checkpoint and maintained it round the clock. Many hundreds of vehicles and their occupants were checked. A man seen moving near a checkpoint in the early hours was fired on when he was challenged but failed to halt. A blood trail followed by a tracker dog at first light led to the border. Whatever the sum of useful intelligence gathered during operations such as this, it is seizure of the initiative from local terrorist groups that has significant impact – on both sides.

The tercentenary of the founder regiments, formed on 22 June 1685, fell during the Ballykinler tour. While the principal celebrations were in York, the 1st Battalion held a families' sports day and an all ranks' dance on the evening of 22 June. Earlier, B Company had received a tercentenary cake at Bessbrook Mill amidst wide press coverage. Even the Provisionals tried to join in, albeit a touch cynically. On 27 June, the *Republican News* reported, 'On Sunday the IRA had the honour of blowing out the candles when two birthday cards in the shape of mortar bombs arrived by airmail at Crossmaglen. They read:

Happy birthday to you; happy birthday to you.

Happy birthday, dear Charlie, happy birthday to you.

Although the 'birthday cards' were sent to the wrong place, on the wrong date and for the wrong reason, it was the thought that mattered!

Visitors to the battalion during this period were invariably struck by the strong sense of community spirit. Some anxiety for the menfolk manning the OPs or on patrol in South Armagh was inevitable, but Ballykinler was seemingly remote from the violence seen on the television screens. As in Palace Barracks during the earlier resident tour, families were drawn even more closely together than in the usual garrison station. Care for the wives and children of the men away needed no special arrangements, as they were part of the clubs, sports teams and activities which kept everyone interested and involved. The Ladies Cross-Country team and the Ballykinler Bunny Warren, for small girls too young to become Brownies, are just two examples of the host of activities designed to ensure that no one was at any time left out or forgotten.

The Colonel-in-Chief, Her Royal Highness The Duchess of Kent, made her first visit to the battalion on a bitingly cold February day in 1986. The previous evening Sergeant Jack Parnell and Privates Herman Hunter and Alan Topliss had been wounded in a Provisionals' bomb attack in Castlewellan. Immediately on her arrival, Her Royal Highness requested news of the injured and asked to meet their wives. A brief demonstration of battalion capabilities by men drawn from all companies, under command of Major Nigel Waistell, was followed by informal meetings with soldiers and families. It was an emotional day, with the Colonel-in-Chief listening with quiet attention to all that the men, wives and children had to tell her about their lives in the Province. Claire Highfield, the five-year-old daughter of Lance-Corporal David and Sybil Highfield, presented her with a homemade bouquet on behalf of all the children. A few days later Colonel Forsyth sent an account of the visit to the author ending with the words, 'HRH looked beautiful and I think everyone fell in love with her.'

At Aldershot on the day of the visit of the Colonel-in-Chief the battalion cross-country team, led by Captain Dave Moffat, won the Army Championship for the third year in succession.

Command of the 1st Battalion changed on 24 March 1986, when Lieutenant-Colonel Duncan Green succeeded Lieutenant-Colonel Rory Forsyth. It was an easy transition between men who had enjoyed a friendship and a similar humour over twenty years.

Around this time Protestant opposition to the Anglo-Irish Agreement began to make demands on the security forces. This was especially so during the marching season, but the extra tasks brought an end to a much more tedious one of guarding RUC stations against an intensified PIRA threat against the RUC. Emergency reinforcement units were brought in from England for this purpose.

Expectation of serious trouble in Portadown during the lead up to the anniversary of the Battle of the Boyne required the battalion's redeployment there from 5 to 12 July. Portadown is a mainly Protestant town situated in predominantly Republican Armagh. The place has a special significance for the Unionist cause, as the Orange Order was first established there towards the end of the eighteenth century. The initial local march, which by long-standing tradition passes through a Republican district, took place on Sunday 6 July. Although the RUC Divisional Commander was shouted down by the crowd and had his skull fractured in a melee, order was otherwise maintained. For the principal march on 12 July, 2nd Grenadier Guards and 1st Prince of Wales's Own were both deployed in the Republican area to support the RUC in preventing a Protestant invasion. Again order was generally kept, largely through strict control by the stewards organizing the march.

The close of the year was marked by a series of incidents involving PIRA attacks and exchanges of fire. A sapper protection group from Support Company under command of Sergeant Ken McFadden came under mortar fire from across the border in the early evening of 28 October. The baseplate position was indicated by tracer from a GPMG mounted in the sustained fire role, allowing the riflemen to engage with their SLRs. Sergeant McFadden's group thus won the fire-fight decisively and no casualties were sustained. Elements of the COP, intelligence platoon and the signal platoon based in the Middletown RUC station were rudely awakened early on 28 November by a mortar attack on the station. Three bombs fell inside the compound and serious damage was done. Miraculously no one was injured.

The tour of duty in Ballykinler ended in May 1987. There had been two more mortar attacks early in the new year, Lord Justice Gibson and his wife were murdered in a Provisionals' ambush south of Armagh city on 25 April and the other Republican terrorist group, the Irish National Liberation Army (INLA), conducted a useful internal feud, which left quite a few of their number dead. Reflecting on the two years of the tour, credit could be claimed for siting and building the hilltop observation posts, which had significantly limited terrorist freedom of movement, successful support for the RUC in Portadown and domination of the countryside and border crossing points in South Armagh, mainly by a varied and aggressive patrol programme. The battle against the Provisionals had not been won but their activities had been closely contained in the battalion's area of operational responsibility.

Several members of the battalion had been wounded during the two-year period, some seriously, but no fatal casualties were sustained. As is often the case when a battalion keeps a tight grip on its operational area, very little media attention was attracted. The battalion's performance and that of individuals were properly recognized, however. Lieutenant-Colonels Rory Forsyth and Duncan Green were both mentioned in despatches, as were Company Sergeant-Major Phil Stainthorpe, Sergeants Jack Parnell and Kim Fowler and Corporals Kevin Burton and Terry Hudson. In addition to the MBE for Captain Henry Middleton and the BEM for Sergeant Donald McBurney for their services with the close observation platoon, Major Michael Watson was appointed MBE for his resolute and forward leadership of Support (Patrol) Company under command of Headquarters 39th Brigade.

Belfast 1991–2

The second resident tour in Northern Ireland was followed by a gap of four years before the 1st Battalion returned to the Province – on this occasion to Belfast for a six-month roulement tour from November 1991 to May 1992. At this time based in Osnabrück in Germany, as part of 12th Brigade in 1st Armoured Division, the battalion had to retrain for the security role. The final test for this took the form of the Geddes Cup competition in October 1991.

The task of a Belfast roulement battalion lived up to its reputation of being both tough and exacting. Now commanded by Lieutenant-Colonel Alastair Duncan, who had led a platoon in Belfast in 1973 and commanded C Company in Ballykinler 1985–7, the battalion faced an upsurge in PIRA activity. This was primarily targeted on Belfast and the main security force concern was to prevent the bombs from getting into the city centre, which had received a major face-lift since the 1970s.

To make best use of available manpower, B Company was placed in suspended animation for six months and its platoons sent to reinforce A and Support Companies. The area of operational responsibility was the Catholic part of west Belfast. Battalion Tac HQ and Support Company (Major Pat Tracy) were based at the Catholic-Protestant interface of North Howard Street mill, A Company (Major Duncan Barley) in Girdwood Park, C Company (Major Simon Caley) in Fort Whiterock and the Echelon (Captain and Quartermaster Brian Crummack for the first half of the tour and Captain Byron Cawkwell for the second) in Musgrave Park. Reinforcement companies from the 1st Queen's Lancashire Regiment and 1st Argyll and Sutherland Highlanders were essential for the battalion to give requisite support to the RUC. At one stage the battalion group was 1,200 men strong.

During the closing weeks of 1991 A Company was involved in a series of shooting incidents while supporting the RUC D Division. Corporal 'Scouse' Davies-Rockliffe was wounded by a blast from a 12-bore shotgun and was lucky not to be more seriously hurt. Number 1 Platoon of A Company commanded by 2nd Lieutenant Richard Lockwood was shaken by a blast bomb after investigating a hoax warning on New Year's Eve. Although several members of the platoon suffered shock, no one was injured.

The start of 1992 saw weapons and ammunition finds that were a just reward for thorough training in search techniques and not a few intuitive guesses as to where to look. A team from C Company led by Lieutenant Boris Cowen uncovered bomb-making equipment beneath a gravestone in Milltown cemetery and another, led by Corporal Tim Binns, discovered a GPMG in the loft of a house in Andersonstown. A third team, working under the seemingly inspired direction of Corporal Kevin Blagdon found an RPG-7 rocket launcher and two automatic rifles.

In apparent retaliation, PIRA blast bomb attacks and shots at patrols and search teams intensified. The 'Mark 15' coffee jar bomb was a weapon favoured by the Provisionals during this period, but fortunately none was thrown close enough to cause injury. Fire was returned by Private Chris Aspel of C Company on New Year's Eve, when his patrol encountered a small group of PIRA gunmen. He fired three shots and a Special Branch source later confirmed that a wounded terrorist had tried to find refuge in the Turf Lodge Estate.

The searches continued relentlessly and more successes were recorded. In all, the battalion found forty-two weapons and several thousand rounds of ammunition during the six-month period, as well as bomb-making equipment and explosives.

A new operational experience arose in the form of manning the OPs on the top of the multi-storey blocks of Divis flats and the Broadway tower. The former, in particular, had been used by the Provisionals in the past to monitor security force patrols and permanent occupation of the building denied them this advantage, while allowing the battalion excellent twenty-four-hour surveillance over much of Falls Road area and that surrounding the Royal Victoria Hospital. Colour-Sergeant Frank Menzies and Corporal Andy Williamson were the landlords of the Divis flats OP, while Sergeant Chris Doyle and Corporal Kevin Horton manned Broadway. Other than for occasional relief to ensure continued mental stability, these NCOs lived in flatlets below the OPs for the entire tour, reinforced by lodgers who came to help out with the observation duties for a week at a time. OP Broadway was engaged by two or three bursts of automatic fire from the corner of Iveagh Crescent just before midnight on 23 October. No target was visible, so fire was not returned.

Private Paul Shirt was wounded by a command wire bomb while on patrol in the Falls Road soon after 2100 hours one evening. His account of the incident will strike a chord in a few memories. 'The world went white, then black and I came to in the middle of the road. Shaken but not stirred. [Gordon] Thornton was shouting at me but I could not hear him. I tried to stand up but fell back. My foot was bleeding badly and beginning to hurt. I was bundled into the back of the QRF[3] and within seconds I was being given a cup of tea by the CO and the RSM was being nice to me – I could get used to this.' A suspect was arrested while trying to leave a house in the Falls Road shortly after the explosion. Private Shirt returned to duty after making a full recovery.

Colonel Alastair Duncan summed up the tour in laconic style with the words, 'We trained, we deployed and we all returned.' Although several men of the battalion were wounded as a result of terrorist action during the tour, once again intensive training and a resolutely professional attitude to operations had avoided any fatal casualty. The battalion had undoubted success, especially in terms of terrorist arrests and finds of weapons and ammunition. In the subsequent list of operational awards, the commanding officer was made an OBE and Major Pat Tracy an MBE. Major Duncan Barley, Corporal Kevin Blagdon and Lance-Corporal Phil Wignall were all mentioned in despatches.

The regiment had continued to provide officers and soldiers to serve on the staff or with specialist units in Northern Ireland both during and between the battalion tours described in this chapter. Majors Ken Peacock and Graham Binns were both appointed MBE for services as chief of staff (brigade major) of 39th Infantry Brigade in Belfast in 1986 and 1991 respectively. Captain Kevin Robbin received the same award for service as staff captain (Intelligence) Headquarters 8th Brigade in Londonderry in 1974. Major Tony Bostock was made an MBE in recognition of his service with the Northern Ireland Intelligence and Security Group in 1987. Captain Tony Blanch was mentioned in despatches for service with Headquarters 8th Brigade in 1982 and Company Sergeant-Major George Jaszynski received the BEM for his intelligence work with Headquarters Northern Ireland. Many others also served as individuals on hazardous duty in the Province without receiving any special recognition.

In addition to Staff-Sergeant Arthur Place, killed by an IRA bomb in 1973, and Private David Wray, shot by a sniper in 1975, Major Christopher Dockerty[4] of the regiment was killed in the Chinook helicopter which crashed on the Mull of Kintyre while taking Intelligence staff members, of which he was one, from Belfast to Inverness for a conference on 2 June 1994. These were the only fatal casualties sustained by the regiment in the Province, over a period of twenty-five years.

Those who served in Northern Ireland during the troubles that began in 1969 will almost certainly look back at the curious combination of courage, humour and obduracy that typifies the people of the Province. As this chapter comes to its close, a ceasefire is again in place in Northern Ireland and, in spite of many uncertainties and difficulties to be overcome, there is at least a prospect of lasting peace. There is a story that as God was making the world, the angels protested when they saw the forming of Ireland. 'How can the people here be favoured in this way – with such a beautiful country, such gentle hills and crystal streams?' they asked. 'Ah,' replied the Maker, 'wait until you see their neighbours.'

8
In Yorkshire

'Wheers'as ta bin sin' ah saw thee?'
From 'ILKLA MOOR'

A serving soldier visiting the county during the early 1970s might well have asked, 'Where has everyone gone?' The days of the Regimental District with a headquarters, depot and a couple of Territorial battalions parading the name of the regiment in the main towns were no more. Only a small headquarters remained, tucked away in what had once been the depot commanding officer's quarter in Imphal Barracks, York and an outstation in a Georgian house in Beverley. Each establishment had a museum containing medals, pictures and other treasures of the two former regiments and exuded a comfortable and gentlemanly aroma of pipesmoke and the past. As with other regiments, recruit training was centralized at Strensall, while the former Territorial Army battalions had been absorbed into one large regiment – The Yorkshire Volunteers.

This period was the low point of representation of The Prince of Wales's Own in the county from which it draws virtually all its recruits. With characteristic resistance to change, the civilian population seemed unable to comprehend the regiment's provenance. 'We know the Green Howards, of course, they're at Catterick [they weren't but that scarcely helped] and the Duke of Wellington's at that place where the cakes come from!' What a mess the contractions and expansions had left behind.

The two regimental associations were almost exclusively concerned with their own affairs, in spite of their expressions of intent at the time of amalgamation to form one association. The West Yorkshire Association had extended its title and mandate to allow men leaving The Prince of Wales's Own to join, but only a few were doing so. The old hands claimed 'Young 'uns today just aren't interested.' They were but, first, attitudes had to change.

Early developments in Territorial Army reorganization were positive. Reductions in the number of regular units, made in consequence of the 1956-7 Defence Review, left little doubt that the TA could only expect similar treatment. Sensibly, the War Office allowed the regular amalgamations to get well under way before applying the technique elsewhere. For the main part, the first phase of TA reorganization was well thought out. On 15 February 1961, 3rd Battalion the Prince of Wales's Own was formed from the 5th West and 4th East Yorkshires. The unit headquarters was established in Hull, where the volunteer spirit had been consistently strong for decades, balancing the consolidation of the two former Leeds Rifles battalions based on Leeds. 7th (Leeds Rifles) Battalion The West Yorkshire Regiment and 466 Light Anti-Aircraft Regiment Royal Artillery, formerly 8th Leeds Rifles, also amalgamated on 15 February 1961 to become The Leeds Rifles, The Prince of Wales's Own Regiment of Yorkshire.

These arrangements worked well. The two new battalions enjoyed a clear-cut identity and were strongly supported by their TA Associations and local communities. The regular battalion of the regiment continued to supply adjutants, quartermasters, permanent staff instructors and, when required, the occasional commanding officer. The 3rd Battalion, under command of Lieutenant-Colonel Paddy Bryan, gave a demonstration of an air-landing force with support weapons, in collaboration with RAF Dishforth, before their inauguration parade on 15 July 1961. The battalion team represented 49th Infantry Division in the individual TA Boxing Championships in London, where Private Dickie Barker became the lightweight champion for 1961 and Private Dickie Young the light-welterweight runner up.

The Leeds Rifles, under command of Lieutenant-Colonel Ewart Clay, exercised against the 12th/13th Parachute Regiment in May and concentrated for a rifle meeting in June. The two battalions were organized identically with companies based on drill halls in areas with, in the main, good reputations for recruiting. The Leeds Rifles had A Company (Major Gerry Jarratt) in Morley, B Company (Major Brian Davenport) based in Carlton (Old) Barracks, Leeds, C Company (Major Maurice England) at Castleford and both D Company (Major John Harrap) and Headquarter Company (Major Alfie Wood) co-located with Battalion headquarters in Carlton (Old)

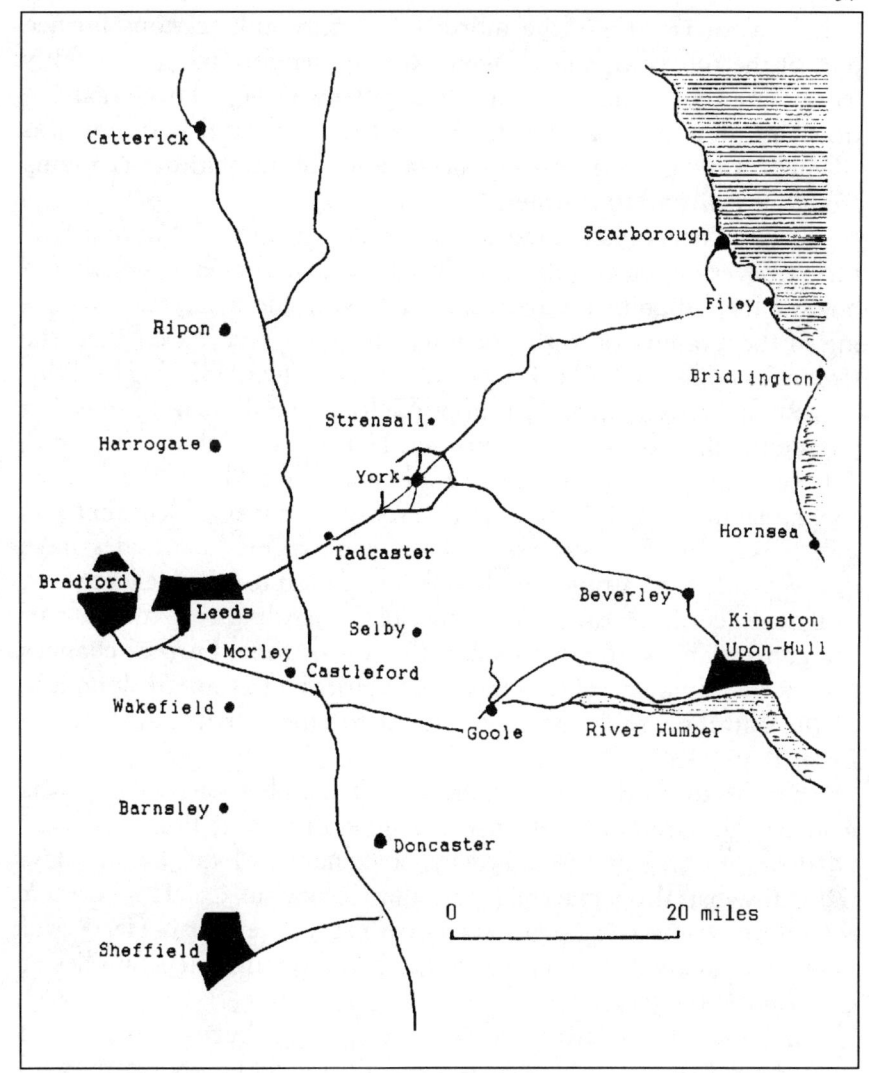

Map 12 *Yorkshire*

Barracks, Leeds. The 3rd Battalion was similarly dispersed, with A Company (Major George Cooke) in Hull, B Company (Major Douglas Beal) in Beverley, C Company (Major Charles Rennie) in York and D Company (Major Teddy Denison) in Tadcaster. Headquarter Company (Major Johnny Bull) was co-located with battalion headquarters in Londesborough Barracks, Hull. As in regular battalions at this time, the mortars and anti-tank sections formed part of the rifle companies, each of which therefore had a capability to operate as a semi-independent company group. This organization had an additional advantage for the Territorial battalions, as riflemen could graduate to support weapon duties without changing from one drill hall to another.

The 3rd Battalion's inauguration parade was held in Victoria Barracks, Beverley on 15 July. Five hundred invited guests including a host of local dignitaries attended. Following the inspection, trooping of the Colours of both previous battalions and march past, the Colonel-in-Chief of The Prince of Wales's Own, HRH The Princess Royal, addressed the battalion. Before complimenting those on parade for their bearing and turnout, Her Royal Highness declared, 'The amalgamation of the Territorial battalions is the final act in the reorganization which began three years ago. I am confident that you will make the same success of it as your regular comrades have done.' While the battalion had doubtless got off to an excellent start, sadly the words of the Colonel-in-Chief regarding the 'final act of reorganization' were not to stand the test of time. Further changes lay not too far ahead but, as if to keep spirits high, Captain John Rae of the battalion took the Silver Jewel for the Territorial Army at Bisley that year.

A parade to mark the inauguration of the new Leeds Rifles was held on the battalion's return from annual camp at Proteous, near Ollerton, on 22 July 1961. Led by Lieutenant-Colonel Ewart Clay, the entire battalion marched past the Colonel-in-Chief, who took the salute on the steps of Leeds Town Hall. Afterwards Her Royal Highness attended a tea party for the battalion and their families at Carlton (Old) Barracks.

Command of the 3rd Battalion changed in August 1962 when Lieutenant-Colonel Peter Steel succeeded Colonel Paddy Bryan, who was appointed OBE in the Queen's Birthday Honours list in recognition of his outstanding period of six years in command. Peter Steel was a regular officer who had fought with 2nd West Yorkshires in the Eritrean and Burma campaigns and recently served with 1st Battalion The Prince of Wales's Own in Aden and Gibraltar.

The operational roles of the two Territorial battalions in the event of general war were, as a first priority, the reinforcement of the British Army of the Rhine (BAOR) either as formed units or by provision of individual reinforcements. These roles were welcome, as they ensured that organization and equipment would be the same as or close to those of regular infantry battalions – and training visits to Germany would be undertaken from time to time. Senior officers had to adopt a flexible view, however. The GOC of 49th Division (TA), Major-General Peter Glover, wrote to all his unit commanders with commendable candour explaining, 'It is impossible exactly to predict the role of the Territorial Army in war; it might well be called on for Home Defence or for World-Wide operations, conventional or non-conventional in nature.' After that, no one could claim that training was restricted in scope.

Training was seriously addressed. The personal weapons range course was completed before each annual camp, which could then be chiefly devoted to an exacting programme of tactical training and exercises. In 1962 both battalions held their annual camp on Dartmoor where, whatever the weather, a truly rugged experience was inevitable. Prior to camp, the Leeds Rifles had participated in a NATO exercise on Fylingdales Moor with elements of the Special Air Service Regiment (SAS) acting as the escape and evading enemy. Subsequently the exercise was carried out with the riflemen in the escape and evasion role in snow which drifted to a depth of ten feet.

Annual camp that year marked the final stage in a four-year training cycle with the concentration of all the units of 146th Infantry Brigade TA under command of Brigadier John Deedes. Tactical training and exercises at battalion level led up to a brigade exercise incorporating an approach march across Dartmoor to the north coast of Devon. There each battalion was embarked in amphibious landing vehicles to cross Bideford Bay and make an assault landing further north for the establishment of a bridgehead for a major landing. Few regular battalions had the advantage of such facilities at that time.

Towards the close of the 1962 annual camp, a competition for the Foljambe Trophy – presented many years earlier by Captain the Honourable Bertie Foljambe – was conducted for the first time since 1937. The trophy, a handsome silver horse, is for a flat race over six furlongs. The six starters were given the off by Major-General T. H. Birbeck – the new GOC 49th Division – after Brigadier Deedes had decided the handicaps. The trophy was won by Major Teddy Denison riding his Freebooter's Ghost, with Major Billy Robinson, the 3rd Battalion's regular Training Major, second and Lieutenant Dan Rodwell a very close third.

A new category of Territorial engagement was introduced in 1962 termed the Army Volunteer Reserve II (AVR II) or 'Ever-Readies'. The ending of National Service on 31 March 1962 had left the standing army dependent on men willing to enlist for a minimum of three years with the Colours and, as insufficient numbers were coming forward, many units were falling below their establishment strength. Territorials entering into the new AVR II commitment were liable to be called up to fill the ranks of regular battalions in an emergency, which might be one short of general war. Both Territorial battalions filled their allocation of Ever-Ready volunteers without difficulty. In addition to attending annual camp, each volunteer was required to complete a fixed minimum number of training days each year to qualify for an extra bounty payment of £150.

Shooting, sport and a wide variety of competitions featured in the annual programme, exactly as in the regular battalion. The 3rd Battalion won the Queen's Challenge Cup for the best sporting record for the seasons 1962, 1963 and again in 1968. This cup was competed for annually by all TA units in Great Britain and Northern Ireland, the winner being the unit which scored the most competition points for athletics, boxing, cricket, cross-country running, rugby, soccer and swimming. A battalion team went to Bisley each year and Sergeants 'Nobby' Clarke and Steve Holtby both reached the Army (first) Fifty in 1962. That October, the 3rd Battalion shooting team won the Northern Command Infantry Challenge Cup. Next to shooting, boxing was probably their principal sporting preoccupation.

The Leeds Rifles were equally competitive but in a less gladiatorial fashion. As to be expected in a rifle battalion, priority was accorded to shooting and the annual inter-company competition was the individual training highlight of the year. Records show that the competition was invariably won by Gerry Jarratt's well over a hundred-strong A Company at Morley.

Each battalion had its own Band and Corps of Drums. These played the traditional part in unit activities and also provided musical accompaniment for civic events such as Remembrance Day parades, fêtes and race meetings. There was both rivalry and co-operation between the two bands, with one helping out the other when an essential musician could not perform when required. The 3rd Battalion won the Lincolnshire and East Riding TA Association Band Competition in 1962 and 1963. The Leeds Rifles won the band competition organized by the West Riding Territorial and Auxiliary Forces Association three times in the four years 1960–4.

The Colours of the 5th West and 4th East Yorkshires, having been carried by 3rd Battalion The Prince of Wales's Own since 1961, were replaced by new Colours on 27 June 1964. The parade was held in Queen Elizabeth Barracks, Strensall, the Yorkshire Brigade Depot and the presentation was made by the Colonel-in-Chief, Her Royal Highness The Princess Royal. There were more than a thousand invited guests, including the Lord Lieutenants of the North, East and West Ridings, together with the Lord Mayors or Mayors of the cities and towns of which the regiment held the Freedom.

It was a fine June day with a breeze to lift the Colours when they were allowed to fly during the Royal salutes and march past; it also helped to keep everyone cool during one and a half hours of complex drill. After the old Colours had been marched off parade for the last time, the new ones were consecrated by the Chaplain-General, the Venerable Archdeacon Ivan Neill. Then the parade was addressed by the Colonel-in-Chief. Her Royal Highness referred back to the inauguration parade of three years before saying, 'You have shown yourselves a worthy part of my Prince of Wales's Own Regiment of Yorkshire and I compliment you on the standard of your parade.' The Colours were then marched into the battalion to begin what was intended to be twenty-five years of service.

At the time of the presentation of new Colours, four pairs of side drums were presented to the battalion, one pair each by the Cities and Counties of York and Kingston-upon-Hull and by the Boroughs of Beverley and Harrogate, all of which had previously conferred their Freedoms on the regiment. In addition to regimental emblazoning, each drum bore the coat of arms and inscription plate of the City or Borough which presented it.

Being a rifle battalion, the Leeds Rifles carried no Colours which, as someone irreverently pointed out, saved quite a lot of bother. They nonetheless maintained close touch with the Colonel-in-Chief. Her Royal Highness dined with the officers at Carlton (Old) Barracks on 8 January 1965, when Lieutenant-Colonel Derek Rawlings presided with the Honorary Colonel – Brigadier Kenneth Hargreaves

– in attendance. The battalion also provided the Guard of Honour for the visit of Her Majesty The Queen to the City of Leeds on 22 October the same year. It was a typical West Riding autumn day, with grey cloud reaching to every horizon. There was one shaft of sunlight during Her Majesty's inspection of the Guard – commanded by Major Gerry Jarratt – which appeared to fall on her alone, as may be seen from the photograph facing page 112.

Throughout this period excellent work was done by the Yorkshire Brigade Depot at Strensall, just north of York. It had become clear from the ending of National Service, with a much-reduced recruit intake for an all-regular Army, that the old single-regiment training depots were no longer viable. The training and sports facilities of Queen Elizabeth Barracks at Strensall, modern accommodation and the close by availability of small-arms ranges all contributed to the depot's success. There were individuals, not of the depot staff, who argued for training companies or wings each dedicated to one of the regiments for which the depot provided reinforcements. This concept was rejected as wasteful of instructors and resources.

When it was appreciated that junior soldiers aged sixteen or seventeen represented the best source of future senior NCOs and warrant officers for the Army, the depot rose well to the challenge. Yorkshire and more distant Scotland and Wales were used for adventurous training exercises, character-building for recruits and junior soldiers alike. Particular care was taken in the selection of NCO instructors, to ensure that discipline was tempered with humour and understanding for youths and boys living away from home for the first time. A posting to the depot training staff was not always welcomed, particularly by the more ambitious NCOs. Opportunities for promotion were better in a battalion and there was the risk of being passed over while at the depot.

Care was also taken to maintain an even balance of representatives of the four Yorkshire regiments in the depot permanent staff. This avoided suspicion arising that the more promising recruits were being syphoned away into one regiment that might otherwise have become predominant. The depot was a lieutenant-colonel's command with an administrative structure comparable to that of a regular battalion. This allowed the depot to give support for such events as the presentation of new Colours to the 3rd Battalion, described earlier. Facilities for regimental associations, and for their annual dinners in particular, were generously provided by the depot, although these could not be used by associations with branches remote from York.

The one-armed Lieutenant-Colonel Malcolm Cubiss of the regiment commanded the depot at Strensall for a while. On the day before the initial visit of a new GOC, the General's ADC telephoned expecting to speak to the adjutant. He had gone out, however, and left his telephone switched through to the CO's office. 'How is your CO known to his friends?' inquired the ADC, believing he was addressing the adjutant. 'Piggy,' replied Cubiss, quick as a knife, and put down the telephone.

Next morning, exuding bonhomie, the General leaped from his car with the cheerful greeting, 'Good morning, Piggy.' Cubiss allowed his undamaged left arm to fall from the salute, leaving the stump of the right one grimly extending a drooping, half-empty sleeve, so that he appeared not unlike a partly-dismasted frigate after receiving a broadside. 'Piggy!' he gasped, 'My name is Malcolm, always has been – unabbreviated.' The General remained at a marked disadvantage throughout the visit and the ADC was shortly found alternative employment.

Regimental Sergeant-Major Pat Savidge of the 3rd Battalion distinguished himself on 21 June 1966 whilst supervising the throwing of grenades at Willsworthy range in Devon. He was later to receive a commendation for gallantry from the General Officer Commanding-in-Chief Northern Command for pushing to safety a young soldier who had dropped a grenade in the throwing bay. The citation read 'Had it not been for this Warrant Officer's presence of mind, swift action and disregard for his own safety there could have been a serious accident.' RSM Savidge was a regular soldier and the son of Regimental Sergeant-Major Harry Savidge, late of the West Yorkshire Regiment.

A Government-inspired review of the Territorial Army and Emergency Reserve structure during 1966 resulted in a major upheaval for both TA battalions of the regiment. The Territorial Army in its then current form came to an end on 31 March 1967 by amalgamation with the Army Emergency Reserve to form the Territorial and Army Volunteer Reserve (TAVR).

The underlying theory behind the change was to make best use of the substantial numbers of AVR II volunteers – the 'Ever-Readies' –

by forming them into complete units. Their primary role would be reinforcement of the Army of the Rhine on mobilization for general war in Europe, at that time expected to be of a very short duration. Levels of training and operational readiness were to be enhanced by working more frequently with regular units, either as company groups or during annual camps held in Germany on a rotational basis. Weapons, uniform and equipment were to be virtually the same as for the regular Army. The increased equipment and training costs were to be met, however, by a drastic reduction in the number of units.

It was an attractive proposition from a political standpoint, as it allowed the Government to profess a greater readiness to deal with the threat posed by the Warsaw Pact while actually reducing defence expenditure. Defence of the United Kingdom in General War was accorded the lowest priority, as the appreciation at the time was that the conflict would be fought out on the Continent.

A gesture was made towards the maintenance of links between the new TAVR II units and regular regiments by subtitling TAVR companies after them. In Yorkshire the new infantry structure at first comprised a single battalion – The Yorkshire Volunteers – based on York, with A Company (The Prince of Wales's Own) commanded by Major Bill Sheppard, also in York and similarly linked companies in Middlesbrough (The Green Howards), Halifax (The Duke of Wellington's) and Sheffield (The Hallamshires). Headquarter company was based in York and comprised TAVR II volunteers from all the former TA battalions. Under a curiously ill-judged policy, regular permanent staff serving with the Yorkshire Volunteers were obliged to cease wearing their own regimental insignia and adopt those of the Volunteers, a practice which became intensely unpopular with the pemanent staff, not least because it made them appear to be Territorial rather than regular soldiers.

On concentration of the Ever-Ready volunteers in the new TAVR II battalion, the 3rd Prince of Wales's Own and the Leeds Rifles were graded TAVR III with responsibility for 'defence of the United Kingdom against actual or apprehended attack when national danger is imminent or a great emergency has arisen. For service in the United Kingdom only.' Each battalion was granted an establishment of only 341 all ranks, on which a recruiting ceiling of eighty percent was imposed. The allocation of training days for which an officer or soldier could be paid was reduced to four per year.[1] One positive aspect of this entire upheaval was the encouraging number of officers and men who volunteered to become TAVR II to serve under the new and more demanding obligation. Around seventy percent of both battalions so volunteered and were accepted.

Titles were also changed. The 3rd Battalion became The Prince of Wales's Own Yorkshire Territorials in Hull with a detachment in York, while the Leeds Rifles became the Leeds Rifles Territorials based in Leeds with a detachment at Castleford. As so many TA soldiers had volunteered for TAVR II service, The Prince of Wales's Own Territorials were reduced to a strength of 118 all ranks but were permitted to retain use of Londesborough Barracks in Hull, with which they had a long historical connection. The Leeds Rifles Territorials were reduced to a strength of 104 all ranks and a Band of thirty-three. They were obliged to leave what had been their home since 1887, Carlton (Old) Barracks, to share Harewood Barracks, Leeds with various sub-units of the Royal Corps of Signals.

These very significant organizational changes followed two exceptionally successful periods for both the 3rd Battalion and the Leeds Rifles, when they were commanded by Lieutenant-Colonel Teddy Denison and Lieutenant-Colonel Gerry Jarratt respectively. It says a great deal for the wisdom and determination of those who served on with the TAVR III battalions, with their reduced establishment and status, that the units survived. Gerry Jarratt continued in command of the Leeds Rifles Territorials until the completion of his full term on 31 March 1969, while Lieutenant-Colonel Tom Farrell took over command of The Prince of Wales's Own Yorkshire Territorials.

They and a handful of remaining officers, warrant officers and NCOs did their damnedest to keep the volunteer spirit alive in spite of loosely defined operational tasks, drastically reduced equipment tables and precious little other resources or training incentive. Their energies and enthusiasm were taken up trying to rebuild their unit strengths against a background of threatened disbandment. While this period was inspirational for the much-reduced TAVR III units, with recruits applying to join in spite of pay for only four days of the year, representation of The Prince of Wales's Own in Yorkshire was eroded almost to the extent set out at the beginning of this chapter. But not quite; there was worse to come.

Looking at events in retrospect, one is driven to the conclusion that Ministry of Defence policy immediately following the TA reorganization of 1967 must have been so to starve the residual TAVR III units, up and down the country, of resources that they would eventually elect to disband. Authority for the four paid training days per year was cancelled from 1 April 1968 and all regular army instructors and civilian support staff were withdrawn by the end of June. Annual camps that year had to be held on the basis of 'no cost to public funds'. Those who attended camp received no pay or allowances and the costs of food, transport and virtually all else had to be met either by the men themselves or from battalion private funds. Even so, the Leeds Rifles had a strength of 137 in camp at Rolston, near Hornsea, in July. Later that same month, thirty-five past and present members of the Leeds Rifles made a pilgrimage to the British military cemetery at Montagne de Bligny near Reims to honour those of 8th Battalion The West Yorkshire Regiment (Leeds Rifles) who had stormed the Montagne under a hail of fire fifty years earlier, on 28 July 1918. The action led to a citation signed by the Commanding General of the French 5th Army, referring to 'This Battalion *d'élite*' and the award of the Croix de Guerre to the battalion for gallantry. In 1968 the Prince of Wales's Own Yorkshire Territorials won the Queen's Challenge Cup, for the Territorial Army unit with the most outstanding record, for a third time. They were also asked to stage the Regular Army versus the TAVR boxing competition at Londesborough Barracks in November.

Notwithstanding these triumphs current and from the past, The Prince of Wales's Own Yorkshire Territorials and the Leeds Rifles Territorials were ordered to disband, in common with all other TAVR III battalions, on 31 December 1968. Each was permitted to form a cadre of eight men to provide administrative assistance to TAVR II battalions in peace, act as their rear parties on mobilization and to provide a framework for any sudden requirement for expansion. The Prince of Wales's Own Cadre formed at Londesborough Barracks, Hull under command of Major Bill Sheppard and the Leeds Rifles Cadre at Carlton New Barracks, Leeds under command of Major Harry Bury.

The Leeds Rifles were told that their title was not to be carried forward, in this third reorganization, to any sub-unit of the TAVR II. A campaign against this decision was orchestrated by Colonel Gerry Jarratt, aided by Colonel Ewart Clay, by then Editor of the

Yorkshire Evening Post. The Secretary of State for Defence, Dennis Healey, found himself hard-pressed as the Member for Leeds East. Well-turned-out riflemen presented themselves at his Saturday afternoon surgeries over a four-week period. Company Sergeant-Major Alan Gaines was received on the first Saturday, two corporals on the next, then two lance-corporals and finally two riflemen. Shrewdly Jarratt kept his commissioned officers in the wings, from where they organized 'Operation Grand Slam' to gather signatures to a petition of public support. Planning paid. E (Leeds Rifles) Company The Yorkshire Volunteers was formed in Leeds, under command of Major Brian Brook, comprising riflemen who had volunteered for the TAVR II 'Ever-Ready' commitment.

There were other compensations in a seemingly endless downward spiral of change. The cadres were allowed to resume their former titles of 3rd Battalion, The Prince of Wales's Own Regiment of Yorkshire and The Leeds Rifles and retain their Honorary Colonels: Colonel The Right Honourable The Earl of Halifax, DL and Colonel John Taylor. There was no sense of despair. The 3rd Battalion cadre took on recruiting for The Prince of Wales's Own company of the Yorkshire Volunteers, based in Hull and York, while the Leeds Rifles cadre gave the newly formed E (Leeds Rifles) Company training and administrative support. The cadres were invited to keep their eyes on enough likely candidates to form battalions in their respective areas. Once again, spirits rose. Recognizing that he could not win The Queen's Challenge Cup with a team of eight, Major Bill Sheppard led the Reserve Army 'A Team' to victory in the Inter-Allied Show Jumping Competition at Fontainebleau in March 1970.

Change of Government in 1970 brought with it a new concern about home defence. The Warsaw Pact invasion of Czechoslovakia in 1968 had intensified Cold War tensions, while intelligence revealed the development of Soviet *Spetznaz* special forces, allegedly responsible for sabotage and assassination.[2] Whitehall suddenly got the breeze up when a Ministry of Defence appreciation proved that, once all TAVR II battalions had been mobilized and sent to the Continent, no one would be left to meet the new threat. 'We must expand the TA,' growled Prime Minister Edward Heath, who had commanded a TA Gunner regiment. So the nadir point passed and re-expansion began.

The military appreciation suggested a requirement for three extra Territorial battalions in the North-East Defence Region. Arguments that the need could be met by each of the remaining regular Yorkshire regiments reforming a TA battalion met objections from those concerned for other regiments, still with a foothold in the county, and the powerful Gunner lobby. The end result was the formation of two more battalions of Yorkshire Volunteers, of which B and C Companies of the 2nd Battalion were raised respectively by the two regimental cadres and E Company by a cadre of the King's Own Yorkshire Light Infantry. Two companies of the new 3rd Yorkshire Volunteers were formed from TA Gunner batteries in Bradford and Rotherham.

On the face of it, and in common with the other regular Yorkshire regiments, The Prince of Wales's Own had gained only the raising of its two cadres to company status, but appointment of one individual in the new structure was to prove significant. Major Bill Sheppard was selected to command the new 2nd Battalion The Yorkshire Volunteers. This former regular officer had won the Military Cross in Korea as a 2nd lieutenant and had been adjutant of the 1st Prince of Wales's Own in Aden in 1958, before leaving the Army to become a businessman. He served with the 3rd Battalion from 1962 and then commanded A Company 1st Yorkshire Volunteers 1967–8 and the 3rd Battalion cadre throughout its existence. Sheppard was to have a remarkable Territorial Army career, eventually becoming a brigadier and the TA Adviser to the Commander-in-Chief United Kingdom Land Forces. As the first CO of 2nd Yorkshire Volunteers, he set about establishing close links with The Prince of Wales's Own. Those links never had official status but that cost them nothing in their effectiveness.

The Territorial Army structure in Yorkshire remained largely unchanged for more than twenty years, providing a much-needed period of stability. The Prince of Wales's Own and Leeds Rifles companies formed part of the 1st and 2nd Yorkshire Volunteers.

Lieutenant-Colonel Harry Ford was the first regular officer of the regiment to command the 1st Yorkshire Volunteers in 1972–4 and Lieutenant-Colonel Michael Wilson, late the 3rd Battalion, commanded the 2nd Volunteers 1978–80. In turn with other regiments of the King's Division, in which Lancastrian, Yorkshire and Irish regiments were grouped from 1969, The Prince of Wales's

Own provided training majors, adjutants, quartermasters, regimental sergeant-majors, permanent staff instructors and the occasional commanding officer for the Volunteers and for other Territorial battalions of the King's Division.

An unexpected development during the early 1980s precipitated significant changes at Regimental Headquarters and brought the two Regimental Museums together. A need for further economy in defence spending resulted in the return of the 2nd Division from Germany and establishment of its headquarters in Imphal Barracks, York. From the moment that Headquarters 2nd Division announced that the Regimental Headquarters building would be needed for expansion of their officers' mess, an inevitable progression towards a single RHQ and museum began. Negotiations were conducted in a gentlemanly manner. The Regimental Secretary – Major Bob Tomlinson – was invited by District Headquarters to choose a new RHQ building from a range of Army property due to be vacated or sold. He knew York like the back of his hand and, after viewing several prospective sites, recommended No. 3 Tower Street.

This Georgian town house facing the historic Clifford's Tower close to the City centre, with a TA drill hall large enough to accommodate both Regimental Museums to the rear, had undeniable advantages. There were also serious objections. The building exceeded the regiment's entitlement of space for a museum and headquarters, it would be needed by a company of the Yorkshire Volunteers until a new custom-built drill hall could be funded and provided and the cost of buying it from the TAVR Association, to whom it belonged, and converting it to its proposed new use would be £250,000. Undeterred by difficulties, the Regimental Secretary made inquiries and discovered that the 4th/7th Royal Dragoon Guards and 13th/18th Royal Hussars were both prepared to move their respective Home Headquarters into the building and the former were keen to share the drill hall as a museum. Thus the excess space objection was overcome.

The question of the Volunteers' drill hall and conversion costs still looked like formidable problems until the Ministry of Defence's Assistant Under-Secretary for quartering matters had occasion to call on the chief of staff at Headquarters UKLF, who was Colonel of the Regiment at the time. 'Ah, but you have considerable assets on your side of the balance sheet,' said the AUS taking a crumpled envelope from his pocket when the subject was broached during lunch. 'The present York RHQ is worth £180,000 and sale of the lease on the Beverley outstation £95,000 – so there is your quarter of a million. All that is necessary is for you to move 2nd Yorkshire Volunteers' new drill hall up the UKLF list of building priorities.' 'And what about the £25,000 left over?' queried the chief of staff, who had been watching the back of the envelope. 'Ten percent conveyancing charge,' chortled the AUS, shoving it back into his pocket.

What was agreed over tenants and costs in a few months took some years to bring to a conclusion. Regimental Headquarters opened at No. 3 Tower Street on 15 February 1985 but deep heart-searching attended the closure of the outstation at Beverley. The regimental presence in the East Riding's county town reached back to 1782 and it was still the Mecca for the pilgrims of the East Yorkshire Regimental Association, many of whom had begun their service as recruits at Victoria Barracks. It fell to Brigadier Bill Sheppard, the Association's chairman, to bring about a gradual change of heart and alignment with the headquarters of The Prince of Wales's Own in York.

Meanwhile the Beverley outstation had to be closed. This unenviable task fell to another remarkable personality, Major 'Spud' Taylor. He had been Regimental Sergeant-Major to Boris Garside in the 1st Battalion in 1958–61 and would eventually succeed him as chairman of the combined Regimental Association. No one who knew him in 1958 would have thought of 'Spud' as a man of sentiment, but the care and tact with which he closed the outstation at No. 11 Butcher Row will be long remembered.

The drawing together of the two Regimental Associations was accomplished with surprising ease and lack of rancour, once a clear lead was given. There were two long-standing objections to amalgamation. The first was that the rules of the Charity Commissioners precluded the pooling of their respective funds. While this was correct, there was nothing to prevent the funds of the Associations being administered separately, within a combined Association. The second objection was more difficult to solve. It concerned the location of future annual reunions for the East Yorkshire Old Comrades, which had been held at Beverley since the Association was founded in 1912.

Speeches were made at branch dinners. Diehards were quietly lobbied, not least by Mrs Ellen Tomlinson – the wife of the

Regimental Secretary – whose influence in the West Yorkshire Association was remarkable, thanks to her many years' service to its interests. Quite suddenly, the tide began to turn. The year 1980 saw adoption of new titles: The Prince of Wales's Own and West Yorkshire Regimental Association and The East Yorkshire and Prince of Wales's Own Regimental Association. At the suggestion of George Hardaker of Leeds branch, the 1st Battalion hosted both associations at Bulford over the weekend 18–20 June 1980 when, despite long-held beliefs to the contrary, startling similarities of outlook were revealed. Before handing over as chairman of the East Yorkshire and Prince of Wales's Own Association in 1982, Colonel Andy Edgar had given his branches in Beverley, Hull, London and Newcastle a clear indication that the future lay in a combined body. Bill Sheppard took up this lead with enthusiasm, so he and Boris Garside were able to draw the final strands together in The Prince of Wales's Own and West Yorkshire Association. Their annual general meeting on 2 October 1982 proposed that the two associations should amalgamate to form The Prince of Wales's Own (West and East Yorkshire) Regimental Association.

On the other side of the county, only Hull branch was opposed to a similar motion. Whereupon their President, Mr Harry Burnett, who supported an amalgamation, resigned and joined the ranks of Beverley Branch. Some urgent discussion behind closed doors ensued and then, on the twenty-fifth anniversary of amalgamation of the two old regiments, one Association came into being on 25 April 1983. It comprised branches from Beverley, Bradford, Hull, Leeds, London, Newcastle, Sheffield and York, with Selby coming up fast on the outside rail to form a new branch. The Chairman was Boris Garside and Bill Sheppard Vice-Chairman. Harrogate formed a branch and was welcomed into the Regimental Association on 2 April 1984.

Work on the Regimental Museum building was completed in time for it to be taken over by Brigadier Malcolm Cubiss, the new Regimental Secretary and curator, on 21 May 1985. Creation of the combined museum was exclusively his work. He methodically selected items for display, sought expert advice on presentation and grouped the treasures and trophies with meticulous regard for their period and significance. The museum was formally opened by the Colonel-in-Chief, Her Royal Highness The Duchess of Kent, on 17 May 1987.

Her Royal Highness had made her first visit to the regiment since her appointment as Colonel-in-Chief on 7 May 1985 to mark the Tercentenary. Several events were arranged in York, of which the laying up of the old Colours of the 1st Battalion in the Minster was the centrepiece. The service was preceded by a formal luncheon in the Mansion House attended by Her Royal Highness, the Lords Lieutenant of North, West and South Yorkshire and of Humberside and their wives, the Lord Mayors and the Lady Mayoresses of the Freedom Cities and the Mayors and Mayoressess of the Freedom Boroughs.

A guard from the 1st Battalion, commanded by Major Nicholas Allbeury, escorted the old Colours through York, exercising the Freedom right of marching with bayonets fixed and Colours flying. The old Colours were received by the Dean of York, the Right Reverend John Southgate, and laid on the altar for the service, which was attended by a congregation of 1,900 people, including 450 members of the Regimental Association and many relatives of those serving in Northern Ireland with the 1st Battalion. Afterwards Her Royal Highness inspected the 1st Battalion guard and old comrades of the Association and took tea with them together with a large number of regimental families in St William's College and the York Assembly Rooms.

A remarkable thing happened in early May 1987. 1st Battalion The Prince of Wales's Own was posted to Yorkshire from Northern Ireland for a two-year tour in Catterick as part of 24th Air-Mobile Brigade commanded by Brigadier Peter Woolley. Not only had the battalion never previously served in the county, neither of the founder regiments had been stationed there, except in transit, since 2nd West Yorkshires were in Catterick, and then only briefly, in 1938. An account of the 1st Battalion's adventures in the airmobile role is included in chapter 6. Those aside, the years 1987–90 were of value in placing The Prince of Wales's Own on the map in Yorkshire.[3]

An even more remarkable event occurred on 25 April 1993. At Catterick, in pouring rain, the Yorkshire Volunteers disbanded and the three battalions were assigned to the three regular Yorkshire regiments. After twenty-five years of service, the Volunteers greeted this change, part of the Territorial Army reorganization under the 1990–2 'Options for Change' defence review, with decidedly mixed feelings. Their reputation as a strong and effective TA regiment was second to none but one of the requirements arising from 'Options for Change' was to strengthen the affiliation of regular and part-time volunteer units. Consequently the Army Board decided that the three battalions of the Yorkshire Volunteers would disband and reform as TA battalions of the three regular Yorkshire county regiments.

3rd Battalion The Prince of Wales's Own was thus restored to the Territorial Army order of battle and, in 1994, became one of only eight TA battalions to be part of the new NATO Allied Rapid Reaction Force (ARRC),[4] organized on a basis of three rifle companies, a reconnaissance platoon and a support group of anti-tank, machine-gun and mortar platoons. Lieutenant-Colonel Tony Blanch, who had been commanding the 2nd Yorkshire Volunteers, had assumed command on 25 April of the previous year and established battalion headquarters at Worsley Barracks, York. A Company (Major Fred Frewster) was also based at York, in Lumley Barracks, with a platoon at Goole. B Company (Major David Potter) was located in Mona House, Hull and C (Leeds Rifles) Company (Major Richard Booker) in Harewood Barracks, Leeds with a platoon at Castleford. The battalion Support Group set up its headquarters in York, co-located with the anti-tank platoon but with the mortar and reconnaissance platoons in Beverley, the machine-gun platoon at Castleford and the assault pioneer platoon in Hull.

Immediately following formation, the 3rd Battalion launched into a characteristic burst of activity, winning the march and shoot phase of Exercise Martial Merlin, 15th (North-East) Brigade's inter-unit skills competition, and gaining first and second places in the night navigation phase in May. A and B Companies camped at Folkstone to host an exchange group of US National Guardsmen, while C Company flew to Indiana to train with the National Guard's 1/152 Regiment.

A further review of the Territorial Army was announced by Malcolm Rifkind, the Secretary of State for Defence, in July 1994 and an intense period of behind-the-scenes consultation began. The number of infantry battalions was to be reduced and four converted into 'fire support' battalions, with responsibility for providing heavy weapons support for former 'national defence' battalions, with no support weapons of their own, which were being re-roled to the ARRC. This role was not without its attractive side, as virtually every man would become a support weapon or other form of specialist.

Unfortunately the fire support battalion establishment turned out to be well below that for an ARRC-roled battalion of 540 all ranks. When it was decided that the 3rd Battalion would convert to the fire support role, their authorized establishment shrank to only 377. Aside from a loss of men that this would entail, some of the drill halls would have to go – with inevitable penalties for the regiment's local connections. As the new establishment called for only two heavy weapons companies, each with integral signals, transport and administrative sub-units, the commanding officer – Lieutenant-Colonel Christopher Wood – faced some difficult decisions in implementing the new organization while conserving main bases in York, Leeds and Hull.

After a detailed appreciation, he decided that A and C Companies would combine to form A (Leeds Rifles) Fire Support Company based on York, but with its mortar platoon in Harewood Barracks, Leeds and its machine-gun platoon in Castleford. B Fire Support Company was formed from the rifle company in Hull and the mortar platoon at Beverley, which would have a detachment in Goole. Both companies were to be equipped with nine 81 mm mortars, six Milan anti-tank launchers and nine 7.62mm GPMGs (tripod-mounted) in the sustained-fire role. At the time of writing, the future of the smaller outstations at Castleford and Goole is still open to question, as the countrywide review of TA centres has yet to complete its work.

The years between 1968, when the 3rd Battalion and the Leeds Rifles were both reduced to cadre status, and the reorganization of the Territorial Army in 1993–4, reflected a steady rise in the fortunes of The Prince of Wales's Own in Yorkshire. Regimental Headquarters acquired a site in the historic centre of York with a much-visited museum; and the main base of the 3rd Battalion again displayed the regimental signboard title on the Fulford Road, as well as in Hull, Leeds, Beverley, Castleford and Goole. A strong and united Regimental Association, having forged close links with the 1st and 3rd Battalions, is having publishing a newsletter to keep in touch with its members who, should they so choose, could parade in their thousands.

9
On Detachment

'You have been selected from a host of applicants
to go on detachment to....'

'Sidi Barrani' – or to wherever the fashionable trouble spot happens to be – announces the man on the seat of authority. As often as not, the call for volunteers has been subdued or not publicized at all. This is not in trepidation that few would be forthcoming but in case the number wishing to set themselves up in positions remote from the seat of authority turns out to be embarrassingly large. The chances are that announcement of his selection will be the first that the lucky man has heard of the requirement and, not improbably, of the place to which he is to be detached.

The first recorded detachment from the recently formed 1st Battalion was from Aden to Karachi, in January 1959. Captain James Yeo took a party comprising Colour-Sergeant Mac McManus, Sergeant 'Chick' Doran Thorp, Corporals Pete Barley and Geoff Duke and fourteen soldiers to carry out security duties for the British delegation attending a meeting of the now-defunct Baghdad Pact. The group flew by Canadair in uniform but each man was provided with an outfit *de rigueur* for Karachi: white shirts, grey flannel trousers and shoes.

This turned out to be one of the hardship detachments. The party was accommodated in the North-Western Hotel. No one was allowed to make his own tea or clean his shoes or bedroom, as 'bearers' were on hand to do these jobs round the clock. Tax free English beer was provided by the British High Commission, together with Chevrolet staff cars to take those of the party not on duty sightseeing or for a swim. The security duties were demanding but not exhausting and shoulders were rubbed with the politically world-famous.

Selection of the commander of any detachment is crucial to the success of the mission and James Yeo was the man to whom any commanding officer would naturally turn. Brought up in Switzerland, he spoke English, French and German with equal fluency, he was an all-round sportsman and an exceptional leader. He had won the Military Cross as a subaltern in Korea where he was also mentioned in despatches, as he was again in Malaya; but it was his outstanding ability to make friends and inspire confidence in those around him that made him a natural choice as a detachment commander. When he was killed in a motor accident while an instructor at the School of Infantry in 1962, a group of warrant officers of the regiment initiated the presentation of a silver rose bowl as the prize for the annual rifle match named in his memory.

With few exceptions, life on detachment lives up to the best of expectations and most people are willing to go, if only in pursuit of the principle that the next place must be better than the present one. Detachments may be for individuals, for small groups or for complete companies or more. Until the larger grouping of military musicians was introduced in 1994,[1] the best of the detachment market was cornered by the Regimental Band and Corps of Drums.

Strictly speaking, a Regimental Band was a unit of its own, as bandmasters were wont to point out when commanding officers raised eyebrows as yet another attractive and lucrative detachment required them to be without military music. The Band did not go to Aden in 1958 but moved to Gibraltar in April of the following year ready to greet the 1st Battalion 'rejoining from detachment', as Bandmaster Ray Pinkney whimsically remarked, very nearly forfeiting his long service and good conduct medal in consequence. Scarcely had the reunion been accomplished when the Band left for Casablanca to play at the British Trade Fair before boarding HMS *Ulysses* when she took the Flag Officer Gibraltar to meet the Spanish Captain-General at Cadiz.

Thus began a career of spectacular detachments that saw the Regimental Band travelling worldwide during the thirty-six years of its existence. Frequently accompanied by the Corps of Drums, an intregal part of the battalion with an operational role as battalion headquarters defence platoon, the Band was in almost constant demand to carry the flag for the United Kingdom or British industry abroad. Both Band and Drums were three times detached to Abyssinia, or Ethiopia as the country became more generally known after the Second World War. While on detachment with the Somaliland Scouts in the late 1950s, Captain Dick Glazebrook[2] of the regiment had had a hand in mapping the Somali-Ethiopian frontier region, but that was not the reason for the visit of the Band and Drums.

Oddly embarked in HMS *Eskimo*, flying the flag of Flag Officer Middle East, Bandmaster 'Dixi' Richards, Drum-Major Alan Ashby and their musicians sailed up the Red Sea from Aden to Massawa in sweltering heat in January 1966. The purpose was to perform during the passing out parade of the Ethiopian Imperial Navy Training College, at which the salute was taken jointly by His Imperial Majesty Haile Selassie and King Olav V of Norway. 'Few have the privilege of parading before two monarchs simultaneously,' Ashby remarked on return – which cost him a glass or two. Pleased with their enjoyable expedition, the musicians were taken aback to be sent again on detachment, immediately on their return to Aden, to the barren and stony island of Perim off the heel of Arabia to guard the Diplomatic Wireless Station there. Reward was at hand, however. They had so impressed the British Ambassador to Addis Ababa during the Massawa visit that he requested them to play at his reception to mark Her Majesty The Queen's Birthday in April of the same year.

The third detachment to Ethiopia, from Cyprus in 1972, was to take part in the same event as the first but, apart from His Imperial Majesty Haile Selassie who again took the salute, many of the key personalities had changed. Bandmaster Trevor Platts was wielding the baton and Drum-Major Nigel Elliott, transferred from the Coldstream Guards on payment of an undisclosed fee, the mace. This detachment allowed more to be seen of the country. The party flew from Cyprus to Asmara, which is almost 8,000 feet above sea level and the next station down the railway from Keren, where 2nd West Yorkshires fought the Italians in 1941. The seventy-mile drive down the mountainside to Massawa on the coast was a delight for all concerned. After the parade, the Drum-Major was presented with a gold medallion by the Emperor himself, in appreciation of the Band and Drums' performance. (See the photograph between pages 112 and 113.)

Detachments of the Band and Drums from Cyprus to Israel in 1970 and in 1971 were Anglo-Israeli good relations visits sponsored and arranged by the British Embassy in Tel Aviv. These were exhausting affairs, involving two and sometimes three performances each day, usually for the benefit of audiences of several thousand. Detachments aboard the liner *Canberra* in 1980 and 1981, when the Band entertained passengers during Mediterranean cruises, were not surprisingly enjoyed by the musicians and passengers alike. When a third such cruise, planned for 1982, had to be cancelled because *Canberra* was needed as a troopship for the Falklands campaign, the Band adopted a staunchly anti-Argentinian stance. But tours by both the Band and Drums in the United States for performances in Washington and Oregon in 1988 helped to heal the wounds. These highly prestigious cruise and American engagements were organized by Bandmasters Richard Martin and Steven Thompson, assisted by Band Sergeant-Majors Eddie Hinchcliffe, Mervin Warrington and John Cocker respectively. The Band and Drums were frequently the envy of those who had to soldier on in less attractive surroundings. Musical tours abroad demanded great stamina and dedication, however, and the musicians carried the flag for the regiment as well for Britain, wherever they went.

Training detachments are always welcome, as they provide opportunities to meet new friends and to develop a sense of independence in circumstances where individuals can learn by mistakes which are seldom likely to have serious consequences. Remarkable in this category were the detachments of companies from the 1st Battalion under command of 1st Lancashire Fusiliers, in 1962 and 1963, for exercises to test the combat readiness of units of the Danish Army in defence of their homeland, described in chapter 3. These established a regimental link with Denmark, which was renewed when the 1st Battalion exercised there as part of the NATO ACE Mobile Force between 1978 and 1983.

The detachment of a company group under Major Dick Glazebrook to Andalsnes at the head of the Romsdal fjord on Norway's west coast, in the late summer of 1968, was a barter arrangement with the Norwegian Tourist Board. In exchange for clearing the remains of a hotel destroyed by an avalanche and dynamiting parts of the rockfall, the party spent four weeks climbing the surrounding peaks under instruction from the Romsdal Corps of Mountain Guides, or boating on the fjord. Towards the end of the expedition a two-sided counter-insurgency exercise was run, for which the rugged contryside was ideal. Every man who went to

Norway was a volunteer and, although the clearance work was tough going, there were no complaints. The Norwegian Army and local population proved most generous hosts, confirming the nature of Nordic hospitality first gained from the Danes.

Operational detachments were more serious stuff but no less welcome to those chosen. During the first Aden tour of 1958–9 every company was detached at some point but remained under command and had the full support of the battalion structure. The same situation applied again in Aden, in 1965–6, when A Company was detached to Mukeiras throughout the tour, initially under command of Captain Tony Nevile and later under Major Peter Wade. C Company commanded by the author was detached first to the Radfan area, under command of 1st Welsh Guards, and later to Dhala under command of an FRA battalion. While the Welsh Guardsmen were friendly and helpful to a man, at Dhala it was felt necessary to have a 'hostage' of some kind from the FRA within the company perimeter whenever an officer was required to visit the FRA headquarters. Relations were uncertain and grenades had been thrown into the tents of British NCOs attached to local units elsewhere.

One extraordinarily interesting individual detachment, first to the Foreign and Commonwealth Office[3] and then to the Malaysian Border Scouts, was undertaken by Captain Bill Battey during 1965–6. This was the period of Indonesia's 'confrontation' with Malaysia as to which country had rightful claim to the territories of Sabah and Sarawak, previously under British control. Battey had an exciting time in the contested frontier region, for which he was subsequently mentioned in despatches.

Detachment of senior NCOs as weapon-training instructors to the Sultan's Armed Forces during the Marxist insurrection in Oman proved a mixed blessing. All signals or weapon specialists, the men were already filling important roles in the 1st Battalion, then in Cyprus during the 1970–2 garrison tour. Detachments were each for several months and the NCOs were left largely to their own devices with full responsibility for training Omani recruits of unpredictable motivation. These were not detachments of the more popular variety, although all but one of the NCOs selected excelled while virtually alone.

In what subsequently became known as 'Black September' 1970, King Hussein of Jordan decided that his army would restore his authority in those areas of the country where the PLO was busy usurping it. The fighting was intense and casualties severe. The 1st Battalion was asked to send six volunteers with a warrant officer in charge to help with burying the dead and supporting the injured in a half-completed Jordanian hospital near Amman. Sergeant-Major Lance Miles had made first aid his lifelong hobby and was on the point of ending his service. Together with Corporal 'Amos' Burke and five men, he left for Amman in an RAF Hercules on 4 October. This was a grim detachment, codenamed Operation Shoveller. The party returned after a month having witnessed more than enough death, maiming and suffering. It was to the particular credit of Privates Sam Clutterbuck and Bob 'Primus' Lawrence that they managed to get to Petra, covering the final leg on horseback, during a brief break in dealing with the dead and injured. Every man received a gold medal inscribed 'With the grateful thanks of the Hashemite Kingdom of Jordan' in appreciation of his work.

While a basis to bring Rhodesia back from the brink of civil war was being hammered out in Lancaster House in the autumn of 1979, the Ministry of Defence was struggling to put together a force to monitor any agreement reached. So delicate was this mission expected to be that the extraordinary decision was taken to set up teams using the commanding officer and several company commanders from almost every battalion of the United Kingdom Strategic Reserve. The 1st Battalion was not so called on, however, as their NATO ACE Mobile Force role kept them at the disposal of SACEUR. Instead, the battalion sent a party of one officer and eight NCOs to man a collecting point for guerrillas of the Patriotic Front wishing to surrender.

2nd Lieutenant David Hill, Company Sergeant-Major Pip Hall with Corporals Rob Agar, Ken Ainsworth, Paul Bennett, Graham Theaker and Lance-Corporals Paul Handley, Steve Rhodes and 'Paddy' Williams arrived at the ruined Muchinjikki Methodist School, in the Mrewa district, immediately before Christmas. The school had been abandoned after a guerrilla attack some eighteen months previously but, after a bit of self-help and collection of furniture from other buildings, Collecting Point 'Delta One' was ready to receive guests. The group donned the white armbands of the monitoring force and took the group's liaison officer with the Patriotic Front – 'Comrade Chris' – off into the bush in search of his friends.

On Christmas Day Graham Theaker astonished the rest of the team by producing a fully iced cake. When pressed, he conceded to having 'found it' in the battalion cookhouse at Bulford on the day the party left. It had been an individual entry for the 'Best-decorated cake' competition due to be judged by Holly Filor, the commanding officer's wife, that very afternoon. It was a good cake and the group decided that, given the opportunity, it might have won first prize.

The subsequent main event became the most publicized of the entire monitoring operation. Sitting side by side at their six-foot table in the sun in the early evening of 29 December, David Hill and Pip Hall suddenly realized that the bush around them was alive with men. 'Put your rifle down on the table, sir,' said Hall, 'then go out and welcome them in.' Hill did exactly that, holding up his empty hands and calling 'Welcome, welcome.' Armed to the teeth with AK 47s and the like, the guerrillas came out of the bush in their hundreds, at first incredulous that the small group of white soldiers was there to guide them to safety. The tension was broken by David Hill suggesting a cup of tea! He subsequently received the Queen's Commendation for brave conduct for his action. The whole party returned to England after three busy weeks in Rhodesia, shortly to become Zimbabwe.

After giving up command of the 1st Battalion to become an instructor at the Staff College in 1983, Lieutenant-Colonel Peter Woolley was suddenly selected to command the British component of the Multi-National Force in Lebanon. Before the British element had been added, this force had successfully overseen a Saudi-Syrian plan for evacuation of some 10,000 members of the PLO bottled up in west Beirut by the Israelis. When the Lebanese President-elect, Bashir Gemayel, was killed in a bomb blast, Britain agreed to provide a small contingent of 120 officers and men as part of the force. The aim was political: to have a seat at the table at any peace conference on Lebanon and, meanwhile, to put about goodwill by armoured car patrols and protection of a ceasefire committee representing the various factions.

The situation deteriorated rapidly after a renewed outbreak of fighting in April 1983 and, in October, 241 American and 58 French soldiers of the force were killed in separate bomb attacks by extremist Muslim groups. Desertion of many Muslim soldiers from the Lebanese Army – as fighting intensified – made clear that the

Multi-National Force had little if any further job to do. The Chief of the General Staff, General Sir John Stanier, personally selected Colonel Woolley to take command of the British contingent and evacuate it as soon a political formula could be agreed with the other contributing nations.

A decision to withdraw to the Royal Fleet Auxiliary *Reliant* was taken at 0200 hours on 8 February 1984 and the contingent left by road for the port of Junieh, north-east of Beirut, at 0830 hours, travelling through an area which had seen heavy fighting during the night of 7 February. The plan to evacuate the scout cars and other vehicles by ferry had to be abandoned due to the sea conditions. Instead, the complete withdrawal was accomplished by Sea King helicopter direct to the vehicle ferry and RFA *Reliant* by last light, except for two vehicles too heavy to lift which were left on the quayside. There were no casualties in spite of indiscriminate shelling of Junieh by unidentified artillery during much of the day. Colonel Woolley was subsequently mentioned in despatches in recognition of his gallant and distinguished services in the Lebanon.

The Iraqi invasion of Kuwait, in the early hours of 2 August 1990, led to the largest-scale and potentially most hazardous detachment that The Prince of Wales's Own had been called on to provide up to that date. Iraq's claim to sovereignty over Kuwait was implausibly based on a British statement of 1863, which included Kuwait amongst 'territories nominally recognizing the suzerainty of the Turkish (Ottoman) government but in practice independent under their own chiefs'. A subsequent Anglo-Turkish Convention of 1913, designed to grant formal independence to Kuwait, was never ratified and division of the Ottoman Empire by the Paris Peace Conference of 1919 brought Iraq into existence under a British mandate. Iraq's frontiers drawn up by Britain during the Cairo Conference of 1921 have been disputed by successive Iraqi governments, as has reliance on the unratified Anglo-Turkish Convention of 1913 as the authority for Kuwait's independence and frontiers.

Discovery of rich oil deposits in Kuwait in 1938 guaranteed the small state's prosperity but attracted envious attention. Kuwait gave significant financial support to Iraq during the Iran-Iraq War of 1979–87 but this did not prevent President Saddam Hussein from seeking a dispute with his small neighbour. The Rumailah oilfield lies below the common frontier and both countries have access to its products. Saddam accused the Kuwaitis of stealing part of Iraq's share of the Rumailah oil and demanded a cash refund in recompense, otherwise he would 'do something effective'. Shuttle diplomacy by King Fahd of Saudi Arabia, King Hussein of Jordan and President Mubarak of Egypt failed to persuade Saddam to take a conciliatory stance.

The invasion was launched in defiance of world opinion and international law. Saddam proclaimed Kuwait an Iraqi province and established a puppet regime to administer it in a brutally ruthless fashion. The annexation of Kuwait was condemned by the United Nations Security Council, at a meeting which began before dawn in New York on 2 August, when Resolution 660 was passed demanding the immediate withdrawal of Iraqi forces. Two further Resolutions were passed on 6 August. Resolution 661 called for mandatory international sanctions against Iraq and Resolution 662 declared Iraq's annexation of Kuwait null and void. Other resolutions followed but without any perceptible impact. On 29 November the Security Council authorized member states 'to use all necessary means' to uphold and implement Resolution 660 and set a deadline of 15 January 1991 for Iraq to comply with all the United Nations resolutions dealing with the dispute.

Meanwhile the American-led Coalition Force was being built up in Saudi Arabia and the Arabian Gulf to contain any Iraqi move south from Kuwait towards the Saudi oilfields at Dhahran, and later – given a UN mandate – to liberate Kuwait. British naval and air force units were assigned to the force from 9 August, but a decision to commit 7th Armoured Brigade, the 'Desert Rats' formation of Second World War Western Desert fame, was not taken until 14 September. 4th Armoured Brigade was added in December and the two were formed into 1st (British) Armoured Division for the Coalition operation to free Kuwait.[4]

Those serving in the British Army of the Rhine when the Gulf crisis began knew that a decision to use British ground forces would bring 1st British Corps to a standstill. Financial restrictions on armoured vehicle spares, in particular, meant that units not selected for the Gulf would have to give up many of their vehicles to equip fully those that were. 1st Prince of Wales's Own had moved from Catterick to Osnabrück in August 1990 to begin what was expected to be a six-year tour of duty in the armoured infantry role in 12th Armoured Brigade.

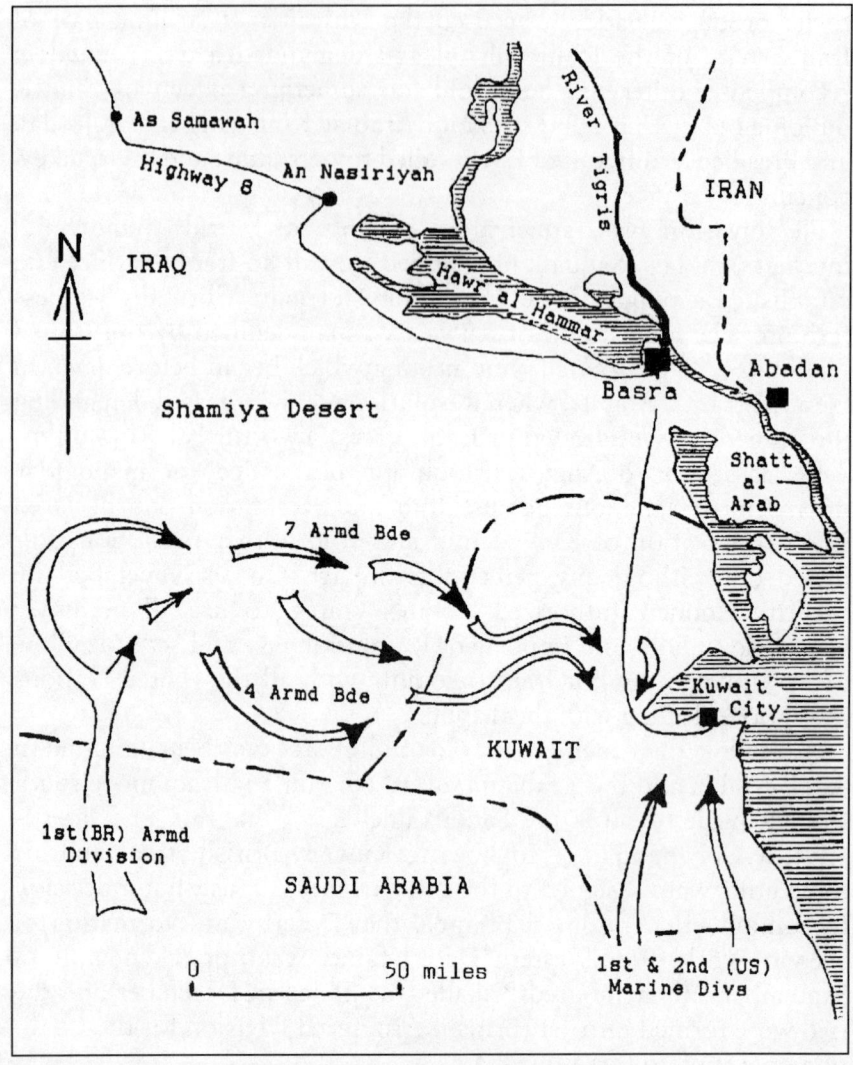

Map 13 *The Liberation of Kuwait 1991*

On the day after the announcement that 7th Armoured Brigade was to go to the Gulf, the battalion received instructions to send four officers, a warrant officer and thirty-six junior ranks to reinforce 1st Staffordshires, who were already preparing to move. And so the great detachment began. The commanding officer, Lieutenant-Colonel John King, was promoted to colonel and despatched to join

Headquarters 1st Armoured Division as Chief of External Affairs with responsibility for relations with war correspondents representing the news media. Eventually 149 officers and men of the battalion joined units in the Gulf for the ground battle. A number of vehicles of the battalion's fleet also went to war, although not with those who usually drove or travelled in them.

The largest detachment from the 1st Battalion during the Gulf War served with 1st Staffordshires, an armoured infantry battalion of 7th Armoured Brigade equipped with the new Warrior armoured fighting vehicles. The Coalition forces' plan for the ground battle is shown on Map 13. On the extreme right, 1st and 2nd (US) Marine Divisions were tasked to break through the Iraqi minefields and fight their way due north towards Kuwait City. On the extreme left, XVIII (US) Corps with units of the French Army under command were to make a wide sweep through the desert to cut Highway 8, which offered the swiftest means of Iraqi reinforcement, or retreat. At the same time, the helicopter-borne 101st (US) Airborne Division was to establish a forward base eighty miles inside Iraq, while the Coalition naval forces shelled the coast, as if in preparation for an amphibious landing which the Iraqis had been led to expect.

The second phase, which was advanced by fifteen hours due to the rapid advances achieved in the first, was for VII (US) Corps including 1st (British) Armoured Division to breach the frontier minefields and drive north before turning sharply to the east towards Kuwait City. At the last moment, Commander 1st Division changed the plan to lead with 4th Armoured Brigade, as it was stronger in infantry, and unleashed 7th Brigade with its two armoured regiments and 1st Staffordshires.

Private Andrew Kelly with A Company of the Staffordshires gave the following account:

> For us, the battle started late at night – an enemy position with a few scattered vehicles. The dark sky lit up with machine-gun fire and tracer bouncing everywhere in front of our position. When we were on our third attack, we dismounted right [from the Warrior] and landed on top of the enemy position. The section 2IC and one of the lads ran to the first bunker while I and another lad gave covering fire right up until they threw the grenades in. They did not go off, so I changed magazines and

ran forward firing at the bunker. When the next lot of grenades went off, we found that the section commander had been hit in the stomach and had shrapnel wounds in his arms and legs. We gave him first-aid until the company aid post arrived.

Captain Tom Wagstaff, Sergeant-Major Shaun Byrne and Lance-Corporal Chris Wright were part of the Alternate HQ of 1st Staffordshires' battle group. After assisting with around thirty prisoners of war, many of whom were wounded, the Alternate HQ was monitoring radios during the 7th Brigade advance when Wright shouted, 'We're being opened up on by 7.62 coax, sir!' 7.62 mm coaxial machine-gun fire is used to fire ranging rounds for a tank main armament. Sure enough, seconds later a 120 mm HESH struck the command Warrior in which Wagstaff was travelling, from which he immediately threw himself before the tank fired again. This was a 'blue on blue' incident which did not receive publicity, although a Royal Green Jackets officer was badly injured.

One aspect of the Warrior design, the 'Chobham' protective armour, undoubtedly saved the lives of Captain Wagstaff and his crew. Equally, intensive training of all ranks in first aid and use of intravenous drips very probably avoided the wounded Green Jackets officer bleeding to death. He was given the drips by Corporal Wright while the vehicle crew applied field dressings. The wounded man was evacuated and a new Warrior was provided to replace the one struck by the round of HESH. Captain Wagstaff and his team were back in action with the Staffordshires' battle group within twenty-four hours.

Not everyone from the regiment detached to the Gulf had such an exciting time as those serving with 1st Staffordshires, but no complaints were heard. Colonel John King, at Headquarters 1st Armoured Division, kept an eye on as many of the regiment as possible. These included Captain Andrew Broadbent with HQ 7th Armoured Brigade, Sergeant-Major Micky Braybrook, Corporal Tom Berry and eight men with Divisional Main HQ and Captain Mark Bower at Divisional Rear HQ. Sergeant Sammy Arzu, Corporal 'Diddly' Fawcett and others had the unglamorous role of waiting as battle casualty replacements in a holding unit formed by 1st Scots Guards. When visited by his former commanding officer, Arzu complained that the NAPS (nerve agent pre-treatment set) tablets, which everyone was obliged to take, were beginning to turn him white and his dog wouldn't recognize him when he got home.

The Gulf War was successful in liberating Kuwait, if not in removing the aggressor – Saddam Hussein. Those who took part saw the impact of modern weapon systems technology in a most dramatic fashion. Casualties amongst the Coalition forces were remarkably light, chiefly due to incompetent Iraqi leadership and training which caused their defences to collapse once the ground offensive began. There were no casualties amongst those on detachment from The Prince of Wales's Own, although Captain Tom Wagstaff and his team were very lucky not to be injured.

This chapter would be seriously lacking without an account of the experiences of Regimental Sergeant-Major (now Captain) Michael Haynes and his family during the Gulf War. He was the Regimental Sergeant-Major of the British Liaison Team in Kuwait responsible for technical and training support to the Kuwaiti army and air force. As soon as the Iraqis reached the Liaison Team camp at Fahaheel, thirty miles south of Kuwait City, the men of the team were rounded up and taken to the Headquarters of the invading Army. From there they were almost immediately bussed to Baghdad.

Mrs Elaine Haynes and their two sons Thomas and James were left in the Liaison Team camp together with all the families of the Liaison Team, where they were subjected to a regime of harassment and terror by the Iraqi occupation force for two weeks. The families were eventually reunited with their husbands in Baghdad on 17 August, only to be taken next day to strategic facilities where they became human shields against possible attack by the Coalition air forces. The Haynes family was put into a hut at a satellite communications centre known as Victory Station, some forty kilometres south of Baghdad. At the end of August Saddam Hussain staged his public relations stunt with some of the hostage families, following which the wives and children were allowed to leave for home.

RSM Haynes was later moved from Victory Station to one some fifty miles north of Baghdad. Conditions improved gradually but uncertainty about the future of the hostages was ever-present. News of their release was received on 6 December and the servicemen flew home five days later. In what must go down as *the* laconic comment of the whole campaign Haynes remarked, 'When the Iraqis march you out of your quarter you do not have to clean your cooker!'

10

In Competition

'Nec Aspera Terrent.'
REGIMENTAL MOTTO[1]

Active service in Aden in 1958–9 confined sport in the newly formed 1st Battalion to the parochial setting of South Arabia, leaving one of the Territorial battalions to steal the limelight. The 4th East Yorkshires won The Queen's Challenge Cup[2] for the Territorial Army unit with the outstanding sporting record for the season 1957–58. The margin over the runners-up, 6th North Staffordshires, set a post-Second World War record. Points were awarded for athletics, boxing, cricket, cross-country, soccer and swimming. Individuals representing the TA against the regular Army or the other services also gained points. 4th East Yorkshires excelled in athletics and boxing but – except for swimming – competed in everything.

Later, the 1st Battalion established a great sporting reputation but a TA battalion was the first to set an Army-level standard. Credit for this success lay chiefly with Major 'Lakri' Wood, quartermaster of 4th East Yorkshires and later of 3rd Prince of Wales's Own, and Regimental Sergeant-Major John McCullough. Together they masterminded the selection and coaching of the teams and individual competitors.

Sporting achievement was a key aspect of the traditions of the British and Indian Armies until the Second World War – and in some instances for long afterwards. A regiment would decide on a sport or particular trophy on which to set its sights and train teams over periods often extending into decades. Second only to operational ability, the spirit of competition became the theme central to regimental life but the struggle towards victory became as valuable as the trophy itself.

Selection of the sports in which a regiment elects to excel might be a matter of circumstance, dictated by the climatic or ground conditions of a foreign station. More usually, choice arises out of the dedication of a handful of enthusiasts. The story of the sporting achievements of The Prince of Wales's Own calls up the same group of names time and again. Over the years these men can be seen moving from being key performers to become team captains and then coach-managers and, finally, dedicated supporters in retirement. Underlying all these factors and the foundation on which all aspirations depend is the Yorkshireman's love of sport and his competitive instinct.

Aden held a few surprises for the 1st Battalion in 1958. Expecting to be committed to operations throughout an emergency tour barely extending to one winter season, enthusiasts found that South Arabia had some good sporting facilities, together with keen opponents. Members of the battalion were just getting to know each other, following amalgamation, so the informal discipline of the rugger and soccer fields and of the boxing ring had a useful part to play. In spite of having three companies detached up-country, the battalion won the British Forces Aden Protectorate team boxing competition, dominated the individual bouts and won the soccer and seven-a-side rugby leagues. Training of an athletics team began for the summer season in Gibraltar.

Only men competitive to their fingertips turned out to play rugby. With the thermometer at ninety, any discoverable shade was a tempting alternative to a pitch of sand and shale. But it was just these conditions that fostered the will to win. Led by Captain James Yeo, the battalion team lost its first two games of Aden's brief winter but won the remaining nine. British Petroleum and RAF Khormaksar were defeated 21-8 and 20-0, allowing the battalion to take the league trophy with ease. The team was strong in officers, setting a pattern for later years, with Lieutenants Allan Bower, David Dodd, Tony Nevile and 2nd Lieutenants Edwin Beckett and Ivan Scott Lewis providing the core of the team. Scott Lewis and Sergeant Brian Fogarty were to prove the long-term stayers, their names featuring in regimental rugby sides for almost two decades.

Gibraltar's more settled routine promised conditions better suited to sporting achievement. But the turnover of National Service junior ranks and posting out of regular officers and NCOs demanded an average of sixty percent new team members each season, so an unremitting search for new talent became essential. The Rock was home to Royal Engineers Gibraltar and RAF Gibraltar, both with sporting traditions that attracted high-quality sportsmen to their ranks.

Despite courageous running in the deciding 4 x 400 metres relay, the battalion was beaten into third place overall in the 1959 Gibraltar athletics competion. This narrow but very public defeat was humiliating. Preparations for the winter season began with near-professional care. Only rugby had to be set aside, as the Rock had no pitch.[3] Training brought success. The battalion took the Gibraltar swimming and novices' boxing trophies in what remained of 1959, won the open boxing, the soccer league, athletics championship and swimming competition in 1960 and all of them again in the 1961 season, before leaving for Germany.

Gibraltar had provided the opportunity to form a battalion ski team. Sergeant Geoffrey Broadman of the regiment, Inter-Services Ski Champion at St Moritz in 1951, took a ski hut in Le Moyen Atlas Mountains of Morocco for the winter of 1960–1. There was no shortage of volunteers to take advantage of his expert instruction and a team began to take shape in anticipation of competitions as part of the Army of the Rhine.

At first, Germany presented a dismal prospect. Demands on the 1st Battalion trickling back from post-Gibraltar leave were extensive and the bronzed and fit National Servicemen were being replaced by pallid new regular soldiers. With competition brought to a much broader canvas, it was clear that it would be some time before the 1st Battalion could make any significant impression. Fortunately, both Territorial battalions were able to claim successes at home. Private Dicky Barker of the 3rd Battalion became the Territorial Army's lightweight boxing champion, later to be declared the TA 'Sportsman of the Year', and the Leeds Rifles celebrated joining 49th Division with a decisive 9–0 defeat of 5th/8th Sherwood Foresters in the final of the Divisional knockout Soccer Cup.

It was Colour-Sergeant Mick Dillon who who started the 1st Battalion on the road to success in cross-country and other team running competitions, although Colonel Peter Taylor was to be held responsible for the weekly runs by the entire battalion, begun in Wuppertal. Lance-Corporal Johnny Redfern was an early star in cross-country competition. He led a well-trained team to victory in the 12th Brigade competition at Osnabrück in January 1962, conceding first individual place only through losing a shoe halfway round the course. From that point, team distance running became the 1st Battalion's primary sport, sometimes obscuring rising strengths in athletics, boxing, cricket, rugby, soccer and swimming.

After the 3rd Battalion had won the Queen's Challenge Cup for 1961–2, the 1st Battalion thoughtfully returned Sergeant Mick Garrigan to them as a permanent staff instructor. He was thus able to coach his four boxing brothers, plus two more up and coming with the Army Cadet Force. Garrigan senior had won the 2nd Division welterweight championship before leaving, and was very narrowly defeated in the BAOR final. Another individual success was scored when Private 'Smiler' Horsely won the 200 metres breast-stroke in the BAOR Swimming Championships and in the Germany Inter-Services match.

Exercises far from home base curtailed the 1st Battalion's sporting effort while with the 2nd Division in Germany 1961–3. But all field force units of 1st British Corps suffered similarly, so rather than grounds for complaint the difficulty became an accepted challenge. The 1962–3 rugby season saw the making of a useful team, with Majors Bill Todd and Tony Sherratt and Sergeant Brian Fogarty being joined by Captain John Filor, Lieutenant Jimmy Vickers, Corporal 'Ginger' Pell and Privates Trevor Bailey, Anthony 'Tosh' Burton and Bob Padget.

Shortage of talent amongst regular soldier players held the soccer team back from consistent progress, despite the dedicated attention of Captain Lew Borrett as the team's selector, coach and manager. Even so, wins were notched up against 24th Regiment RA (10–1) and 1st Royal Hampshires (1–0) in the preliminary rounds of the 1962–3 BAOR Major Units Challenge Cup. Unfortunately, the more experienced 1st Royal Warwickshires' team took the next round with a 1–0 victory in a well-fought game at Wuppertal in foul weather. The cross-country team retained the 12th Brigade trophy with a margin of seventy points over the runners-up. There were some fine individual performances, but no significant team impact was made in boxing, cricket, hockey or swimming. Everyone was looking forward to better conditions in the next station – Berlin.

The 3rd Battalion won the Queen's Challenge Cup for a second successive season: 1962–3. Sixty-seven units had entered the competition and excitement reached a high pitch when the 3rd Battalion and 5th/6th North Staffordshires returned equal scores. The Cup was awarded to the 3rd Battalion on grounds of their having competed in more competitions. This was Major 'Lakri' Wood's final triumph in a career as player, referee, coach and tireless sporting organizer, spanning thirty years.

Meanwhile, the 1st Battalion had moved to Berlin where sporting rivalry was intense. As the East's window on the West, anything done well there won restrained applause but anything done less than well tended to be unhelpful. Since taking over command in November 1962, the commanding officer – Lieutenant-Colonel Peter Taylor – had led the weekly battalion cross-country run, at least for the first fifty yards or so, thereby lending fashion to the sport.

On arrival in Berlin the battalion cross-country team beat 1st Somerset and Cornwall Light Infantry by the exceptionally narrow margin of five points, over a gruelling course through the Grünewald forest, to win the Berlin Brigade Championship. Private Mick Conroy was the individual winner, crossing the line with a clear lead in the Olympic Stadium. The team result was notable, as the Somersets had enjoyed an Army-wide reputation for cross-country for many years. The battalion went on to win the BAOR 1963–4 Championship, when Lance-Corporal Paddy O'Brien was only seconds behind the individual winner. A subsequent fourth place in the Army Championships at Aldershot marked the 1st Battalion's break into Army-level cross-country competition. Much credit for this was due to Sergeant Russ Pask, the team captain, but also to Herman Brecht, the team's German ex-Olympic coach.

Some fine individual performances aside, swimming had not featured in 1st Battalion achievements since leaving Gibraltar. An enthusiast of experience was needed to revive interest in the sport and one arrived in the form of Lieutenant 'Cobber' Rushworth, who joined the battalion in Berlin. He captained the team which was very narrowly beaten into second place by 1st King's in the Berlin Brigade Championship in June 1964 – but both teams went forward to the BAOR final. The BAOR Championship, held at the Olympic pool in Berlin, was a nail-biting event. Closely watching performances in every race, Rushworth made subtle changes to the battalion team as the day progressed, with the result that victory was snatched from the 1st King's by the margin of half a point.

Boxing also made a come-back during 1964–5. Sergeant Mick Garrigan had rejoined the 1st Battalion in time for the autumn 1964 Berlin Brigade Championship held in the Kuppelsaal, site of the 1936 Olympic Boxing Championships. 3rd Royal Anglians contested the match at every stage and the outcome hung on the last bout, in which Garrigan was to box as first string welterweight. Skill and experience paid and Garrigan outboxed his opponent to bring his team victory by a single point. A photograph facing page 49 shows him receiving the trophy from the Commander Berlin Brigade.

The 1st Battalion soccer team won the Berlin 1964–5 league competition under Corporal George Potter's captaincy while, taking the 1st Battalion's cue, the 3rd won the 49th Division cross-country championship at Catterick, where Lance-Corporal James Hargreaves of the battalion took the individual trophy. Berlin provided the environment in which the 1st Battalion first established a challenging position on the Army sporting scene. Operational tours aside, the distance running teams never had cause to look back. In early 1965 the cross-country team won the 1st Division Cross-Country Championship without difficulty, Sergeant Russ Pask taking individual second place just behind the winner. As runners-up in the BAOR final, the battalion qualified for the Army Championship at Aldershot, where the team improved on its previous year's fourth position to run the champions, the 1st Parachute Regiment, to a very close finish. That rivalry lasted for several years.

The operational tour in South Arabia, from September 1965 to September 1966, effectively excluded the 1st Battalion teams from Army competition. Moreover, the greatly increased tempo of operations in both Aden and the Western Protectorate, compared with 1958–9, localized sporting events almost entirely to company level. Even so, battalion runners managed to keep sufficiently in training to win the Middle East Command Cross-Country title. In the Command Athletics Championships, 2nd Lieutenant Michael Garside won the high jump trophy and Lance-Corporal Johnny Redfern individual first place in the mile.

England won the World Football Cup in 1966 and, deployed in the Radfan area of the Western Protectorate, the 1st Battalion listened to the tense period of extra time relayed by BBC World Service as darkness fell. At Dhala on the Yemeni frontier, C Company was standing-to ready to rehearse defensive fire tasks just before last light. Sergeant

George Prosser, captain of C Company's soccer team, broke the attentive hush with a shout to the company commander, 'Can we hold fire till the finish, sir? The dizzies [dissident tribesmen] must be listening too.' Fire was held until England had scored the winning goal against West Germany. Those were the days!

Cricket, boxing and swimming were all kept going during the the 1st Battalion's Aden tour. Private Ed Kilkenny became the Middle East Command light-welterweight boxing champion and Lance-Corporal Jim Neil the featherweight champion. The annual Victor Ludorum competition was run in the continued search for new sporting talent. Starved of opportunity to develop team performances, individuals trained where and whenever they could, determined to keep their form in anticipation of the coming winter season at home.

The 3rd Battalion kept in the public eye by winning the Scarborough Cup in the TA Team Boxing Championship, providing nine members of the 49th Division team and no less than four individual Territorial Army champions. Private Roger Tighe of the 3rd Battalion became the British Empire and Commonwealth Games light-heavyweight Gold Medallist, ABA and Territorial Army Champion 1966. The 3rd Battalion also won the Northern Command TA cross-country competition, in which the Leeds Rifles came third, running 8th Durham Light Infantry very closely for second place.

The period between the 1st Battalion's return from Aden in September 1966 and departure for a two-year tour in Cyprus in early 1970 seemed ideal for a resumption of sporting achievement at Army level. The battalion was stationed at Colchester, with excellent facilities for major sports and high-quality opponents in abundance in the garrison and throughout the southern counties. Contrary to expectations, development of sporting standards was upset by two further emergency operational tours, one in Aden and the first in Northern Ireland, plus exercises in Cyprus, Kenya and Norway. While no complaint can be raised against emergency tours and the overseas exercises were stimulating and offered valuable training, these diversions made it difficult for battalion sportsmen to keep a foothold on the Army's competitive ladder. Uncertainties of a different kind hung over both TA battalions in the form of the 1967 reorganization of the Reserve Army.

Boxing began another upturn in the 1966–7 season under the continuing captaincy of Sergeant Mick Garrigan. The 3rd Royal Green

Jackets were beaten by a single point in the Army Zone D final at Colchester in February 1967. The decision hung on the final bout which Garrigan won, as he had done in Berlin. But against the 1st Parachute Regiment in the next round, the battalion team was beaten 11–0 in spite of intensive training by Mick Garrigan and Corporal Ken Bolton. Access to Army-level boxing remained elusive. The Army Cross-Country Championship was run that year over a flat dry course at Blackdown, which did not suit the 1st Battalion team accustomed to heavy going in Essex. Only a disappointing fourth place was achieved. The 3rd Battalion again won the 49th Division Cross-Country trophy but were runners-up to 8th Durhams in the Northern Command Cup

Briefly free from sudden emergency tours, the 1st Battalion started 1968 well by winning the East Anglian District Rugby Cup. The 3rd Battalion (briefly titled The Prince of Wales's Own Territorials) responded by winning The Queen's Cup for the third time – for the 1967–8 season. This was was especially commendable, as the unit had recently been reduced to a much much smaller establishment and allocation of financially supported training days. The 3rd Battalion also won five individual titles in the TAVR boxing championships.

The 1st Battalion faced a difficult situation in the 1969–70 season. The spring and summer of 1969 were spent on an emergency tour in Northern Ireland while the winter was interrupted by the early 1970 move to Cyprus. There, at least, auguries were good. The sports facilities were outstanding and the two RAF Stations of Akrotiri and Episkopi, each more than twice the battalion's strength, offered high-quality competition.

The end of the 1960s also saw the first sea change in the way that sport was organized and encouraged in the 1st Battalion. While everyone took part in the Friday afternoon cross-country race over the Essex countryside, it was a small, tightly-knit group of dedicated enthusiasts who were ambitious for the regiment's reputation in the field of distance running. Although the commanding officer 1967–9, Colonel Bill Todd, had done more than any other to put cross-country high in 1st Battalion priorities, it was Peter Blyth, soon to become a youthful Company Sergeant-Major, who was the mainspring of this group. His principal lieutenant was Sergeant Dave Moffat. Together, and with others, they later extended their scope to athletics and eventually Moffat succeeded Blyth in the management of both teams.

There was a close but not exact parallel in soccer. Captain Frank Walker had coached and managed the football team since the early 1960s and continued to do so throughout the Cyprus period. But Corporal Benny Bates, attached from the RAPC, put enough effort of his own into the team to give Walker breathing space. When Bates left the battalion in 1971, Corporals John Bateman and Byron Cawkwell were more than ready and eager to take on his role. Between them, or separately when one or other was posted away, they kept soccer in the forefront of 1st Battalion sporting effort for two decades, although never with the spectacular success at Army level achieved by the distance runners.

Boxing suffered severely when Sergeant Mick Garrigan left for service on secondment, but recovered in the mid-1970s when a group of dedicated enthusiasts equal to the distance runners emerged. While Dave Moffat managed the team in Celle, Sergeant Dave Frank provided the driving force and, together with fellow boxers Terry 'Huddy' Hudson, Jimmy Hyam and Errol Tyrell, kept up the pressure until Captain Danny Matthews took over the management of boxing in Catterick. As we shall see, the team under his management became the Grade II novices' Army Champions in 1989.

We are running a little ahead in the story but it is of significance that the principal *effort* in the organization of the 1st Battalion sports teams, except for rugby which had always been officer-dominated, came from the relatively junior levels during the 1970s. The prominent figures, Blyth, Moffat, Matthews and Cawkwell, were all commissioned and continued to bring their influence to bear, even when retired. The next sea change began with Colonel Peter Woolley's period in command, when officers were drawn to the regiment by its sporting reputation and competed hard to become members of teams, athletics teams in particular, representing the 1st Battalion at command and Army level.

Cyprus, to where the 1st Battalion was moving when we began the diversion into the sources of sporting initiative, offered a stable routine while denying participation in Army-level competitions. Every sport benefited from the excellent facilities and opportunity to exploit them but soccer kicked off to a brisk start. The battalion formed two teams to compete throughout the island. These were the 'Lions', captained by Corporal Benny Bates, and the 'Tigers', captained by Corporal John Bateman. In the final two of his eight years as battalion soccer officer, Captain Frank Walker saw these two teams take a collection of trophies and lead the Western SBA League in both seasons. Matches were also played against highly competitive local civilian sides. Battalion teams won the Polemidhia six-a-side competition in 1970-1 and the Limassol summer league in 1972. With Sergeant Byron Cawkwell, Privates Tony Glossop, Mick Keeney and Tommy Rusk from the 1st Battalion in the team in 1971, the Army beat the RAF Cyprus soccer team for the first time in fifteen years.

Athletics, boxing, cricket, swimming and distance running teams were selected, trained and tested against every possible opponent. The Near East Command Army versus RAF Cyprus Athletics meeting in 1971 saw victory by the Army team for the first time in eleven years. The Army team was organized by Captain Michael Garside and comprised battalion athletes almost exclusively. The sun, the enthusiasm of sportsmen old and new, the time and the facilities were all most valuable investments for the sporting future. Even the ski team, neglected since the battalion left Berlin in 1965, was able to make a fresh start during the short season on Mount Olympus.

From Cyprus the 1st Battalion went direct to Northern Ireland to begin an eighteen month so-called 'resident' tour. As the Province reserve battalion, there were good opportunities to maintain and indeed increase the sporting momentum. The 1972 Northern Ireland Cricket Cup was won and the team reached the Army final in the same year. The battalion won the Northern Ireland Soccer League in 1973 and took part in the Army Ski Championships at Oberjoch, Bavaria, in early 1974. Attention was paid to developing the soccer and rugby sides in particular, with temporary neglect of athletics and cross-country.

On arrival in Celle in 1974, the 1st Battalion soccer team set its sights on winning the Army Challenge Cup – in due course – with the Infantry Challenge Cup as the immediate goal in the 1975-6 season. But the team was knocked out in the first round of the Army Cup by the 1st Black Watch. In the Infantry Cup the team captained by Corporal John Bateman reached the BAOR final after defeating the 1st King's Own Border, the 1st Parachute Regiment and the 2nd Light Infantry. The final was played at Sennelager against 1st Queen's Own Highlanders, a regiment with a name in soccer. The 1st Battalion beat the Highlanders three goals to one but the other finalists in the infantry-wide final were none other than 1st Black Watch. The match was played at Aldershot and revenge was not taken. A four goals to one defeat made clear that the battalion team had more to learn. It took five more years to reach the final of the Army Cup.

The struggle to reach the final and win the 1st Division novices' competition in 1977–8 kept boxing on the map. The first round against 16th/5th The Queen's Royal Lancers was won by seven bouts to nil. The account in the regimental journal *The White Rose* caught the atmosphere rather well. 'Not to be outdone, Private Poss Poessl volunteered to take on the 16th/5th heavyweight, who they put a lot of faith in. This guy looked a fighter on his toes, like a young Ali. Robbo[4] had Poss tied to the corner post with his muzzle on. Bong, round one, Poss hit him; end of fight.' This round also saw Jimmy Hyam emerge as a battalion boxer at light-middleweight. He was to become a mainstay of the team and later served as selector and coach. In the second round, to their astonishment, the 1st Coldstream Guards were also defeated seven bouts to nil. The final against 49th Field Regiment Royal Artilley produced a five bouts to two win for the battalion and the Divisional Cup.

Return of the 1st Battalion to England from Celle, in 1978, led to a determined revival of distance running. Stationed at Bulford on the edge of Salisbury Plain, the battalion had an operational role requiring the highest standards of physical fitness. As part of the AMF(L),[5] the battalion was on stand-by to reinforce the NATO flank in Norway, on skis. Learning to ski and spending two months in Norway's Arctic snow each winter soon got everyone fit. Captain Peter Blyth set the pace by becoming the Army 5,000 metres veteran individual champion in 1981. In 1982 the battalion won the Army Team Marathon Championship, achieved third place in the Army Cross-Country Championship and were runners-up in the Army Cross-Country Relay Competitition.

Boxing was not allowed to slide. Lance-Corporal Terry 'Huddy' Hudson, who had won all his light-heavyweight bouts in the 1st Division competition, boxed at that weight for the Army throughout the 1978–9 season and, having shed the necessary pounds, at middleweight in the 1979–80 season. He reached the Army middleweight individuals' final but the fight was stopped by a previous collar-bone injury.

The relentless dedication of the 1st Battalion footballers, dating from Cyprus and enhanced by the competition opportunities of Celle, brought the team to the final of the Army Challenge Cup in 1981. Mention has already been made of this event in chapter 6. Company Sergeant-Major Byron Cawkwell had prepared his team for the final, to be played against the School of Electrical and Mechanical Engineers, with infinite care. He knew that the odds were stacked against him, as the SEME had concentrated sporting effort on soccer for more than a generation.[6] Once a star player got on the SEME strength, he was unlikely – to say the least – to be posted away. It was a spectacular game but, after a two-all score at the end of the second half, the REME side produced a third during extra time. This was a deep personal disappointment for Cawkwell, but he went on to captain the Army side in the 1981–2 and 1982–3 seasons. He was capped for the Army more than a hundred times.

Boxing also had some setbacks. The South-West District novices' competition of 1982 found the 1st Battalion facing the 3rd Parachute Regiment in the second round. By the interval the score was three bouts to two in the battalion's favour, Kevin Pickering, Errol Tyrell and Colin Sharp having defeated their featherweight, lightweight and light-middleweight opponents decisively. The first two fights after the break were lost and the battalion team was a point down at the start of the heavyweight bout. Fighting a man a foot taller than himself, John Slater scored steadily with blows to the head and body and won on points. The welterweight bout became the decider, which was won by Sergeant Dave Frank when the referee stopped the fight in his favour at the end of the second round. The battalion won the next round but did not reach the final that year.

Proof that concentration on distance running was beginning to pay became apparent in 1983 with victory for the first time in the Army Cross-Country Relay. Battalion teams were runners-up in both the Army Marathon and the Army Cross-Country Championship, improving on the 1982 result. The athletics team, which had begun serious training in 1981, won the South-West District competition with ease for the second successive year in 1982 and the Berlin Brigade competition shortly after their arrival there in the summer of 1983.

Berlin outclassed Cyprus for sporting opportunities. Not only were the facilities outstanding and local competition keen but access to

Army-level competitions was afforded through Rhine Army. Captain Roy Hunter was by this stage assisting Peter Blyth in the management and training of 1st Battalion athletics and distance runners. The regiment's sporting reputation was attracting ambitious young athletes, like Privates Graham Birdsall and Aiden Hill, from junior leaders units and the team had an athlete and coach of international standard in the dynamic form of Sergeant Kris Akabusi.

The combination of five years' training with the AMF(L) and a concentration of key regimental sporting figures in Berlin brought the 1st Battalion exceptional sporting success. Aside from such local achievements as victory in the Berlin Brigade Rugby Simper Cup, the Soccer A and B League Championships and the BAOR Infantry Cricket Cup, the battalion won the Army Cross-Country Championship in 1984 and 1985, the Army Cross-Country Relay Competition in 1983, 1984 and 1985 – the first hat-trick – and were runners-up in the BAOR Intermediate Boxing Championship in 1984. Could the momentum be maintained, everyone asked, as preparations were made to move to Northern Ireland for a second resident tour, this time for two years in Ballykinler of happy memory for a few from 1969.

The battalion won the Northern Ireland Cricket Cup and Tennis Championship on arrival in the summer of 1985. Dave Bennett had been the linchpin of the cricket team since being a junior member of the 1st Battalion orderly room staff in Cyprus and, as one of the team that reached the Army final in 1972, this return of the battalion's cricketing fortunes was especially welcome. The cricket team was captained over this period by Lieutenant Peter Germain, a first-rate individual player, who also represented the Army and the Combined Services. On moving to Catterick in May 1987, the cricket team won the Yorkshire Army League Cup that summer.

The 1985–6 season brought victory in the Army Cross-Country Championship for the third consecutive year, the second distance running hat-trick under the successive captaincies of Blyth and Moffat. Moffat was also the Army Veteran Champion. In 1987, 1st Battalion teams won the Army Cross-Country Championship for the fourth consecutive year, regained the Army Cross-Country Relay title and, for the first time, achieved runners-up position in the Army Athletics Competition.

The winter of 1987–8 boxing season began with a decisive win over the formidable 38 Engineer Regiment from Ripon, bringing victory to the 1st Battalion in the North-East District Grade III Novices' Team Championship. Credit for this belonged to Captain Danny Matthews who had rejoined from the 2nd Yorkshire Volunteers in 1987. This success should not be underrated just because it was in a novices' contest. Army boxing had undergone a long-overdue reform to separate experienced 'open' fighters from three grades of up-and-coming novices. This encouraged young new boxers to compete on equal terms, rather than face massacre by technically superior fighters.

Matthews saw this change as an opportunity to inspire new boxers for the battalion. Corporal 'Taff' Curtis was his chief coach. Between them, they trained teams that brought victory in the Northern Zone Novice Team Championship in 1987–8, the runners-up place in the UKLF Grade III Novices' final in 1988 and victory in the Army Novices' Grade II Inter-Unit Team Championship in 1989. Corporal Errol Tyrell of the 1st Battalion became the Army individual featherweight champion in the same year. The teams also boxed for charity, raising £1,000 for the Army Benevolent Fund during a sponsored event in 1988.

Captain Roy Hunter captained the team that took the 1988 Army Marathon title and the battalion were runners-up in the Army Cross-Country Championship, the Cross-Country Relay Championship and – for the second year – in the Army Athletics Championship. Would-be sailors won the Infantry Keel Boat Sailing Regatta and Colour-Sergeant Tom Copperwaite added the United Kingdom title to that of Army surf canoe champion.

The 1st Battalion also produced five Army individual athletic champions in 1988, with six titles altogether: Army junior 100 metres and 200 metres champion, Drummer David Blair; Army long jump champion, Private Paul Fogg; Army triple jump champion, Lance-Corporal Nigel Bulmer – who was to win the title for the next four years; Army pole vault champion, Lance-Corporal Bobby Lyons and the Army steeplechase champion, Private Richard Simpson. These were strenuous challenges but, just for fun, 2nd Lieutenant Rupert Crowfoot and Lance-Corporal Martin Wingrove won the 24th Brigade tennis doubles, also in 1988.

The record of the regiment's sporting achievements is set out in Appendix 6 and of individual champions in Appendix 7. 1st

Battalion teams did not feature outside the top two places in one or other of the distance running competitions in the years 1982–92. The Army Team Marathon Championship was won in 1982 and the Army Cross-Country Relay Championship for the three successive years 1983–5. The Army Cross-Country Team Championship was won four years in succession, between 1983 and 1987, and again in 1991 and 1992. Since 1982 the 1st Battalion has kept up intense pressure on athletics, gradually moving up the lists and achieving the runners-up position in the Army Championships on four occasions between 1986 and 1992. Although the Championship has yet to be actually *won*, individual champions have kept the regiment's name prominent in Army athletics.

Athletics, boxing and distance running are the sports that have made the regiment known Army-wide in recent years. It is the name that will continue to attract young athletes, boxers and endurance runners with ambition to reach Army standard to join from Sandhurst, junior leader and recruit training units.

Although finalists in the Army Football Challenge Cup in 1981 and in the BAOR final ten years later 1991, the battalion soccer team has yet to match the regiment's immense enthusiasm for the game by winning at Army level. Perhaps this is really less important than the bedrock of company-level games, played with the passion with which the 1966 World Cup final was heard on the Yemeni frontier nearly thirty years ago. Fierce competition at company level is certainly a dynamic as valuable as the thrill of cheering eleven battalion heroes on to victory – or to try even harder next season.

Exciting though they are, there is always a danger that games can become too much a spectator sport. Athletics, boxing and distance running call for individual determination within an overall team effort. So much depends on sustained training in the pauses between competitions. These, akin to operational lulls on active service, can so easily sap the personal will to win. In any sport, the satisfaction of winning has only a transitory place. The key, which the regiment has found, is to involve as many people as possible in the selection, training, performance and support of competition.

11
Wives and Children

> 'Alice is marrying one of the guard
> "A soldier's life is terrible hard,"
> Says Alice.'
>
> A. A. MILNE

Had she but known, Alice might have gone on to explain to Christopher Robin, 'But sometimes not half as hard as for his wife and children.' By the late 1950s the Army had a fairly good reputation for looking after soldiers' families, but performance was patchy. In cases of crisis or hardship the Soldiers', Sailors' and Airmen's Families Association (SSAFA) provided immediate support, but only in emergency or on the brink of one. The all-regular Army of the early 1960s brought with it an increasing number of wives, including many in their late teens or early twenties, who had never lived away from their mothers and needed advice on such things as having babies and how to react when their brand-new husbands were being beastly to them. SSAFA consequently widened its scope of care significantly. In addition to providing professional advice to young mothers and mothers-to-be, SSAFA sisters tried to foresee and so prevent problems by regular contact with all families, including those *not* in distress.

Good communications lay at the heart of making wives and children feel secure, cared about and, above all, truly part in the regimental scheme of things. When the 1st Battalion left Dover for operational duty in Aden in 1958, no base in England was maintained or set aside for its return. Although a handful of wives and children of the more senior officers, warrant officers and NCOs stayed in quarters in and around Dover, the rest dispersed to the homes of their parents or were put into hired accommodation in Yorkshire or elsewhere. Communication with those dispersed was possible only through the not entirely reliable means of letters from husbands in Aden. Fortunately in this respect, after seven months the battalion and the families were reunited in Gibraltar.

The confines of the Rock brought the wives and children into the regimental family in a way that might have taken years to achieve elsewhere. In spite of the Mediterranean holiday expectations, the Atlantic weather could be dismally cold and wet and then the claustrophobic aspects of the Rock became apparent. Families living in sub-standard quarters and with no transport to take them into Spain, were completely dependent on arrangements made by the battalion and quickly came to appreciate the companionship of others similarly placed. At the same time, the wives who had served with one of the two former regiments were getting to know each other, beginning to set aside old loyalties – often deeply held – and turn their attention to the young wives new to Army life. These were the circumstances, more than any other factor at that time, which brought the wives' club into being.

This was doubly fortunate because, initially at least, Germany was to provide a grim contrast two years later. It was in Wuppertal, from the autumn of 1961, that large numbers of young wives who had never been far away from home before began to come within the battalion's care. Strangeness of customs and language were not always sympathetically appreciated by the young husbands, some of whom appeared reluctant to allow 'the regiment' to intrude too far into their jealously guarded domestic affairs. The need for regimental support became clear when the men were away on exercises, sometimes for several weeks, while the rain poured down relentlessly on the married quarter areas stuck on a hillside at the edge of the Ruhr.

Gibraltar proved its worth with the formation of the White Rose Club, although it did not have that title at first. Wives who had become firm friends took care to bring the new wives into the regimental family, so that loneliness could first be shared and then dismissed. Shyness remained a barrier sometimes difficult to overcome. Just as in any group, individuals ready to lead and have a go at anything were quick to emerge, while others hung back saying, 'I don't want to be organized,' or 'I've got nothing to say to *her*,' – usually a wife about whom, for one reason or another, the speaker was apprehensive. It was seldom plain sailing and the sails of the White Rose could be trimmed only for the squalls immediately ahead. Tried and trusted members of the crew left when their husbands were posted, leaving gaps for which new stalwarts had to be found.

The key figures were the wives of the commanding officer and the regimental sergeant-major who, like as not, had known each other for years and already had a close rapport. But without the enthusiasts not a lot could be done. Enthusiasts are valuable for their ideas and vigour, no matter how far out or seemingly unprofitable the projects for which they enthuse. The danger that they present is that they will, in the main, attract only other enthusiasts, leaving 'timid Tina' still on the sidelines. This was where the battalion command structure became of value to the Club. The company commanders' wives were invited to get stuck in too. In particular, each set up an informal network through the wives of men in her husband's company to befriend new wives or those who appeared most alone when the men were away. Delegation being crucial to success in any organization, company commanders' wives were each given a special responsibility or put in charge of a project or two, with two or three of the enthusiasts to help them. It was surprising how this combination opened up challenging vistas!

The initiatives and stimulus always came from the wives or sometimes from one of the children. Husbands inclined to smile just a touch indulgently at a new idea or project soon found themselves having to quicken their pace to keep up with the bandwagon. Having watched the battalion small-bore rifle team narrowly beat the team of HMS *Gambia* 584 points to 564 in Gibraltar in 1960, a group of wives formed their own team and within weeks the company teams found they faced a formidable new challenger. More wives turned up to witness the men's discomfiture. The hushed quiet of an indoor range, broken only by the confidential low-key crack of the .22 rifle, is not a bad environment for making new friends – rather like a bowling alley but less stressful.

Curious to know why the men had decided to spend Whitsuntide 1962 at Haltern which, apart from being a training area, had a reputation for nothing more than being somewhere just off the Wuppertal-Münster autobahn, the wives decided to find out. Penelope Armour telephoned her husband to say that they would be arriving in 'buses from Wuppertal at 1030 hours on Whit Sunday, 'So please make all arrangements, as the children will be coming too.' 'Good,' he replied, 'we've been racking our brains how to spend Sunday.'

After a week of uncertain weather for field firing, brilliant sunshine greeted the wives and children arriving from the rain-sodden Ruhr, giving unwarranted support to the suspicion that the men were engaged in a surreptitious 'jolly' of some kind. It was a remarkably successful outing which lost nothing due to the rough and ready arrangements of a temporary camp, while gaining a great deal from the spontaneity of the expedition. For a few years, 'Haltern' remained a watchword amongst the wives, even though the place never achieved a status higher than being just somewhere off the Wuppertal-Münster autobahn.

Children were always an important consideration. Christmas and other parties brought not only them together but also the wives and husbands who made the arrangements. Thought was given to other children too. Adoption by the battalion of a house run by the SOS Children's Homes for orphans in 1962 led to a round-trip of 1,300 miles to Moosburg, in Austria, over Easter the following year. Regimental Sergeant-Major Tommy Wall and his wife Muriel had inspired this foray back to a part of Carinthia he remembered from his service there with 1st West Yorkshires after the war, before they were married. A phenomenal quantity of toys and other presents had been contributed by the families of the battalion. These were taken by a group of well-wishers, led by Captain John Filor, in the battalion's minibus via Münich, Bad Gastein, Villach, Klagenfurt and other places of happy memory to Moosburg, where the travellers were received with warmest Austrian hospitality.

Berlin in 1963–5 brought the wives and children of the 1st Battalion together in much the same way as Gibraltar had done. There was so much to see and do that it was difficult to know where to begin. Making the best of opportunities was hindered by the majority of the families living in quarters or hired flats in the Charlottenburg district, some eleven miles by road from Montgomery Barracks at Kladow. A number of families were obliged to move into 'mobile homes' as a temporary expedient – and then found them so convenient that they were reluctant to leave when a proper quarter became available.

The search for a meeting place ended in a room, once used as a Corporals' Club, in a building scheduled for demolition. It was not in good condition. After scraping the hardened compost of beer and mud from the floorboards, the enthusiasts colour-washed the walls, painted the woodwork and curtained the cracked and broken windows. The wives' first meeting was attended by a dramatic thunderstorm but no one appeared to mind. At the suggestion of Pamela Taylor, wife of the commanding officer, the *White Rosette* newspaper was introduced to advertise future activities and to publish recipes, household hints, a wanted column and a crossword. Not many wives troubled themselves to read this so long as it was supplied free. But, unaccountably, all copies were quickly taken at a charge of five pfennigs each.

The Brownie pack, started in Wuppertal, thrived in Berlin under the guidance of Joan Sherratt and Bridget Crowfoot to such an extent that it was decided to risk a complementary venture for the boys. Peggy Hardaker assisted by 'Jimmie' Brooks and the battalion's physical training instructor, Sergeant Tommy Lunt, formed the 2nd (Berlin) (PWO) Cub Pack, who wore neckscarves in the regimental colours of maroon and old gold. A combined meeting of all the Berlin Cub packs was held in the battalion gymnasium, when the 'grand howl' at the close of proceedings shook the ancient wooden structure. The highlight of the Brownies' season was meeting the World Chief Guide, Olave Lady Baden-Powell, at Berlin's Templehof airport.

The wives, children and the whole battalion were shocked when Doris Carrington, the very popular wife of Major Stan Carrington, was killed instantly when an oil-tanker's brakes failed and crashed into the car in which she and Pamela Taylor were travelling on the Berlin Heer Strasse. Although trapped in the wreckage, Mrs Taylor was miraculously uninjured and was freed by a passing German worker using a crowbar. Writing about this incident more than thirty years afterwards, she remarked, 'It was after the accident that I personally experienced the support that the Regiment and the wives club can give to anyone in trouble.' The two wives had been on their way into the city to take their turn working in the Berlin Brigade thrift shop.

On return to England from Berlin in April 1965 the battalion faced a year-long operational and unaccompanied tour in Aden. In contrast to the earlier period of service in South Arabia, a home base was maintained in Roman Barracks, Colchester, to which the battalion moved for three months' intensive counter-insurgency training. This allowed everyone to find their feet in the new station before the men left for Aden in September.

This period saw the introduction of the 'families officer' into the regimental life of the British Army. It had initially been intended that such officers, appointed exclusively for the administration and welfare of families, would serve only with units on unaccompanied tours of duty abroad. Quite soon, however, they were added to the establishment of all units having a liability for unaccompanied service overseas. In the early days, officers selected to serve as families officer were almost invariably those who had reached their promotion ceiling at the rank of major. The thought behind this policy rested partly on the argument that such men would not feel unfairly sidelined from the mainstream and that the wives and children would feel at home with a fatherly figure. This selection policy was not an unqualified success and, at a later stage, 'late-entry' officers commissioned from warrant rank were to prove themselves outstanding in this role.

A year-long unaccompanied tour, unthinkable in the last decade of the twentieth century – other than in extreme national crisis, put a strain on those left behind. Concern about the lonely year stretching ahead was heightened when the battalion was involved in the suppression of violent rioting immediately on arrival in Aden. These events were widely reported on television and in the press, with particular emphasis on the battalion because the serious violence occurred in Aden's Crater for which the battalion was responsible. After the first few weeks there was little or no reporting by the news media, leaving an uneasy silence broken only by occasional snippets of news that someone had been killed, wounded or injured.

No news is not necessarily good news in circumstances where messages had to pass through the Ministry of Defence and the local District headquarters before they could reach the rear party. Sometimes unofficial news or rumour got there first, usually through a letter home from a soldier serving in Aden, sometimes with disquieting results. It was unfortunate that the battalion had not become part of 19th Infantry Brigade in Colchester before leaving for Aden but, instead, remained a responsibility of the not over-active District staff, some of whom clearly regarded the battalion's wives and children as an additional tax on their time. There was a marked contrast in attitude in June 1967, when the battalion was despatched

Berlin 1984. ABOVE Presentation of new Colours to the 1st Battalion by Field-Marshal Sir Edwin Bramall. The Ensigns were Lieutenants Christopher Dockerty and Graham Jackson.

BELOW, LEFT Allied Forces' Day Parade. Lieutenant-Colonel Rory Forsyth leads the 1st Battalion down Strasse des 17 Juni. Number 1 Guard is commanded by Major Neil Porter. RIGHT Private Graham Birdsall, Army Junior Champion Steeplechaser.

ABOVE, LEFT Lieutenant-Colonel Peter Woolley and Corporal Dale Archer in the Lebanon 1984. RIGHT Brigadier Bill Sheppard.

BELOW 1st Battalion cross-country team 1986. Back row: Nobby Clark, Robbo Robson, Jimmy Clune, Paul Margison, Lieutenant-Colonel Rory Forsyth, Graham Birdsall, Andy Phillips, Lieutenant Dave Moffat; front row: Chris Smithson, David Wray, 'Ginge' Chippendale, Paul Medley, Phil Quantock, Richard Simpson, Geoff Wade and Aiden Hill.

ABOVE 1st Battalion athletics team 1986. Back row: Tony Wilson, Don McBurney, Lieutenant Steve Padgett, Paul Clark, 'Scouse' Halliday, David Hyde, Lieutenant Dave Moffat, Tommy Copperwaite, Dave Prew, Paul Dobson, Andy Bowland, Peter Stirk and Dave Crowther; front row: Corporal Reid (REME), Geoff Wade, Graham Birdsall, Andy Phillips, Bob Hope, Wilks Wilman, Lieutenant Dominic Hancock, Steve Thompson, Jack Frost, Neil King and Chris Smithson.

BELOW 1st Battalion ladies cross-country team 1986. Back row: Michelle Ellison, Jamie Kent-Payne, Karen Scott and Tracy Smelt; front row Joy Frank and Angela Quantock.

Ballykinler 1985-7. ABOVE, LEFT Sergeant Paul Wood being greeted on his return from Bessbrook by his son James. RIGHT. Middleton RUC station after a Provisionals' mortar attack.

BELOW. C Company emplanes in a Chinook helicopter for their final operation in South Armagh, April 1987.

Catterick. ABOVE Her Royal Highness The Duchess of Kent watches a demonstration of a helicopter-borne assault with Major-General Tony Crowfoot (left) and Lieutenant-Colonel John King, while visiting the 1st Battalion, 30 March 1990.

BELOW 1st Battalion boxing team; Army Major Units Grade II Novices' Champions 1988-9. Back row: Dave Wilson, Colin Sharp, Dave Licence, Adrian Thorne, Dave Reid, Vic Vickers; front row: Bob Baynes, Errol Tyrell, Lieutenant-Colonel John King, Captain Danny Matthews, Jamie Yule and Steven Dickman.

The Gulf War 1990-1. ABOVE, LEFT RSM Michael Haynes, his wife Elaine and their sons Thomas and James shortly before being taken as Iraqi hostages. RIGHT The 1st Battalion exercising the Freedom of Osnabrück, 8 June 1991.

BELOW Captain Tom Wagstaff and Corporal Chris Wright with their 'Warrior' after it had been struck by friendly fire during the liberation of Kuwait.

ABOVE 1st Battalion cross-country team, Army Champions 1991-2. Back row: Dave Beckett, Chris Smithson, Dave Wilson, Ian Cain, Richard Bingley, Richard Watson and Karl Hutchinson; front row: Lee Haywood, Darren Stephenson, Captain Dave Moffat, Lieutenant-Colonel Alastair Duncan, Paul Margison, Richard Thomas and Tony Nevet.

BELOW, LEFT B Company of the 3rd Battalion exercising at Otterburn in October 1993. (Left) Lance-Corporal Margaret French and (right) Lance-Corporal Mark Brown. RIGHT Belfast 1992, Private Steve Naylor 'dominating'. (Note the contrast in weapon, equipment and dress with those of August 1969 in earlier photographs).

Bosnia 1993. ABOVE, LEFT Warrior patrol through a ruined village. RIGHT Lieutenant-Colonel Alastair Duncan with an HVO (Bosnian Croat) militia commander.

BELOW, LEFT Clearing the corpses from the streets of Vitez, Captain Lee Whitworth and Private Paul Weldrand. RIGHT Corporal Paul Dobson, MC.

to Aden on the third and last occasion while on Spearhead stand-by. Brigadier Dick Bishop commanding 19th Brigade, to which the battalion by then belonged, was quick to interest himself and his staff in the wives' and children's morale and welfare.

There was not an especially strong collective spirit amongst the wives and children during the five years the 1st Battalion was based in Colchester. There were several reasons for this, most prominently the fact that they were living in their own country with no language or cultural barriers to surmount. Not a few of the very young wives returned to their parents in Yorkshire during the battalion's service abroad. Those who remained were protected from any serious sense of isolation by being intermingled with families of other regiments in the extensive married quarter areas. The character of the White Rose Club changed, in that it became reactive to problems as they arose, rather than a means of banding together to foresee difficulties before they became acute.

A conclusion drawn from the Colchester period, which embraced the first emergency tour in Northern Ireland as well as two in Aden and several lengthy exercises overseas, was the essential need for a centre to which wives would be drawn once or twice each week through a common interest or hobby, keep-fit class, demonstration or talk, or as the start-point for excursions organized by the White Rose Club. At such a centre, calm and rational dissemination of news could become a matter of routine. These were the means by which a strong sense of community spirit and commitment were developed during later emergency and resident tours in Northern Ireland, at the time of the Gulf War and while the battalion was in Bosnia.

After Colchester, there was a general expectation that Cyprus would bring the wives and children into the regimental fold in much the same manner as Gibraltar and Berlin had done. But the circumstances were curiously different, at least in the early stages. Having been assured of being allocated a quarter or a local hiring there, many young soldiers took the opportunity to marry very shortly before the battalion left Colchester in February 1970. A total of 465 families were booked on flights due to arrive at the Akrotiri RAF airbase or Nicosia airport over a ten-day period. There was housing available for only 350 of them. The entire officer and warrant officer complement of the advance party ceased doing whatever they had gone to Cyprus to do and set out for Limassol and its suburbs to seek houses to let. The recently joined 2nd Lieutenant John Knopp achieved the record of finding, inspecting and negotiating the rent for twenty-four houses in a single day – so establishing his entrepreneurial reputation. Every family was housed on arrival, although not all to their satisfaction.

Once again, many of the new wives were in their teens and had previously left Yorkshire only on holiday with their parents. In the main the new wives were the ones who found themselves in the newly acquired, widely dispersed houses without neighbours whom they knew or felt they could trust. Many Cypriots speak English and are by nature friendly and helpful, but where and how to go shopping, the financial pitfalls to avoid and the unwelcome attention that a mini-skirt may attract all required careful explanation. Distance and undependable public transport made it difficult to draw these younger wives into a central point. They were therefore visited by the wives of officers, warrant officers and senior NCOs living not too far away and, more important than the visits themselves, a means of communication established for use in distress or emergency. Such visits were not welcomed by a few house-proud young ladies, who regarded them as 'inspections', but the majority enjoyed the chat and the contact.

The battalion was fortunate in its new-image families officer and his small staff. Captain Frank Walker[1] had been the regimental quartermaster-sergeant and more recently the motor transport officer. He therefore knew exactly how to get the best out of the Army system. More significantly, he had a different outlook and aspect from his gruff and grizzled predecessors. Although capable of giving a cold blue stare to anyone attempting to take advantage of his good nature, he had the welfare of the wives and children completely at heart and never spared himself in their service. His ability and dedication won their confidence from the outset, while his knack of foreseeing problems before they became acute was especially valuable. His assistant, Lance-Corporal Dennis Jolly,[2] had a similar personality and a mature outlook for so youthful an NCO. 'I'll be old before my time,' he would ruefully remark. 'Sometimes I feel like a grandfather already.'

Cyprus provided a splendid variety of activities for wives and children and places of excitement and interest to visit. It could be a place full of enjoyment but the autumn of 1970 brought intense sadness. Within little more than a month, four infant children died cot-deaths, causing understandable alarm amongst all families of the battalion. Even less was understood about this heart-breaking occurrence than is the case twenty-five years later and the blameless parents were desolate in their grief. One of the first to die in this way was the child of Corporal John Procter and his wife Carol. Then, very shortly afterwards, their four-year-old daughter was struck by a car on the Limassol bypass and died in hospital. As the commanding officer's wife, Angela Tillotson, tried to comfort her for a second time, Carol Procter looked up and said, 'We'll start again.' Their son, Stephen John Procter, was born in Akrotiri hospital on 23 August the following year.

When the 1st Battalion left Cyprus in March 1972, the White Rose Club had regained its former purpose and vigour. So many wives had contributed to this situation, but perhaps no one more than Sandra, wife of Regimental Sergeant-Major Laurie Linskey. Unhesitatingly forthright, she rescued many a tense situation with her warm-heartedness, laughter and common sense. On 6 November 1972 the Linskeys' younger daughter Angela married Sergeant Michael Sullivan in the church of St Pius X in Episkopi. One of the hymns sung to modern tunes was 'Michael, Row the Boat Ashore'. Sullivan did as he was bid and, in due course, became the regimental sergeant-major of the 1st Battalion himself.

Belfast in 1972 presented yet another new situation. At least everyone knew where they were – in Northern Ireland for a year and a half, complete with wives and children! This was the period when urban rioting was at its worst and the television screens daily showed the hatreds and horror of it all. While so close, the wives and children were insulated from the violence by being together in quarters within the battalion's base at Palace Barracks, five miles from the city centre. The chief advantage of being so near and yet so far was that the wives and children could be kept in close touch with what was really happening, rather than seeing the worst bits on television and anxiously waiting to hear whether husband and father was safe and well.

The battalion was the Province Reserve and so on-call at very short notice to despatch companies and platoons to reinforce other units in Belfast, Londonderry or elsewhere. The penalty was uncertainty as to what might happen next. A husband leaving his quarter at 0730 hours, hoping to be home in time for his daughter's birthday party, could find himself away from home for the night, or even for several days. Under these circumstances the White Rose Club became essential for the dissemination of news on what was happening, of when the men could be expected back and as a place where wives could seek advice and help in anxiety or difficulty.

The security situation limited access to facilities outside barracks that would have been commonplace and expected in England. The facilities were therefore built or developed within the safety of Palace Barracks. A kindergarten was open on weekdays, an indoor heated swimming pool was built and the tennis courts and gymnasium, there for the men in 'peacetime', were put at the disposal of wives and children for as much time as they could use them. There were 2,000 men, women and children living in the barracks. With the men so often deployed on security duties, it was essential that they felt confident that their wives and children were safe and cared for. The strength and value of the regimental family became apparent in Belfast to an extent not felt before.

Politicians able to grasp the crude essentials of their brief with an attorney's guile are apt to short-change the regimental system with a perfunctory nod. Their indifference arises not from hostility but lack of experience of any long-term commitment which could override personal aspiration. Theirs is the loss. The experience drawn by the 1st Battalion from Belfast in 1972–3 was carried forward to the next accompanied tour in Ballykinler in 1985–7, not just by the men but by their wives. The situation was similar in some ways and utterly different in others. The campaign had changed and rural south Armagh was the battalion's principal area of operations. Periods away from barracks were more predictable but potentially more dangerous. Watching and documenting the movements of a ruthless enemy had replaced containing mindless violence on the streets. These were the differences, but a visitor to Ballykinler in 1986 who had known Palace Barracks thirteen years earlier immediately felt on familiar ground. The regimental family appeared much younger but was clearly just as strong.

The intervening years in Celle and Bulford brought stresses of their own. Two unaccompanied tours in Londonderry, each of four months' duration, disrupted battalion life in Celle that was both professionally invigorating for the men and enjoyable for their families. The separation seemed less easy to accept, possibly because the wives and children were themselves in a foreign, albeit friendly, environment. Activity to keep everyone busy and unworried was clearly the key. To help in this endeavour, the wife of the Colonel of the Regiment, Penelope Armour, went to Celle to stay with the wives while her husband visited the men in Londonderry. This gesture had an effect beyond all expectations. Everyone had a sense of shared commitment and enjoyed themselves as well. It was a success to be repeated in later years, with an equally effective outcome.

Although the 1st Battalion was debarred from service in Ulster while at Bulford, due to their NATO AMF(L) role, the wives and children still had to face long periods of separation from husbands and fathers. The annual Hardfall exercises, held in Norway or some other extremity of the NATO area, took up all of February and March. Thus the wives and children were thrown onto their own resources during what are often the dreariest months of the English winter. The White Rose Club again became the focus for activity, with visits to such varied points of interest as the Poole Pottery and the Southampton ice-rink alternating with events at home.

Suddenly these valued trips away from not very exciting Bulford were curtailed by demise of the battalion's aged minibus. Months passed as the promptly ordered replacement failed to materialize. The commanding officer's wife, Holly Filor, was not constrained by any undue regard for those in positions of authority, particularly if they were failing to live up to her expectations. Exasperated by the minibus situation and noticing a full-page *Daily Telegraph* advertisement urging readers, 'Don't knock the British Bulldog – buy British Leyland', she wrote a sharp letter to Sir Michael Edwardes, then in charge of BL, from whom the new bus had been ordered. '*Mr* Edwardes,' she demanded, 'I wish to know why the White Rose minibus is eighteen months late in delivery.' Edwardes, of course, had not the least idea why, but the bus was delivered – insured and licensed – at the beginning of the following week.

The families officer and his small staff continued to play an important part in all this activity. Major Michael Orum ran the office in Berlin 1983–5 and was assisted, at least in the early stages, by Corporal Alan Whiting who had served with the 1st Battalion for as long as anyone wished to remember. Whiting knew every*one*, if not absolutely every*thing*! His work in the families office brought him into contact with service youth clubs and, through them, into contact with Berlin youth clubs. This work seized an imagination that had clearly lacked adequate stimulation in the past. Before long, Corporal Whiting became 'Mr Youth Clubs Berlin'. He organized a vast jamboree of youth clubs and sent an invitation to the General Officer Commanding beginning 'Corporal Whiting requests the pleasure . . .' The General turned up, properly dressed and bang on time. It came as no surprise, other than to himself, when Corporal Whiting received the British Empire Medal in the New Year Honours list for 1986.[3]

During the remaining years of the span of this story, men of the 1st Battalion endured two periods of separation from their wives and children when the men were felt to be in greater danger than when in Aden or Ulster. These were the periods of the Gulf War in 1990–91, when 149 officers and men of the 1st Battalion served with other units during the liberation of Kuwait, and when the entire battalion served with the United Nations Protection Force in Bosnia in 1993. Both situations received relentless coverage by the news media and were attended by an atmosphere of suspense, due to constantly changing political circumstances, threats by the Iraqis and by the Bosnian Serbs and restrictions on news of operational movements. Although only part of the battalion went to the Gulf, contingents were sent away from Osnabrück to guard Operation Granby garrisons left empty by whole units deployed and to Emden to guard port facilities.

During the period of the build-up and actual operations of the Gulf War, the wives and children of the men sent to Saudi Arabia had the support of battalion headquarters and the rest of the wives to help sustain them. Again the White Rose Club provided the centre for up-to-date information and the point to which wives needing advice or help could turn. Sergeant Brian 'Knocker' Knowles ran a special course at Tiefenbach in Bavaria to teach the wives and children of those serving in the Gulf how to ski. When Her Royal Highness The Duchess of Kent visited the battalion on 12 February 1991, her first request was to meet the wives and children of the men in the Gulf. Mercifully, all the men returned safely.

Between the Gulf War and deployment to Bosnia, from November 1991 to May 1992, the 1st Battalion served on a six-months' emergency tour in Belfast. An incident during this period casts light on the strong sense of family commitment of which everyone was conscious. Private Paul Shirt was wounded and blown across the road by a remotely controlled bomb. As he was to put it afterwards, he was 'shaken but not stirred'. Quickly evacuated to the command post at North Howard Street Mill, he was being handed a cup of tea by Regimental Sergeant-Major Michael Haynes when the commanding officer, Alastair Duncan, had the idea that Paul should telephone his wife in Osnabrück. The call was put through. Joanne Shirt was also shaken but stirred only by the thoughtfulness of her husband in letting her know that he was not seriously hurt.

Other than for a small rear party under command of Major Terry Darley,[4] the entire battalion went to Bosnia, leaving the wives and children in Osnabrück in the care of the families officer. This was Captain Paul Mizon for the first three months and then Captain Alan Wright for 'the second half', so to speak. The strength of the White Rose Club had been tested and not found wanting during the battalion's tour in Belfast but Bosnia provided the Club with its sternest test to date. As in the past, the Club became the information centre for the wives. A fortnightly newsletter was published and outings to places of interest were arranged. The local German community demonstrated the appreciation felt for the men serving in Bosnia. The local Volkstruppen (Army Reservists) association and Anglo-German Club in Osnabrück organized outings for the wives and children and the local Euro-MP attended a champagne and strawberry picnic for them.

The Club's chairman was Chrissy Watson, wife of the battalion second-in-command. The citation for the Certificate of Commendation which she received from the General Officer Commanding 1st Armoured Division after the men's return read: 'Mrs Watson became the focus for all welfare activities throughout the traumatic six months' tour. Despite the obvious needs of her own family, her commitment to the families was total and selfless. Mrs Watson made an outstanding contribution to the overall success of the battalion's achievements in Bosnia.' On hearing of her award, Chrissy Watson remarked, 'I wish that this was a joint award, as none of this would have been possible without a team effort. Luckily for me, we had a great team.'

12
In Bosnia

'Weary of war, but cheered by hopes of peace
and quite determined to see the matter out.'
W. S. CHURCHILL[1]

There are some who say that the Muslims of Bosnia-Herzegovina brought disaster on themselves. The Bosnian Serbs would argue that separation of Bosnia from Yugoslavia was Muslim-inspired – something only the Muslims wished to see. The truth is less straightforward but there was a catastrophe just the same.

Yugoslavia emerged from the Second World War as a federal republic led by the Croat-Slovene Josip Broz (Tito). His Communist guerrillas had defeated the Serbian 'Chetniks' in a bitter civil war that the occupying German-led Axis forces attempted to control only so far as suited them. The defeated Serbs had to wait until Tito's death before they could renew their centuries-old struggle for supremacy. Anticipating a struggle for power, Tito decreed that he should be succeeded by a collective presidency of the leaders of the six federated states.[2] This worked well enough until the resurgence of Serbian nationalism under Slobodan Milosevic in the late 1980s. When it was the turn of the President of Croatia to succeed to the chair of the collective presidency, Milosevic engineered a majority to block the change and Yugoslavia began to fall apart.

The population of Serbia proper, excluding the northern province of Vojvodina and Kosovo in the south-west, is virtually homogeneous. Croatia was much the same but with a Serbian minority of some 600,000 settled along the border regions and around Krajina. (See Map 14 on page 219.) The blocking of Croatia's turn to chair the collective presidency led to a Croat-Serb confrontation in 1991 and fierce fighting broke out in the Croatia-Serbia border areas as soon as Croatia received diplomatic recognition as an independent state.[3] The United Nations first became involved with the formation of the United Nations Protection Force (UNPROFOR) to provide humanitarian aid to Croats and Serbs in the disputed regions on the state borders. Under Security Council Resolution 743 of 21 February 1992, the UN Force was given a mandate 'to create the conditions of peace and security required for the negotiation of an overall settlement of the crisis'.[4] Sarajevo, the nearby capital of Bosnia-Herzegovina, then still at peace, was chosen as the site for the UN headquarters because it is well situated in relation to the disputed Croatian and Serbian border areas without being in either country.

In contrast to both Serbia and Croatia, Bosnia-Herzegovina has a history as a separate state dating only from 1945 and a more evenly divided ethnic grouping. Before the civil war that began in March 1992, forty-four percent were Muslims, thirty-two percent Serbs and seventeen percent Croats. The Government which came to power following the first post-Communist, multi-party elections in 1990 was a Muslim-Serb-Croat coalition led by Alija Izetbejovic, a Muslim.

Shortly before the state elections of November 1990, Serbs in Bosnia-Herzegovina (the Bosnian Serbs) formed the Serb Democratic Party (SDS) and declared a policy of a 'seamless Serbian nation'. This implied some form of union between the Bosnian Serbs and Serbia proper and, by inference, a challenge to any future Government of Bosnia-Herzegovina. An SDS 'Serb national council' set itself up at Banja Luka and began charting the Serbian populated areas of Bosnia-Herzegovina, linking them by actual or potential corridors under Bosnian Serb control. This group of so-called 'autonomous regions' was referred to by the Bosnian Serbs as the 'Serb Republic of Bosnia-Herzegovina' – a wholly unofficial title quickly abbreviated in general usage to the 'Serb Republic'. In consequence, no little confusion arose in the minds of journalists and politicians, particularly those remote from the scene, between Slobodan Milosevic's Republic of Serbia and the groups of Bosnian Serbs led by the increasingly confident and intransigent Radovan Karadzic.

Although a part of the 1990 coalition Government of Bosnia-Herzegovina (hereafter referred to simply as Bosnia), the SDS obstructed all significant political business. Amongst legislation awaiting approval were measures to enhance the status of Bosnia as one of Yugoslavia's sovereign, but not at that stage 'independent', states. When a vote on the inviolability of Bosnia's frontiers was called, Karadzic led his deputies from the chamber. Outside, he declared that sovereignty for Bosnia (separate from Yugoslavia) was impossible without their consent, helpfully adding that in any case consent would not be forthcoming. Frustrated, President Alija Izetbegovic requested the European Community's recognition of a sovereign and independent Bosnia to echo the status already granted to Slovenia and Croatia. This request was repudiated by Karadzic, with a rider that should Bosnia receive international recognition as an independent state, his 'Serb Republic' would remain part of federal Yugoslavia.

At this delicate stage, European Community political leaders were looking increasingly impotent. Unanimity of view extended no further than a wish not to become involved in the murder and mayhem taking place in the Croatia-Serbia border regions. Propelled by a wish to be seen by the rest of the world to be doing something, as a precondition of recognition of Bosnia-Herzegovina as an independent state, they invited Izetbegovic to conduct a referendum on the question of Bosnia's independence from Yugoslavia. While this proposal had a constitutional legitimacy consistent with Western European practice, it took no account of the volatility of Balkan political passions.[5]

On Sunday, 1 March 1992 the electorate was asked to answer the question: 'Are you in favour of a sovereign and independent Bosnia-Herzegovina, a state of equal citizens and nations of Muslims, Serbs and Croats, and others who live in it?' It was a question that could scarcely have been more fairly or clearly put. Almost two-thirds of the electorate voted 'Yes'. On the day following international recognition of Bosnia-Herzegovina as a sovereign independent state, the Bosnian Serbs opened hostilities against both the Bosnian Muslims and the Bosnian Croats. At the same time, advance parties of UN-PROFOR, tasked with helping Croats and Serbs in Croatia, began arriving in Sarajevo.

The outbreak of civil war in Bosnia presented the UN with a new dimension of horror which, initially at least, they had no means to curb. April and May were wasted in bickering between the UN and the European Community as to which of them should grasp the Bosnian nettle. Finally, on 8 June, the Security Council adopted Resolution 758(1992). This enlarged UNPROFOR to allow delivery

Map 14 *Bosnia-Herzegovina (courtesy* The Times)

of humanitarian supplies to besieged communities in Bosnia, with the deployment of troops 'contingent upon an effective and durable cease-fire in Sarajevo', where the fiercest fighting was taking place. This qualification also reflected an intention to use Sarajevo airport as the principal means of delivering the aid. Deployment of UN military observers was to be followed by one of a 1,000-strong infantry battalion 'to maintain security of the airport'. The emphasis was solely on humanitarian aid for refugees.

By the time the Security Council had approved resolution 776 (1992) three months later on 14 September, it was estimated that

100,000 people had died in interfactional fighting in Bosnia and many thousands more had been injured or driven from their homes. Bosnian Serb militias[6] had established control over almost seventy percent of the country, leaving the Croats and Muslims squeezed into the enclaves shown on Map 14. The UN resolution authorized an expansion of UNPROFOR to a strength of 'four or five battalions' to provide armed escort for humanitarian convoys of the UN High Commission for Refugees (UNHCR) in Bosnia and to protect detainees to be released from two Serb-controlled camps and escort them to safety. It did not authorize UN troops to use force, except when their own lives came under immediate threat or to prevent the aid supplies from being stolen. But the act of escorting detainees to safety gave further credence to the local false belief that UNPROFOR was there to protect the population.

The British contribution to the new initiative took the form of a battle-group based on the 1st Cheshires and a squadron of the 9th/12th Royal Lancers on a six months' tour of duty, beginning in early November 1992. Codenamed Operation Grapple, the primary task of the British contingent was to escort humanitarian aid convoys, provided by the UNHCR, to besieged enclaves of Bosnians of any faction in desperate need. Towards the end of 1st Cheshires' tour of duty, the rules for the use of force by UN troops were modified so that they could afford some protection for civilians but only if they were seeking sanctuary in certain designated areas. In implementation of this policy, the Security Council approved resolution 824 (1993), which declared Sarajevo, Bihac, Foca, Goradze, Srebrenica, Tuzla and Zepa 'safe havens' free from armed attack. UN troops were committed 'to monitor' the security of these areas.

The 1st Prince of Wales's Own, having returned from a six months' emergency tour in Ulster in May 1992, was stood-by to relieve 1st Cheshires in Bosnia in May 1993. Based in the German city of Osnabrück in the armoured infantry role, the battalion was in the process of converting to the use of Warrior armoured fighting vehicles, which had already proved their worth in Bosnia. Confirmation was received with a sense of professional satisfaction in January; but only three months remained for testing the Warrior crews and weapons and for the briefing, training and administrative preparations essential for a dangerous and demanding commitment.

All was accomplished with the customary expenditure of sweat and expletives. The Warriors were painted white and despatched by sea for the Adriatic port of Split. (To avoid the local population being misled into thinking that the UN had taken over their country or that German soldiers were being sent to Bosnia, the blue 'UN' signs were not allowed to be added until after the vehicles had arrived in theatre – but no one seemed in the least concerned about the signs when the vehicles returned six months later.) The battalion and the wives and children who were to be left behind were greatly heartened when the Colonel-in-Chief, Her Royal Highness The Duchess of Kent, visited them in Osnabrück on 23 April to wish the men a successful humanitarian mission in Bosnia and a safe return.

The region of central Bosnia in which the then single British battle-group was deployed underwent a dramatic and significant break in local allegiance in April 1993. Until then, Bosnian Croats and Muslims had fought alongside each other against the Bosnian Serbs, who surrounded the Croat and Muslim redoubt on three sides. In a sudden switch in alliance, believed in this instance to have arisen from a Croat suspicion that the Serbs and Muslims were about reach an overall agreement, the Croats turned against their Muslim partners. Ninety-two civilians, including women and children, were massacred in the Muslim village of Ahmici, south-east of Vitez, and the whole place set ablaze. On the day before responsibility passed to his battle-group, Lieutenant-Colonel Alastair Duncan helped to remove the charred bodies of a Muslim family from the remains of their house in Armici.

Speaking to the press shortly after this incident, Duncan pointed to the area on the map that he assessed as his first major trouble spot – the Lasva valley, which runs south-east from Turbe before turning south-west towards Kiseljak, fifteen miles west of the capital Sarajevo. Croats and Muslims in the Turbe-Kiseljak valley had begun competing in the odious practice of 'ethnic cleansing', that is murdering or driving out people of the other faction to make the village homogenous.

The 1st Prince of Wales's Own battle group comprised the battalion reinforced by three platoons, one each from the 1st Queen's Lancashires, 1st Gordon Highlanders and the 1st Argyll and Sutherland Highlanders, with B Squadron The Light Dragoons[7] and a field troop of the Royal Engineers under command. Battle-group

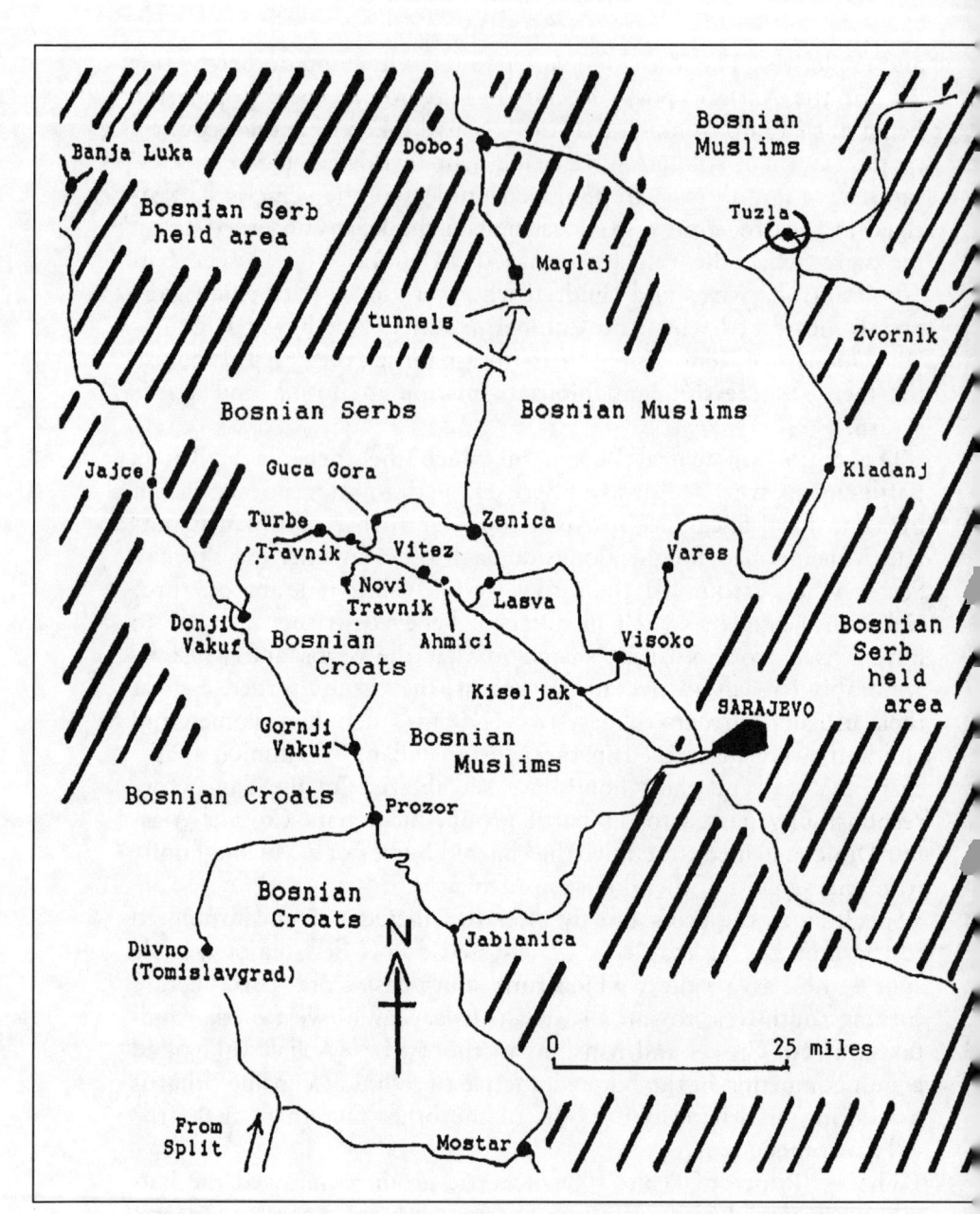

Map 15 *Central Bosnia*
1st Prince of Wales's Own battle-group territorial area of responsibility (TAOR), which excluded Sarajevo. (The Bosnian Croat controlled area extended north of Travnik to Guca Gora and eastwards towards Zenica.)

headquarters was established at Vitez, in the centre of the territorial area of responsibility (TAOR). The three rifle companies and B Squadron Light Dragoons were each allocated to a specific area and made into balanced, all-arms sub-units by allocation of troops of the Dragoons' Scorpion light tanks and sections of Milan anti-tank guided missiles and 81 mm mortars from the battalion's Support Company, reinforced by support weapon specialists from the 1st Argylls. As Support Company was broken up, Major David Hill became the Operations Major at battle-group headquarters.

A Company Group (Major Roy Hunter) was initially based at Vitez with a troop of Light Dragoons and the platoon of 1st Queen's Lancashires. B Company (Major Graham Binns), with the battalion reconnaissance platoon under command, deployed to Gornji Vakuf, some fifteen miles from Vitez down a tortuous track running south from Novi Travnik. C Company (Major Vaughan Kent-Payne) was also at Vitez with a troop of Light Dragoons and a platoon of 1st Gordons. B Squadron Light Dragoons, commanded by Major Marcus Browell, was initially deployed to Tuzla in the extreme northern sector of the TAOR and was reinforced by a Warrior platoon from the battalion. The Lancashire and Scottish reinforcements got on very well with everyone, helped by good-humoured banter about what various things are called. The Geordies in the Dragoons were universally popular, although only the Bosnians made any pretence of understanding what they were talking about.

In all, the battle group's TAOR covered territory extending over 5,400 square kilometres. Deployment coincided with the breakdown of the alliance of convenience, already explained, between the militias of the Croat HVO (Hrvatska Vijece Obrane or Croat Defence Force) and the BiH (Bosnian-Muslim Army) against the Bosnian Serbs. While the breakdown did not apply to the whole area, Tuzla being the principal exception, it led to most of the fighting in central Bosnia becoming three-sided. This made it more difficult than previously for UN detachment commanders to set up local arrangements for safe passage of the UNHCR aid and food convoys they were charged to protect.

Soldiers deployed on United Nations peacekeeping or protection duties face a dilemma when dealing with the armed factions in any conflict and the civilian population intermingled with them. No matter how carefully or frequently the UN mandate is explained, the faction at a disadvantage, even if only temporarily, cannot comprehend why the armed UN troops do not fight to support or at least protect them. Equally, the faction with the upper hand will be quick to accuse the UN troops of being partisan if they try to shelter soldiers or civilians of the weaker side. Impartiality of approach is a fine principle but often a trial to maintain under personal stress or insult, or when some horrific outrage has been committed by one side or another. It is sometimes said that British troops excel in these trying circumstances. If this is so, then it is a credit to their sense of fairness and sympathy for others in danger or distress, as much as to their professionalism and training.

Colonel Duncan defined the battle-group's mission as being 'to create the conditions whereby humanitarian aid could be delivered into and through the area of responsibility'. From the outset he recognized that success would crucially depend on possession of information on local attitudes, conditions and vehicle routes. For this information Duncan depended on his day-to-day personal contacts with the now-opposing local BiH and HVO commanders, on information from the European Community Monitoring Mission,[8] on patrols mounted by the battle-group and perhaps to the greatest extent, on liaison officers with the various factions. These were young captains from the battalion or detached from other units in Britain or Germany. Their tasks were to establish themselves with their factional group, move about in the region under that group's control, keep a lookout for trouble and for potential alternative routes for the delivery of humanitarian aid.

Captain Lee Whitworth of the battalion was the LO for Vitez and found himself under unremitting pressure, despite the close proximity of battle-group HQ. His own account of just one series of incidents requires no embellishment:

> For some months, the front line between the Croat HVO and Muslim BiH militias ran 100 yards from the battalion camp at Vitez. Much of my time was spent trying to persuade the local militia commanders not to fire in the immediate vicinity, so to avoid UN soldiers being caught in the cross-fire. The BiH held the high ground and claimed many successes in sniping attacks on the local Croat community. Several Croats had been shot dead and their bodies left on the road nearby. Exasperated by

this, after their own compliance with a locally arranged ceasefire, the HVO exacted swift retribution. At 0100 hours a barrage of shells fell in an area which included the camp perimeter and HVO rocket launchers pounded the Muslim-held village of Grbavica. After fifteen minutes of shelling, I drove in a Warrior with my Croat interpreter, Suzanna Hubjar, to appeal to the HVO for a halt to the onslaught. As we drove through Grbavica, few Muslim militiamen were apparent and, at the Croat HVO headquarters, staff officers blandly refused to accept that any bombardment was taking place.

Next morning, we emerged to find local Muslims seeking refuge and our protection. The Croat assault continued throughout that and the following day, with HVO infantry clearing the village house by house. By afternoon of the second day, every building was on fire, a few bodies were apparent and HVO militia were walking round the former BiH trenches. One group waved their weapons jubilantly as I passed. Aware that a group of about thirty Muslims were hiding in a house under UN protection, Suzanna and I managed to divert the attention of the HVO away from the house until the Muslims could be evacuated to Travnik. Suzanna and I entered the house to find men, women and children crying hysterically, on their knees begging for protection. Suzanna, herself a Croat,[9] was in tears. We quickly relieved the Muslims of their weapons and military clothing and, through the prompt arrival of four Warriors from C Company, managed to get them to the Travnik refugee centre. A happy ending of sorts.

Captains Lee Whitworth and Mark Bower were both awarded the Queen's Gallantry Medal for their work as liaison officers.

Crossfire became direct fire into the Vitez camp during the night of 28 May. Lance-Corporal Steve Bingley of A Company fired three aimed shots at the Croat trenches from which the fire had come. Commenting on this incident to the press, Colonel Duncan pointed out that this was the first occasion on which any of his men had opened fire but concluded by saying, 'If the camp is engaged, I'll fire again.' During the entire six months in Bosnia, fire was returned by the battle-group on sixty-nine occasions.

The UNHCR convoy routes for which the battle group was

responsible were varied in difficulty and in risk. There were two main UNHCR warehouses in the area – one at Zenica and the other at Tuzla. Zenica received resupply convoys from Croatia along the Sapper-improved Diamond and Triangle routes through Dunvo (Tomislavgrad) to Prozor and then along the road Gornji Vakuf–Turbe–Travnik–Zenica and also from Zagreb through Banja Luka, Donji Vakuf and Turbe. Supplies to Tuzla came either from Belgrade through Zvornik or were uplifted from Zenica, along the main road south-east through Visoko and then through the hills via Vares and Kladanj. The battle-group was chiefly concerned with escorting resupply convoys to Zenica and Tuzla. From these main distribution centres, aid convoys had to be escorted along the front of the Serbian lines to Kladanj, south of Tuzla, and from Vitez northwards to Maglaj and south-eastwards to Kiseljak.

An account of one convoy escort tells what each one might expect. This is given in the words of Lance-Corporal Michael Brown, one of the individual reinforcements from the 1st King's.

> We had been warned that Maglaj had been shelled but the UNHCR was determined to get the convoy through the tunnels south of the town. There was no room in the last tunnel to turn round, so we went in two at a time. My Warrior, callsign D32, paused at the far exit just as the shelling started again with a direct hit on the UNHCR depot in the town. I told the UNHCR drivers to move their trucks back into the tunnel and shouted for them to get moving when a mortar round landed in front of my vehicle. They started to take photographs instead. Another explosion ripped through the tunnel, rocking my vehicle. I ordered the crew to close down, then we heard screams from the UNHCR drivers and staff.
>
> Once the shelling stopped, we had a chance to treat the casualties. The tunnel smelled of death, limbs were hanging off, steam was coming off the blood. The dead still had their eyes open. We moved the injured back to Warrior D33 and I checked that the rest of the casualties were dead. I ordered the men into D33, telling Lance-Corporal Andy Grant to get in touch with battle-group HQ. Only Corporal Dave Gillett and me were left in D32. More rounds landed and an UNHCR land cruiser came up and blocked us in; its driver got into the back of the Warrior

suffering from shock. We had noticed a railway tunnel which offered us a chance to turn round. We moved out, flattening the land cruiser on the way, and picked up D33 for the journey back to Zenica. The company commander tasked us to go back and collect the dead. On the way home we hardly spoke to each other; everyone was thinking about what had happened and how boring we thought the day was going to be.

Corporal Dave Gillett was subsequently mentioned in despatches for his organization of the evacuation of casualties from the Maglaj tunnel on this occasion.

Mines were a constant source of concern, either because they were placed on the road to halt a convoy and for all to see or, more insidious as a threat, buried on the track edges and verges. In all, eleven vehicles of the battle-group struck mines on roads or their verges. A reconnaissance party from B Company, under command of 2nd Lieutenant Gary Payne, set out from Gornji Vakuf on 31 May to find an alternative route to bypass Prozor to the south-east. The village was held by Bosnian Croats and B Company had found difficulty in negotiating safe-passage for aid convoys. After slowing for a bend in the route running north-east from the main road, the leading Warrior stuck a mine which blew off a section of track and threw several road wheels around. Apart from a few bruises, none of the crew was hurt. Sappers mine-cleared the road and a REME recovery vehicle was about to hitch up to the Warrior when another mine was struck. Miraculously, there were no casualties. Some weeks later Private Lee Furniss was seriously injured when the Warrior he was driving struck a mine just off the main supply route, some five kilometres from Gornji Vakuf.

Not infrequently it was necessary for the battle-group to send Warrior patrols to investigate the situation in areas being shelled or mortared, or where fighting was reported. Lieutenant Jason Medley of A Company led such a patrol to the Croat village of Guca Gora, ten miles north-west of Vitez, on 8 June. He takes up the story.

Mortars bracketed the village as heavy small-arms fire was exchanged between the advancing Muslims and defending Croats. We proceeded cautiously and found two groups of stranded and helpless civilians. Disabled people and a three-day old child were among those whom we escorted into the monastery under the Warriors' protection. A mortar bomb injured an elderly civilian. We gave him immediate first aid, pending his evacuation to hospital, together with the tiny baby. Major Hunter arrived in the late afternoon with Padre Carson Nicholson, whose calm approach eased the victims' confusion and despair. Blankets, hot soup and baby food were brought to see the group through the night in the candle-lit monastery.

During the night a Muslim attack was thwarted as we engaged them entering a firing point. Grenades were thrown against the Warriors' sides and tracer rounds flashed around us. There were no friendly casualties and fire was returned. Dawn broke and the civilian dead were laid to rest by the padre in a simple service. Muslim heavy machine-gun fire penetrated the monastery cloisters. Some 200 rounds of 7.62 mm chain-gun fire was returned while the commanding officer negotiated safe passage for the casualties and refugees. Eventually, thirty armoured vehicles from C Company moved the civilians to safety. We had saved 186 lives. [The total was actually 187, including the three-day-old child.]

UN soldiers were sometimes fired on by the side they were trying to help. In Vitez C Company drew up a plan to escort half-a-dozen Muslims to their houses, from which they had been 'ethnically cleansed' by Croat HVO militia on the previous day, to collect a few sacks of flour. Escorted by a couple of Warriors and a rifle section on foot, the Muslims pulled their barrow down the seemingly deserted street. Suddenly, HVO militiamen appeared in the path of the party waving Kalashnikovs and shouting. As the company commander went forward to negotiate, three sniper rounds were fired into the group by Muslim militia on the nearby high ground. 'I'm not prepared to get one of my soldiers shot for the sake of a few sacks of flour,' he concluded. After further negotiation with both sides, five men of C Company and the Muslim interpreter pulled a load of flour and potatoes back for the Muslims. No shots were fired.

Virtually all the major and minor incidents in which the battle-group became involved concerned inter-ethnic conflict between Croats and Muslims. Negotiations with Bosnian Serbs occurred only where the main supply routes crossed from areas under their control. The principal point of contact was at Travnik, through which the supply route from Zagreb ran via Banja Luka and the southern supply route from Prozor and Gornji Vakuf. It was also at Travnik that negotiations were made with the Bosnian Serbs for the transfer of several hundred displaced persons, which was accomplished without serious incident. This procedure, codenamed Operation Slaven, absorbed a great deal of staff planning effort and patience in carrying out. But the results were worthwhile, even when those exchanged or evacuated carried the grief of a lifetime on their faces and all their possessions in a single plastic bag. After the Muslims had made their main thrust southwards towards Vitez and Gornji Vakuf in May, following the collapse of the Croat-Muslim alliance, the strategic situation stabilized in central Bosnia and became one of deadlock. Vitez and Gornji Vakuf were UN pockets between the confronting Croat and Muslim militias. It was around Gornji Vakuf, astride the main supply line from the south, that the most serious inter-ethnic fighting took place. B Company's base was on the confrontation line and was shelled by accident and, on occasions deliberately, by both sides. Private Pete Woodward narrowly escaped death or serious injury when a mortar bomb fell through the roof above his fortunately empty bed space. Small-arms fire was frequently directed into the base and B Company were often obliged to take cover in their hard shelters. Even so, an intensive patrol programme was maintained and the southern supply route for aid convoys was kept open.

In early September the Croat HVO militia harassed B Company vehicles with heavy machine-gun fire for five successive days and use of wire-guided missiles against the Warriors threatened the continued use of the convoy route. Fire was returned but Major Graham Binns commanding the company, at significant personal risk, visited the militia units on both sides, told them of his wish to de-escalate the tension and placed his Warrior with the gun-turret pointing at neither but with the gun aligned between them. He remained in this situation for three hours to demonstrate his determination. For his coolness under fire and resolute leadership in detached command at Gornji Vakuf, Major Binns was subsequently awarded the Military Cross.

Croats and Muslims were equally guilty of sniping at each other, at civilians and into the UN bases and at UN vehicles. Sergeant Andy Williamson was dropping off a group of interpreters in the centre of

Gornji Vakuf when his party was engaged by small-arms fire. He was hit by one round in the shoulder but subsequently made a complete recovery. The proximity and therefore degree of danger of sniper fire was informally categorized by the expletive it produced. A shot which whistled only close enough to make everyone look up or turn round was classed simply as a 'bugger you'; but one which was close enough to cause real alarm was a 'bugger me'! Fire was returned against either category, whenever the point of fire could be identified.

On 3 July a patrol commanded by Corporal Paul Dobson from C Company came across a group of civilians trapped in a blazing apartment block in Novi Travnik, just to the west of the road from Vitez to Gornji Vakuf, where there was heavy fighting between the Croat and Muslim militias. Corporal Dobson positioned his Warriors to give cover and began to shepherd the terrified civilians into the vehicles to take them to safety. The HVO militia, realizing his intention, opened direct fire onto the Warriors causing the last civilian, a woman, to panic and dash out into the open. Dobson ran after her and brought her to the vehicle shielded by his body. For his leadership and example of selfless bravery, Paul Dobson was awarded the Military Cross. This was the first occasion that this decoration was awarded to any soldier below the rank of warrant officer.

During the whole six months of the battle-group's service in Bosnia, the area in and around Tuzla remained stable. As a safe haven for Croats in a mainly Muslim region, where both were being pressed by the Bosnian Serbs, it provided a convincing reason for continuation of the Croat-Muslim alliance that had collapsed elsewhere. B Squadron Light Dragoons, although conscious of the vulnerability of the 'finger' of Muslim-held territory stretching north-eastwards from the town, felt that their potential was perhaps wasted at Tuzla. They were therefore relieved by A Company from Vitez and redeployed to picket the main supply route north through Dunvo (Tomislavgrad). Tulza was later handed over to the UN Scandinavian contingent, allowing A Company to return to Vitez.

The situation in Vitez alternated between periods of relative calm and bursts of intense activity. These could be of an operational nature, such as the orchestration of aid convoys down the Lasva valley to Kiseljak and then up through Vares to Tuzla, or dealing with the stream of visitors and inquiries from press, radio and television reporters. It was decided to give frequent background briefings to the press, so that every reporter had a clear idea of what was happening and what was likely to happen next. Reporters' questions were given clear and straightforward answers, as is the Yorkshire custom, which bred the mutual confidence essential for good press relations. The day-to-day tasking of the battle-group was primarily driven by the need to get the aid convoys through to their destinations. For this Colonel Duncan depended on the regular flow of current information from his young liaison officers and the local agreements that he or his staff could set up between the BiH and HVO militias. A total of 923 primary convoys, from the outside supply points to the distribution centres at Zenica and Tuzla, turned up and were successfully escorted to their destinations. Some were delayed for as long as six hours and a few for twenty-four hours, while safe-passage was negotiated, but every one got through. This achievement represented delivery of 35,000 tonnes of aid. In addition, half a million displaced persons were fed.

In an effort to restore a brief element of normality in an otherwise desperately abnormal atmosphere, the battalion ran tea parties for some 4,000 children within the TAOR. A Warrior patrol would escort a couple of soft-skinned vehicles into a village, set up a few stalls and serve tea and buns. Soldiers would talk to the children, show them over the Warriors and probably enjoy the brief excursion into normality as much as the children themselves.

The battle-group was provided with a (male) psychiatric nurse to advise and help anyone who became seriously distressed by any horror that they had witnessed. Unfortunately, there were horrors in abundance, of which probably the worst was digging up bodies and returning them to relatives who had been forced out of their homes and moved elsewhere. This was a gruesome task but one which was of significant importance to the local people. Around one hundred men visited the psychiatric nurse. Twenty-five of these returned for a second consultation and three for a third. After a while visits to the nurse became of no great account. Asked where he had just been by a friend, one soldier retorted, 'I've been to see the psychiatric nurse, mate, because I've seen some action and you haven't.' And that was bloody that, as they would say. In all, fourteen men of the battalion were wounded or seriously injured as a result of action by one or other of the factions, or by mines.

Speaking after his return from Bosnia, Colonel Alastair Duncan reported, 'I was fortunate in the quality of my soldiers and that of my young officers.' He then went on to describe an incident when one of his subaltern officers drove round a corner in his Warrior to be rammed by the vehicle of General Praliac, commander of the Croat HVO. Praliac leaped out brandishing a pistol and shouting with rage. The subaltern removed his helmet, climbed out, called his interpreter and said, 'General, I don't know what you are doing but officers should not behave like that. Put that pistol away, calm down and behave like a gentleman.' General Praliac did as he was asked.

Shortly before The Prince of Wales's Own battle-group completed its tour of duty, Alastair Duncan called on General Praliac to say good-bye. At the close of the conversation, Praliac ventured, 'The British are very, very professional, they are very, very cold and you are also very arrogant.' Musing on this afterwards, Duncan decided that he could live with the personal description; his battalion had got the job done.

Epilogue

'The only contingency for which one can plan
with certainty is the unexpected.'
ADMIRAL OF THE FLEET LORD FIELDHOUSE

This was how that calm and and forthright Yorkshireman, who had commanded all the forces engaged in the 1982 Falklands War, concluded his lecture – as CDS – to the Staff College, Camberley in 1988. It is a message that might usefully be printed in blocks, starkly framed and hung opposite the desk of every politician and civil servant whose responsibilities could conceivably touch on matters of national defence. The fashion of 'fitting forces to contingencies' has proved to fail on every occasion, either because the contingency has manifested itself differently from what was expected or the danger has come from an entirely unexpected quarter. Iraq and Bosnia are the most obvious recent examples.

The cynically titled *Options for Change* defence review of 1990–2 was based not on the realistic conclusion that there is no clear forecast of what Britain's future defence commitments will be, which would suggest a need for balanced and flexible armed forces, but on a Treasury demand for reductions in the defence budget. While it was sensible to cut the Army's tank fleet to match the reduced threat in central Europe, the scale of reductions in other arms and supporting services had no equally compelling rationale. More dangerously, the planned reductions in naval and air force capabilities, short of extensive modernization programmes, will finally dispose of the pretence that Britain has any significant national 'clout' in defence matters on the international scene.

This story spans thirty-six years during which the British Army has changed from battledress to combat kit, from field dressings to drip-feeds administered in the field by a comrade, from struggling in the dark and rain with a grubby map to satellite navigation.

The conscripted National Serviceman has made way for the regular professional soldier, trained for war and to keep the peace. For sixteen of the same thirty-six years, the 1st Battalion of the regiment has spent time on active service and, aside from the periods in Gibraltar and Cyprus, all the rest 'fighting' the Cold War in one role or another. The Territorial battalions have had a part in this, by their contribution to NATO's readiness to confront the now-defunct Warsaw Pact.

Reviewing the tasks that the regiment has faced since 1958, only Aden – now in economic and political chaos – can be rated a failure, but that was due to lack of sound political perceptions and skill. Berlin is a free and flourishing city without a foreign garrison; Germany is united and reasonably friendly; Iraq is contained; and the ceasefire in Northern Ireland is holding, while the negotiators follow their wisely cautious minuet. Bosnia presents the primary current problem, but a settlement there can come only through dogged economic and political pressure on the Serbs – while soldiers of the United Nations try to buy time for the politicians – and save lives.

Experience in South Arabia pointed the way towards a more professional outlook than had been previously apparent. The wilderness of the Western Aden Protectorate gave everyone a feel for a naturally hostile environment, dangerous enough before the enemy put in an appearance. The need for ceaseless vigilance against the urban terrorist was learned in Crater – and did not have to be relearned for Londonderry and Belfast.

Six well-spaced tours of duty in Ulster provided education in techniques and technologies of terror and counter-terrorist operations, the penalties of competing intelligence structures, the gains to be made by planned community relations, thinking leadership at every level and constant attention to the morale and well-being of the wives and children left behind. War in the Gulf brought those there face-to-face with the advantages and risks of high technology weapons. Bosnia brought patience and compassion.

Gibraltar is no longer an infantry battalion station. Once Hong Kong has been returned to China in 1997, Cyprus will be the only garrison outside Continental Europe where an infantry battalion will be able to serve accompanied by wives and children. Currently, there appear to be sound politico-strategic arguments for keeping watch from a base there, on the edge of a still unsettled Middle East.

The colonial legacy of overseas garrison service has gone. So where should the much-changed, well-educated modern Army, with its wives and children, video television sets, good cars and high holiday expectations go from here? Should it look forward to becoming part of an international gendarmerie, rather than being an imperial one as during the nineteenth century and until the late 1930s? Such a role would continue to draw good men to the Colours in search of adventure, travel and advancement. Sport would still be keenly and fairly played, no doubt to new peaks of excellence. The unexpected would be matched by energy, resource and humour as it has always been.

The regiment is known in Yorkshire for what it represents in terms of professionalism and competitiveness. The reforming of the Territorial Army battalion is of exciting significance, because it restores the full concept of the integrated regiment, with both regular and volunteer battalions sharing a common territorial identity. It is a concept which has proved highly successful in the past and one which will be given an even sharper focus when the new Reserve Forces Act, allowing greater flexibility in the use of reserves, comes into force. Of particular relevance will be the powers to call out reservists for 'wider' humanitarian operations and disaster relief. Had the Act been in force in 1993, the forty volunteers from the 3rd Battalion would have been able to accompany the 1st Battalion to Bosnia. The future is alive with promise.

Throughout the period, the character of the Yorkshire soldier has stood undiminished. Although he can be perversely glum on the sunniest day, blunt of speech and scornful of pomp and show, his caustic wit inspires that final effort when the going really gets rough, while his resourcefulness and grit are surpassed only by a gentle humanity. He will not be the one caught out by the unexpected; he will have seen it coming, from way back, and told us all about it – several times.

APPENDIX I

Citation for the George Cross

The George Cross. Lieutenant Terence Edward Waters (463718) (deceased), The West Yorkshire Regiment (The Prince of Wales's Own), attached The Gloucestershire Regiment.

Lieutenant Waters was captured subsequent to the Battle of the Imjin River, 22nd-25th April, 1951. By this time he had sustained a serious wound in the top of the head and yet another most painful wound in the arm as a result of this action.

On the journey to Pyongyang with other captives, he set a magnificent example of courage and fortitude in remaining with wounded other ranks on the march, whom he felt it his duty to care for to the best of his ability.

Subsequently, after a journey of immense hardship and privation, the party arrived at an area west of Pyongyang adjacent to P.W. Camp 12 and known generally as 'The Caves' in which they were held captive. They found themselves imprisoned in a tunnel driven into the side of a hill through which a stream of water flowed continuously, flooding a great deal of the floor, in which were packed a great number of South Korean and European prisoners-of-war in rags, filthy, crawling with lice. In this cavern a number died daily from wounds, sickness or merely malnutrition: They fed on two small meals of boiled maize daily. Of medical attention there was none.

Lieutenant Waters appreciated that few, if any, of his numbers would survive these conditions, in view of their weakness and the absolute lack of attention for their wounds. After a visit from a North Korean Political Officer, who attempted to persuade them to volunteer to join a prisoner-of-war group known as the "Peace Fighters" (that is active participants in the propaganda movement against their own side) with a promise of better food, of medical treatment and other amenities as a reward for such activity – an offer that was refused unanimously – he decided to order his men to accede to the offer in an effort to save their lives. This he did, giving the necessary instructions to the senior other rank with the British party, Sergeant Hoper, that the men would go upon his order without fail.

Whilst realising that this act would save the lives of his party, he refused to go himself, aware that the task of maintaining British prestige was vested in him. Realising that they had failed to subvert an officer with the British party, the North Koreans now made a series of concerted efforts to persuade Lieutenant

APPENDIX I: CITATION FOR THE GEORGE CROSS 237

Waters to save himself by joining the camp. This he steadfastly refused to do. He died a short time after.

He was a young, inexperienced officer, comparatively recently commissioned from The Royal Military Academy, Sandhurst, yet he set an example of the highest gallantry.

London Gazette, 9 April 1954

APPENDIX 2
Roll of Honour

KILLED OR DIED OF WOUNDS OR INJURIES ON ACTIVE SERVICE

Sergeant Wilfred Sanderson Saville	Aden	1958
Lance-Corporal Bryan Foley	Western Aden Protectorate	1966
Private Frederick Walter Langrick	Aden	1966
Lance-Corporal Trevor Jeremy Holmes	Aden	1967
Lance-Corporal Leslie Thomas Roberts	Aden	1967
Staff Sergeant Arthur Place	Northern Ireland	1973
Private David Anthony Wray	Northern Ireland	1975
Major Christopher John Dockerty	Northern Ireland	1994

APPENDIX 3
A: *Honorary Appointments*

COLONELS-IN-CHIEF

Her Royal Highness Princess Mary The Princess Royal, CI, GCVO, GBE, RRC, TD, CD, DCL, LL. D	1958–65
Her Royal Highness The Duchess of Kent, GCVO	1985–

AIDES DE CAMP TO HER MAJESTY THE QUEEN

Brigadier T. R. Birkett, OBE	1974–75
Brigadier W. P. Sheppard, MC, TD	1977–81
Brigadier J. M. Cubiss, CBE, MC	1982–83
Colonel G. B. Smalley, OBE, TD	1994–

COLONEL COMMANDANT OF THE KING'S DIVISION

Major-General E. H. A. Beckett, CB, MBE	1988–94

COLONELS OF THE REGIMENT

Brigadier R. J. Springhall, CB, OBE	1958–60
Brigadier G. H. Cree, CBE, DSO	1960–70
Brigadier W. S. G. Armour, MBE	1970–79
Major-General H. M. Tillotson, CB, CBE	1979–86
Major-General A. B. Crowfoot, CB, CBE	1986–

HONORARY COLONELS OF TERRITORIAL BATTALIONS

3rd Battalion

Colonel R. B. Holden, DSO, TD, DL	1961–62
Colonel H. P. Robson, TD	1962–65
Colonel The Right Honourable The Earl of Halifax, DL	1965–71
Colonel E. A. K. Denison, OBE, TD	1993–

The Leeds Rifles

Brigadier J. N. Tetley, DSO, TD, DL	1961–63
Brigadier K. Hargreaves, CBE, TD, DL	1963–66
Colonel J. H. Taylor, CBE, TD, MA	1967–71
Colonel Sir Marcus Worsley, Bt, TD	1988–93

B: Regimental Appointments

COMMANDING OFFICERS
1st Battalion

Lieutenant-Colonel B. R. D. Garside, MC	Apr 1958 –Jun 1960
Lieutenant-Colonel W. S. G. Armour, MBE	Jun 1960-Nov 1962
Lieutenant-Colonel P. E. Taylor	Nov 1962–Apr 1965
Lieutenant-Colonel T. R. Birkett, OBE*	Apr 1965–Apr 1967
Lieutenant-Colonel W. A. E. Todd, OBE*	Apr 1967–Sep 1969
Lieutenant-Colonel H. M. Tillotson, OBE	Sep 1969–Oct 1971
Lieutenant-Colonel D. W. Hanson, OBE*	Oct 1971–Nov 1973
Lieutenant-Colonel A. B. Crowfoot, MBE	Dec 1973–Jun 1976
Lieutenant-Colonel E. H. A. Beckett, MBE	Jul 1976–Sep 1978
Lieutenant-Colonel F. J. W. Filor	Oct 1978–Apr 1981
Lieutenant-Colonel P. E. Woolley, OBE*	Apr 1981–Sep 1983
Lieutenant-Colonel R. H. J. Forsyth	Sep 1983–Mar 1986
Lieutenant-Colonel D. A. H. Green	Mar 1986–Sep 1988
Lieutenant-Colonel J. C. L. King, MBE	Sep 1988–Nov 1990
Lieutenant-Colonel A. D. A Duncan, DSO,* OBE*	Dec 1990–Nov 1993
Lieutenant-Colonel C. G. Le Brun	Dec 1993–

3rd Battalion

Lieutenant-Colonel N. H. Bryan, OBE,* TD	Feb 1961–Aug 1962
Lieutenant-Colonel P. P. Steel, MC	Sep 1962–Feb 1965
Lieutenant-Colonel E. A. K. Dennison, TD	Mar 1965–Mar 1967
Lieutenant-Colonel T. H. F. Farrell, TD	Apr 1967–Mar 1969 (Apr 1969–Apr 1993)†
Lieutenant-Colonel A. C. G. Blanch	Apr 1993–Sep 1993
Lieutenant-Colonel C. J. M. Wood, TD	Sep 1993–

The Leeds Rifles

Lieutenant-Colonel E. W. Clay, MBE	Feb 1961–Jan 1964
Lieutenant-Colonel D. H. Rawlings, TD	Jan 1964–Jul 1966
Lieutenant-Colonel G. Jarratt, TD	Jul 1966–Mar 1969 (Apr 1969–Apr 1993)†

* Award made for service while in command of the battalion.
† Battalion incorporated as companies of the Yorkshire Volunteers.

APPENDIX 3: REGIMENTAL APPOINTMENTS

ADJUTANTS

1st Battalion

Captain W. P. Sheppard, MC	Apr 1958–Nov 1958
Captain J. Halmshaw	Dec 1958–Aug 1960
Captain D. H. Dodd	Aug 1960–Jul 1962
Captain S. J. Burnip	Aug 1962–Jul 1964
Captain A. B. Crowfoot	Aug 1964–Jun 1966
Captain F. J. W. Filor	Jun 1966–Jun 1968
Captain T. C. E. Vines	Jul 1968–Apr 1970
Captain P. E. Woolley	Apr 1970–May 1972
Captain P. D. Orwin, MC	May 1972–Jun 1974
Captain D. B. St J. Lyburn	Jun 1974–Sep 1976
Captain N. S. Porter	Sep 1976–Jul 1978
Captain J. L. Davies	Jul 1978–Feb 1979
Captain A. D. A. Duncan	Feb 1979–Dec 1980
Captain C. G. Le Brun	Dec 1980–Aug 1983
Captain D. A. Barley	Sep 1983–Jul 1985
Captain G. J. Binns	Jul 1985–Dec 1986
Captain A. J. Stevenson	Dec 1986–Jul 1987
Captain K. Howard	Jul 1987–Feb 1988
Captain S. Padgett	Feb 1988–Oct 1989
Captain C. J. Schofield	Oct 1989–Aug 1991
Captain A. T. Jackson	Aug 1991–May 1993
Captain T. E. Wagstaff	May 1993–

3rd Battalion

Captain P. T. Ryan	Feb 1961–Mar 1963
Captain D. A. Rodwell	Mar 1963–Oct 1965
Captain M. R. Jackson	Oct 1965–Dec 1968
Captain J. J. Brasher	Apr 1993–Oct 1994
Captain H. Newson	Oct 1994–

QUARTERMASTERS

1st Battalion

Major G. Watson, MBE	Apr 1958–Oct 1962
Captain L. K. Borrett, MBE	Oct 1962–Jun 1963
Captain S. Gibson	Jun 1963–Feb 1966
Captain H. Rushworth	Feb 1966–Jan 1968
Captain J. Long, MBE*	Jan 1969–Jun 1974
Major F. Walker	Jun 1974–May 1977
Major E. Bostock	May 1977–Jun 1979
Captain J. M. P. Dillon	Jun 1979–Aug 1981

* Awarded for service while Quartermaster of the battalion.

QUARTERMASTERS
1st Battalion (continued)

Captain P. Blyth	Aug 1981–Apr 1985
Major K. W. Miles	Apr 1985–Dec 1987
Major T. H. Senior	Dec 1987–Sep 1989
Captain D. A. Matthews	Sep 1989–Aug 1991
Captain B. J. Crummack	Aug 1991–May 1992
Captain B. Cawkwell	May 1992–

3rd Battalion

Major L. J. Wood, MBE	Feb 1961–Feb 1963
Lieutenant E. Mottram	Feb 1963–Dec 1964
Lieutenant-Colonel C. J. Robinson, MBE	Dec 1964–Dec 1968
Captain B. Atkinson	Apr 1993–Jan 1994
Captain M. T. Haynes	Jan 1994–

The Leeds Rifles

Captain J. Blagdon	Feb 1961–Dec 1961
Captain M. Emmott	Dec 1961–Jan 1963
Lieutenant-Colonel G. Watson, MBE	Jan 1963–May 1965
Lieutenant H. Rushworth	May 1965–Jan 1966
Captain G. S. Hutchinson	Jan 1966–Dec 1968

REGIMENTAL SERGEANT–MAJORS
1st Battalion

Regimental Sergeant-Major N. D. Taylor	Apr 1958–Jul 1961
Regimental Sergeant-Major C. L. Wiley	Aug 1961–Sep 1962
Regimental Sergeant-Major W. T. Wall	Oct 1962–Jul 1965
Regimental Sergeant-Major B. Campey	Aug 1965–Feb 1968
Regimental Sergeant-Major R. C. Fenn	Mar 1968–Jan 1970
Regimental Sergeant-Major L. Linskey	Feb 1970–Oct 1972
Regimental Sergeant-Major J. M. P. Dillon	Jan 1973–Dec 1974
Regimental Sergeant-Major P. Blyth	Jan 1975–Dec 1977
Regimental Sergeant-Major A. Bostock	Dec 1977–Jul 1979
Regimental Sergeant-Major T. R. Darley	Aug 1979–Aug 1982
Regimental Sergeant-Major M. L. Sullivan	Sep 1982–May 1985
Regimental Sergeant-Major B. J. Crummack	May 1985–Mar 1987
Regimental Sergeant-Major B. Cawkwell	Mar 1987–Jan 1989
Regimental Sergeant-Major B. Atkinson	Jan 1989–Feb 1991
Regimental Sergeant-Major M. T. Haynes	Feb 1991–Jul 1992
Regimental Sergeant-Major A. Adair	Jul 1992–Jul 1994
Regimental Sergeant-Major C. W. Lister	Jul 1994–

APPENDIX 3: REGIMENTAL APPOINTMENTS

REGIMENTAL SERGEANT-MAJORS

3rd Battalion

Regimental Sergeant-Major N. Maddocks	Feb 1961–Nov 1963
Regimental Sergeant-Major J. Peterson	Nov 1963–Apr 1964
Regimental Sergeant-Major P. Savidge	Apr 1964–May 1967
Regimental Sergeant-Major H. A. Howard	May 1967–Dec 1968
Regimental Sergeant-Major M. H. Robinson	Apr 1993–Jun 1993
Regimental Sergeant-Major R. F. Cantrell	Jun 1993–

The Leeds Rifles

Regimental Sergeant-Major H. C. Smith	Feb 1961–Jun 1962
Regimental Sergeant-Major J. Guthrie	Jul 1962–Jul 1963
Regimental Sergeant-Major P. Suddaby	Jul 1963–Mar 1967
Regimental Sergeant-Major P. H. Bullen	Mar 1967–Dec 1968

BANDMASTERS

The Regimental Band

Bandmaster A. R. Pinkney, ARCM	Apr 1958–Jan 1965
Bandmaster P. G. Richards	Jan 1965–Apr 1968
Bandmaster T. P. Platts, ARCM	Apr 1968–Sep 1972
Bandmaster R. A. Martin	Sep 1972–May 1981
Bandmaster K. C. Shell, ARCM	May 1981–Sep 1984
Bandmaster S. A. Thompson, ARCM	Jan 1985–Jun 1993
Bandmaster D. J. Bertie	Jun 1993–Jul 1994

The Band of the 3rd Battalion

Bandmaster E. Nicholson*	Feb 1961–Feb 1965
Bandmaster C. Dennis	Jul 1965–Aug 1967
Bandmaster M. Hardman	Apr 1995–

The Leeds Rifles Band

Bandmaster A. S. Swain, MBE	Feb 1961–Aug 1967

REGIMENTAL SECRETARIES

Major H. A. V. Spencer	Apr 1958–Nov 1976
Major R. F. Tomlinson	Nov 1976–Nov 1983
Brigadier J. M. Cubiss, CBE, MC	Nov 1983–Sep 1993
Lieutenant-Colonel T. C. E. Vines	Sep 1993–

* Bandmaster Nicholson died while conducting a concert in February 1965.

APPENDIX 4
Battalion Locations 1958–1994

1st Battalion

Dover	19th Infantry Brigade	Apr 1958–Aug 1958
Aden	Aden Garrison	Sep 1958–Apr 1959
Gibraltar	Gibraltar Garrison	Apr 1959–Aug 1961
Libya	Training exercise	Oct 1960–Nov 1960
Wuppertal	12th Infantry Brigade	Sep 1961–Jun 1963
Berlin	Berlin Brigade	Jun 1963–Apr 1965
Colchester	Colchester Garrison	Apr 1965–Sep 1965
Aden	Aden Brigade	Sep 1965–Sep 1966
Western Aden	Protectorate 24th Infantry Brigade	Jun 1966–Aug 1966
Colchester	19th Infantry Brigade	Oct 1966–Jun 1967
Aden	Aden Brigade	Jun 1967–Oct 1967
Colchester	19th Infantry Brigade	Nov 1967–Feb 1970
Cyprus	Training exercise	Jul 1968–Aug 1968
Kenya	B Company training exercise	Feb 1969–Mar 1969
N. Ireland	39th Infantry Brigade	Apr 1969–Aug 1969
Cyprus	HQ Dhekelia Area	Feb 1970–Mar 1972
Kenya	Training exercise	Jun 1971–Jul 1971
Belfast	HQ Northern Ireland	Mar 1972–Nov 1973
Dover	Dover Garrison	Jan 1974–Jun 1974
Celle	7th Armoured Brigade	Jun 1974–Aug 1978
Londonderry	8th Infantry Brigade	Jul 1975–Nov 1975
Canada	All-Arms training area Suffield	Apr 1976–Aug 1976
Londonderry	8th Infantry Brigade	Mar 1977–Jul 1977
Bulford	Allied Command Europe Mobile Force (Land),	Aug 1978–Jun 1983
Berlin	Berlin Brigade	Jun 1983–Apr 1985
Ballykinler	39th Infantry Brigade	Apr 1985–May 1987
Catterick	24th Infantry Brigade	May 1987–Dec 1987
	24th Air-Mobile Brigade	Jan 1988–Aug 1990
Osnabrück	12th Armoured Brigade	Aug 1990–Aug 1994
Arabian Gulf	Detachments totalling 149 all ranks 1st Armoured Division	Sep 1990–Feb 1991
Belfast	39th Infantry Brigade	Nov 1991–May 1992
Bosnia	United Nations Protection Force	May 1993–Nov 1993

APPENDIX 4: BATTALION LOCATIONS 1958–1994   245

Canada	All-Arms training area Suffield	Jan 1994–Jun 1994
Warminster	Combined Arms Training Centre Battle Group as the Demonstration Battle Group	Aug 1994–

3RD BATTALION*

Hull	Battalion Headquarters and HQ Company; A Company in Hull; B Company in Beverley; C Company in York; D Company in Tadcaster, under command 146 Infantry Brigade (TA)	Feb 1961–Mar 1967

Formed on 15 February 1961 on the amalgamation of the 5th Battalion The West Yorkshire Regiment (TA) with 4th Battalion the East Yorkshire Regiment (TA)

THE PRINCE OF WALES'S OWN TERRITORIALS OR 3RD BATTALION CADRE

Hull	With a detachment at York–total establishment 341 all ranks	Apr 1967–Dec 1968

3RD BATTALION CADRE

Hull	Establishment 8 all ranks	Jan 1969–Mar 1971

THE LEEDS RIFLES (PWO)*

Leeds	146th Infantry Brigade (TA) Battalion Headquarters in Leeds A Company in Morley B Company in Leeds C Company in Castleford D Company in Leeds HQ Company in Leeds	Feb 1961–Mar 1979

Formed on 15 February 1961 on the amalgamation of the 7th (Leeds Rifles) Battalion The West Yorkshire Regiment with 466 Light Anti-Aircraft Regiment RA, formerly the 8th (Leeds Rifles) Battalion The West Yorkshire Regiment

THE LEEDS RIFLES TERRITORIALS

Leeds	With a detachment at Castleford – –total establishment 341 all ranks	Apr 1967–Mar 1969

THE LEEDS RIFLES CADRE

Leeds establishment 8 all ranks: Apr 1969–Mar 1971

2ND BATTALION THE YORKSHIRE VOLUNTEERS

York BAOR reinforcement on Home Defence Apr 1971–Apr 1993
    A (Prince of Wales's Own)
      Company in York
    B (Prince of Wales's Own)
      Company in Hull
    C (The Leeds Rifles)
      Company in Leeds

3RD BATTALION–REBADGED FROM 2ND BATTALION THE YORKSHIRE VOLUNTEERS

York 15th (North East) Brigade* Apr 1993–Apr 1995
    Battalion HQ in York
    A Company in York with a
      platoon at Goole
    B Company in Hull
    C (The Leeds Rifles) Company
      in Leeds with a platoon
      in Castleford
    HQ Company and Milan anti-tank
      platoon in York
    Reconnaissance and mortar
      platoon in Beverley

    *Battalion dedicated to the
    NATO AlliedRapid Reaction
    Corps (ARRC)

3RD BATTALION
(FIRE SUPPORT ROLE, DEDICATED TO THE ARRC)

    Battalion HQ & HQ Company
      in York April 1995–
    A (The Leeds Rifles) Heavy Weapons
      Company in York with detachments
      in Leeds and Castleford
    B Heavy Weapons Company in Hull
      with detachments in Beverley and
      Goole

APPENDIX 5

Honours and Awards

Dates refer to the year of publication in the *London Gazette*

COMPANIONS OF THE ORDER OF THE BATH

Major-General H. M. Tillotson, CBE	Chief of Staff UKLF	1983
Major-General E. H. A. Beckett, MBE	Chief of Staff BAOR	1988
Major-General A. B. Crowfoot, CBE	General Officer Commanding North-West District	1991

COMMANDERS OF THE ORDER OF THE BRITISH EMPIRE

Colonel C. Nixon, MBE	Commander Aden Garrison	1961
Colonel A. W. Cowper, OBE	HQ Far East Land Forces, Singapore	1964
Brigadier H. E. Boulter, DSO	Deputy Fortress Commander, Gibraltar	1965
Colonel J. H. Taylor, TD, MA	late The Leeds Rifles, Yorkshire	1974
Colonel H. M. Tillotson, OBE	HQ Land Forces Hong Kong	1976
Colonel J. M. Cubiss, MC	HQ Northern Ireland	1979
Brigadier M. A. Atherton	Deputy Constable Dover Castle	
Brigadier A. B. Crowfoot, MBE	Commander 39rh Infantry Brigade, Northern Ireland	1981
Brigadier W. P. Sheppard, MC, TD, DL	Territorial Army Advisor to C-in-C UK Land Forces	1982

COMPANION OF THE DISTINGUISHED SERVICE ORDER

Lieutenant-Colonel A. D. A. Duncan, OBE	1 PWO, Bosnia	1994

OFFICERS OF THE ORDER OF THE BRITISH EMPIRE

Lieutenant-Colonel R. S. MacG. Laird, MBE	Staff Ghana	1962
Lieutenant-Colonel N. H. Bryan, TD, DL	3 PWO, Yorkshire District	1962
Lieutenant-Colonel M. R. R. Turner, MBE	HQ Singapore District	1963

Lieutenant-Colonel T. R. Birkett	1 PWO, Aden	1967
Lieutenant-Colonel W. A. E. Todd	1 PWO, Northern Ireland	1970
Lieutenant-Colonel H. M. Tillotson, MBE	MoD London	1970
Colonel E. W. Clay, MBE	late The Leeds Rifles, Yorkshire	1971
Lieutenant-Colonel D. W. Hanson, MBE	1 PWO, Northern Ireland	1973
Lieutenant-Colonel G. M. Longdon, MBE	Commander Belize Defence Force	1983
Lieutenant-Colonel P. E. Woolley	1 PWO AMF(L), Bulford	1984
Lieutenant-Colonel E. A. K. Denison, TD	late 3 PWO, Yorkshire	1986
Lieutenant-Colonel A. D. Frais, TD	2 Yorks, late Leeds Rifles, Yorkshire	1986
Lieutenant-Colonel G. B. Smalley, TD	2 Yorks, Yorkshire	1991
Captain P. D. Orwin, MC	Foreign & Commonwealth Office, Israel	1992
Lieutenant-Colonel A. D. A. Duncan	1 PWO, Northern Ireland	1993

MEMBERS OF THE ORDER OF THE BRITISH EMPIRE

Major L. J. Wood	4 E Yorks, Yorkshire	1960
Major L. Tolmie	War Office, London	1961
Major P. T. J. Tidman	1 Y&L, UK & BAOR	1964
Major J. Halmshaw	MA to the Governor of Gibraltar	1966
Major R. Glazebrook	HQ Federal Regular Army, Aden	1967
Major D. W. Hanson	1 PWO, Aden	1967
Bandmaster A. S. Swain	The Leeds Rifles, Yorkshire	1967
Captain C. L. Wiley	Royal Hong Kong Regiment	1968
Captain E. Crowcroft	Staff Band WRAC, Guildford	1969
Captain J. W. Green	3 PWO, Yorkshire	1970
Captain G. M. Longdon	1 PWO, Northern Ireland	1970
Major C. W. Crossland	British High Commission, Lagos	1971
Captain G. Long	1 PWO, Northern Ireland	1973
Major A. B. Crowfoot	MoD, London	1974
Captain K. F. Robbin	HQ 8 Brigade, Northern Ireland	1974
Major E. H. A. Beckett	HQ 11th Armoured Brigade, Germany	1975
Major B. Campey	5/8 Kings, Lancashire	1978
Major M. G. Orum	1 PWO, Berlin	1985
Major J. M. P. Dillon	Sennelager Training Centre, Germany	1985
Major K. A. Peacock	COS HQ 39th Infantry Brigade, Northern Ireland	1986

APPENDIX 5: HONOURS AND AWARDS

Major M. J. Watson	1 PWO, Northern Ireland	1986
Major A. Bostock	Intelligence & Security Group, Northern Ireland	1987
Major R. Hunter	BRIXMIS, East Germany	1987
Captain K. H. Middleton	1 PWO, Northern Ireland	1988
Major S. Ashby	1 Yorks, Yorkshire	1989
Major H. A. Robinson	Royal Brunei Armed Forces	1990
Major G. J. Binns	COS HQ 39 Infantry Brigade, Northern Ireland	1991
Major E. P. Tracy	1 PWO, Northern Ireland	1993
Major D. A. Hill	1 PWO, Bosnia	1994
Major F. Frewster	3 PWO, Yorkshire	1994
Major N. Le B. Allbeury	Staff, Yorkshire	1995
Band Sergeant-Major P. J. Watts	Regimental Band, Germany	1995

MILITARY CROSS

Lieutenant P. D. Orwin	1 PWO, Western Aden Protectorate	1966
Major G. J. Binns, MBE	1 PWO, Bosnia	1994
Corporal P. S. Dobson*	1 PWO, Bosnia	1994

MILITARY MEDAL

Corporal A. G. Auker	1 PWO, Western Aden Protectorate	1966
Sergeant R. Bradley	1 PWO, Aden	1968
Private P. Davison	1 PWO, Aden	1968

QUEEN'S GALLANTRY MEDAL

Captain M. W. Bower	1 PWO, Bosnia	1994
Captain L. K. Whitworth	1 PWO, Bosnia	1994

BRITISH EMPIRE MEDAL

Colour-Sergeant G. W. Exelby	4 Yorks, Yorkshire	1958
Colour-Sergeant H. Moxon	1 PWO, Berlin	1964
Colour-Sergeant L. Wilkinson	1 PWO, Aden	1967
Sergeant C. Jackson†	1 PWO, Aden	1968
Warrant Officer II J. G. Cape	1 PWO, Colchester	1968
Sergeant E. Ross	1 PWO, N. Ireland	1970
Corporal D. B. Gee	King's Division Depot, Yorkshire	1973
Colour-Sergeant J. Wood	1 PWO, N. Ireland	1973
Sergeant B. K. Dent	1 PWO, N. Ireland	1973
Warrant Officer II G. R. Jaszynski	HQ, N. Ireland	1980
Warrant Officer II R. A. White	HQ 1st (British) Corps	1982

*This was the first award of the Military Cross to any soldier in the Army below the rank of Warrant Officer.
†British Empire Medal for Gallantry.

Sergeant P. J. O'Brien	1 PWO, Bulford	1984
Corporal A. R. Whiting	1 PWO, Berlin	1986
Corporal D. McBurney	1 PWO, Northern Ireland	1987

MENTIONED IN DESPATCHES

Lieutenant-Colonel A. M. Cooper, OBE	HQ 17th Gurkha Division, Malaya	1958
Major W. C. A. Battey	Malaysian Border Scouts, Borneo	1966
Lieutenant-Colonel W. A. E. Todd	1 PWO, Aden	1968
Major D. C. Hall	1 PWO, Aden	1968
Captain E. H. A. Beckett	1 PWO, Aden	1968
Captain F. J. W. Filor	1 PWO, Aden	1968
Lieutenant C. D. Parr	Intelligence Corps attached, 1 PWO, Aden	1968
Lieutenant A. J. Phelan	1 PWO, Aden	1968
Corporal W. J. Fuller	1 PWO, Aden	1968
Lance-Corporal M. D. P. Nokes	1 PWO, Aden	1968
Private D. J. Watts	1 PWO, Aden	1968
Colour-Sergeant A. F. Simpson	1 DWR, Northern Ireland	1972
Major C. R. Day	1 PWO, Northern Ireland	1973
Major F. J. W. Filor	1 PWO, Northern Ireland	1973
Major H. R. Goble	1 PWO, Northern Ireland	1973
Major M. H. Sharpe	1 PWO, Northern Ireland	1973
Company Sergeant-Major M. J. Barham	1 PWO, Northern Ireland	1973
Colour-Sergeant P. N. Hinds	1 PWO, Northern Ireland	1973
Sergeant R. Bradley, MM	1 PWO, Northern Ireland	1973
Colonel J. M. Cubiss, MC	Deputy Commander 39th Infantry Brigade, Belfast	1974
Lieutenant C. G. Le Brun	1 PWO, Northern Ireland	1975
Corporal D. Austin	1 PWO, Northern Ireland	1975
Lance-Corporal B. D. McAnulty	1 PWO, Northern Ireland	1975
Private B. P. Kelly	1 PWO, Northern Ireland	1975
Major P. L. W. Wood	662 Squadron AAC, Northern Ireland	1976
Lieutenant-Colonel E. H. A. Beckett, MBE	1 PWO, Northern Ireland	1977
Colour-Sergeant D. Moffat	1 PWO, Northern Ireland	1977
Captain A. C. G. Blanch	HQ 8th Infantry Brigade, Northern Ireland	1982
Lieutenant-Colonel P. E. Woolley, OBE	Commander British Force in Lebanon	1984
Lieutenant-Colonel R. H. J. Forsyth	1 PWO, Northern Ireland	1986

APPENDIX 5: HONOURS AND AWARDS

Sergeant P. Parnell	1 PWO, Northern Ireland	1986
Company Sergeant-Major P. A. Stainthorpe	1 PWO, Northern Ireland	1987
Sergeant K. Fowler	1 PWO, Northern Ireland	1987
Corporal K. J. Burton	1 PWO, Northern Ireland	1987
Corporal T. A. Hudson	1 PWO, Northern Ireland	1987
Lieutenant-Colonel D. A. H. Green	1 PWO, Northern Ireland	1988
Colonel J. C. L. King, MBE	Headquarters 1st Armoured Division, Arabian Gulf	1991
Captain E. P. Tracy	HQ 8th Infantry Brigade, Northern Ireland	1991
Major D. A. Barley	1 PWO, Northern Ireland	1993
Corporal K. A. Blagdon	1 PWO, Northern Ireland	1993
Lance-Corporal P. G. Wignall	1 PWO, Northern Ireland	1993
Captain A. G. P. Hay	Gordons, attached 1 PWO, Bosnia	1994
Lieutenant R. Lockwood	1 PWO, Bosnia	1994
2nd Lieutenant G. Payne	1 PWO, Bosnia	1994
Colour-Sergeant K. J. Burton	1 PWO, Bosnia	1994
Lance-Corporal D. I. Gillett	1 PWO, Bosnia	1994

HM THE QUEEN'S COMMENDATION FOR BRAVE CONDUCT

Sergeant K. Johansson	1 PWO, Germany	1962
Major H. M. Tillotson, MBE	1 PWO, Aden	1966
Captain S. G. Lucas	1 PWO, Aden	1966
Lieutenant D. A. Hill	1 PWO, Rhodesia	1979
Corporal C. Pearce	1 PWO, Yorkshire	1988
Lieutenant J. C. Medley	Adjutant General's Corps attached 1 PWO, Bosnia	1994
Corporal A. D. Donlon	Gordons attached 1 PWO, Bosnia	1994

HM THE QUEEN'S COMMENDATION FOR VALUABLE SERVICE

Major C. J. Dockerty (posthumous)	8th Infantry Brigade, Northern Ireland	1995

COMMANDER-IN-CHIEF'S OR GENERAL OFFICER COMMANDING'S CERTIFICATES OF COMMENDATION

Regimental Sergeant-Major P. Savidge*	3 PWO, Devon	1966
Warrant Officer Class 2 K. D. Morris	1 PWO, Aden	1966
Colour-Sergeant E. Harrison	1 PWO, Aden	1966
Colour-Sergeant J. E. Thornton, BEM	1 PWO, Aden	1966

*Commendation for Gallantry.

Colour-Sergeant J. G. Cape	1 PWO, Aden	1966
Sergeant P. Michael	1 PWO, Aden	1966
Sergeant G. E. Potter	1 PWO, Aden	1966
Lance-Corporal P. Ralph	1PWO, Aden	1966
Regimental Sergeant-Major B. Campey	1PWO, Aden	1967
Sergeant A. Place	1PWO, Aden	1967
Sergeant J. Wood	1PWO, Aden	1967
Corporal K. A. Bolton	1PWO, Aden	1967
Corporal A. Calverley	1PWO, Aden	1967
Corporal H. G. Pearce	1PWO, Aden	1967
Lance-Corporal M. Jowsey	1PWO, Aden	1967
Lance-Corporal R. Sleight	HQ, Northern Ireland	1973
Company Sergeant-Major H. Alderson	1PWO, Northern Ireland	1975
Sergeant T. Copperwaite	1PWO, Northern Ireland	1975
Corporal D. Craze	1PWO, Northern Ireland	1975
Lance-Corporal P. G. O'Shaughnessy	1PWO, Germany	1976
Sergeant P. A. Stainthorpe	1PWO, Northern Ireland	1977
Corporal M. Braybrook	1PWO, Northern Ireland	1977
Lance-Corporal D. Hawes	1PWO, Northern Ireland	1977
Sergeant M. H. Robinson	Depot King's Division, Yorkshire	1980
Corporal F. E. Peacock	Depot King's Division, Yorkshire	1980
Lieutenant S. Padgett*	1PWO, Norway	1983
Lieutenant N. R. M. Parker*	1PWO, Norway	1983
Corporal K. A. Blagdon*	1PWO, Norway	1983
Corporal C. Harland*	1PWO, Norway	1983
Lance-Corporal A. Whittingham	1PWO, Northern Ireland	1986
Sergeant C. V. Drowley	1PWO, Northern Ireland	1987
Private R. Singleton*	1PWO, Hull	1989
Major M. J. Barham	1 Green Howards, Northern Ireland	1990
Corporal D. O. M'Benga	Depot King's Division, Yorkshire	1990
Lance-Corporal N. Birkinshaw	1PWO, Yorkshire	1992
Lance-Corporal F. Rodland	1PWO, Yorkshire	1992
Lance-Corporal M. Wyrill	1PWO, Yorkshire	1992
Captain R. M. Bruce	1PWO, Northern Ireland	1993
Lance-Corporal R. M. Balderson	1PWO, Northern Ireland	1993
Private D. Booker	1PWO, Northern Ireland	1993
Mrs Christine Watson	1PWO, Germany	1994

*Commendation for Gallantry.

APPENDIX 5: HONOURS AND AWARDS

UNITED NATIONS JOINT COMMANDER'S COMMENDATION

Major R. J. Watson	1PWO, Bosnia	1994
Captain B. Cawkwell	1PWO, Bosnia	1994
Lieutenant J. A. J. Calder	Gordons attached 1PWO, Bosnia	1994
Company Sergeant-Major S. W. Emerson	1PWO, Bosnia	1994
Sergeant S. J. Eley	REME, attached 1PWO, Bosnia	1994
Sergeant N. B. White	1PWO, Bosnia	1994
Corporal J. B. Denison	1PWO, Bosnia	1994
Corporal J. G. Haley	Intelligence Corps attached 1PWO, Bosnia	1994
Corporal R. Holton	Gordons, attached 1PWO, Bosnia	1994
Lance-Corporal S. P. Bingley	1PWO, Bosnia	1994
Lance-Corporal R. E. Dixon	1PWO, Bosnia	1994
Lance-Corporal A. Grant	1PWO, Bosnia	1994
Lance-Corporal P. A. Urey	QLR, attached 1PWO, Bosnia	1994
Private M. B. Barnett	1PWO, Bosnia	1994
Private J. T. Shannon	QLR, attached 1PWO, Bosnia	1994

UNITED NATIONS FORCE COMMANDER'S CERTIFICATE OF COMMENDATION

Company Sergeant-Major M. C. Clark	1PWO, Bosnia	1994
Company Sergeant-Major N. F. Clarke	1PWO, Bosnia	1994
Sergeant G. R. Whitton	Royal Logistic Corps, attached 1PWO, Bosnia	1994
Corporal N. Bulmer	1PWO, Bosnia	1994
Corporal P. A. Hodgson	1PWO, Bosnia	1994
Corporal D. Robinson	1PWO, Bosnia	1994
Lance-Corporal M. Brown	Kings, attached 1 PWO Bosnia	1994
Lance-Corporal K. A. Raby	QLR, attached 1 PWO Bosnia	1994
Private C. M. Beardow	1PWO, Bosnia	1994
Private A. K. Davis	1PWO, Bosnia	1994
Private A. M. Denham	1PWO, Bosnia	1994
Private A. M. Morley	1PWO, Bosnia	1994
Private M. Nicholson	1PWO, Bosnia	1994
Private C. M. Spottiswood	1PWO, Bosnia	1994

APPENDIX 6
Sporting Achievements

1958

1ST BATTALION

Winners of the British Forces Aden Protectorate Major Unit Team Boxing Competition.
Winners of the British Forces Aden Protectorate Football League.
Winners of the British Forces Aden Protectorate Rugby seven-a-side League (nine games to two).

4TH EAST YORKSHIRES TA

Winners of The Queen's Challenge Cup (Territorial Army unit with the year's most outstanding sporting record).

1959

1st Battalion

Winners of the Gibraltar Garrison Novices' Boxing Championships (ten bouts to two).
Winners of the Gibraltar Command Major Units Swimming Competition.

1960

1ST BATTALION

Winners of the Gibraltar Command Athletics Championships.
Winners of the Gibraltar Command Open Boxing Championships.
Winners of the Gibraltar Command Major Units Football League.
Winners of the Gibraltar Command Major Units Swimming Competition.

4TH EAST YORKSHIRES TA

Winners of the 50th Division Open Boxing Championships (eight bouts to one).

APPENDIX 6: SPORTING ACHIEVEMENTS

1961

1ST BATTALION

Winners of the Gibraltar Command Athletics and Gibraltar AAA Championships.
Winners of the Gibraltar Command Open Boxing Championships.
Winners of the Gibraltar Command Major Units Football League.
Winners of the Gibraltar Command Minor Units Football Knockout Cup (B Company).
Winners of the Gibraltar Command Major Units Swimming Competition.

3RD BATTALION

Winners of the Hull and District Sunday League Football Championship.

1962

1ST BATTALION

Winners of 12th Infantry Brigade Group Cross-Country Competition.

3RD BATTALION

Winners of The Queen's Challenge Cup (Territorial Army unit with the year's most outstanding sporting record).

THE LEEDS RIFLES

Winners 49th Infantry Division (TA) Football Cup.

1963

1ST BATTALION

Winners 12th Infantry Brigade Group Cross-Country Competition.
Winners Berlin Brigade Corss-Country Championship.

3RD BATTALION

Winners of The Queen's Challenge Cup (Territorial Army unit with the year's most outstanding sporting record).

1964

1ST BATTALION

Winners Berlin Brigade Team Boxing Championship.
Winners BAOR Cross-Country Team Championship.
Winners BAOR Swimming Team Championship Trophy.

1965

1ST BATTALION

Winners 1st Division Major Units Cross-Country Championship.
Winners Berlin Brigade Football League.

3RD BATTALION

Winners 49th Infantry Division (TA) Cross-Country Championship.

1966

1ST BATTALION

Winners Middle East Command Cross-Country Championship.

3RD BATTALION

Winners Scarborough Cup TA Team Boxing Championship.
Winners Northern Command TA Cross-Country Championship.

1967

1ST BATTALION

Winners Southern Command Cross-Country Championship.

3RD BATTALION

Winners 49th Infantry Division (TA) Cross-Country Championship.

1968

1ST BATTALION

Winners 19th Infantry Brigade Football Challenge Cup.
Winners of the East Anglian District Rugby Cup.

3RD BATTALION

Winners Northern Command TA Cross-Country Championship.
Winners of The Queen's Challenge Cup (Territorial Army unit with the year's most outstanding sporting record).

1971

1ST BATTALION

Winners Near East Land Forces Athletics Competition.
Winners Cyprus Western Sovereign Base Area Football Competition:
  1 PWO 'Lions'.

1972

1ST BATTALION

Winners Near East Land Forces Cross-Country Championship.
Winners Northern Ireland Cricket Cup.
Finalists in the Army Cricket Cup.

1973

1ST BATTALION

Winners of the Northern Ireland Major Units Football League.

1976

1ST BATTALION

Winners Infantry Football Challenge Cup BAOR.
Finalists Infantry Football Challenge Cup.

1977

1ST BATTALION

Winners 1st Division Football League

1978

1ST BATTALION

Winners 1st Armoured Division Novices' Boxing Competition.
Winners 1st Armoured Division Football League.

1980

1ST BATTALION

Winners Salisbury Plain Services Football League.

1981

1ST BATTALION

Winners South-West District Athletics Competition.
Winners South-West District Football League.
Finalists Army Football Challenge Cup (Score 3–2 in extra time).

1982

1ST BATTALION

Winners South West District Athletics Competition
Winners Army Zone B Athletics Championship.
Winners Army Team Marathon Championship.
Runners-up Army Cross-Country Relay Championship (A Team).
3rd place Army Cross-Country Championship.
Winners South-West District Cross-Country Competition.

1983

1ST BATTALION

Winners Berlin Brigade Athletics Championship.
Winners Berlin Brigade Cross-Country Championship.
Winners 3rd Armoured Division Cross-Country Championship.
Runners-up Army Cross-Country Championship.
Winners Army Cross-Country Relay Championship (A Team).
Runners-up Army Team Marathon Championship.
Winners BAOR Infantry Cricket Cup (Private J. Willerton taking six Royal Green Jackets' wickets for seven runs).

1984

1ST BATTALION

Winners Berlin Brigade Athletics Championship.
Winners Berlin Brigade Inter-Company Boxing Competition. (Support Company.)
Finalists BAOR Intermediate Boxing Championships.
Winners Berlin Brigade Cross-Country Championship.
Winners 3rd Armoured Division Cross-Country Championship.
Winners Army Cross-Country Championship.
Winners Army Cross-Country Relay Championship. A Team (second consecutive year).
Winners Berlin Brigade Rugby Simper Cup Competition.
Winners 3rd Armoured Division Tennis Doubles Competition.

1985

1ST BATTALION

Winners Army Cross-Country Championship (second consecutive year and setting a new Army record of 55 points).
Winners Army Cross-Country Relay Championship: A Team (third consecutive year).

1985 (continued)

Winners Berlin Brigade Soccer A and B League Championships:
1 PWO A Team and 1 PWO B Team.
Winners Northern Ireland Athletics Championships.
Winners Northern Ireland Cricket Cup.
Winners Northern Ireland Tennis Championship.

1986

1ST BATTALION

Winners Army Cross-Country Championship (third consecutive year).
Runners-up Army Cross Country Relay Championship (A Team).
Winners Northern Ireland Cricket Cup.
Winners Northern Ireland Football League.

1987

1ST BATTALION

Runners-up Army Athletics Team Championship.
Winners Army Cross-Country Championship (fourth consecutive year).
Winners Army Cross-Country Relay Championship (A Team).
Winners Yorkshire League Cricket Cup.

1988

1ST BATTALION

Runners-up Army Athletics Team Championship.
Winners North-East District Grade III Novices' Boxing Championships 1987–8.
Winners Northern Zone Novices' Team Boxing Championship 1987–8.
Runners-up Army United Kingdom Grade III Novices' Boxing Championships 1987–8.
Runners-up Army Cross-Country Championship.
Runners-up Army Cross-Country Relay Championship (A Team).
Winners Army Team Marathon Championship.
Winners Infantry Keel Boat Sailing Regatta.
Winners North-East District Dinghy Team Race.

1989

1ST BATTALION

Winners Army Major Units Grade II Novices' Boxing Championship 1988–9.
Runners-up Army Cross-Country Championship.
Winners Army Team Marathon Championship (second consecutive year).
Winners 24th Air-Mobile Tennis Doubles Competition.

1990

1ST BATTALION

Runners-up 1st Division Grade III Novices' Team Boxing Championship 1989–90.
Winners Army Team Marathon Championship (third consecutive year).
Winners North-East/North-West/Scotland Districts Rugby Championship.

1991

1ST BATTALION

Winners 1st and 3rd Division Athletics Championships.
Runners-up BAOR Athletics Championships.
Runners-up Army Athletics Team Championship.
Winners BAOR Cross-Country Championship.
Winners Army Cross-Country Championship.
Runners-up Army Cross-Country Relay Championship.
Runners-up Army Team Marathon Championship.
Finalists BAOR Football Championship.

1992

1ST BATTALION

Runners-up BAOR Athletics Championships.
Runners-up Army Athletics Team Championship.
Winners BAOR Cross-Country Championship.
Winners Army Cross-Country Championship.
Runners-up Army Half Marathon Championship.

APPENDIX 7
Individual Sporting Champions

1958

BRITISH ARMY ADEN PROTECTORATE OPEN BOXING CHAMPIONS

Flyweight Champion: Private G. Callan, 1 PWO.
Bantam weight Champion: Private N. Wilkin, 1 PWO.
Featherweight Champion: Corporal D. S. Kenny, 1 PWO.
Lightweight Champion: Private B. Neal, 1 PWO.
Light welterweight Champion: Corporal K. A. Bolton, 1 PWO.
Middleweight Champion: Corporal P. J. Russell, 1 PWO.
Heavyweight Champion: Private N. Burns, 1 PWO.

1961

TERRITORIAL ARMY BOXING CHAMPIONS

Lightweight Champion: Private R. Barker, 3 PWO.

TERRITORIAL ARMY SPORTSMAN OF THE YEAR

Private R. Barker, 3 PWO.

1962

BAOR INDIVIDUAL SWIMMING CHAMPIONS

200m Breast Stroke Champion: Private M. Horsley, 1 PWO.

2ND INFANTRY DIVISION INDIVIDUAL BOXING CHAMPIONS

Welterweight Champion: Sergeant M. Garrigan, 1 PWO.
Light Heavyweight Champion: Private D. Davis, 1 PWO.

1964

BERLIN BRIGADE CROSS-COUNTRY CHAMPIONSHIP

Individual Champion: Private M. Conroy, 1 PWO.

BAOR INDIVIDUAL SWIMMING CHAMPIONS

200m Breast Stroke Champion: Private M. Horsley, 1 PWO.
400m and 800m Free Style Champion: Lance-Corporal J. A. Devenish, 1 PWO.

1965

49TH INFANTRY DIVISION (TA) CROSS-COUNTRY CHAMPIONSHIP

Individual Champion: Corporal J. Hargreaves, 3 PWO.

1966

MIDDLE EAST COMMAND INTER-SERVICE ATHLETICS CHAMPIONS

One Mile Champion: Lance-Corporal J. Redfern, 1 PWO.
High Jump Champion: 2nd Lieutenant M. V. Garside, 1 PWO.

MIDDLE EAST LAND FORCES INDIVIDUAL BOXING CHAMPIONS

Light Welterweight Champion: Private E. Kilkenny, 1 PWO.
Featherweight Champion: Lance-Corporal J. Neil, 1 PWO.

TERRITORIAL ARMY INDIVIDUAL BOXING CHAMPIONS

Lightweight Champion: Private J. Silvester, 3 PWO.
Middleweight Champion: Private S. Garrigan, 3 PWO.
Welterweight Champion: Private K. Hawkins, 3 PWO.
Light Heavyweight Champion: Private R. Tighe, 3 PWO.

BRITISH EMPIRE AND COMMONWEALTH GAMES LIGHT HEAVYWEIGHT GOLD MEDALLIST & ABA CHAMPION

Private R. Tighe, 3 PWO.

1968

TERRITORIAL ARMY & AVR INDIVIDUAL BOXING CHAMPIONS

Featherweight Champion: Private R. Blowman, 3 PWO.
Lightweight Champion: Private M. Murray, 3 PWO.
Light Middleweight Champion: Private F. Bagshaw, 3 PWO.
Light Welterweight Champion: Private A. Cook, 3 PWO.
Welterweight Champion: Private K. Hawkins, 3 PWO.

APPENDIX 7: INDIVIDUAL SPORTING CHAMPIONS

1972

NEAR EAST COMMAND INTER-SERVICE CHAMPIONSHIPS

400m Champion: Private S. Arzu, 1 PWO.
800m Champion: Sergeant B. Cawkwell, 1 PWO.
1500m Champion: Sergeant D. Moffat, 1 PWO.

1977

NORTH-EAST DISTRICT INDIVIDUAL BOXING CHAMPIONS

Middleweight Champion: Private R. Williams, E (Leeds Rifles) Company 1st Yorkshire Volunteers.

1981

ARMY 400M CHAMPION

Sergeant K. Akabusi, 1 PWO.

ARMY 5,000M INDIVIDUAL VETERAN CHAMPION

Captain P. Blyth, 1 PWO.

ARMY JUNIOR STEEPLECHASE CHAMPION

Private G. Birdsall, 1 PWO.

1983

ARMY SURF CANOE CHAMPION

Colour-Sergeant T. Copperwaite, 1 PWO.

ARMY JUNIOR STEEPLECHASE CHAMPION

Private G. Birdsall, 1 PWO

1984

ARMY CROSS-COUNTRY INDIVIDUAL CHAMPIONSHIPS

Army Junior Champion: Private P. A. Hill, 1 PWO.

1985

ARMY INDIVIDUAL ATHLETICS CHAMPIONSHIPS

2000m Steeplechase Champion: Private R. Simpson, 1 PWO.
5000m Veteran Champion: Lieutenant D. Moffat, 1 PWO.

1986

ARMY CROSS-COUNTRY INDIVIDUAL CHAMPIONSHIPS

Army Veteran Champion: Lieutenant D. Moffat, 1 PWO.
Army Senior Champion: Sergeant G. Wade, 1 PWO.
Army Junior Champion: Private R. Simpson, 1 PWO.

INTER-SERVICES CROSS-COUNTRY INDIVIDUAL CHAMPIONSHIPS

Junior Champion: Private R. Simpson, 1 PWO.

1988

ARMY INDIVIDUAL ATHLETICS CHAMPIONS

3000m Steeplechase Champion: Private R. Simpson, 1 PWO.
Junior 100m & 200m Champion: Drummer D. Blair, 1 PWO.
Long-Jump Champion: Private P. Fogg, 1 PWO.
Triple-Jump Champion: Lance-Corporal N. Bulmer, 1 PWO.
Pole-Vault Champion: Lance-Corporal R. A. Lyons, 1 PWO.

ARMY BOXING CHAMPION

Featherweight: Corporal E. Tyrell, 1 PWO.

ARMY SURF CANOE CHAMPION AND UNITED KINGDOM CHAMPION

Colour-Sergeant T. Copperwaite, 1 PWO.

1989

ARMY INDIVIDUAL ATHLETICS CHAMPIONS

Long-Jump Champion: Private P. Fogg, 1 PWO.
Triple-Jump Champion: Lance-Corporal N. Bulmer, 1 PWO.
Pole-Vault Champion: Lance Corporal R. A. Lyons, 1 PWO.

1990

ARMY INDIVIDUAL ATHLETICS CHAMPIONS

400 metres Champion: Lance-Corporal N. Bulmer, 1 PWO.
3000m Champion: Private D. R. A. Stephenson, 1 PWO.
Triple-Jump Champion: Lance-Corporal N. Bulmer, 1 PWO.

APPENDIX 6: SPORTING ACHIEVEMENTS

1991

ARMY INDIVIDUAL ATHLETICS CHAMPIONS

100m and 200m Champion: Captain D. S. Hancock, 1 PWO.
400m Champion: Private N. Bulmer, 1 PWO.
Triple-Jump Champion: Private N. Bulmer, 1 PWO.
Pole-Vault Champion: Corporal R. A. Lyons, 1 PWO.
Junior Triple-Jump Champion: Private M. Waltham, 1 PWO.

ARMY CROSS-COUNTRY CHAMPIONSHIP

Army Junior Champion: Private D. R. A. Stephenson, 1 PWO.

ARMY HALF MARATHON INDIVIDUAL CHAMPIONSHIPS

Army Champion: Private D. R. A Stephenson, 1 PWO.

1992

ARMY INDIVIDUAL ATHLETICS CHAMPIONS

100m Champion: Captain D. S. Hancock, 1 PWO.
Triple-Jump Champion: Corporal N. Bulmer, 1 PWO.

ARMY CROSS-COUNTRY INDIVIDUAL CHAMPIONSHIP

Junior Champion: Private D. R. A Stephenson, 1 PWO.

Notes

CHAPTER I

1 Military service in Aden was never keenly sought. When a group of British soldiers raped a woman in Burma in 1899, the Viceroy of India – Sir George Curzon – ordered their entire battalion to spend two years in Aden as a punishment.
2 Fears that France coveted Perim Island, off the heel of Arabia, led to the Union Flag being hastily raised there in 1857. For the same reason, the Al Burayqah promontory was bought from the Aqrabi Sheikh for £30,000 and renamed Little Aden in 1862. Acceptance of Ottoman protection by the Emir of Dhala in 1873 led to an Anglo-Turkish confrontation there, but tension was defused by diplomacy.
3 Appointment of the far-sighted Sir Richard Luce as Governor of Aden 1956 brought a fresh political impetus to the region. Perceiving that Aden could never be secure with a hostile hinterland, he put forward a ten-year programme for political and social reforms in Aden and the Protectorates in parallel. Beyond these developments, he foresaw the emergence of an independent South West Arabia, within which the Aden base might be retained under a treaty negotiated with a newly independent state. His proposals were coolly received in London.
4 The newly elected British Labour Government of October 1964 grasped the South Arabian nettle by calling a constitutional conference in London for March 1965, to which the now moderate-seeming Abdullah al-Asnaj was invited to represent the ATUC/PSP. The independent rulers of the Eastern Protectorate states refused to sit down with al-Asnaj and the conference was abandoned when the NLF declared that any Arab who attended would be killed on his return.
5 Abdull al-Qawi Meccawi, an ardent nationalist, had been appointed President of the Federation's Supreme Council by Sir Richard Turnbull, the Governor who succeeded Travaskis, when the previous moderate President resigned over cancellation of the proposed March 1965 constitutional conference. Meccawi promptly declared his support for a 1963 UN General Assembly Resolution, calling for an abrogation of the South Arabian constitution and new elections based on universal suffrage leading to independence.
6 Major Spencer Holtom, RA, was later awarded the Air Force Cross for the rescue of seventy-eight people trapped on their house rooftops by a flash

NOTES 267

flood of the Sungei Mengkibol in Kluang, Malaysia, in December 1969. Driving rain had reduced visibility only to yards under a cloud base of 100 feet but, with his helicopter stripped to flying essentials, Holtom returned time and again to the scene until he had lifted every man, woman and child to high ground safe from the flood.

7 The following message was read out over Arabic and English language radio networks on the evening of the explosion in the Khusaf Valley: 'By the will of Allah a treacherous member of the so-called NLF destroyed himself in an explosion in the Khusaf Valley at 12.20 pm today. The explosion was caused when this man was attempting to fix a time fuse device to the explosive and, due to his amateurish knowledge of these dangerous materials, he blew away his face and arms and split open his insides. Let us all now look at our neighbours and make sure that they are true friends of Aden and the Arabs. If your suspicions are aroused, inform the police at once so that the suspected one may either clear his name or be arrested.'

8 Monks Field, named by a battalion of the Coldstream Guards, was almost certainly intended to be known as 'Monck's Field' but the spelling used in this book is that used on the Ordnance Survey maps.

9 Peter Hinchcliffe was later British Ambassador in Amman, Jordan.

10 The supertanker *Torrey Canyon* ran aground off the Cornish coast in the spring of 1967 and spilled its cargo of mainly crude oil into the sea. The Army and fire services from many parts of the country were called on to clean the Cornish beaches and to help rescue wildlife. It was the first disaster of its kind in Europe.

CHAPTER 2

1 The United States' initiative arose out of concern that Greece and Turkey would renew their ancient feud and so weaken the south-eastern arm of the NATO alliance.

2 During the period before the outbreak of fighting around Christmas 1963, the British, Greek and Turkish Governments had attempted to reconcile the two Cypriot communities without success. Major-General Peter Young, the GOC British Troops in Cyprus, devised the 'Green Line' dividing the Greek and Turkish Cypriot areas of Nicosia. It was green simply because that happened to be the colour of the chinagraph pencil with which he drew the line on his map.

3 The Treaty of Establishment ended the period of British Colonial rule in Cyprus and recognized her an an independent state.

4 The Akrotiri airbase had been expanded to allow two or more nuclear strike bomber squadrons to operate from there as a measure of support for the Baghdad Pact. When the latter collapsed and was replaced by CENTO, it was judged necessary to maintain the base in support of the new alliance.

5 The Haggan brothers were known in the battalion only by the last two of their regimental numbers: 16, 48 and 81.

6 The provenance of the Inniskilling Cup has not been established beyond doubt. It is thought to have been presented by The Inniskillings (6th Dragoons) to mark their winning the Delhi Durbar Polo Tournament in 1911. It is believed that the cup was moved to Egypt when the British garrison withdrew from India in 1947 and later from Cairo to Cyprus, when GHQ Middle East moved there in 1954.

7 Glavkos Clerides was elected President of Cyprus in 1993.

CHAPTER 3

1 The division of Germany into four zones of occupation, by armies from Britain, France, the Soviet Union and the United States, was drawn up by Churchill, Roosevelt and Stalin during their meeting at the Black Sea port of Yalta in February 1945.

2 Sea trooping having been replaced by air trooping during the 1st Battalion's period in Gibraltar, the Ministry of Defence economized further by flying the men and their families direct on leave and from leave to Germany, thereby avoiding the expense of providing accommodation in the United Kingdom.

3 See Prologue, page 14.

4 The Geddes Cup was presented to 2nd Battalion The East Yorkshire Regiment by Colonel Guy Geddes, DSO, in 1928 to be competed for by all platoons in a annual marching and shooting competition.

5 George I had married Sophia Dorothea of Zell (Celle) in 1682 before his accession, but they were divorced in 1694 and she spent the rest of her life in seclusion.

6 Operation Granby was the deployment of British forces to the Arabian Gulf. Granby Garrisons were those in BAOR left empty, except for small rear-parties and families.

CHAPTER 4

1 When President John Kennedy made his dramatic pledge as a citizen of Berlin, he should have said 'Ich bin Berliner'. Probably only the solemnity of the moment prevented some audible laughter when he declared himself '*Ein Berliner*', for this is a round, hollow, sugar-coated bun sold throughout Germany. The President had declared himself to be a doughnut!

2 The Victory Column in the Tiergarten was erected in 1873 to commemorate the Prussian victories over Denmark in 1864 and Austria in 1866 and in the Franco-Prussian War of 1870–71.

3 Except possibly by the speed with which he began removing the more extreme economic measures of the Brezhnev era, it was not immediately apparent that the able President Yuri Andropov had only a short time to live. He lasted only until February 1984. Fortunately, President Konstantin Chernenko – who was of the old guard – dutifully died after thirteen months in office, leaving the way open for Mikhail Gorbachev to succeed.

4 The Battle of the Boyne actually took place on 1 July 1690 but the eleven-day change from the Julian to the Gregorian calendar in Britain, in September 1752, moved the date to 12 July. Although less well remembered, it was at the Battle of Aughrim in Galway on 2 July 1691 that the Jacobite army was finally defeated in Ireland.
5 Bandmaster Kenneth Shell died in the British Military Hospital, Hannover on 3 September 1984 after being taken seriously ill while returning from holiday with his family. He was appointed Bandmaster of the Regimental Band in May 1981 after graduation from the Royal Military School of Music and proved himself outstanding in that role.

CHAPTER 5

1 The Liberal Government of H. H. Asquith (1908–16) failed to persuade the Protestant population of Ulster to accept Irish Home Rule, with Dublin as the seat of Government, and groups of 'Ulster Volunteers' formed with the object of retaining independence from Dublin by force. Continued opposition by the Protestants led to the the division of Ireland into the Irish Free State, with Commonwealth status, and the British Province of Northern Ireland by the Anglo-Irish Treaty of 1921. A Boundary Commission determined the border in 1924.
2 The doctrine of 'equivalent force' required that a soldier could shoot only if the person at whom he fired was seen to be about to do something equally drastic to him personally.
3 At a time before anyone had been killed in this phase of Irish troubles, the Government of Harold Wilson was understandably cautious of making any move that would leave them open to a charge of precipitate military action or favouring one community in the Province over the other.
4 See chapter 4, note 4.
5 The Tribunal of Inquiry headed by the Hon. Mr Justice Scarman, set up by the British Government to inquire into and report on violence and civil disturbances in Northern Ireland in 1969, was presented to Parliament in April 1972.
6 More significant than the haphazard participation of members of the IRA in the Londonderry riots was the part played by anarchists and professional terrorists from Europe in the organization and planning of the disturbances.
7 The IRA had become virtually moribund following defeat of a badly bungled bombing campaign during 1956–62. Internment of the known key figures in both the north and south caught most of the leaders. No support was received from the Catholic population and the campaign was abandoned after two terrorists had been shot by the RUC and nine others killed in 'own-goal' accidents while handling explosives.
8 A system was introduced in 1972 whereby any soldier who required medical attention as a result of riot or terrorist action could claim compensation under the Criminal Injuries Act.

CHAPTER 6

1 There were seven AMF(L) contingency plan areas: Northern Norway, Zealand (Denmark), Greek Thrace, Turkish Thrace, the Turkish border area with Syria, the Turkish Armenian region around Kars (adjacent to Soviet Armenia) and the Italian/Yugoslav border in the area of the Gorizia gap.
2 'The Green Machine' was the term used by Canadian servicemen to describe the unified services, all of which wore the same green uniform. Captains in the RCN became 'colonels' and army colonels and below wore naval-type badges of rank. Regiments regarded as representing old colonial links, such as the Black Watch of Canada, were reduced to 'nil strength'.
3 The 1st East Yorkshires were defeated 2–1 in the 50th final of the Army Football Cup also by a REME training unit – the 4th Training Battalion – in 1951, when an East Yorkshire goal was disallowed. The REME side included five professionals.
4 2nd and 3rd Battalions The Parachute Regiment were selected to join the Falklands task force because the 2nd was Spearhead battalion when the Navy asked for reinforcement for 3 Commando Brigade RM and had been replaced as Spearhead, in normal sequence, by the 3rd when the Navy asked for more infantry. When 5 Airborne Brigade was ordered to follow, its two parachute battalions were replaced by 2nd Scots Guards and 1st Welsh Guards because both were handy for Aldershot, where their commanding officers were summoned for briefing on the exercise, hastily arranged in Wales, before 5 Brigade sailed. 'Elitism' did not enter discussions as to which units should join the force.
5 The *motti* tactics employed by the Finns during the Winter War of 1939/40 derived their name from the Finnish word for a cubic metre of logs cut and stacked on forest tracks awaiting collection. In similar fashion, the columns of invading Soviet troops were cut up and isolated on the same narrow tracks, besieged and starved either to death or to surrender.

CHAPTER 7

1 Lieutenant-Colonel Duncan Green carried his enthusiasm for the canine species into civilian life by becoming the Director of the Battersea Dogs' Home.
2 The 'Arms Plot' is the plan, revised each year, for the routine movement of field force units of the Army through the various stations at home and abroad. To prevent any unit receiving favourable treatment, the Plot is checked at every level up to the Chief of the General Staff. Even so, those responsible for drawing up the initial plan are subjected to intense lobbying of varying degrees of subtlety.
3 The QRF (Quick Reaction Force) was usually of section strength, standing by at immediate notice to move to the scene of any emergency.

4   In the Armed Forces operational honours list of 9 May 1995, Major Christopher Dockerty was posthumously awarded The Queen's Commendation for valuable service. This was a newly instituted award ranking with a mention in despatches and The Queen's Commendation for brave conduct.

CHAPTER 8

1   The allocation of 'man-training days' for individual members of the Territorial Army varied according to a need to encourage training, on the one hand, and exercise financial restraint on the other. The average annual usage was around thirty-four days, of which fourteen days were allocated for the annual camp. Dedicated individuals fulfilled many more days work than the average, utilizing the allocation of days not taken up by other men of the same unit.
2   The Russian *Spetznas* special forces were reputably modelled on the British SAS Regiment methods of training, initiative and self-reliance.
3   An affiliation with the destroyer HMS *York* began in 1992 in recognition of allegiance to the city shared by the ship's crew and the regiment.
4   The Allied Rapid Reaction Corps was established by NATO, after the collapse of the Warsaw Pact in 1990, to provide a structure to deal with any new threat to peace in Europe.

CHAPTER 9

1   Under the *Options for Change* defence review of 1990–92 the manpower allocation to regular army bands was reduced to an extent that individual cavalry and infantry regimental bands could no longer be sustained. The band of The Prince of Wales's Own was disbanded at a parade held at Osnabruck on 9 July 1994 and the musicians dispersed to the newly formed Normandy and Waterloo Bands, the latter becoming affiliated to the three Yorkshire infantry regiments.
2   Major, later Lieutenant-Colonel, Dick Glazebrook was a determined seeker of unusual detachments. His work in the Somali-Ethiopian frontier region arose from a detachment *from* the Somaliland Scouts to the Foreign and Commonwealth Office.
3   Captain W. C. A. Battey, having been trained in sabotage, terrorism and counter-terrorism, and operating under the auspices of the FCO, trained a group of ex-Indian Army officers and NCOs in these techniques in the Indian Himalayas in 1965 with a view to their use by the Indian Army against any invading Chinese force at that time. For a year from April 1965 he commanded a force of the Malaysian Border Scouts in cross-border operations against military camps used by Indonesian raiding parties penetrating into Sarawak, East Malaysia.
4   By a remarkable coincidence, 4th and 7th Armoured Brigades fought together in the British Army's first victory in the Second World War –

General Sir Richard O'Connor's lightning defeat of Marshal Graziani's much larger force in Cyrenaica in the winter of 1940–41.

CHAPTER 10

1. *Nec aspera terrent* – the regimental motto usually translated as 'Nor do difficulties deter' – is used as a shout of encouragement to those on the sports field and, in particular, on the cross-country course.
2. The Queen's Challenge Cup was presented for competition by Territorial Army units by King George VI and renamed The Queen's Challenge Cup in 1952.
3. A rugby pitch was found in Spain and used by the 1st Battalion team in the last season before leaving Gibraltar.
4. Sergeant Melvin 'Robbo' Robinson continued as the boxing coach for the 1st Battalion almost without break until appointed RSM of 2nd Battalion The Yorkshire Volunteers in 1991.
5. AMF(L). See chapter 6.
6. SEME. See chapter 6, note 3.

CHAPTER 11

1. Of officers first commissioned into The Prince of Wales's Own since 1958, Frank Walker was the first to be appointed a Lieutenant-Colonel Quartermaster.
2. Captain Dennis Jolly himself served as Families Officer 1989–90, while the 1st Battalion was in Catterick, and in Osnabruck until 1991.
3. Having left the service by the time his award was made public, Corporal Whiting first heard the news on the morning programme of Radio Teesside.
4. Major Terry Darley was due to leave the battalion for resettlement training and terminal leave halfway through the battalion's time in Bosnia, but remained at his post until the battalion had returned.

CHAPTER 12

1. This quotation is taken from a despatch by Winston Churchill, while a war correspondent for the *Morning Post* during the South African War 1899–1902, after he had witnessed the march of British troops through Pretoria.
2. Aside from the Muslim Albanians in Kosovo, the Croats, Muslims and Serbs of former Yugoslavia are all ethnic Slavs. The six states of the federation were Bosnia-Herzegovina, Croatia, Macedonia, Montenegro, Serbia and Slovenia.
3. Slovenia, the first to leave the federation, struggled free with only token protest from Belgrade.
4. The title of UN Protection Force (UNPROFOR) was (possibly intentionally) misleading. The 'protection' was only for the humanitarian aid and, later, for detainees whom the factions agreed from time to time to release. Hardly

surprisingly, in view of the title of the force, the bulk of the population believed it had arrived to protect *them*.

5 The referendum proposal put President Izetbegovic in an unenviable position. If he declined, friends and enemies would accuse him of fearing the verdict of the people. If he accepted, he knew that a 'no' vote would vindicate the Bosnian Serbs' opposition to his independence bid and strengthen their hand in seeking to become a part of 'Greater Serbia'. A 'yes' vote would alienate the Serbs completely and lead to the violence already seen across the border in Croatia. He took the statesman's option and the consequences that would follow.

6 Units of the Yugoslav National Army (JNA) were stationed in Bosnia but tanks, artillery and heavy mortars were held under close Serbian control, as were stockpiles of weapons for reserve units of the Teritorijalna Odbrana. When the JNA withdrew from Bosnia, the stockpiles were handed over to Bosnian Serb reservists, leaving the Croat and Muslim reservists with smallarms only and a handful of mortars and artillery pieces.

7 The Light Dragoons were formed from the amalgamation of the 13th/18th Royal Hussars (Queen Mary's Own) and 15th/19th The King's Royal Hussars following the 1990-2 *Options for Change*.

8 Locally known as the 'cricket team', the European Community Monitoring Mission (ECMM) wore white suits and were unarmed. They were described by Lieutenant-Colonel Alastair Duncan as 'a catalyst across all levels and an invaluable source of good advice and useful information'.

9 Miss Suzanna Hubjar, the 1st Battalion's Croat interpreter at Vitez, had interrupted her medical studies at Guy's Hospital to be in Bosnia. The battalion arranged for her to return to London to complete her degree.

List of Abbreviations

AFV	armoured fighting vehicle
AMF(L)	Allied Command Europe Mobile Force (Land)
APC	armoured personnel carrier
ATUC	Aden Trades Union Confederation
BAOR	British Army of the Rhine
BEF	British Expeditionary Force (1914–18 & 1939–40)
BiH	Bosna I Hercegovina (Bosnian Muslim Army)
BOAC	British Overseas Airways Corporation
CENTO	Central Treaty Organization
CND	Campaign for Nuclear Disarmament
COP	close observation platoon (Northern Ireland)
CPX	command post exercise
DF	defensive-fire task (usually pre-registered)
EAP	Eastern Aden Protectorate
ECMM	European Community Monitoring Mission
ENOSIS	desired Hellenic union of Cyprus with Greece (correctly 'Hénosis')
EOKA	National Organization of Greek Cypriot fighters
FAC	forward air controller (with ground forces)
FIBUA	fighting in built-up areas
FLOSY	Front for the Liberation of South Yemen
FNG	Federal National Guard (South Arabia)
FRA	Federal Regular Army (South Arabia)
GPMG	general purpose (7.62 mm) machine-gun
HESH	high-explosive squash-head (armour-penetrating) ammunition
HVO	Hrvatska Vijece Obrane (Bosnian Croat militia)
IGB	Inner-German border (prior to unification)
INLA	Irish National Liberation Army (terrorist group)
IRA	(The 'official') Irish Republican Army
LAD	light aid detachment (of the REME)
LST	landing ship (tank)
LSW	light support weapon (SA 80 5.56 mm machine-gun)
NICRA	Northern Ireland Civil Rights Association
NLF	National Liberation Front (South Arabia)
OIRA	'official' Irish Republican Army

LIST OF ABBREVIATIONS

OP	observation post or point
PIRA	Provisional (Army Council of the) Irish Republican Army
PLO	Palestine Liberation Organization
PSP	Peoples' Socialist Party (South Arabia)
RFA	Royal Fleet Auxiliary (vessel)
RHA	Royal Horse Artillery (now mechanised)
RUC	Royal Ulster Constabulary
SACEUR	NATO Supreme Allied Commander Europe
SAL	South Arabian League
SAS	Special Air Service Regiment
SBA	Sovereign Base area(s) of Cyprus
SHAPE	Supreme Headquarters Allied Powers Europe
SLR	self-loading (7.62 mm) rifle
SMG	Sterling sub-machine-gun
Tac HQ	tactical headquarters
TAOR	tactical area of responsibility
TAVR	Territorial Army & Volunteer Reserves
UDA	Ulster Defence Association (Protestant)
UDR	Ulster Defence Regiment
UKLF	United Kingdom Land Forces (now Land Command)
UNF	United National Front (Aden)
UNFICYP	United Nations Force in Cyprus
UNHCR	United Nations High Commission for Refugees
USC	Ulster Special Constabulary
VOPO	Volkspolizei (East German security police)
WAP	Western Aden Protectorate
WETC	Weekend Training Centre (used by Territorial Army units and cadets)

Bibliography

Balfour-Paul, Glen, *The End of Empire in the Middle East*, Cambridge University Press, 1991.
Barker, Lieutenant-Colonel A. J., *The East Yorkshire Regiment*, Leo Cooper, 1971.
Barker, Lieutenant-Colonel A. J., *The West Yorkshire Regiment*, Leo Cooper, 1974.
Barber, Tony; Bellamy, Christopher and Cathcart, Brian, 'Bosnia – Why They Are Killing Each Other', *The Independent on Sunday* 16 August 1992.
Barzilay, David, *The British Army in Ulster*, vols. 1 to 4, Century Books, Belfast, 1973–81.
Bidwell, Robin, *The Two Yemens*, Longman Group and Westview Press, 1983.
Bowen, Roderic, QC, *Procedures for the Arrest, Interrogation and Detention of Suspected Terrorists in Aden*, HMSO, 1966
Chant, Christopher, *Handbook of British Regiments*, London and New York, Routledge, 1988.
de la Billière, General Sir Peter, KCB, KBE, DSO, MC, *Storm Command: A Personal Account of the Gulf War*, HarperCollins, London, 1992.
Dewar, Lieutenant-Colonel Michael, *The British Army in Northern Ireland*, Arms and Armour Press, London, 1985.
Duncan, Colonel A. D. A., DSO, OBE, 'Operating in Bosnia', *RUSI Journal*, June 1994.
Graves, Robert, *Goodbye to All That*, London, Jonathan Cape, 1929.
Hasek, John, *The Disarming of Canada*, Toronto, Key Porter, 1987.
Historical Record of 1st Battalion The Prince of Wales's Own Regiment of Yorkshire, 1959–1994.
Horne, Alastair, *Macmillan 1957–1986*, Macmillan, London, 1989.
Kitson, General Sir Frank, *Bunch of Five*, Faber and Faber, London, 1977.
Magas, Branka, *The Destruction of Yugoslavia*, Verso, London, 1993.
Nightingale, Lieutenant-Colonel P. R., *A History of the East Yorkshire Regiment in the War of 1939–45*, York and London, William Sessions, 1952.
Podmore, Major A. J., MBE, TD, *Volunteer Artillery and Volunteer Infantry in the County of York 1859–1993*. privately published, 1994.
Sandes, Lieutenant-Colonel E. W. C., DSO, MC, *From Pyramid to Pagoda: The Story of the West Yorkshire Regiment (The Prince of Wales's Own) in the War 1939–45*, F. J. Parsons, London and Hastings, 1951.

Spencer, Major H. A. V., *A Short History of the Prince of Wales's Own Regiment of Yorkshire (XIV and XV Foot) 1685–1966*, privately published, 1966.

Vines, Lieutenant-Colonel T. C. E., *A Handbook on Northern Ireland*, published by Headquarters 8th Infantry Brigade.

White Rose, The, The Journal of The Prince of Wales's Own Regiment of Yorkshire, 1959–1994.

Index

A (Leeds Rifles) Fire-Support Company, 3rd Battalion, The Prince of Wales's Own Regiment of Yorkshire, 174
abbreviations, 274–5
Abercorn Barracks, Ballykinler, 146
Abraham, Heights of, 4
Abram, The Reverend Paul, 96, 119
ACE Mobile Force (AMF(L)), 91, 97, 121–31, 132, 133, 145, 178, 180, 198, 200, 213, 270; Northern Contingencies Region, 124 (Map 11); contingency plan areas, 270
Adair, A., Appx 3, illus
Addis Ababa, 177
Addlington, T., 39
Aden, xiii, 15, 16 (Map 1), 17–46, 47, 51, 53, 57, 59, 97, 99, 101, 114, 117, 146, 168, 175, 176, 179, 189, 203, 207, 208, 209, 234, 266, Appx 4
Aden Armed Police, 22, 28, 42
Aden Brigade, 30, 46
Aden Protectorate Levies (APL), 19–20, 27
Aden Trades Union Confederation (ATUC), 18, 22, 26, 28, 32
Adenauer, Chancellor Konrad, 82
Adjei, A. P. 'Adj', illus
Agar, R., 180
Ahmici, 221, 222 (Map 15)
Ainsworth, K., 180
air-mobile operations, 131–7
Aisne, River, 5
Akabusi, K., 127, 130, 200, Appx 7
Akamas peninsula, 58 (Map 5), 63
Akrotiri, 58 (Map 5), 62–3, 267
Al-Asnaj, Abdullah, 26, 27

Al Burayqah (Little Aden), 16 (Map 1), 17, 266
Al Mansoura (detention centre), 16 (Map 1), 28–9, 41, 43
Al Milah, 21 (Map 2), 33, 34, 35, 36
Al Waht, 27
Alamein, Battle of, 8, 77
Alberta, 74, 75
Aldershot, 149, 192, 193, 198
Alderslade, M. 'Boo-Boo', illus
Alderson, H., Appx 5
Alexander-Sinclair, Maj-Gen David, 76
Ali, Sultan of Lehej, 19, 25
Allbeury, N. Le B., 76, 172, Appx 5, illus
Allen, J., 75; Mrs J., illus
Allied Forces' Day (Berlin), 85, 91, 94, illus
Allied Rapid Reaction Corps (ARRC), 173, 271, Appx 4
Altnagelvin Hospital, 106 (Map 9), 139, 140, 143
Am Nu'am, 22
Ambler, P., illus
Amherst, General The Lord, 4
Amman, 180
Andalsnes, 178
Andersonstown, 111 (Map 10), 113, 114, 115, 152
Andrew, HRH Prince, 52
Andrews, N., illus
Andropov, Yuri, 90
Anglo-Irish Agreement, 149
Anglo-Irish Treaty of 1921, 269
Anglo-Turkish Convention of 1913, 182
Anthony, J., 40

INDEX

Aosta, General Duke of, 8
Apprentices Boys' March, 99, 105, 145
Ar Rikab, 21 (Map 2), 36
Arakan, 9, 131
Archer, D., illus
Arctic, the, 121–131
Argyll and Sutherland Highlanders, The, 1st battalion, 41, 42, 152, 221, 223
Armagh (City or County), 76, 110, 147, 150
Armalite (carbine), 139
Armies, 8th, 8; 5th French, 166; 14th, 9, 50
Armour, Mrs P., 205, 213, illus
Armour, W. S. G., 53–4, 68–9, 70–1, Appx 3, illus
'Arms Plot', 145, 270
Army Benevolent Fund, 201
Army Regulation Act of 1871, 2
Army Volunteer Reserve II (AVR II), the 'Ever-Readies', 160, 163, 164
Arnold, M. 'Arnie', illus
Arzu, S., 186, Appx 7
Ashby, A., 177
Ashby, S., Appx 5
Asmara, 177
Aspel, C., 152
Astbury, P., 75, illus
Athabasca Glacier, 75
Atherton, M. A., Appx 5
athletics, 127, 130, 133, Gibraltar Championships 1959–61, 55, 190, Appx 6; Middle East Command Individual Championships 1966, 193; Near East Land Forces Competition 1971, Appx 6; Near East Command Inter-Service meeting 1971, 197; South West District Competition, 1981, 1982, 127, 199, Appx 6; 1983, Appx 6; Zone B Championships 1982, Appx 6; Berlin Brigade Competition 1983, 90, 199, Appx 6; 1984, Appx 6; Northern Ireland Championships 1985, Appx 6; Army Team Championship 1987, 1988, 201, Appx 6; 1st and 3rd Divisions Championships 1991, Appx 6; BAOR Championships 1991, 1992, Appx 6; Army Team Championship 1991, 1992, Appx 6; Army individual champions 1985, Appx 7; 1988, 201, 202, Appx 7; 1989, 1990, 1991, 1992, Appx 7
Atkin, W., 86
Atkinson, B., 136, Appx 3, illus; Mrs J., 136
Atkinson, Private, illus
Aughrim, Battle of, 269
Auker, A. G., 35–6, Appx 5, illus
Austin, D., 141, Appx 5
Australia, 50
Austria, 4, 10, 50, 77, 98, 206

B Fire-Support Company, 3rd Battalion, The Prince of Wales's Own Regiment of Yorkshire, 174
B Special Constabulary, 107, 108
Baden-Powell, Olave, Lady, 207
Baghdad, 187
Baghdad Pact, 175, 267
Bagnall, General Sir Nigel, 135
Bagshaw, F., Appx 7
Bahrein, 32
Bailey, T., 191
Baker, General Sir George, 100
Balderson, R. M., Appx 5
Ballykinler, 102–3 (Map 8), 104, 105, 132, 133, 135, 145–51, 200, 212, Appx 4
Ballymacarret, 111 (Map 10), 115
Ballymoney, 102–3 (Map 8), 108
Ballynahinch, 102–3 (Map 8), 104
Baltic Sea, 124 (Map 11), 126
Bandar Tawahi, 16 (Map 1), 17
Banja Luka, 217, 219 (Map 14), 222 (Map 15), 226, 229
Bardufoss, 124 (Map 11), 127
Barents Sea, 121, 124 (Map 11)
Barham, M. J., 120, Appx 5
Barker, M., 44
Barker, R. 'Dickie', 156, 190, Appx 7
Barley, D. A., 152, 154, Appx 3, Appx 5
Barley, P., 175
Barlow, Mrs L., illus
Barnett, M. B., Appx 5

Bateman, J., 196, 197
Bates, B., 61, 196
Battey, W. C. A., 52, 179, 271, Appx 5, illus
battle honours, 4–6, 8–9
Baynes, R., illus
Beal, D., 157
Beardow, C. M., Appx 5
Beaumont, Lance-Corporal, illus
Beckett, D., illus
Beckett, E. H. A., 45, 56, 75, 76, 113, 122, 136, 141, 142, 145, 189, Appx 3, Appx 5, illus
Beckett, J., 53
Beirut, 181–2
Belfast, 64, 72, 78, 79, 101, 104, 105, 108, 109, 110, 111 (Map 10), 112–20, 138, 140, 145, 146, 151–4, 211, 215, 234, Appx 4
Belgrade, 219 (Map 14), 226
Benares (Varanasi), 3
Bennett, D., 200, illus
Bennett, J. H., illus
Bennett, P., 180
Bergen, 123, 124 (Map 11)
Berlin, 5, 72, 81–98, 83 (Map 7), 129, 145, 191, 192, 192, 200, 206, 213, 234, Appx 4
Berlin Brigade, 84, 87, 88, 90, 92, 98, Appx 4
Berlin Wall, 78, 81, 82, 89, 90
Berry, J., illus
Berry, T., 186
Berryman, J., 37
Bertie, D. J., Appx 3
Bessbrook, 102–3 (Map 8), 147; Mill, 148
Beswick, The Lord, 32
Beverley, 77, 155, 157 (Map 12), 158, 161, 170, 171, 173, 174, Appx 4
Biggs, D., 95
BiH (Bosna I Hercegovina) militia or 'Armija', 223–4, 231
Bihac, 219 (Map 14), 220
Bingley, R., illus
Bingley, S. P., 225, Appx 5
Binns, G. J., 92, 154, 223, 229, Appx 3, Appx 5

Binns, T., 152
Birbeck, Maj-Gen T. H., 159
Bird, M., illus
Birdsall, G., 130, 200, Appx 7, illus
Birkett, T. R., 27, 29, 31, 32, 38, 39, 40, 42, Appx 3, Appx 5, illus
Birkinshaw, N., Appx 5
Bishop, A., illus
Bishop, Brigadier Dick, 209
Bisley, 76, 133, 158, 160
Black Watch, The, 1st battalion, 75, 197–8
'Black September', 179
Blackfoot, Chief of the, 74, illus
Blackmountain School, 118
Blagdon, J., Appx 3
Blagdon, K. A., 152, 154, Appx 5, illus
Blair, D., 201, Appx 7
Blanch, A. C. G., 63, 96, 154, 173, Appx 3, Appx 5
'Bloody Sunday', 110, 112
Blowman, R., Appx 7
'blue on blue', 186
Blyth, P., xiv, 61, 88, 94, 95, 113, 127, 195, 196, 198, 200, Appx 3, Appx 7, illus
Blythe, R., 39
Bogside, 106 (Map 9), 99, 107–8, 141, 142, illus
Bolton, Captain Philip (RAMC), 143
Bolton, K. A., 45, 46, 51, 195, Appx 5, Appx 7, illus
Booker, D., Appx 5
Booker, R., 173
Bordon, 72
Borrett, L. K., 191, Appx 3
Bosnia, 78, 80, 209, 214, 215, 216–32, 219 (Map 14), 222 (Map 15), 233, 234, Appx 4
Bosnia-Herzegovina, 216, 217, 218
Bosnian Croats, 218, 220, 221, 227, 228, 230, 272
Bosnian Muslims, 218, 220, 221, 227–8, 230, 272
Bosnian Serbs, 216, 218, 220, 221, 228, 229, 272
Bostock, A., 154, Appx 3, Appx 5
Bostock, E., Appx 3

Boston, USS, 50
Boulter, H. E., Appx 5
Bowen, Rodrick QC, 29
Bower, A. B., 52, 54, 104, 189, illus
Bower, M. W., 186, 225, Appx 5
Bowland, A., illus
Bowman, K., illus
boxing, 133, 134, 137; BFAP Team competition 1958, 189, Appx 6; BFAP Open Individual Championships 1958, Appx 6, illus; Gibraltar Novices' Competition 1959, 190, Appx 6; Gibraltar Open Championships 1960, 1961, 190, Appx 6; 50th Division Open Championships 1960, Appx 6; 2nd Division Individual Championships 1961–2, 191; Berlin Brigade Team Championship 1964–5, 193, Appx 6; Aden 1965–6, 194, Appx 7; Scarborough Cup TA Team Boxing Championship 1965–6, 194, Appx 6; Army Zone D Competition 1966–7, 194–5; Celle, 1st Division Novices' Competition 1977–8, 198, Appx 6; South West District Novices' Competition 1982, 199; Berlin Brigade Inter-Company Competition 1984, Appx 6; BAOR Intermediate Championship 1984, 200; North East District Grade III Novices' Championships 1987–8, 133, 201, Appx 6; Northern Zone Novices' Team Championship 1987–8, 133, 201, Appx 6; Army (UK) Grade III Novices' Championship 1987–8, 201, Appx 6; Army Grade II Novices' Champions 1988–9, 196, Appx 6; 1st Division Grade III Novices' Team Championship 1989–90, Appx 6
Boyne, Battle of the, 95, 105, 150, 269
Boynton, K., illus
Bradford, 12, 72, 77, 157 (Map 12), 168, 171
Bradley, R., 46, 117, 120, Appx 5, illus
Bramall, Field-Marshal Sir Edwin, 4, 94, 95–7, 98, illus

Brandenburg Gate, 80, 81, 85
Brandywell estate, 106 (Map 9), 141, 143, 143
Brasher, J. J., Appx 3
Braybrook, M., 186, Appx 3
Brecht, H., 192, illus
Brezhnev, Leonid, 73, 90
Brigades: 1st Guards, 11; 3rd Commando, 129, 270; 3rd Infantry, 110, 116; 4th Guards, 69; 4th Armoured, 79, 183–5, 271–2; 5th Airborne, 270; 7th Armoured, 72, 73, 79, 138, 183–6, 271–2, Appx 4; 8th Infantry, 110, 143, 154, Appx 4; 12th Armoured, 78, 151, 183, Appx 4; 12th Infantry Brigade, 69, 70, 86, 87, 191, Appx 4; 15th (North-East), 173, Appx 4; 19th Infantry, 14, 208–9, Appx 4; 24th Air-Mobile, 78, 133, 135, 172, Appx 4; 24th Infantry, 132; 26th Gurkha, 12; 39th Infantry, 110, 145, 146, 147, 148, 151, 154, Appx 4; 48th Gurkha, 12; 99th Gurkha, 12; 146 Infantry TA, 159, Appx 4
Brindle, Lance-Corporal, illus
British Army of the Rhine (BAOR), 65, 73, 77, 79, 80, 87, 97, 110, 112, 138, 158, 164, 183, 190, 200
British Expeditionary Force (BEF) 1914–18, 5, 8
British Petroleum, 24
Broadbent, Sir Andrew, Bt, 186
Broadhurst, 'Blackie', illus
Broadman, G. M., 56, 190
Broadway tower, 153
Brook, B., 167
Brooke Barracks, 83 (Map 7), 90
Brooke Park, 106 (Map 9), 140
Brooks, Mrs 'Jimmie', 207, illus
Browell, Major Marcus (Light Dragoons), 223
Brown, Lance Corporal M. (King's), 226, Appx 5
Brown, M., illus
'Brownies', 119, 149, 207, illus
Browning, CSMI (APTC), illus
Broz, Josip (Tito), 216
Bruce. R., 114, illus

Bruce, R. M., Appx 5
Bryan, N. H. 'Paddy', 156, 158, Appx 3, Appx 5
Buckley, K. 'Moose', illus
Bulford, 122, 125, 128, 130, 133, 145, 171, 181, 198, 212, 213, Appx 4
Bulgaria, 121
Bull, J. W. C., 157
Bullen, P. H., Appx 3
Bulmer, N., 201, Appx 5, Appx 7
Burgin, R., 34, 39
Burke, P. 'Amos', 76, 180, illus
Burma Campaign, 7, 9, 10, 53, 96
Burnett, H., 171
Burnip, S. J., Appx 3, illus
Burns, N., Appx 7, illus
Burntollet, 100, 102–3 (Map 8)
Burton, A. J. 'Ginger', 135
Burton, J. A. 'Tosh', 191
Burton, K. J., 147, 151, Appx 5
Bury, H., 166
Butel, D., illus
Byrne, S. J., 186

C (Leeds Rifles) Company, 3rd Battalion, The Prince of Wales's Own Regiment of Yorkshire, 173
'Ça Ira', 5
Cadiz, 176
Cain, I., illus
Cairo Conference of 1921, 182
Calder, Lieutenant J. A. J. (Gordons), Appx 5
Caley, S. R., 94, 137, 152
Callan, G., Appx 7, illus
Calverley, A., Appx 5
Calvert, A., illus
Cambridge University, 51–2
Campbell, M., 38
Campey, B., 27, Appx 3, Appx 5, illus
Canada, 73, Appx 4
Canberra, SS, 178, illus
Cantrell, R. F., Appx 3
Cape, J. G., Appx 5
Cardwell, Edward, 2, 7
Carinthia, 206
Carn Hill estate, 140

Carlton (New) Barracks, 166
Carlton (Old) Barracks, 156, 158, 161, 165
Carrington, S., 207; Mrs D., 207
Carter, T., 46
Casablanca, 176
Castleford, 156, 157 (Map 12), 165, 173, 174, Appx 4
Castlereagh, 100, 102–3 (Map 8), 140
Castlewellan, 102–3 (Map 8), 149
Catterick, 78, 80, 131–7, 157 (Map 12), 172, 183, 193, 196, 200, Appx 4
Cawkwell, B., xiv, 61, 75, 127, 152, 196, 197, 199, Appx 3, Appx 5, Appx 7, illus
Celle, 66 (Map 6), 72–7, 78, 122, 138, 145, 196, 197, 198, 213, Appx 4
Central Treaty Organization (CENTO), 58, 267
Ceremony of the Keys (Gibraltar), 48
Charity Commissioners, 170
Charlottenburg, 83 (Map 7), 90, 206
Cheshire Regiment, The, 1st battalion, 220
'Chetniks', 216
Chappelow, Lance-Corporal, illus
Charles II, King, 2
Charles, Sir Arthur, 27
Chichester-Clark, Rt. Hon. James, 101, 105, 107
Chinook helicopter (s), 135, illus
Chippendale, P. 'Ginge', illus
Chippendale, T. S. 'Chippy', illus
'Chobham' protective armour, 186
Christison, General Sir Philip, 9
Churchill, Sir Winston S., 88, 99, 100, 216, 268, 272
Clark, Corporal, illus
Clark, M. C., Appx 5
Clark, P., illus
Clarke, N. F., Appx 5
Clark, M. C. 'Nobby' (1st battalion), illus
Clarke, 'Mack', illus
Clarke, 'Nobby' (3rd battalion), 160
Clay, E. W., 156, 158, 166, 167, Appx 3, Appx 5
Cleopatra, HMS, 126

Clerides, Glavkos, 63, 268
Clifford's Tower, 169
Clifton's Regiment of Foot (Sir William), 2
Clocktower Hill, 43, 44 (Map 4), 45
close observation platoon (COP), 146, 147, 148, 150
Clune, J., illus
Clutterbuck, S., 180
CND, 132
Cocker, D., xiii
Cocker, J., 178
Coffee, P., 108
Colchester, 42, 61, 63, 100, 105, 108, 194, 195, 207, 208–9, Appx 4
Cold War, 80, 82, 90, 96, 138, 167, 234
Coldstream Guards, 177; 1st battalion, 198; 2nd battalion, 28
Coldstream Regiment of Foot Guards, 2
Colley, Private, illus
Colours, Presentation of, 52–4, 93, 96–7, 161, 162, illus
Command Hill (Aden), 16 (Map 1), 31, 43
Commandos, Royal Marines, 42 Commando, 35, 130; 45 Commando, 46
Conroy, M., 192, Appx 7, illus
Convent, the (Gibraltar), 48, 52
Conway, 'Paddy', illus
Cook, A., Appx 7
Cooke, G., 157
Cooper, A. M., Appx 5
Copenhagen, 71, 124 (Map 11), 127
Copperwaite, T., 130, 201, 255, Appx 7, illus
Cornell, G., 37–8
Corps, 1st British, 67, 72, 73, 92, 132, 133, 183, 191; VII (US), 185; XV British, 9; XVIII (US), 185
Corps of Drums, 48, 56, 176–8; Territorial battalions, 160
Corunna, 4
Cossens, S. J. V., illus
Cowen, A. B., 136, 152
Cowper, A. W., Appx 5
Coyle, J., 140

Craigavon bridge, 106 (Map 9), 142, 143; camp, 142; Paisley march over, 143
Crammond, A., illus
Crater, 22, 23 (Map 3), 26–33, 34, 35, 38, 39, 41, 42, 43, 45, 101, 208, 234
Craze, D., Appx 5
Cree, G. H., 9, 14, 15, 39, 54, Appx 3, illus
Creggan estate, 106 (Map 9), 107, 139, 140, 141, 142
cricket, 137; Army Competition 1972, 119, 197, Appx 6, illus; Northern Ireland Cup 1972, 197, Appx 6; BAOR Infantry Cup 1983, 200, Appx 6; Northern Ireland Cup 1985, 200, Appx 6; 1986, Appx 6; Yorkshire Army League Cup 1987, 200, Appx 6
Crimea, 4
Criminal Injuries Act, 269–70
Croatia, 216, 217, 218, 219 (Map 14), 273
Croat-Muslim alliance, 221, 229, 230
Crom Castle, 117
Cross, C., 139
cross-country, 130, 149; 12th Infantry Brigade Competition 1962, 69, Appx 6; 1963, 191, Appx 6; Berlin Brigade Championship 1963, 87, 192; 1964, 192, Appx 6; 1st Division Championship 1965, 193, Appx 6; 49th Infantry Division TA Championships 1965, 193, Appx 6; 1967, 195; BAOR Team Championship 1964, 87; 1965, 193; Army Championship 1965, 193; 1966, 195; Middle East Command Championship 1966, 88, 193, Appx 6; Northern Command TA Championship 1966, Appx 6; 1967, Appx 6; 1968, Appx 6; Southern Command Championship 1967, Appx 6; Near East Land Forces Championship 1972, Appx 6; South West District Competition 1982, Appx 6; Army Championship 1982, 198, Appx 6; 3rd Armoured Division Championship 1983, Appx 6; 1984,

Appx 6; Army Championship 1983, 88, 199, Appx 6; Berlin Brigade Championship 1984, Appx 6; Army Championship 1984, 1985, 1986, 88, 200, Appx 6; 1987, 88, Appx 6; 1988, 201, Appx 6; 1989, Appx 6; BAOR Championships 1991, 80; 1992, Appx 6; Army Championships 1991, 1992, 202, Appx 6 cross-country relay, 133; Army Championships 1982, 198, Appx 6; 1983, 130, 199, 200, Appx 6; 1984, 1985, 1986, 149; 1987, 200, Appx 6; 1988, Appx 6; 1991, 1992, 202, Appx 6
Crossland, C. W., Appx 5
Crossmaglen, 102–3 (Map 8), 147, 148
Crowcroft, E., Appx 5
Crowfoot, A. B., xiii, 60, 73, 74, 137, 138, 140, 145, Appx 3, Appx 5, illus; Crowfoot, Mrs B., 207, illus
Crowfoot, Chief of the Blackfoot Tribe, 74
Crowfoot, R. J., 201
Crowther, D., illus
'Cruisewatch', 132
Crummack, B. J., 152, Appx 3
Cubiss, J. M., xiii, 13, 123, 163, 171, Appx 3, Appx 5
'Cub' Pack, 207, illus
Cunningham, M., illus
Curtis, A. 'Taff', 201
Curzon, Sir George, 266
Cyprus, 15, 19, 47, 57–64, 58 (Map 5), 97, 177, 179, 195, 199, 209–11, 234, Appx 4
Cyrenaica, 79
Czechoslovakia, 167

D-Day (1944), 9
Daly, Bishop Cahal, 144
Dallas, 84
Dar am 'Umayrah, 22
Dardanelles, 6
Darley, T. R., 215, 272, Appx 3, illus
Davenport, B., 156
Davidson, P. (REME), 134
Davies, J. L., Appx 3, illus
Davies-Rockcliffe, C. 'Scouse', 152

Davis, A. K., Appx 5
Davis, D., Appx 7
Davis, P. 'Danny', 51
Davis, Private, illus
Davison, P., 43, 46, Appx 5
Davison, R., 37, illus
Day, C. R., 120, Appx 5
de Gaulle, President Charles, 82
de Guingand, Maj-Gen Sir Francis, 77
Dean, P., illus
Deedes, Brigadier John, 159
'defence of the river line', 66, 67, 68
Defence Review 1956–7, 67, 156
Denham, A. M., Appx 5
Denison, E. A. K., xiv, 157, 159, 165, Appx 3, Appx 5
Denison, J. B., Appx 5
Denmark, 71, 126, 131, 178
Dennis, C. Appx 3
Dent, B., 117–18, 120, Appx 5, illus
Desmond, J. H., 139, illus
Devonish, J. A., Appx 7
Devonshire, HMT, 19
Dhala, 20, 21 (Map 2), 33, 34, 35, 37, 179, 193
Dhala, Emir of, attack on palace, 38; Ottoman protection of, 266
Dhekelia, 58 (Map 5), 58, 60, Appx 4
Diamond, J. 'Legs', 76, 95, 143, illus
'Diamond' route, 226
Dickman, S., illus
Dickson, R., 76
Digest of Service (1st Battalion), 61
Dilcock, B., illus
Dillon, J. M. P., 39, 190, Appx 3, Appx 5
Dimapur, 9
Dingy Team Race, North East District, Appx 6
Divis flats, 111 (Map 10), 153
Divisions, 1st, 72, 73, 75, 78, 88; 1st Armoured, 138, 151, 183–6, 215, Appx 4; 1st Federal, 12; 1st and 2nd (US) Marine, 185; 2nd, 9, 169, 191; 3rd, 8, 14; 5th Indian, 8, 9; 6th, 5, 6; 7th Armoured, 11; 10th (Soviet) Guards Tank, 87, 89; 11th, 6; 15th Japanese, 9; 17th Gurkha, 12; 17th

INDEX

Indian, 9, 10; 33rd Japanese, 9; 49th Infantry TA, 156, 190, 193, 194, 195; 50th (Tyne Tees), 8; 101st (US), 185
Dixon, R. E., Appx 5
Dobson, P. S., 230, Appx 5, illus
Dockerty, C. J., 96, 154, 271, Appx 2, Appx 5, illus
Dodd, D. H., 53, 56, 189, Appx 3, illus
dogs, 144
Donji Vakuf, 222 (Map 15), 226
Donlon, A. D. (Gordons), Appx 5
Doran, G., illus
Doran Thorpe, B. 'Chick', 71, 175
Dover, 15, 72, 203, Appx 4
Down (County), 101, 102–3 (Map 8), 104, 117
Dowson, B., illus
Doyle, C., 153
Doyle, Colonel Welbore Ellis, 5
Doyle, M., illus
Dransfield, M. J. A., 92
Drake, E., illus
Drowley, C. V., Appx 5
Duke, G., 175
Duke of Wellington's Regiment, The, 155, 164; 1st battalion, 120, 137
Duke of York, HRH, 3
'Duke of York's Own, The', 3
Duncan, A. D. A., 79, 151, 153, 215, 221, 224, 225, 231, 232, 273, Appx 3, Appx 5, illus
Dundrum Bay, 102–3 (Map 8), 146
Dungiven, 102–3 (Map 8), 105
Dunkirk, 8
Dunne, P., illus
Durham Light Infantry, The, 1st battalion, 82; 8th battalion, 194, 195
Duvno (Tomislavgrad), 222 (Map 15), 226, 230

E (Leeds Rifles) Company, The Yorkshire Volunteers, 167
East Riding, 12
East Surrey Regiment, The, 14
East Yorkshire Regiment, The, 3, 6, 14, 15, 71, 119; 1st battalion, 5, 7, 10, 11, 12, 13, 50, 57, 270; 2nd battalion, 7, 8, 9, 10; 4th battalion, 7, 8, 15, 156, 188, Appx 4; 5th battalion, 7, 8, 9; 6th battalion, 6
East Yorkshire Regimental Association, 170
Eastern Aden Protectorate (EAP), 18
Eastern Sovereign Base Area (Cyprus), 58 (Map 5), 60
Eastridge, C. L., 6
Eastwood, S., 114–15
Eaton, J. S., illus
Eddison, C. S., 77
Eden, Rt. Hon. Sir Anthony, MP, 14
Edgar, A. W., 171
Edwardes, Sir Michael, 213
Edwards, J., 'Smiler', 39
Egypt, 6, 41; Canal Zone of, 11, 13
Eisenhower, General Dwight, 65
Eley, S. J., Appx 5
Elliott, C., 30
Elliott, Sir George, 48
Elliott, N., 177, illus
Ellison, Mrs M., illus
Elsey, Corporal, illus
Emerson, S. W., Appx 5
Emmott, M., Appx 3
Emms, J., 61
Empire Guillemot, LST, 55
'Enclave', the, 102–3 (Map 8), 139, 140
England, M., 156
Enniskillen, 102–3 (Map 8), 119, 136
Enosis, 57
EOKA, 57
Episkopi, 58 (Map 5), 58, 60
'equivalent force', 101, 269
Esbjerg, 124 (Map 11), 127
Eskimo, HMS, 177
Ethiopia (Abyssinia), 8, 176, 177
'ethnic cleansing', 221
Europa Point (Gibraltar), 52, 54, 95
European Community, 218; Monitoring Mission (ECMM), 224, 273
Evans, J., illus
Evans, N. R. H., 136
'Ever-Readies', see Army Volunteer Reserve II (AVR II)
Exelby, G. W., Appx 5
Exercises: Agate Exchange, 126; Alloy Express, 129; Hardfall, 122, 127, 131,

213; Keystone, 132; Last Straw, 70, 71; Red Rat, 73; Martial Merlin, 173; Rocking Horse, 87; Snow Queen, 77, 79; Shooting Star, 92; Spring Gallop, 92

Fahaheel (Kuwait), 187
Fahd, King of Saudi Arabia, 183
Falkland Islands, 8
Falklands War, 128–9, 178, 233, 270
Falls, Falls Road, 109, 111 (Map 10), 114, 153
Famars, 5
families officer (s), 208, 213, 272
Farrell, T. H. F., 165, Appx 3
Fawcett, M. T. 'Diddly', 186
Federal National Guard (FNG) South Arabia, 28, 34–5, 36, 42; 2nd battalion, 35
Federal Regular Army (FRA) South Arabia, 27, 28, 34–5, 42, 179
Federation (of South Arabia) Supreme Council, 27
Fenn, R. C., Appx 3
Fermanagh, 102–3 (Map 8), 110, 117, 136
Fieldhouse, A., 89
Fieldhouse, Admiral of the Fleet The Lord, 233
15th/19th The King's Royal Hussars, 273
Filor, F. J. W., 112, 120, 122, 123, 125, 127–8, 191, 206, Appx 3, Appx 5, illus; Filor, Mrs H., 181, 213
Finland, 121
1st Division and Signal Regiment, 75
First World War (the Great War), 5–6, 18, 110
Fitzgerald, 'The Baron', 37
Fletcher, B., illus
Fletcher, J., illus
FLOSY, 32, 34, 35, 39, 41, 43, 45, 46
Foca, 219 (Map 14), 220
Fogarty, B., 189, 191
Fogg, P., 201, Appx 7
Folan, M., illus
Foley, B., 37, 38, Appx 2

Foljambe, The Hon. Bertie, 159; Trophy, 159
football (soccer), 127, 134, 137; Aden 1958–9, 189; BFAP Competition 1958, Appx 6; Gibraltar Major Units League 1960, Appx 6; 1961, Appx 6; Gibraltar Minor Units Knock Out Cup 1961, Appx 6; Hull and District Sunday League 1961, Appx 6; BAOR Challenge Cup 1962–3, 191; 49th Division TA Cup 1962, Appx 6; Berlin Brigade League 1964–5, 193, Appx 6; 19 Brigade Challenge Cup 1968, Appx 6; Cyprus 1970–2, 196–7; Western SBA Competition 1971, Appx 6; Northern Ireland Major Units League 1973, 197, Appx 6; Army Challenge Cup, 127, 197; Infantry Challenge Cup BAOR and Army final 1975–6, 75, 197, Appx 6; 1st Division League 1977, 1978, Appx 6; Salisbury Plain Services League 1980, Appx 6; South West District League 1981, Appx 6; Army Challenge Cup 1981, 199, Appx 6; Berlin Brigade 'A' and 'B' League Championships 1984–5, 200, Appx 6; Northern Ireland League 1986, Appx 6; BAOR Championship 1991, Appx 6; Army Challenge Cup, 202, 270
Ford, General Sir Robert, 125
Ford, H., 168
Forsyth, J. W. D., 91
Forsyth, R. H. J. 39, 88, 91, 92, 94, 97, 145–6, 149, 151, Appx 3, Appx 5, illus
Fort George, 106 (Map 9), 139
Fort Lewis USA, 134
Fort Morbut, 16 (Map 1), 30
Fort Whiterock, 111 (Map 10), 152
Forward Air Control unit No. 609, 123, 127
Fossli, 131
Four Corners Guard (Gibraltar), 48
4th Cruiser Squadron USN, 50
4th/7th Royal Dragoon Guards, 35, 36, 169
Fowler, K., 147, 151, Appx 5

INDEX

Foyle, River, 100, 106 (Map 9), 138, 141, 142, 145
Foyle Road, 106 (Map 9), 143
Fox, B., illus
Frais, A. D., Appx 5
France, 4, 8
Frank, D., 196, 199, illus; Mrs J., illus
Frankfurt am Main, 65
French, M., illus
Frewster, F., 173, Appx 5
Froggart, A., 95, illus
Front Bay, 16 (Map 1), 22
Frost, J., illus
Fulda Gap, 65, 66 (Map 6)
Fuller, W. J., Appx 5
Funen Island, 71, 124 (Map 11)
Furniss, L., 227
FV 432, 67, 72, 74, 78, 80

Gaines, A., 167
Gambia, HMS, 205
Garen, Olav, 131
Garnett, M., illus
Garrigan, M., 191, 193, 194–5, 196, Appx 7, illus; Mrs B., 119, illus
Garrigan, S., Appx 7
Garside, B. R. D., 19, 20, 47, 49, 53, 54, 98, 170, 171, Appx 3, illus
Garside, M. V., 38, 193, 197, Appx 7
Gazala Line, 8
Gazelle helicopter, 129
Geddes Cup, 71, 134–5, 151, 268, illus
Gee, D. B., Appx 5
Gemayel, Bashir, 181
General Service Medal (1918), 25; (1962), 34, 41, 108, 120, 145
George Cross, 13, Appx 1
George I, King, 268
George III, King, 4
George V, King, 3, 4
George VI, King, 272
Germain, P. S., 200
German Democratic Republic (GDR), 81, 82–3, 90
Germany, 7, 11, 50, 65–80, 66 (Map 6), 122, 135, 145, 190, 234
Gibbons, P., illus
Gibraltar, xiii, 47–57, 67, 69, 87, 92, 95, 97, 176, 190, 192, 204, 205, 234, Appx 4; Great Siege of, 48
Gibraltar Chronicle, 54
Gibraltar Regiment, The, 49
Gibson, Lord Justice, 150
Gibson, S., Appx 3
Gillett, D. I., 226, 227, Appx 5
Girdwood Park, 111 (Map 10), 152
Girl Guides, 119
Glazebrook, R., 45, 177, 178, 271, Appx 5
Glossop, A., 197
Gloucestershire Regiment, The, Appx 1
Glover, Maj-Gen Peter, 159
Goble, H. R., 120, Appx 5
Gold Mohur Bay, 16 (Map 1), 20; Camp, 22
Goodall, V., 43
Goole, 157 (Map 12), 173, 174, Appx 4
Goradze, 219 (Map 14), 220
Gorbachev, Mikhail, 73, 90, 269
Gordon Highlanders, The, 93, 1st battalion, 221, 223
Gornji Vakuf, 219 (Map 14), 222 (Map 15), 223, 226, 227, 229, 230
GPMG (7.62 mm machine-gun), 55, 67, 68, 150, 152
'Granby Garrisons', 79
Grannum, R., illus
Grant, A., 226, Appx 5
Gratangen Fjord, 124 (Map 11), 129
Graves, Robert, 2
Graz, 10
Graziani, Marshal, 79, 272
Grbavica, 225
'great motormower drama', 104
Great War, The (First World War), 5, 6, 7, 65
Greece, 57, 122, 126
Greek-Cypriot National Guard, 63
Greek-Cypriots, 57
Green, D. A. H., 34, 89, 133, 135, 141, 144, 149, 151, 270, Appx 3, Appx 5, illus
Green, J. W., Appx 5
'Greenfinch' women soldiers of the UDR, 115

Green Howards, The, 15, 78, 135, 155, 164
Grenade No. 36, 33, 55
Grenadier Guards, 2nd battalion, 150
Grivas, Colonel George, 57
Grosvenor Road, 111 (Map 10), 119
Gruenther, General Al, 65
Grünewald, 83 (Map 7), 86, 192
Guca Gora, 222 (Map 15), 227
Gulf of Aden, 16 (Map 1), 24
Gulf War, 78, 79, 184 (Map 13), 209, 214, 234
Gurkha Rifles, 12
Gurney, Sir Edward, 11
Guthrie, J., Appx 3
Gwilliams, J., illus

Habilayn, 20, 21 (Map 2), 33, 34, 35, 36, 37, 38
Haggan brothers ('16, '48 and '81), 59, 267–8
Hague Conference of 1929, 65
Haile Selassie, Emperor, 177, illus
Haines, Commander Stafford, 17, 22
Hales's Regiment of Foot (Sir Edward), 2
Haley, Corporal J. G. (Intelligence Corps), Appx 5
Halifax, Rt. Hon. The Earl of, 167, Appx 3
Hall, D. C., 45, Appx 5
Hall, P. 'Pip', 180–1, illus
Hallamshires, The, 164
Halliday, J. P. 'Scouse', illus
Halmshaw, J., Appx 3, Appx 5
Haltern training area, 66 (Map 6), 205–6
Hamburg, 65, 66 (Map 60
Hamelin, 66 (Map 6), 66
Hamilton, D., 39
Hancock, D. S., Appx 7, illus
Handley, P., 180
Hannover, 66 (Map 6)
Hanover, 4
Hanover, Horse of, 4, 50
Hanover, House of, 4
Hanson, D. W., xiii, 27, 40, 61, 64, 99, 104, 112, 113, 117, 120, Appx 3, Appx 5, illus; Mrs A, 119
Happy Valley (Cyprus), 61
Hardaker, G., 171, illus; Mrs P., 207, illus
Hardman, M., Appx 3
Hare, E., 114
Harewood Barracks, Leeds, 165, 173, 174
Hargreaves, J., 193, Appx 7
Hargreaves, K., 161, Appx 3
Harland, C., Appx 5
Harrap, J., 156
Harris, Lt-Gen Sir Ian, 101
Harrison, E., Appx 5
Harrison, P., illus
Harrogate, 77, 157 (Map 12), 161, 171
Hart, J. A. D., 87
Haushabi Tribe, 20, 21 (Map 2), 34
Haussmann, Baron Georges Eugène, 22
Havelsee, 81, 83 (Map 7), 86
Hawes, D., Appx 5
Hawes, M., 76, illus
Hawkins, K., Appx 7
Hay, Captain A. G. P. (Gordons), Appx 5
Haynes, M. T., 79, 187, 215, Appx 3, illus; Mrs E., Thomas and James, 187, illus
Haynes, P., 75, illus
Haywood, L., illus
Healey, Rt. Hon. Dennis, MP, 167
Heath, Rt. Hon, Edward, MP, 110, 115, 167
Heaton, P., illus
Heckler-Koch rifle, 131
Hegney, T., 129
Hejaf cemetery, 25
Helmstedt (checkpoint), 66 (Map 6), 84
Henderson, A., illus
Henderson, George, 26
Hepworth, C. F., 96
Hepworth, L., 45
Hess, Rudolf, 84, 90
Hickinbotham, Sir Tom, 25
Highfield, David (ACC), Mrs S., Claire, 149
Highland Light Infantry, The, 14

INDEX

Hill, A., 200
Hill, D., 95
Hill, D. A., 180–1, 223, Appx 5, illus
Hill, P. A., Appx 7, illus
Hinchcliffe, E., 178
Hinchcliffe, Peter, 38, 267
Hincks, A. D., 61, 139
Hindle, M., illus
Hinds, P. N., 117, 120, Appx 5, illus
Hochsauerland, 92
Hodgson, P. A., Appx 5
Holden, R. B., Appx 3
Holland, 4, 5
Hollingsworth, S. W. 'Olly', illus
Holmes, D. H., illus
Holmes, T. H. J., 117, illus
Holmes, T. J., 45, Appx 2
Holroyd, H. D., 142, 143
Holtby, S., 160
Holtom, Captain Spencer (RA) 29, 266
Holton, Corporal R. (Gordons), Appx 5
Homs, 55, 56, illus
Hope, S. J. 'Bob', illus
Hopkinson, B., illus
Hopper, G., illus
Hornby, L., illus
Horseley, M. 'Smiler', 191, Appx 7
Horton, K., 153, illus
Howard, H. A., Appx 3
Howard, K., Appx 3
Howell, D., 75
Hubjar, Suzanna, 225, 273
Hudson, T. A. 'Huddy', 151, 196, 198, Appx 5, illus
Hughil, A. N. W. 'Huggy', 46
Hull, 12, 77, 157 (Map 12), 157, 161, 166, 167, 171, 173, 174, Appx 4
'human shields', 187
Humber armoured 'Pig', 67, 132
Hunt, General Sir Peter, 73
Hunt, Lt-Col Ashton (Somerset Light Infantry), 9
Hunter, B., illus
Hunter ground-attack aircraft, 35, 36
Hunter, H., 149
Hunter, R., 200, 201, 223, 228, Appx 5, illus
Hussain, King of Jordan, 179, 183

Hussain, Saddam, 79, 182–3, 187
Hutchinson, C. F., 9
Hutchinson, G. S., Appx 3
Hutchinson, K., illus
Hutton, L., 61
HVO (Hrvatska Vijece Obrane) (Bosnian Croat militia), 223–5, 228, 229, 230, 231, 232
Hyam, J., 196, 198, illus
Hyde, D., illus
Hyman, C. R. 'Clint', illus

Iceland, 8
Idris, King of Libya, 55
Imam of Yemen, 18
Imjin River, Battle of, 13, Appx 1
Imphal, 9, 50, 86, 96, 131; Imphal Day, 9
Imphal Barracks, York, 155, 169
India, 6, 7, 8, 9, 10
Indiana, 173
Indonesia, 179
Infantry Keel Boat Sailing Regatta, 201, Appx 6
Inner German Border (IGB), 65, 66 (Map 6), 72
Inniskilling Cup, 61, 268
Inter Allied Show Jumping Competition, 167
Ipoh, 12
Iran-Iraq War, 182
Iraq, 6, 8, 9, 182–7, 184 (Map 13), 233, 234
Irish Guards, 1st battalion, 69
Irish Home Rule, 99, 269
Irish National Liberation Army (INLA), 150
Irish Republican Army (IRA), 100, 108, 109, 269
Irvin, H., 34, 39, 46
Isles, H., illus
Israel, 177
Italy (Italians), 8
Iveagh Crescent, 111 (Map 10), 153
Izetbejovic, Alija, 217–18, 273

Jackson, A. T., Appx 3
Jackson, C., 44, 117, Appx 5

Jackson, D., illus
Jackson, F., illus
Jackson, G. L., 96, 131, illus
Jackson, M. R., Appx 3
Jackson, P. A. C., illus
James, 'Jesse', 104, illus
James II, King, 2
Jarratt, G., xiv, 156, 160, 162, 165, 166, 167, Appx 3, illus
Jarvis, K., illus
Jasper, S., 53, 86
Jaszynski, G. R., 154, Appx 5
Jeapes, Maj-Gen Tony, 146
Jebel Lassat, 21 (Map 2), 37
Jebel Miswarah, 21 (Map 2), 37
Jebel Shamsan, 16 (Map 1), 43, 44 (Map 4), 46
Johansson, K., 69–70, Appx 5
Johnson, A., illus
Johnson, J., 127
Johnson, R., illus
Johnson, R. M., illus
Johnston, The Venerable Archdeacon Frank, Chaplain-General to the Forces, 96
Johore, 12, 13
Jolly, D., 210, 272
Jones, A., illus
Jordan, 18, 62,
Jowsey, M., Appx 5
Judenburg, 10
Junieh, 182

Kabul to Kandahar, the march from, 4
Karachi, 175
Karadzic, Radovan, 217–18
Kathendini forest (Kenya), 64
Kattegat, 124 (Map 11), 126
Keeney, M., 197
Keightley, General Sir Charles, 52
Kelly, A., 185
Kelly, B. P. 'Jock', 141, Appx 5
Kennedy, President John F., 81, 82, 86, 268

Kennedy, S. A., xiv, 108; Mrs J., illus
Kennerdale, G., 56

Kenny, D. S., Appx 7, illus
Kent, HRH The Duchess of, 79, 98, 137, 149, 171, 172, 214, 221, Appx 3, illus
Kent-Payne, V. R, 223; Mrs J., illus
Kenya, 63–4, Appx 4
Keren, Battle of, 8, 86, 177
Khormaksar, 16 (Map 1), 22, 24; airport, 16 (Map 1), 20, 26, 43
Khrushchev, Nikita, 81
Khusaf Valley, 16 (Map 1), 22, 34, 267
Kilkenny, E., 194, Appx 7
King, B., illus
King, General Sir Frank, 120
King, J. C. L., 78, 135, 136, 137, 184, 186, Appx 3, Appx 5, illus; Mrs S., 136
King, N., illus
King's Bastion (Gibraltar), 50
King's Division, The, 168
King's Own Border Regiment, The, 1st battalion, 147, 197
King's Regiment, The, 1st battalion, 85, 88, 192, 226
Kirk, A., illus
Kiseljak, 222 (Map 15), 221, 226, 230
Kladanj, 222 (Map 15), 226
Kladow, 82, 83 (Map 7), 86, 206
Knopp, J. F., 210
Knowles, B. 'Knocker', 79, 214
Korea, 13, 168, 176, Appx 1
Korotoga, S., illus
Kosovo, 216, 219 (Map 14)
Krajina, 216, 219 (Map 14)
Kranzegg (Bavaria), 77
Kuwait, 78, 79, 184 (Map 13), 182–7, 214
Kuwait (British Army) Liaison Team, 79, 187

La Bassée Canal, 8
La Panne, 8
La Linea, 56
Ladies cross-country team, 149, illus
Ladysmith, 4
Lagan, River, 102–3 (Map 8), 104
Lahej, 19, 25, 27; Lahej, Sultan of, 17, 33; Sultan Ali, 19, 25

INDEX

Laird, R. S. MacG., Appx 5, illus
Lancashire Fusiliers, The, 1st battalion, 71, 178
Lancaster House, 180
Langrick, F. W., 40, Appx 2
Lasva valley, 221, 222 (Map 15), 230
Latto, R., illus
Laverick, A., 40
Lawrence, R. 'Primus', 180
Le Brun, C. G., xiv, 141, Appx 3, appx 5
Le Fanu, Admiral Sir Michael, 31
Ledgeway, R., illus
Leeds, 12, 72, 77, 157 (Map 12), 139, 156, 162, 171, 174, Appx 4, illus
Leeds Rifles (see also 7th and 8th battalions The West Yorkshire Regiment), xiv, 7th and 8th battalions re-roled in 1938 and 1936 respectively, 7; re-roled to infantry post-Second World War, 7; amalgamated to form the Leeds Rifles 1961, 156, Appx 4; initial deployment 156–7, Appx 4; inauguration parade, 158; operational role, 159; sporting achievements, 160, 190, 194; Band and Drums, 160, 161; visit of HM The Queen to Leeds, 162, illus; becomes a TAVR III unit, 164–5; change of title, 165, Appx 4; regimental pilgrimage to Montagne de Bligny, 1968, 166; reduced to cadre of eight men, 166–7, Appx 4; campaign to ensure title carried forward, 166–7; formation of C (Leeds Rifles) Company of 3rd Battalion, The Prince of Wales's Own Regiment of Yorkshire, 173; amalgamates with A Company to form A (Leeds Rifles) Fire-Support Company, 174; deployment from end of 1994, 174, Appx 4
Leigh, Mrs H., illus
Leptis Magna ruins, 56
Leslie, Mrs S., illus
liaison officers, 224, 231
Libya, 55–6
Licence, D., illus
Life Guards, The, 20

Light Dragoons, The, 221–3, 230, 273
Light Infantry, The, 2nd Battalion, 138, 197
light support weapon (SA 80), 133
Lightning interceptor aircraft, 62
Ligoniel estate, 111 (Map 10), 118
Limassol, 58 (Map 5), 59, 62, 210
Lincolnshire and East Riding TA Association Band Competition, 161
Linskey, L., 211, Appx 3, illus; Miss A., 211; Mrs S., 211, illus
Lisnaskea, 102–3 (Map 8), 116
Lister, C. W., Appx 3
Little Aden, 16 (Map 1), 17 (Al Buraygah), 24, 40
Lockerbie disaster, 136
Lockwood, R., 152, Appx 5
Lofoten Islands, 123, 124 (Map 11)
Londesborough Barracks, Hull, 157, 165, 166
Londonderry, 109, 211, 212, 213, 234; 1969 first emergency deployment, 74, 76, 99, 104, 105–8, 106 (Map 9), 110, 112; 1975 Operation Banner tour, 74, 138–41; 1977 Operation Banner tour, 76, 141–5, 154; Appx 4
Long, J., 120, Appx 3, Appx 5
Longdon, G. M., 108, 144, Appx 5; Mrs J., 119
Lord Hunt's Commission of Inquiry into Policing in Northern Ireland, 108
Lossiemouth RNAS, 104
Lough Neagh, 101, 102–3 (Map 8), 104, 105
Louisburg, 4
Lubke, President German Federal Republic, 88
Lucas, S. G., 40, Appx 5
Luce, Sir Richard, 266
Lucknow, 3
Lumb, Lance-Corporal, illus
Lumley Barracks, York, 173
Lüneburg Heath, 66 (Map 6), 77
Lunt, T., 207
Lurgan, 102–3 (Map 8), 117
Lusignan Period, 62
Lyburn, D. B. St. J., 130, Appx 3

Lyons, R. A., 201, Appx 7

M'Benga, D. O., Appx 5
Ma'alla, 16 (Map 1), 22, 27, 30, 33, 40, 43
McAnulty, B. D., 141, Appx 5
McBurney, D., 147, 151, Appx 5, illus
McCullough, J., 188
McFadden, K., 150
McGarrell, Mrs B., 119, illus
McKenzie, A. 'Stumpy', 130
McKinder, M., illus
Macleod, Rt. Hon. Iain, MP, 25, 26
McManus, P. 'Mac', 175
McMennum, P., 143
Macmillan, Rt. Hon. Harold, MP, 14, 82
McNichol, C., illus
McSherry, J., 134
Maddocks, N., Appx 3
Magilligan Point, 102–3 (Map 8), 105
Maglaj, 222 (Map 15), 226; tunnels, 226–7
Maifeld (Berlin), 94
Main Pass, 16 (Map 1), 22
Malay Regiment, 12
Malaya, 11, 115, 176
Malayan Communist Party (MCP), 11
Malayan Peoples' Anti-Japanese Army, 11
Malaysia, 179, 266, 271
Malaysian Border Scouts, 179, 271
Malta, 48, 63
Makarios, Archbishop, 57, 62, 63
Mannheim-Seckenheim, 123
marathon, 130, 133; Army Team Championships 1982, 198, 202, Appx 6, 1983, 199, Appx 6; 1988, 201, Appx 6; 1989, Appx 6; 1990, Appx 6; 1991, Appx 6; Army Half Marathon Championship 1992, Appx 6
'marching season', 118
'Mark 15' coffee-jar bomb, 152
Mareth Line, 8
Marienborn checkpoint (Berlin), 84
Margison, P., illus
'Mariandl' (song), 10
Marlborough, 1st Duke of, 4'

Marsh, G., 61
Martin, R. A., 178, Appx 3, illus
Mason, Private, illus
Massawa, 177
Matthews, D. A., xiv, 134, 137, 196, 201, Appx 3, illus
Maungdaw, Battle of, 9
Maze Prison, 140
Meccawi, Abdul al-Qawi, 27, 266
Medley, Lieutenant J. C. (AGC), 227, Appx 5
Medley, P., illus
Mellors, G., 77
Mennell, Godfrey, 36
Menzies, F., 153
Michael. P., Appx 5
Middle East Command, 19
Middlemass, N., illus
Middlesbrough, 164
Middlesworth, A., 108
Middleton, K. H., 95, 147, 151, Appx 5
Middleton, L., illus
Milan anti-tank guided missile (s), 174, 223
Miles, K. W., 92, Appx 3, illus
Miles, L., 180
Military Cross, 13, 37, 168, 176, 229, 230, Appx 5
Military Medal, 36, 46, Appx 5
Milltown Cemetery, 111 (Map 10), 114, 152
Milne, A. A., 203
Milnes, S., 44
Milosevic, Slobodan, 216, 217
Mizon, P., 215
Moffat (Scottish village), 136
Moffat, D., xiv, 61, 75, 88, 135, 145, 149, 195, 196, 200, Appx 5, Appx 7, illus
Monck's Regiment of Foot (General George), 2
Monkman, G. J. 'Monkey', illus
Monks Field, 21 (Map 2), 34, 35, 267
Monmouth Rebellion, 2
Montagne de Bligny, 166
Montgomery Barracks, Berlin, 82, 83 (Map 7), 87, 206
Montgomery, Maj-Gen Bernard, 8

INDEX

Moore, General Sir John, 4
Moorehouse, K., illus
Moosburg, 206
Moran, Monsignor John, 96
Morley, 72, 156, 157 (Map 12), 160
Morley, A. M., Appx 5
Morris, K. D., Appx 5
Morris, The Reverend Edward, 53
Morrison, Mrs C., illus
mortars, 3 inch, 68; 81 mm, 31, 37, 68, 174, 223
Morton, R., illus
Moscow, 121
'motti tactics', 130, 270
Mottram, E., Appx 3
Mount Elliot, 75
Mount Kenya, 64
Mount Olympus (Cyprus), 58 (Map 5), 62, 197
Mountains of Mourne, 146
Moxon, H., Appx 5
Moy, S., illus
Moyen Atlas Mountains, 56
Mrewa District (Rhodesia), 180
Mubarak, President Hosni of Egypt, 183
Muchingjikki Methodist School, 180
Muhammed Ali, Sultan of Egypt, 17
Mukeiras, 24, 31, 32. 34, 179, illus
Mull of Kintyre, 102–3 (Map 8), 154
Multi-National Force in Lebanon, 181
Mulvey, D. A. 'Ginge', illus
Münster, 205
Murmansk Military District, 121, 124 (Map 11)
Murray, M., Appx 7, illus
Musgrave Park, 111 (Map 10), 152

N. A. A. F. I., 89, 143
Nanyuki, 64
NAPS (Nerve Agent Pre-treatment Set), 186
Narvik, 123, 124 (Map 11), 129, 130
National Liberation Front (NLF) (South Arabia), 27, 29, 31, 32, 33, 34, 35, 39, 41, 42, 43, 45, 46, 101, 267
National Service, 10, 11, 12, 14, 38, 87, 119, 160, 162; National Servicemen, 10, 12, 13, 68, 87, 234
NATO, 65, 66, 78, 121, 126, 129, 135, 159, 198, 234, 267, 271
NATO Challenge Cup March and Shooting Competition, 131
Nawbat Dukaim, 20, 21 (Map 2), 22, 24
Naylor, S., illus
Neal, B., Appx 7
Neil, J., 194, Appx 7
Neal, B. 'Rocky', illus
Neill, the Venerable Archdeacon Ivan, Chaplain-General to the Forces, 161
Nevet, A., illus
Nevile, A. J. M., 27, 31, 179, 189, illus
New Model Army, 2
Newry, 102–3 (Map 8), 146, 148
Newson, H., xiv, Appx 3
Newtownhamilton, 102–3 (Map 8), 146, 147
Ngakyedauk Pass (Burma), 9
Nicosia, 57, 58 (Map 5), 61, 62, 209
Nicholson, E., Appx 3
Nicholson, M., Appx 5
Nicholson, The Reverend Carson, 228
9th/12th Royal Lancers, 220
Nixon, C., Appx 5
'No-Go areas', 112, 113, 114
Noakes, M. D. P., Appx 5
Normandy, 8, 9, 96
North East Defence Region, 168
North East District, 133
North Howard Street, 111 (Map 10), 152; Mill, 215
North, Private, illus
North Staffordshire Regiment, The, 14; 5th/6th battalion, 192; 6th battalion, 188
North Ward, 106 (Map 9), 139
North West Frontier, 6; medal, 7
Northern Command Infantry Challenge Cup, 73, 74, 160
Northern Ireland, 13, 63, 64, 67, 80, 97, 98, 132, 194, 195, 197, 200, 209, 211, 234; 1969 emergency, 99–108; 102–3 (Map 8); Province Reserve 1972–3, 109–120; Operation Banner tours in Londonderry 1975, 138–41 and 1977,

141–45; Resident tour Ballykinler 1985–7, 145–51; 1988–9 platoon detachment, 136; Operation Banner tour in Belfast 1991–2, 151–4, Appx 4
Northern Ireland Civil Rights Association (NICRA), 100, 105
Northern Ireland Convention, 141
Northern Ireland Headquarters, 146, 154
Northern Ireland Intelligence & Security Group, 154
Norway, 97, 121–31, 124 (Map 11), 178–9, 198, 213, 270
Novi Travnik, 219 (Map 14), 223, 230

O'Brien, P. J., 87, 88, 192, Appx 5
O'Brien, T., 53
O'Connor, General Sir Richard, 79, 271–2
O'Neill, Rt. Hon. Terence, 100, 101
O'Shaughnessy, P. G., 76, Appx 5
Odense, 71, 124 (Map 11)
'official' IRA, 109, 138, 141
Olav, King of Norway, 177
Oldfield, T., illus
Olympic Games, 56, 127
Olympic Stadium, 83 (Map 7), 94–5
Omagh, 102–3 (Map 8), 117
Oman, 18; Sultan's Armed Forces, 179
1 PWO 'Lions' and 'Tigers', 196–97, Appx 6
Operation Banner, 73, 74, 76, 79, 138; Clamp, 45; Cover Point, 36; Dundee, 147–8; Full Time, 37; Granby, 214, 268; Grand Slam, 167; Grapple, 220; Lollipop, 115–16; Motorman, 113, 139; Random, 114; Segment, 115, 119; Shoveller, 180; Slaven, 229; Springboard, 37; Turner, 148
Options for Change, 78, 80, 172, 173, 233, 271, 273
Orange Order, 105, 150
Oregon, 178
Orum, M. G., 86, 213, Appx 5
Orwin, P. D., 37, Appx 3, Appx 5, illus
Osnabrück, 50, 66 (Map 6), 69, 78–80, 151, 183, 191, 214, 220, 221, Appx 4, illus

Otterburn, illus
Ottoman Empire, 18
Oxley, P., illus

Paddy's Field, 21 (Map 2), 36, 37
Padget, R., 191, Padgett, S., Appx 3, Appx 5, illus
Page, M., illus
Paisley, The Reverend Ian, 143
Palace Barracks, Belfast, 110, 114, 117, 149, 211, 212
Palestine, 6, 7, 8, 10, 115; Liberation Organization (PLO), 62, 180, 181
Paphos, 58 (Map 5), 63
Parachute Regiment, The, 93; 1st battalion, 28, 110, 137, 193, 195, 197; 2nd battalion, 36, 270; 3rd battalion, 118, 199, 270; 12th/13th battalion, 156
Paris Peace Conference of 1919, 182
Parker, C., illus
Parker, N. R. M., Appx 5
Parnell, P. 'Jack', 149, 151, Appx 5
Parr, Lieutenant C. D. (Intelligence Corps), Appx 5
Pask, J. R., 88, 192, 193
Patriotic Front (Rhodesia), 180
Payne, G., 227, Appx 5
Peacock, F. E., Appx 5
Peacock, K. A., 154, Appx 5
Pearce, C., 134, Appx 5, illus
Pearce, H. G., Appx 5
Peel Yates, Maj-Gen David, 85
Peking British Legation Guard, 51
Pell, H., 'Ginger', 191
Peoples' Socialist Party (PSP) of South Arabia, 26, 27, 32
Perak (Malaya), 12–13
Perim Island, 32, 177, 266
Peterson, J., Appx 3
Petra, 180
Phelan, A. J., 37, Appx 5
Phillips, A., illus
Pickering, G., illus
Pickering, K., 199
Picton Barracks, Bulford, 126
Pillars of Hercules, 52
Pinkney, A. R., 176, Appx 3

INDEX

Place, A., 117, 154, Appx 2, Appx 5
Plaice, I., 32
Platts, T. P., 177, Appx 3
Pocklington, 117
Podmore, A. J., xiv
'police primacy', 141, 142, 146
Poessl, R. F., 198
Polhill, M., illus
Port Said, 13
Porter, N. S., 115, Appx 3, illus
Porterdown, 102–3 (Map 8), 150, 151
Pörtshach, 10
Potter, D., 173
Potter, G. E., 193, Appx 5
Praliac, General, 232
Prew, D., illus
Pridgeon, 2nd Lieutenant Claire (WRAC), 136
Prince of Wales, HRH Charles, 93
Prince of Wales, HRH Edward, 3; 'Prince of Wales's Own, The', 3
Prince of Wales's Own (West and East Yorkshire) Regimental Association, The, xiii, 94, 98, 171, 172
Prince of Wales's Own (West Yorkshire) Regiment, The, 3
Prince, Private, illus
Princess Royal, HRH The, 49, 52, 53, 54, 88, 92, 158, 161, Appx 3, illus
Procter, J.; Mrs C.; Stephen John, 211
Proctor, K., 37, 38
Prosser, G., 31, 115, 194
Prosser, J., 115
Proteus camp, 158
Provisional IRA, PIRA, 'Provos', 48, 76, 100, 109, 110, 114, 116, 117, 119, 138, 139, 140–4, 147, 149–54
Prozor, 222 (Map 15), 225, 227, 229
Puma helicopter, 129
Pyongyang, Appx 1

Quantock, Mrs A., illus
Quantock, P., illus
46ème Régiment de l'Infanterie, 5, 91
Quarmby, S., illus
Quebec, 4; Quebec Day, 9
Queen, HM The, 97, 162, illus

Queen Arwa Road, 22, 23 (Map 3), 28, 42
Queen Elizabeth Barracks, Strensall, 161, 162
Queen's Birthday, 50, 177; Parade, 54, 85, 91, 94
Queen's Challenge Cup, 160, 166, 188, 191, 195, 272, Appx 6, Queen's Gallantry Medal, 225
Queen's Lancashire Regiment, The, 1st battalion, 152, 221
Queen's Own Highlanders, 1st battalion, 75, 197
Queen's Own Hussars, The, 46
Queen's Regiment, The, 1st battalion, 100; 2nd battalion, 105
Queen's Regiment, The (West Surrey), 14
Queen's Surrey Regiment, The, 14
Queen's Royal Irish Hussars, The, 126
Quibell, P., illus
quick reaction force (QRF), 153, 271
Quinn, R., illus

Raby, Lance-Corporal K. A. (QLR), Appx 5
Radfan, 21 (Map 2), 31, 37–8, 40, 179; tribesmen, 20, 26, 34
Radio Cairo, 18, 19, 26, 46
Rae, J., 158
RAF Akrotiri, 58 (Map 5), 58, 61, 62, 195, 209
RAF Cyprus, 197
RAF Episkopi, 58 (Map 5), 59, 195
RAF Gatow, 83 (Map 7), 89, 98
RAF Gibraltar, 48, 51, 54, 189, 190
RAF Khormaksar, 189
Ralph, P., 33, 41, Appx 5
Rangoon, 10
Ras Marshag, 16 (Map 1), 17, 28
Rawlings, D. H., 161, Appx 3
Redfern. J., 69, 190, 193, Appx 7
Rees, Rt. Hon. Merlyn, MP, 139
Regimental Band, 48, 87, 176–8; Territorial Army, 160
Regimental Council, 93
Regimental District (s), 2, 155

Regimental Headquarters (RHQ), 51, 88, 169, 170, 174
Regimental Museum, 169
Regimental Tercentenary, 98, 148, 172
Regiments of Foot, Clifton's, 2; Hales's, 2; Monck's, 2; 14th, 3, 4, 5; 14th (Bedfordshire), 3; 14th (Buckinghamshire) (Prince of Wales's Own), 3; 15th, 3, 4, 5; 15th (Yorkshire East Riding), 3; 53rd (Shropshire), 5
Reichstag building, 83 (Map 7), 89
Reid, Corporal (REME), illus
Reid, D., illus
Reliant, RFA, 182
Remblance, H., illus
Remembrance Day, 119, 160
Renardson, B., 40
Render, J., 39
Rennie, C., 157, illus
Republican News, 148
Reserve Forces Act, 235
Rhine, River, 65, 66 (Map 6), 66, 67
Rhineland, 65
Rhodes, S., 180
Rhodesia (Zimbabwe), 180, 181
Richard I, King, 62
Richards, P. G. 'Dixi', 177, Appx 3
Robbin, K. F., 107, 142, 154, Appx 5
Roberts, General Sir Frank, 4
Roberts, L. T., 43, 117, Appx 2, illus
Robinson, C. J., Appx 3
Robinson, D., Appx 5
Robinson, E., 115
Robinson, H. A., Appx 5, illus
Robinson, H. M. P. 'Keith', 27, 33
Robinson, M. H. 'Robbo', 198, 272, Appx 3, Appx 5, illus
Robinson, W. A., 13, 20, 159
Robson, H. P., Appx 3
Rodgers, J., illus
Rodland, F., Appx 5
Rodwell, D. A., 160, Appx 3
Rogerson, P., 70
Roman Barracks, Colchester, 207
Rommel, Field-Marshal Erwin, 8
Romsdal Fjord, 124 (Map 11), 178
Rose, Brigadier Michael, 146

Rosemount estate, 106 (Map 9), 139
Rosenquest, 'Rosie', 89
Ross, E., 108, Appx 5
Rotherham, 168
'roulement', 110, 112
Royal Air Force (RAF), 24, 62
Royal Anglian Regiment, The, 1st battalion, 27; 2nd battalion, 80; 3rd battalion, 193
Royal Artillery, locating regiment, 73; 5th Field Regiment, 20; 24th Field Regiment, 191; 42nd Heavy Regiment, 119; 49th Field Regiment, 198; 'O' battery 2nd Field Regiment, 126; Toombs Troop, 74
Royal Australian Air Force, 62
Royal Canadian Regiment, The, 1st battalion, 87
Royal College of Needlework, 50, 92
Royal Corps of Signals, 165; 9th Regiment, 59
Royal Electrical & Mechanical Engineers (REME), 270
Royal Engineers, Fortress Regiment (Gibraltar), 48, 51, 55, 190; 22 Regiment, 126; 38 Regiment, 133–4, 201; field troop in Bosnia, 221, 227
Royal Green Jackets, The, 186; 1st battalion, 114; 2nd battalion, 91; 3rd battalion, 194–5
Royal Hampshire Regiment, The, 1st battalion, 191
Royal Horse Artillery, The, 1st Regiment, 35, 36; E Battery, 35, 36
Royal Irish Rangers, The, 1st battalion, 136
Royal Lincolnshire Regiment, The, 1st battalion, 19
Royal Montreal Regiment, The, 136
Royal Navy, 48, 51
Royal Northumberland Fusiliers, The, 1st battalion, 41; 'Fifth Fusiliers', 42,
Royal Regiment of Fusiliers, The, 1st battalion, 147; 2nd battalion, 113; 3rd battalion, 134
Royal Scots Fusiliers, The, 14

INDEX

Royal Scots Greys, The, 61
Royal Sussex Regiment, The, 1st battalion, 27
Royal Ulster Constabulary (RUC), 99, 100, 107, 112, 115, 140, 141, 142, 147, 150, 151, 152; 'R' Division, 115
Royal Victoria Hospital, 111 (Map 10), 153
Royal Warwickshire Fusiliers, 1st battalion, 191
Royal Welch Fusiliers, The, 1st battalion, 133
rugby, Aden 1958–9, 189; BFAP seven-a-side competition 1958, Appx 6; Gibraltar 1959–61, 190; Wuppertal 1962–3, 191; East Anglian District Cup 1968, 195, Appx 6, illus; Berlin Brigade Simper Cup 1984, 200, Appx 6; North East/North West/Scotland Districts Championship 1990, Appx 6; pitch found in Spain, 272
Ruhr, the, 66 (Map 6), 68, 204, 206
Rumailah oilfield, 182–3
Rushworth, H. 'Cobber', 88, 192, Appx 3, illus
Rusk, T., 197
Russell, P. J., Appx 7, illus
Ruweisat Ridge, 8
Ryan, P. T., Appx 3

SA (Small Arms) 80, 133
Sabah and Sarawak, 179
SACEUR, 65, 122, 129, 180
'safe havens', 219 (Map 14), 220
Salamanca Barracks, 58 (Map 5), 60
Salisbury Plain, 122, 133, 198
Sancha, Carlos (artist), 77
Sandhurst, Royal Military Academy, xv, Appx 1
Sandys, Rt. Hon. Duncan, MP, 14, 15, 26, 67
Saracen (wheeled APC), 113
Sarajevo, 217, 218, 219 (Map 14), 222 (Map 15), 220, 221
Saudi Arabia, 78, 183
Sauerland, 91
Saunders, C., illus
Savidge, H., 163

Savidge. P., 163, Appx 3, Appx 5
Saville, W. S., 24, Appx 2
Sawtell, R. F., 95
Saxon (wheeled APC), 132, 133
Saywell, E. 'Spike', 53, illus
Scarman Tribunal, 107, 108, 269
Schloss Laer, 92
Schmelz, 10
Schofield, C. J., Appx 3, illus
Scholes, P., illus
School of Electrical and Mechanical Engineers (SEME), 127, 199
Scimitar Hill, 6
Scorpion light tanks, 223
Scotland, 14
Scots Guards, 1st battalion, 186; 2nd battalion, 270
Scott, Mrs C., illus
Scott, V., illus
Scott Lewis, I. R., 73, 84, 86, 139, 189, illus
Sea Eagle, HMS, 104, 105, 106 (Map 9)
Second World War, 7–10, 57, 65, 72, 79, 98, 121, 131, 216
Sedgemoor, Battle of, 3
Seeburger Chaussee, 83 (Map 7), 87
Selby, 171
Senior, T. H., Appx 3
Sennelager, 66 (Map 6), 74, 75, 86, 87, 98
Serb Democratic Party (SDS), 217
Serb Republic of Bosnia-Herzegovina, 217; the 'Serb Republic', 218
Serbia, 216, 217
Seven Years War, 4
17th/21st Lancers, 61
Shannon, Private J. T. (QLR), Appx 5
Shantallow estate, 106 (Map 9), 139, 140
Sharp, C., 199, illus
Sharpe, M. H., 120, 123, Appx 5
Shaw, R., illus
Shaykh 'Uthman, 16 (Map 1), 18, 27, 28
Sheardown, Captain John (RAMC), 129
Sheffield, 157 (Map 12), 164, 171
Shell, K. C., 95, 269, Appx 3
Shepherd, S., illus

Sheppard, W. P., 13, 164, 166, 167, 168, 170, 171, Appx 3, Appx 5, illus
Sherratt, R. A., 191; Mrs J., 207, illus
Sherwood Foresters, The, 5th/8th battalion, 190
Shirach, Baldur von, 84, 90
Shirt, P. N., 153, 215; Mrs J., 215
Short Strand, 109, 111 (Map 10)
Sibyon-Ni, Battle of, 13
Sicily, 8
Silent Valley, 101, 102–3 (Map 8)
Silvester, J., Appx 7
Simpson, A. F., 120, Appx 5
Simpson, R., 201, Appx 7, illus
Singleton, R., 136, Appx 5
Six Days' War, 41
6th US Infantry Regiment, 2nd battalion, 84, 91; 4th battalion, 91
16th/5th The Queen's Royal Lancers, 70, 117, 198
Skelton, D., illus
Skelton, J. F., 20, ski teams, skiing, 56, 61, 76, 77; Cyprus, 197; Army Championships at Oberjoch 1974, 197
Slater, J., 199
Sleight, R., 120, Appx 5
Slim, Field-Marshal Sir William, 9, 50; Lady Slim, 50
Sloans Terrace, 106 (Map 9), 143
Slovenia, 218, 219 (Map 14), 272
SLR (self-loading rifle), 55, 67, 133, 150
Smalley, G. B., Appx 3, Appx 5
Smelt, Mrs T., illus
SMG (Sterling sub-machine-gun, 55, 133
Smith, H. C., Appx 3
Smithson, C., illus
sniper fire, 230
Snowcat (Volvo) snow vechicle, 128
Socotra Island, 17
Soldiers', Sailors' and Airmen's Families Association (SSAFA), 203
Soltau, 66 (Map 6), 70, 73, 86, 87
Somerset and Cornwall Light Infantry, The, 1st battalion, 192
Somaliland Scouts, 177

Somme, Battle of the, 6
South African War, 4, 6, 272
South Arabia, 188–9, 193, 234, 266
South Arabian Armed Forces (SAAF), 42
South Arabian League (SAL), 19, 27, 32
South Armagh, 102–3 (Map 8), 145–51, 212
South Staffordshire Regiment, The, 14
South Wales's Borderers, The, 1st battalion, 13
South West District, 122, 127
Southgate, The Right Reverend John, Dean of York, 172
Sovereign Base Areas (SBAs) (Cyprus), 58 (Map 5), 58, 59
Soviet Army, 66
Soviet Baltic Fleet, 126
Soviet Union, 10, 73
Spain, 47, 48, 51, 56, 204
Spammer, J. P. 'Spam', 37
Spandau Prison, 83 (Map 7), 84, 88, 90, 91
'Spearhead', 42, 136, 209, 270
Special Air Service Regiment (SAS), 159, 271
'Special Guards' (South Arabia), 36, illus
Speer, Albert, 84, 90
Spencer, H. A. V., xiii, 50, 51, Appx 3
Sperrin Mountains, 102–3 (Map 8), 110
Spetsnaz (Soviet) Special Forces, 167, 271
Spittal, 50
Split, 219 (Map 14), 221
Spottiswood, C. M., Appx 5
Sprangle, T., illus
Springfield Road, 111 (Map 10), 112, 118
Springhall, R. J., 14, 15, 54, Appx 3, illus
Srebrenica, 219 (Map 14), 220
Staff College, Camberley, 59, 135, 148, 181, 233
Staffordshire Regiment, The, 14; 1st battalion, 117, 184–6; Stainthorpe, P. A., 151, Appx 5, illus
Stanford Training Area, 100

Stanier, General Sir John, 182
Star of Brunswick, 15
Stead, B. G., 115
Steamer Point, 16 (Map 1), 31, 43, 45, 46
Steel, G., illus
Steel, P. P., xiii, 20, 53, 158, Appx 3, illus
Steeplechase, 130
Stephenson, D. R. A., Appx 7, illus
Stevenson, A. J., Appx 3
Stevenson, M. A., illus
Stier, 'Eggy', illus
Stirk, P., illus
Stirling, General Sir William, 85
Stocks, K. 'Smiler', illus
Stone, Brigadier Patrick, 98
Stormont (Government of Northern Ireland), 100, 107, 109, 110, 143
Strabane, 102–3 (Map 8), 105
Strand, The, 99, 106 (Map 9); Strand Road, 142
Strasse des 17 Juni, 83 (Map 7), 85
Strensall, 155, 157 (Map 12), 161, 162, 163
Suddaby, P., Appx 3
Suez, 13, 14, 38, 53; Canal, 6, 13
Suffield (Alberta), 73, 74
Sullivan, M. L., 94, 95, 211, Appx 3
surf canoeing, Army Champion, 201
Suvla Bay, 6
Swain, A. S., Appx 3, Appx 5
swimming, Gibraltar Competitions 1959–61, 190, Appx 6; BAOR Championship 1963, 191; 1964, 88, 192, Appx 6; Berlin Brigade Championship 1964, 88, 192; 1983, 90
Swingfire command-controlled guided missile, 72
Synon, Mary Ellen, 138
Syria, 121, 270

T-55 (Soviet) tank, 68
Tadcaster, 157 (Map 12), 157, Appx 4
Tallon, J., illus
Tarhuna, 55, 56
Tattersfield, J., 43

Tawahi, 19, 22, 27, 43, 44 (Map 4), 45, 46
Taylor, Brigadier Alan, illus
Taylor, G., illus
Taylor, J. H., 167, Appx 3, Appx 5
Taylor, N. D., xiii, 48, 54, 56–7, 170, Appx 3, illus; Mrs N., 54
Taylor, P. E., xiii, 71, 72, 86, 190, 192, Appx 3, illus; Mrs P., 207
Tel Aviv, 177
Templer, General Sir Gerald, 11
tennis, Northern Ireland Championship 1985, 200; 3rd Armoured Division Doubles competition 1984, Appx 6; Northern Ireland Championship 1985, Appx 6; 24th Brigade Doubles competition 1989, 201, Appx 6
Territorial and Army Volunteer Reserve (TAVR), 163; TAVR II units, 164–6; TAVR III units, 164–6; TAVR Association, 169
Territorial Army, 2, 7, 15, 122, 159, 235; man training days, 164–6, 271; 1994 Review of, 173; TA Centres Review, 174
Territorial Army and Emergency Reserves Review 1966–8, 163–7
Territorial Army Associations, 156
Territorial Army Sportsman of the Year, 190
Tetley, J. N., Appx 3
Thackeray, M., 39
Theaker, G., 180, 181
3rd Battalion The Prince of Wales's Own Regiment of Yorkshire, formation, 156, Appx 4; initial deployment, 156–7; inauguration parade, 158; Presentation of Colours, 88, 161; wins the Queen's Challenge Cup in 1962, 160, 191, Appx 6; in 1963, 160, 191, Appx 6; in 1968, 160, 166, 195, Appx 6; becomes The Prince of Wales's Own Territorials with home defence role, 164–5, Appx 4; reduced to cadre status, 166, Appx 4; resumes 3rd Battalion title, 167; cadre absorbed into The Yorkshire Volunteers, 168, Appx 4; reforms from

2nd Battalion The Yorkshire Volunteers, 172–3, Appx 4; roled to the ARRC, 173; exercises in the United States, 173; re-roled as a fire-support battalion, 173–4, Appx 4; deployment in Yorkshire from 1994, 174, Appx 4; sporting activities, 194–5; forty men volunteer to serve in Bosnia, 235
3rd Battle Squadron, British Home Fleet, 99
Third Crusade, 62
Third Reich, 81
3rd Royal Tank Regiment, 74
13th/18th Royal Hussars, 74, 169, 273
Thomas, R., illus
Thompson, S., illus
Thompson, S. A., 178, Appx 3
Thorne, A., illus
Thornton, G., 153
Thornton, J. E., Appx 5
Thrace, 121
3 Wing Army Air Corps, 29
Tidman, P. T. J., Appx 5
Tidworth, 122
Tiefenbach, 79
Tiergarten, 83 (Map 7), 85
Tighe, R., 194, Appx 7, illus
Tillotson, Mrs A., 211
Tito (Josip Broz), 216
Todd, W. A. E., 42, 46, 57, 100, 101, 107, 108, 191, 195, Appx 3, Appx 5, illus
Tolmie, L., Appx 5
Tomislavgrad (Duvno), 222 (Map 15), 226, 230
Tomlinson, R. F., xiii, 169, Appx 3; Mrs E., 170
Topliss, A., 149
Torrey Canyon disaster, 42, 267
Towle, J., illus
Tracy, E. P., 152, 154, Appx 5
Trant, Maj-Gen Dick, 144
Travnik, 221, 222 (Map 15), 225, 226, 228, 229
Treaty of Establishment (Cyprus), 58, 265
Treaty of Versailles, 65

Trenchard Barracks, Celle, 73
Trevaskis, Sir Kennedy, 26, 266
Trevelyan, Sir Humphrey, 41, illus
'Triangle' route, 226
Trilax X4 sights, 133
Tripoli, 55
Tripolitania, 47
Turbe, 221, 222 (Map 15), 226
Turf Lodge estate, 111 (Map 10), 152
Turkey, 57, 121
Turkish-Cypriots, 57
Turnbull, Sir Richard, 266
Turner, M. R. R., Appx 5
Tuzla, 219 (Map 14), 220, 222 (Map 15), 223, 226, 230, 231
Tyrell, E., 137, 196, 199, 201, Appx 7, illus
Tyrone, 102–3 (Map 8), 110

Ulster, 64, 102–3 (Map 8), 99, 234
Ulster Defence Association (UDA), 112, 113
Ulster Defence Regiment (UDR), 108, 115, 147
Ulster 'loyalists', 100
Ulysses, HMS, 176
UNFICYP, 58
'uniform of the 80s' trial, 125
United Arab States, 18, 19
United Kingdom Land Forces (UKLF), 129
United Kingdom Strategic Reserve, 57, 63, 180
United National Front (UNF), 19, 22
United Nations, 14, 41, 216, 218, 234
United Nations High Commission for Refugees (UNHCR), 220, 223, 225–6
United Nations Security Council, 58; Resolutions 660 (1990), 183; 661 (1990), 183; 662 (1990), 183; 743 (1992), 217; 758 (1992), 218; 776 (1992), 219; 824 (1993), 220
United States, 57, 81, 82, 131, 178
United Ulster Action Council, 143
UNPROFOR, 80, 214, 217, 218, 272, Appx 4
Urey, Lance-Corporal P. A. (QLR), Appx 5

Urqub Pass, 24
Uscroft, M. F., illus

Valenciennes, 5
Varanasi (Benares), 3
Vares, 222 (Map 15), 226, 230
Vickers, J. A., 191
Vickers, P. M. 'Vic', illus
Vickers machine-guns, 68, illus
Victoria Barracks, Beverley, 158, 170
Victoria Cross, 6
Victorious, HMS, 51
Victory Column (Berlin), 85, 268
Victory Station, 187
Vienna, 10–11
Vietnam, 132
Vines, T. C. E., xiv, 100, 104, 139, Appx 3, illus
Visoko, 222 (Map 15), 226
Vitez, 219 (Map 14), 221, 222 (Map 15), 223, 224, 225, 226, 227, 228–9, 230
Vojvodina, 216, 219 (Map 14)
Volks-Polizei (VOPO), 83
Volkstruppen, 215
Volunteer battalions, 2, 6

Waddington, W., illus
Wade, P. W., 46, 179
Wade, R., illus
Wade, Sergeant G. (APTC), Appx 7, illus
Wadi Akarit, 8
Wadi Ayn, 35
Wadi Bana, 21 (Map 2), 34
Wadi Bilah, 21 (Map 2), 36
Wadi Milah, 21 (Map 2), 37
Wadi Taym, 21 (Map 2), 34, 36
Wadi Tiban, 20, 21 (Map 2), Wagstaff, T. E., xiv, 186–7, Appx 3, illus
Waistel, N. J., 149
Walford, W., 45
Walker, F., 196, 197, 210, Appx 3, 272
Wall, W. T., 86, 206, Appx 3, illus; Mrs M., 206
Walters, W., illus
Waltham, M., Appx 7
Warminster, 78, Appx 4

Warringfield hospital, 120
Warrington, M., 178
Warrior AFV, 78, 80, 132, 185, 186, 220–1, 226–7, 228, 229, 230, 231, 232, illus
Warsaw Pact, 73, 78, 90, 164, 167, 234, 271
Wasden, S. J. 'Wassie', illus
Washington DC, 178
Washington State, 134
Waterhouse, A., illus
Waterhouse, 'Jay-Jay', 114
Waterloo Place, 99, 106 (Map 9)
Waters, L., illus
Waters T. E., 13, Appx 1
Waterside estate, 106 (Map 9), 143
Watson, G., Appx 3
Watson, M. J., 63, 151, Appx 5
Watson, R., illus
Watson, R. J., 136, 140, Appx 5; Mrs C., 215, Appx 5
Watts, D. J., Appx 5
Watts, P. J., Appx 5
Webb, B. 'Spider', 37
Webber, D. R. W., illus
Weimar Republic, 65
Weldrand, P., illus
Welsh Guards, 1st battalion, 31, 69, 179, 270
Weser, River, 66, 66 (Map 6), 132
West German Federal Republic (FDR), 66
West Riding, 12, 162
West Riding Territorial and Auxiliary Forces Association, 161
West Yorkshire Regiment, The, 4, 6, 57, Appx 1; 1st battalion, 5, 9, 10, 11–12, 13, 38, 52, 53, 206; 2nd battalion, 8, 9, 86, 131, 158, 172, 177; 5th Battalion, 7, 8, 15, 156, Appx 4; 1/5th battalion, 7; 2/5th battalion, 7–8; 6th battalion converted to searchlight regiment RE, 7; 7th (Leeds Rifles) battalion converted to Royal Tank Corps battalion, 7; 8th (Leeds Rifles) battalion converted to heavy anti-aircraft regiment RA, 7; 9th battalion, 6; 9th

(Over-seas Defence) battalion, 8; 7th and 8th Leeds Rifles battalions amalgamated and re-roled to infantry, 156, Appx 4
West Yorkshire Regimental Association, 140, 155, 171
Westbury, D. 'Wes', illus
Western Aden Protectorate (WAP), 18, 20, 22, 24, 25, 34, 234, Appx 4
Western Desert, 8, 9, 86, 183
Western Sovereign Base Area (WSBA), 59, 62
Westphalen, Graf von, 92
Westphalia, 65
Weyand, Maj-Gen Alexander, 123
White, Lt-Col Gilbert W. (KRRC), 9
White, Mrs P., illus
White, N. B., Appx 5
White, R. A., Appx 5
White Rose, The, xiii, 198
White Rose Club, 69, 119, 204, 209, 211, 212, 213, 214, 215
White Rosette, 207
Whitelaw, Rt. Hon. William, MP, 110
Whiting, A. R., 213–14, 272, Appx 5
Whittingham, A., Appx 5
Whitton, Sergeant G. R. (RLC), Appx 5
Whitworth, L. K., 224–5, Appx 5, illus
Wignall, P. G., 154, Appx 5
Wild, R., illus
Wiley, C. L., Appx 3, Appx 5
Wilhelm II, Kaiser, 5
Wilkes, The Reverend David, 96
Wilkin, N., Appx 7, illus
Wilkins, E. B., illus
Wilkinson, A., 95
Wilkinson, L., Appx 5
Wilkinson Sword for Peace, 117–18
Willerton, J., 91
William III, King, 4
Williams, P. 'Paddy', 180
Williams, R., Appx 7
Williamson, A., 153, 229
Willingham, B., 39
Wilman, L. A. 'Wilks', illus
Wilson, A. J., illus
Wilson, A. P. F., 135
Wilson, D., 137, illus

Wilson, J. M., 168
Wilson, K., illus
Wilson, Rt. Hon. Harold, MP, 89, illus
Wingrove, M., 201
Winspear, M., illus
wives and children, 203–15, 231
Wolfe, Maj-Gen James, 4
Wood, A., 156
Wood, J, 117–18, 120, Appx 5, illus
Wood, C. J. M., xiv, 174, Appx 3
Wood L. J. 'Lakri', xiv, 188, 192, Appx 3, Appx 5
Wood, P., illus; with son James, illus
Wood, P. L. W., Appx 5, illus
Woodhouse, M. 'Woody', illus
Woodvale, 111 (Map 10), 118
Woodward, P., 229
Woolley, P. E., xiv, 27, 35, 86, 90, 128, 130, 133, 135, 142, 172, 181, 182, 196, Appx 3, Appx 5, illus
Woolsey, R. G., 36, illus
Wombat 120 mm anti-tank gun, 31, 67, 68
World Football Cup competition 1966, 193–4
Worrall, I. 'Fritz', illus
Worsley Barracks, York, 173
Worsley, Colonel Sir Marcus, Bt, Appx 3
Worsley, Lt-Gen Sir Richard, 77, illus
Wörthersee, 10, 'du bist die Rose von' (song), 10, 98
Wray, A., illus
Wray, D., illus
Wray, D. A., 139–40, 154, Appx 2
Wright, A., 75, 215, illus
Wright, C., 186, illus
Wupper, River, 68
Wuppertal, 66 (Map 6), 67–72, 86, 87, 190, 191, 204–6, Appx 4, illus
Wyrill, M., Appx 5

Yalta conference, 65
Yates, D., 45
Yemen, 18, 21 (Map 2), 22, 27, 28
Yemeni Royalists, 35
Yeo, J. A., 13, 175–6, 189
Yom Kippur War, 78

INDEX

York, 157 (Map 12), *et passim*
York, HRH Duke of, 3, 5
York, HMS, 271
York and Lancaster Regiment, 1st battalion, 22, 62
Yorkshire, 72, 96, 155–74, 157 (Map 12)
Yorkshire Brigade Depot, 161, 162
'Yorkshire Lass, The', 5
Yorkshire Volunteers, The, 155, 164, 172; 1st battalion, 168; 2nd battalion, 168, 170, 201, 272, Appx 4
Young, Maj-Gen Peter, 267
Young, R., 156

Younghusband, General Sir George, 18
Youngman, Leo Pretty, Chief of the Blackfoot Tribe, 73–4, illus
Yugoslavia, 216, 217, 218; Yugoslav National Army (JNA), 273
Yule, J., 137, illus

Zagreb, 219 (Map 14), 226, 229
Zealand, 71, 124 (Map 11), 126, 127
Zenica, 222 (Map 15), 226, 231
Zepa, 219 (Map 14), 220
Zimbabwe (Rhodesia), 181
Zvornic, 222 (Map 15), 226